MOVING TARGET

THE HISTORY AND EVOLUTION OF GREEN ARROW

MOVING TARGET

THE HISTORY AND EVOLUTION OF GREEN ARROW

RICHARD GRAY

SEQUART ORGANIZATION   EDWARDSVILLE, ILLINOIS

Moving Target: The History and Evolution of Green Arrow
by Richard Gray

First edition, August 2017, ISBN 978-1-9405-8916-9.

Cover by Louie Joyce. Book design by Julian Darius. Interior art is © DC Comics.

Published by Sequart Organization. Edited by Mike Phillips. Assistant edited by Michael Campochiaro, Peter Coogan, Max Nestorowich, Colby Pryor, Lou Tambone, and Matt Walsh.

For more information about other titles in this series, visit Sequart.org/books.

Contents

Foreword

by Phil Hester

I'm constantly apologizing for Green Arrow.

Whenever an eager fan approaches me with a stack of *Green Arrow*s to autograph and mentions that the run Kevin Smith, Ande Parks, and I did on the book got them into comics for the first time, or back into comics after a lapse, I jokingly apologize. Look, it's an expensive hobby. It makes me feel like the crack dealer who gave some poor kid his first eightball.

And occasionally I'll meet a reader who not only proclaims that *Quiver* got them back into comics, but that our take on Green Arrow is their ideal Green Arrow. Then I apologize sincerely.

You see, "my" Green Arrow is the Neal Adams version. I remember reading about those hallowed Denny O'Neil / Neal Adams *Green Lantern/Green Arrow* books before ever actually laying hands on an issue, but when I did I was blown away. I was never one for photorealism in comics art, being raised on Kirby, Staton, and Wrightson, but the dynamism abounding in those layouts, the drama emanating from the acting, the anatomically stringent, yet exuberantly expressive figure drawing, the pure *sturm und drang* of the whole affair cemented that run in my young mind as THE Green Arrow.

Of course, as I grew as both a fan and young professional, my appreciation for the character both broadened and deepened. I enjoyed the Adams-influenced look Mike Grell brought to his first run on the character, then the more nuanced, self-assured take he brought to *The Longbow Hunters*. I was electrified by the primal, macho immediacy of the Trevor Von Eeden mini-series. And as DC began to reprint the classic Golden Age tales, I fell in love with the squeaky clean, yet energetic Weisinger/Papp proto-Batman version, then Jack Kirby's explosive revamping of that version.

As a working pro, I found so much to admire in the virtuosity of Dan Jurgens, Rodolfo DiMaggio, Jock, Scott McDaniel, Tom Fowler, and Will Rosado's runs. Am I missing anyone? Well, I'm jealous of them, too. I never fail to find something enviable about the work of others. I look at my work and see only an amalgamation of mistakes compounding mistakes until the whole thing goes up in flames. But when I see someone else's work, even work that may be objectively less competent than mine, I see only the positives. So it's tough for me to look at my time at the helm of such a storied character with anything less than a little embarrassment.

That doesn't mean I don't cherish that time. Getting to work with such talented collaborators was one of the richest experiences of my career. Meeting and working with Kevin Smith was a heady experience. That guy is a creative dynamo, never failing to find the moment in any adventure story, no matter how grand, that will humanize the hero. A lot of people misread his humor as broad or crude, but it's actually pretty precise in the manner it deflates pretense and grounds the proceedings in reality. Kevin Smith's characters are undeniably human; heroes, villains, monsters, angels, demons, no matter how preposterously larger than life, all become relatable when uttering his unmistakable dialogue.

Kevin was followed by Brad Meltzer and his laser-like plots carving up the character of Oliver Queen like a surgeon, cutting out the superfluous tissue and healing the core of the hero. I learned so much about writing from just reading Brad's scripts as they came in that I feel like I owe him tuition. And of course, Brad is such a huge DC nerd that we got to go running through the DC toy box, grabbing up characters and settings we'd previously only adored as readers, and sending them soaring at one another across the playground.

After Brad came his long-time friend Judd Winick, who writes with more heart and honesty than most any other writer in comics. Judd IS Oliver Queen in many ways, so he slid right into the skin of the hero. That didn't prevent him from putting the poor bastard through his paces, but it assured me, as both collaborator and fan, that every moment was authentic. Even while providing all the explosive action required in super hero comics, Judd made the human moments between Oliver and his makeshift family, especially Mia and Connor, the truly memorable events in our run.

But the highlight of the entire run was finally getting to trot onto the main stage with my long-time collaborator Ande Parks. We had been working together as penciler and inker for over ten years, but the vagaries of staffing at DC had broken us up, me penciling *Swamp Thing* without him, and him inking *Catwoman*, *Wonder Woman*, and other gigs without me. *Green Arrow* was our chance to finally showcase our collaboration for a large audience, and despite all the misgivings I have about my work, I don't for one second feel Ande did anything less than elevate my efforts. He brought a confidence to my rendering that I sometimes lacked, bringing the look of my clunky pencils to a professional finish, but never betraying my intent. Also, he's my best buddy, so getting to share this success with him was nothing but fun.

I also got to work with the talented Guy Major on colors and Sean Konot on letters, both collaborations I will long remember and appreciate. Plus my hero Matt Wagner was doing covers on my comics! Matt Freaking Wagner! You guys, I know Matt Wagner now!

And the man who made it all possible was Bob Schreck, an editor brave enough to cast a big super hero book against type. Bob trusted his instincts, and our unconventional talents, to bring Green Arrow to a modern audience. With gentle encouragement and devastatingly effective heavy sighs, he shepherded us oddballs all the way to the top of the sales charts and into the memories of thousands of readers. I'm sure he and his editorial team of Michael Wright, Nachie Castro, and Morgan Dontanville faced a lot of pressure from executives at DC to staff this book with Wizard Top Ten talent, or maybe even just safely conventional artists, but he stuck with his guys and shielded us from ever even hearing about that pressure.

So please forgive me when I apologize to you about my time on Green Arrow. There is that little bit of self-deprecation I will never be able to shake, but the truth is, it was such a joyous experience it's hard to look at it as something I earned as much as something fortuitous that just happened to me, a kid from Iowa who wanted to draw comics someday. I ultimately don't know how I fit into the tapestry of the history of the character, but I'm glad they weaved me in.

So, for one last time-- sorry!

Introduction

Who is Green Arrow?

Outside of the comic book world, it's a more than reasonable question. The average civilian from beyond the trenches of fandom is just as likely to think a passionate Green Arrow follower is just *really* into Robin Hood or Van Dyke beards. In fact, until relatively recently, it wouldn't have been surprising to find much recognition for the character at all, even if he has over three-quarters of a century of history behind him. That's because Green Arrow has never been just one thing. Even avid readers of the DC Comics archer might find themselves just as perplexed when trying to come up with a definitive set of characteristics for the Emerald Archer. Once a Batman clone, Green Arrow has morphed into an outspoken scourge of the corporate fat cats, a much darker urban hunter, resurrected hero, and in the last few years, a legitimate television star.

The chief purpose of this book, other than being a tribute to one of DC's most enduring heroes on the occasion of his 75th birthday, is to provide some context around decades of stories from different creators with varying agendas. One of the interesting additions to the Batman mythos from writer and super fan Grant Morrison's was to "accept every single era as one guy's biography."[1] In other words, each era represented a different part of the Batman's growth, from the young urban commando of his youth to the jaded Dark Knight of Frank Miller as he approaches a later stage in his life. When Morrison approached

---

[1] Smith, K. and Morrison, G (hosts). (20 Feb 2013). *Fatman on Batman* [Audio podcast]. Retrieved from http://smodcast.com

Batman in this manner, it had never been done before, because few dared read all of the Caped Crusader's adventures as a single piece. While it's not a perfect analogue for the Emerald Archer, even if he was partly inspired by Batman, reading *all* of the Green Arrow stories chronologically creates a wild personal history for his alter ego Oliver Queen.

In the 1940s, Ollie is in his early 20s and a millionaire. After an accident that leaves him stranded on a remote island, he becomes a skilled archer who goes out on formulaic larks in Star City for a distraction, accompanied by his ward Roy 'Speedy' Harper. He even joins the Seven Soldiers of Victory in lieu of actively participating in the war. Then it's the 1950s, and he's in space thanks to Jack Kirby, the post-war world opening up a whole new avenue of possibilities to him, using his vast resources to concoct a bizarre series of trick arrows to aid his extra-curricular activities. He grows up, loses his fortune because he's too distracted by adventuring, but joins the Justice League and finds a conscience in the 1960s. He's a little older now, so he ditches the kid — or maybe the kid ditches him — gets hip new clothes, facial hair, and becomes angry with the system, travelling across the country as part of his belated 'gap year' with his good friend and colleague Hal 'Green Lantern' Jordan. He finds a country that's stricken by a "hideous moral cancer" and the abandoned Speedy is a junkie. By the time we hit the mid-1970s, Ollie's in his 30s, trying to find a steady job as a public relations agent, a newspaper man or as a mayoral candidate. He's in his first long-term relationship with his new partner, Dinah "Black Canary" Lance, troubled at first because he's still finding out about himself, and so is she. He tries to go hang out with his mate Hal again, but it's not the same, and Lantern's now even more of a representation of the authority Ollie rebels against. Then things start to get darker in his late-30s. He's pondered what one man can truly accomplish, and he's found himself wanting. Increasingly at odds with his super friends, Ollie leaves them for his own pursuits. He moves to Seattle in his early 40s, just as the world is turning to a hell filled with corrupt governments, drugs, gangs, and serial murder. He wants to settle down with children, but Dinah doesn't want to make orphans. He hits his ultimate midlife crisis, abandons the trick arrows, gets another new costume and dives deeper into cynicism. He cuts himself off from everyone but Dinah, who is brutally tortured, driving him even further into urban vigilantism, and wilfully murdering. He no longer trusts police, and is betrayed by the authorities. In turn, he betrays the one person *he* trusted by cheating on Dinah, thus completing his mid-life crisis. Exiled and alone, he becomes a tool of the forces he previously decried, is forced to kill his best friend Hal, and discovers he has a son from a college affair. When faced with a critical decision of losing his arm or his life, he stubbornly chooses to make the ultimate sacrifice in a plane over Metropolis, giving the only thing he has left to give rather than lose his ability to be an archer, the only trait he feels has defined him for decades. He is killed, handing the mantle to his son, only to be literally resurrected years later to start anew.

That is, of course, if you consider it all to be one person. Which Green Arrow is decidedly *not*. That origin story on the island wasn't even part of the mythos until 1959, almost two decades after his debut. Green Arrow has never stopped evolving, and those changes represent the changing tastes and attitudes of creators and readers as much as they do the life-cycle of a vigilante hero. Yet what makes Green Arrow unique is precisely that he is so malleable in the hands of an assortment of writers, but consistently human in all of them. Crafted by some of the biggest names in the industry – from Mort Weisinger, Jack Kirby, Denny O'Neill, Neal Adams and Mike Grell through to Kevin Smith, Brad Meltzer, Judd Winick, Jeff Lemire, and even Alan Moore – Green Arrow has shown an amazing ability to not only adapt to the times, but be an outspoken voice in almost every decade. Not too shabby for a typically hirsute man with no powers, armed with nothing but a bow and arrow and his own wits.

While *Moving Target* covers the entirety of Green Arrow's career to date via a series of thematic essays and interviews, what it doesn't do is exhaustively catalogue every single instance and appearance of the Emerald Archer over 75 years. Green Arrow has been around for a long time, and has featured in literally thousands of stories. Short of publishing a multi-volume set on the character, an idea that this author would have willingly spent years producing, there will inevitably be stories that aren't discussed or are simply referred to in passing. On a far more practical level, the first half of this book deals with stories that aren't as readily accessible to modern readers. Many of Green Arrow's early adventures were back-up features in the pages of other character's titles, and the vast pre-*Crisis on Infinite Earths* catalogue of stories are still sadly unavailable in reprints or digital formats. Nevertheless, years of research and countless hundreds of hours of reading, visiting libraries and staring at screens went into this book to ensure that every major appearance of the character from 1941 to 2016 was acknowledged in the compilation.

Green Arrow is the embodiment of what one person can do. It's a theme that comes up repeatedly in this book, one that explains why this powerless archer with a chip on his shoulder appeals to so many people. He wasn't born of the heartbreaking tragedy of a Batman, he didn't fall from the stars to deliver humanity from evil, nor is his origin wrapped in the fabric of Greek myths and legends. He is a human character that struggles with work, love, loss, darkness, death, and the weight of his own sins. Like the rest of us humans, Green Arrow is flawed, and a perpetually moving target.

The Birth of the Battling Bowman: The Many Origins of Green Arrow

Green Arrow would be better if his arrows weren't so versatile and imaginative.

– Jonathan E. Lighter, a fan[1]

Over 100 comic book characters were introduced in 1941, and only the harshest of pub trivia rounds would ask you to name more than a few of them. As a child excitedly going to the newsstand with a hard-earned 10 cents, you'd look up at the wall of dangling magazines, hanging from a peg on overlapping lines surrounding a little man in a booth. Spotting exciting titles like *Wonderworld Comics, Flash Comics* and *Bill Barnes America's Air Ace Comics*, the choice would come down to which brightly coloured cover stood out between the newspapers and copies of *Popular Science*. Briefly, you might ponder the alarmist headline of whether Hitler could invade America, but that was grown up stuff. Besides, you'd just seen Captain America punch out the dictator at that very newsstand a few months ago. You recognize Doctor Fate

---

[1] From the "JLA Mail Room" back-matter of *Justice League of America* Vol 1 #7 (Nov 1961). Please note that all parenthetical dates are cover dates (which typically run in advance of actual publication dates).

on the cover of *More Fun Comics*, so you grab that one, pay your dime, roll up the comic in your back pocket, and rush home to read the adventures of Johnny Quick, The Spectre and these new characters of Aquaman and Green Arrow inside your well-engineered and structurally sound pillow fort.

Flash forward 75 years, and if you are still in the land of the living, you might wish you'd saved some of those comics as an investment. The Green Arrow of the 21st century is many things, not least of which is one of DC Comics' handful of characters that have successfully made the leap from page to screen. Yet he wasn't always fortunate enough to be regarded as a star player, and even the most generous of foresight would not have predicted his longevity. Born into war-time America, Oliver Queen (a.k.a. Green Arrow) spent the first four decades of his career as a supporting player in other hero's books, surviving the changing tastes of the public and editorial responses to them. Like the newsstands of the last century, he was one of many disposable heroes that had the fortune of being committed to precious pulp paper stock, almost absorbing the qualities of the heroes around him in those early days.

Part Batman, cowboy, vigilante, Robin Hood and soldier, the Green Arrow that emerged during the 1940s was a pastiche. He was whatever the publisher needed him to be, and rode on a wave of new characters that emerged in the 1940s to satisfy a growing desire for more heroes like Superman and Batman. As Bob Schreck, legendary Dark Horse and DC editor, once commented, "He's more of an amalgam of various different archetypes," which is perhaps the best description of Green Arrow in his first decade.[2] Modelled on the same formula that made Batman a hit with audiences[3] – complete with an Arrowcar, Arrowcave, an endless supply of trick arrows by the 1950s and, of course, his trusty teen sidekick Speedy – Green Arrow was also part of a heritage that followed Robin Hood, Fawcett Comics' Old West series Golden Arrow, and the serialized film adaptations of Edgar Wallace's The Green Archer. Even Green Arrow's name appears to be an amalgam of these other heroes.[4]

Writer Denny O'Neil, who would later transform the character into someone with a voice and a social conscience, is less kind. When he started

---

[2] Sheffer, R. (Ed). (2007) "The Green Arrow: Legend of the Emerald Archer." On *Smallville: The Complete Sixth Season* [Blu-ray]. Burbank: Warner.

[3] Booker, M. (2014). *Comics Through Time: A History of Icons, Idols, and Ideas*. (p. 166). Santa Barbara, Calif.: Greenwood.

[4] Boney, A. (Oct 2006). "Mike Grell on Green Arrow." *Back Issue*, 35-45.

giving Green Arrow the morally outraged voice of the left in the late 1960s and early 1970s,[5] along with a change in costume and addition of a trademark beard under artist Neal Adams,[6] he found a character that had gone almost three decades without a defining feature. "Green Arrow was a *tabula rasa*, there was nobody really much interested in him. And there was not a whole lot of backstory or continuity to be saddled with."[7] While this is ostensibly true, in that there was no one defining thing that audiences or writers could point to as being unique prior to the 1970s, it's perhaps more accurate to say that Green Arrow was *overburdened* with characteristics. Traversing the pages of *More Fun Comics*, *Adventure Comics*, *World's Finest Comics*, and eventually *Justice League of America*, if Green Arrow was a blank slate in these early days, then he was one that moved effortlessly between genres, taking on popular attributes to keep him on target with audiences.

Over the decades, Green Arrow became so much more than a simple pastiche, but like all characters born during wartime, he was initially built for an audience hungry for escapist entertainment. For this exploration of the first Green Arrow that lasted throughout the Golden Age, he will be considered not just as a response to a desire for more superheroes, but as a Batman archetype, a vigilante cowboy in an urban landscape, and as a soldier.

Dynamic Duo: Mort Weisinger and George Papp

When Green Arrow first appeared in 1941, he was written by Mort Weisinger and illustrated by George Papp. While we still know Jerry Siegel and Joe Schuster for their most famous creation Superman, and Bob Kane and Bill Finger will forever be associated with Batman, it's perhaps telling that Green Arrow co-creator Weisinger is best known for his work on someone else's creation. Indeed, despite being the father of Green Arrow, Aquaman, and a score of other characters – not to mention his other successful non-comics works[8] – Weisinger remains best known for his work as an editor for the 'weird

---

[5] Beginning with *Justice League of America* Vol 1 #66 (Nov 1968) and later more famously in the "Hard Traveling Heroes" arc of *Green Lantern* Vol. 2 #76-89 (Apr 1970 - Apr 1972).

[6] *Brave and the Bold* Vol. 1 #85 (Sept 1968).

[7] Sheffer (2007).

[8] In addition to his comics and sci-fi work, Weisinger was diverse, including *The Journal of the AMA, Reader's Digest*, an article on the Comics Code for *Better*

period' of Superman comics in the 1950s that introduced the likes of Supergirl, Krypto the Super Dog, and the Phantom Zone.[9] It is little wonder that Green Arrow struggled to find an identity for the first few decades of his life when his own co-creator's name is synonymous with someone else's creation.

Weisinger's personal origin story is based in the kind of fandom modern geeks can relate to, and to understand his history is to get a sense of comic book history as well. Born on 25 April 1915 to the son of a Jewish businessman in the garment trade, specifically manufacturing footwear, he was keenly interested in science fiction from an early age. Going against his father's wishes for him to be a doctor, writing was his trade, and he was instantly drawn to the likes of *Amazing Stories* during the 1920s, introduced to comics via an issue featuring Buck Rogers and The Skylark of Space.[10] Weisinger was a keen member of the science fiction fan community, in 1931 (when Weisinger would have been around 16 years of age) he was hosting a sci-fi club called "The Scienceers." Here he'd meet and become friends with Julius "Julie" Schwartz, who would also go on to become one of the key figures responsible for ushering in DC Comics's Silver Age as the editor of *The Flash* and *Green Lantern*.

Wonderfully described by Jones (2004) as a "great slab of a kid,"[11] he goes on to talk about him being "hungry to get somewhere. He saw writing as his route." Write he did, and throughout his career he would write for virtually anybody that would publish him. Speaking with 'letterhack' and fanzine publisher Guy H. Lillian III later in his career, Weisinger boasted that he was "always writing… even while I was editing comics. I guess that I wrote about

---

Homes and Gardens. In 1955, he'd pen *1001 Valuable Things You Can Get For Free*, a book that went on to sell in excess of three million copies.

[9] Honored posthumously during DC's fiftieth birthday celebrations in 1985, his official bio concentrates exclusively on Weisinger's Superman contributions with no mention of Green Arrow or Aquaman. This was for good reason: he served as editor from 1941 until his military service in the Second World War, returning to the role in 1946 until 1970, where he was succeeded by childhood friend Julius Schwartz. That bio can be found in Marx, B., Cavalieri, J., & Hill, T. (1985). Mort Weisinger: The Superman Legend Grows. In B. Marx (Ed.), *Fifty Who Made DC Great* (p. 23). New York: DC Comics.

[10] Booker (2014), p. 98.

[11] Jones, G. (2004). *Men of Tomorrow: Geeks, Gangsters, and the Birth of the Comic Book* (p. 131). New York: Basic Books.

1000 articles in my spare time, moonlighting."[12] The father of Green Arrow was all about reappropriation too. Never pausing in his ambition, Weisinger would hustle his way into writing gigs:

> He'd point to a piece in a magazine with phony-sounding byline and claim he'd written it under a pseudonym. Then he'd use that to talk an editor into assigning him a short piece, retype something from another magazine, and submit it as his own.[13]

Using those connections and his sheer ambition, in 1932 he co-created *Time Traveller*, one of the first science-fiction fan magazines with editor and super fan Forrest James Ackerman, Allen Glasser and childhood friend Schwartz. By 1934, he and Schwartz would form Solar Sales Service, the first literary agency to specialise in sci-fi, horror, and fantasy. Moving into editing, Weisinger was responsible for almost 40 titles in the Standard Magazine line by the time of the Second World War, establishing himself as the darling of Ned Pine's publishing stable of *Thrilling Mystery*, *Thrilling Love*, *Thrilling Adventure*, and just about any other pulp that had "thrilling" in its title. This writer and editor of virtually anything would pull on popular myths, trends, and legends to spin his characters for the periodicals over the coming years. Prior to his service in the war, he moved from Standard to National Periodical, where he would begin editing the Superman and Batman titles. Out of this environment, Green Arrow would emerge.

George Papp, the artist who gave form to Green Arrow and Speedy, remains something more of an enigma. Born around the same time as Weisinger, on 20 January 1916, he worked almost exclusively as an artist for much of his career. Prior to creating Green Arrow with Weisinger, he began his career in comics with some of the early Superman books, including a small feature in *Superman* Vol. 1 #3 (Dec 1939). When he started illustrating for *More Fun Comics*, the eventual birthplace of Green Arrow, he would co-create Congo Bill with Whitney Ellsworth,[14] the character that would later be transformed into an ape named Congorilla. Following service in the Second World War, Papp

---

[12] Lillian III, G. (1975, July 1). Mort Weisinger: The Man Who Wouldn't Be Superman. *The Amazing World of DC Comics* #7, 2-8.

[13] Jones (2004), p.98.

[14] *More Fun Comics* Vol. 1 #56 (June 1940). In a case of swings and roundabouts, Congo Bill would much later be retconned into being present when Oliver Queen's parents were killed by lions on safari in *Green Arrow Secret Files and Origins* Vol. 1 #1 (Dec 2002).

would draw large chunks of the *Superboy* run, including the introduction of the Legion of Super-Heroes. A versatile artist, he would move effortlessly between characters, but with the exception of his stint in the army, he remained the sole artist for Green Arrow until Weisinger shifted him to *Superboy* in the 1950s[15]. Harvey (2005), writing about Papp's Seven Soldiers of Victory work in *Leading Comics*, adds that "Papp was perhaps the most accomplished: his renderings never faltered, and his anatomy was always accurate."[16] While he would remain on *Superboy* until his departure from the publisher in 1968, he was still associated with Green Arrow well into the 1950s under different writers such as Ed Herron. So when we speak of the visual aesthetics of Green Arrow in these early years, we are almost exclusively talking about what Papp brought to the page.

The Green Arrow's Secret Past

It could be said that Green Arrow exists because of an editorial mistake. This might explain why he didn't get his first origin story until 1943, almost two years after his introduction in the pages of *More Fun Comics*.

The year was 1941, and while the real world was at war in Europe, the comic book industry was doing its bit on the home front. Over at Timely Comics, a patriotic super-soldier made his debut in *Captain America Comics* Vol. 1 #1 (Mar 1941), proving once and for all that it was possible for a kid from Brooklyn to sock Hitler in the jaw. Superman and Batman defended their own territories from the threats of war, leaving the US troops to fight the wars in Europe, declaring "United States Army, Navy, and Marines are capable of smashing their foes without the aid of a Superman". DC's home-grown heroes had propaganda style covers asking readers to buy war bonds or support the American Cross. Lois Lane was later seen on the cover of *Superman* Vol. 1 #29 (July 1944) telling a group of enlistees that "You're my supermen!" Yet even the threat of global conflict could scarcely satiate the public desire for more comic book heroes, as newsstands rapidly filled up with National Periodical Publications' *World's Finest Comics* and *Green Lantern*, All-American's *All-Flash Quarterly*, Timely's *Sub-Mariner Comics*, and Fawcett's *Bulletman*. These contemporaries of pulp

---

[15] Morrissey, R. (2004). A King for a Queen. In J. Morrow (Ed.), *Collected Jack Kirby Collector* (Vol. 4, p. 96). Raleigh: TwoMorrows Publishing.
[16] Harvey, R. (2005). "Introduction." In *The Seven Soldiers of Victory Archives Vol. 1*. New York: DC Comics.

heroes addressed what Chambliss and Svitavsky (2013) identify as reader concerns "increasingly shaped by an urban life amidst ethnic diversity and technological change."[17] These stories largely took place in the crime-riddled inner-city, and the costume vigilantes brought with them a sense of certainty and protection that readers so desperately needed in times of urban upheaval and global turmoil. It was this environment that set the scene for the introduction of Green Arrow, as *More Fun Comics* temporarily shifted its focus away from comedy and into the realm of superheroes.

According to an interview in *The Amazing World of DC Comics* Vol. 1 #7 (July-Aug 1975), Green Arrow co-creator Mort Weisinger - then serving as a writer and editor at National Periodicals, part of the company that is now DC Comics[18] - had to "dream up some new characters." Crawford (1978) notes that a "score of superheroes" were introduced "in order to smother what might be interpreted as a publishing blunder", namely the somewhat unexplained alteration of Doctor Fate's helmet and powers and relationship with Nabu the Wise[19]. Despite being called up for boot camp to serve as a sergeant in the military during the Second World War, Weisinger's amazing first week at the company saw the creation of three new heroes in rapid succession, including

---

[17] Chambliss, J. C., & Svitavsky, W. L. (2013). "The Origin of the Superhero: Culture, Race, and Identity in US Popular Culture, 1890-1940." In J. C. Chambliss, W. L. Svitavsky, & T. Donaldson (Eds.), *Ages of Heroes, Eras of Men* (p. 6-27). Newscastle: Cambridge Scholars Publishing.

[18] What is now DC Comics originally started as amalgam of several separate publishers. National Allied Publications formed in 1935 with *New Fun: The Big Comic Magazine*, the book that would eventually become *More Fun Comics*, the first home of Green Arrow. National Allied entrepreneur Major Malcolm Wheeler-Nicholson was in debt to printer Harry Donenfeld, and Wheeler-Nicholson took the latter on as a partner to form Detective Comics Inc. with accountant Jack S. Liebowitz listed as an owner. Here they would publish the first Superman and Batman stories. National Allied Publications merged with Detective Comics Inc. to form National Comics, who in turn absorbed All-American Publications (creators of Atom, Flash, Green Lantern, Hawkman, and Wonder Woman) in 1944. Liebowitz arranged the merge of All-American and Detective Comics into the entity known as National Periodical Publications. Prior to 1977, DC Comics had not officially adopted the name, and confusing matters further, Superman-DC was often used on the publisher's crest during this period. However, from this point forward, the company will mostly be referred to as DC Comics for convenience.

[19] Crawford, H. (1978). *Crawford's Encyclopedia of Comic Books*, p. 39. Middle Village, N.Y.: Jonathan David.

the western-themed Vigilante and the Flash clone Johnny Quick.[20] Then in *More Fun Comics* Vol. 1 #73 (Nov 1941), readers got their full 10 cents worth with the introduction of two brand new heroes: the Atlantean Aquaman, who would also soon be put to good military use fighting Nazi U-boats, and the dynamic duo of archers, Green Arrow and his sidekick Speedy. As such 25 September 1941 became a "green-letter day" in the history of comics publishing, even if it was to sweep some editorial missteps under the rug.

The Case of the Namesake Hero: Green Arrow as Batman with a Bow

If Green Arrow is an amalgam of other characters, the most obvious one – at least with the benefit of hindsight – is that of the Batman model. Weisinger had, after all, spent his first few years at DC editing *Detective Comics*, and the popularity of the character was understandably rubbing off. The opening pages of Green Arrow's first published adventure 'The Case of the Namesake Murders,' sandwiched as it was between Doctor Fate and Radio Squad stories, introduces us to "Green Arrow and Speedy, wizard archers of the century" *in media res*. From the first panel, their costumes were fully formed, and would remain mostly unchanged until the late 1960s. Green Arrow wore the pointed hat with a red feather, modelled after the 'Robin Hood' hat that was a necessity for fictional archers. His matching green smock and pants weren't far from Errol Flynn's costume in *The Adventures of Robin Hood* (1938) film that arrived a few years earlier. His bright red gloves and boots matched his sidekick's similarly fashioned outfit, which was in turn highlighted with a yellow hat, gloves, and boots. Like Batman and his teen sidekick Robin, Green Arrow and Speedy live together under the aliases Oliver Queen and Roy Harper, ready to take a break following the unpublished off-panel 'Case of the Golden Mummy'. At this stage, Ollie and Roy, as we shall often call them, wouldn't justify their own origin story. "I hadn't thought of one," Weisinger would later explain, "so I backtracked."[21] That convoluted origin story would come in *More Fun Comics* Vol. 1 #89 (Mar 1943), which will be discussed in more detail later in this chapter.

---

[20] *More Fun Comics* Vol. 1 #71 (Sept 1941).
[21] "Green Arrow: A Streamlined Robin Hood." (1976). In D. O'Neil (Ed.), *Secret Origins of the Super DC Heroes* (p. 177). New York: Harmony Books.

Green Arrow and Speedy make their triumphant debut in *More Fun Comics* Vol. 1 #73. Art by George Papp. © DC Comics.

In *More Fun Comics* #73, a masked killer stalks the members of the History Club, all of whom conveniently share names with dead historical figures. George Lincoln is shot, for example, while Anthony Caesar is stabbed. Green Arrow and Speedy, apparently "known throughout the world," begin to investigate, but an attempt is made on Green Arrow's life in the process. He gives chase "with the agility" of a cat, clueing into the fact that it was actually the club's treasurer who had been embezzling money from the group. It's a fine first outing, introducing many key aspects of Green Arrow's shtick in the 1940s, including pinning a crook to the wall with deadly accuracy, and the clever use of multiple arrows to make a ladder foreshadowed the numerous 'trick arrows' that would be added to the archer's arsenal in the next few years. Papp's bold primary colored heroes are strikingly different to Batman through their sheer vividness, and the liberal use of the built-in catapult in the bright yellow Arrowcar (inexplicably named the Arrowplane, even if it was entirely grounded[22]) gave the comic a fluid sense of action Vanier (2014) describes as a "dynamic style of drawing that is rather unconventional for the era."[23] Of course, Vanier is also quick to point out that even with this artistic energy, there is something incredibly familiar about 'The Case of the Namesake Murders.' He argues that a close reading of the text follows an almost identical structure to 'The Case of the Chemical Syndicate', the first adventure of Batman.[24] This is difficult to ignore, even if many of the stories of this era were based on familiar formulas. That was no mistake either: in the early 1940s, DC sent a three-page list of Editorial Requirements to its writers. Comparing themselves to "the adult pulpyarn," it set out core tenants around action, locale, menace (including "a worthy opponent"), ingenuity, mystery, caption, and dialogue.[25] However, even if we put this to one side, the similarities with Batman scarcely stop there.

---

[22] The actual Arrowplane, one that *could* fly, would be introduced in the Ed Herron penned story "The Weather Wizard," one of the backup features in *Adventure Comics* Vol. 1 #118 (July 1947). Green Arrow co-creator George Papp continued on art duties.

[23] Vanier, R. (13 Aug 2014). "Retro Review: More Fun Comics #73 (1941) – 'The Case of the Namesake Murders.'" Retrieved 28 Aug 2015 from http://modernmythologies.com/2014/08/13/retro-review-more-fun-comics-73-1941-the-case-of-the-namesake-murders/

[24] In the seminal *Detective Comics* Vol. 1 #27 (May 1939).

[25] Gilbert, M. T. (Summer 1998). "Internal Affairs: DC in the 1940s - The Garden Fox Letters, Part Two." *Alter Ego - The Comic Book Artist Collection*, 2(2), p. 38-41. We

Where Batman had his well-stocked utility belt, Green Arrow eventually had his trick arrows, seemingly one for every situation. Comic book writer and editor Mike Carlin, who began working at DC in the 1970s, once commented that Green Arrow's "gimmicks were even more limited than Batman's – to arrows. But he had an Arrowcar, and an Arrowcave, he was a millionaire, and he had a sidekick and it was really... a blatant emulation."[26] Many of the things that the Golden Age version of Green Arrow is most closely associated with, and indeed is still tied to, were birthed over the course of many years especially in the pages of *World's Finest Comics* (which still prominently featured artist George Papp after his return from war) and *Adventure Comics*, where Green Arrow more appropriately transitioned after *More Fun Comics*. 'Trick arrows' are so much a part of the character's mythology, it scarcely seems to matter that he didn't use them for large chunks of his early career. More often than not, it was the grappling hook Arrow-Line or the Arrowcar's in-built catapult that came into play in most of the stories in the 1940s. One of the first identifiable trick arrows was the relatively humble bolo (or bolas) arrow, appearing as early as 1942's "Doom over Gayland."[27] By the time we get to 1946's "Contest for Champions," the more outlandish boomerang arrow was starting to turn up.[28] However, the infamous Boxing Glove Arrow didn't make its inauspicious appearance until 1947, when he used it against the only appearance of the Storm King.[29] By the end of the decade, his arsenal broadened to include a tracer arrow, a Dynamite Arrow, a siren arrow, a suction cup arrow and no less than five specific underwater jet arrows including the Leech Jet Arrow and a Eel Jet Arrow.[30] Trick arrows, of course, fulfilled the dual purpose of being a non-lethal alternative to sticking enemies with pointy

---

can only wonder how Green Arrow's vast array of trick arrows fit in with the ingenuity guidelines, which steered creators away from hidden weapons and towards natural props.

[26] Sheffer (2007).

[27] *More Fun Comics* Vol. 1 #77 (Mar 1942).

[28] *Adventure Comics* Vol. 1 #108 (Sept 1946).

[29] *Adventure Comics* Vol. 1 #118 (July 1947).

[30] In *World's Finest* Vol. 1 #20 (Winter 1945-46), *World's Finest* Vol. 1 #21 (Mar-Apr 1946), *World's Finest* Vol. 1 #29 (Mar-Apr 1946), *World's Finest* Vol. 1 34 (May-June 1948) and *Adventure Comics* Vol. 1 #134 (Nov 1948), respectively. Other arrows in this period included sleeping gas, flame, wall-climbing spike, fish-hook and blunt-tip arrows.

The debut of the Boxing Glove Arrow from *Adventure Comics* Vol. 1 #118. Art by George Papp. © DC Comics.

objects, along with keeping in line with an internal memo from editor Sheldon Mayer that prohibited showing "anybody stabbed" or any "blood or bloody daggers."[31] Weisinger once commented: "I was afraid a reader would say one day 'How the hell can he carry that many arrows in his little bag?' He had everything from A to Z in there. In real life, he'd need 50 plastic garbage bags to haul them."[32] Despite their rarity in the early part of the decade, from the late 1940s and throughout the 1950s, the trick arrow collection would be more of a prominent feature for Green Arrow as his quiver began to grow exponentially, with their uses become more specific and logic-defying. By 1951's 'The Case of the Taunting Targets', an incredibly silly issue where a wounded criminal hides radium in the shafts of Ollie's special arrows, a whole quiver of very specific arrows are revealed. The baffling criminal plan is to regain the radium by having Green Arrow fire the special arrows back at the crooks. In order to do so, the bad guys have to concoct a series of convoluted scenarios that require Arrow's use of the Armor Piercing, Flame, Windmill, and Oil Spray ("For motor repairs") arrows, along with the Independence Day Arrow ("Shot on the Fourth of July, Contains Fireworks"), the Wedding Arrow (which naturally "contains rice") and most bizarrely, the Annual Sports Day Arrow ("Skywrites Sports Greeting Once a Year").[33]

Even with all this circumstantial evidence, Weisinger maintained that Batman wasn't the motivator. "I wasn't remotely influenced by Batman. My Green Arrow was a streamlined Robin Hood – a law-abiding Robin Hood. Then I added props – the Arrowmobile, for one, and I got into the business of creating new kinds of arrows."[34] Those props just happened to include a raft of Batman inspired ideas, although these would start to become more obvious in the latter part of the 1940s. Batman's Bat-Signal had been there from the beginning, although the infrequently used Arrow Signal would not really appear until 1947, with the majority of people using the newspaper classifieds to get urgent messages to the heroes. The Arrowcraft boat, on the other hand, would actually

---

[31] Gilbert, M. T. (1998). The "Note to Writers and Artists" is undated, but Gilbert surmises it is between 1939 and 1948, during Mayer's tenure as editor of the All-American Comics line. Similar guidelines would have been in place at National.
[32] O'Neil, D. (Ed.). (1976), p. 177.
[33] *World's Finest Comics* Vol. 1 #55 (Dec 1951).
[34] O'Neil, D. (Ed.). (1976), p. 176.

beat the official launch of the Batboat by several years.[35] At the end of every adventure, Green Arrow and Speedy placed a trophy in their cabinet, just as Batman would in the early adventures. Of course, for Batman that would eventually lead to the Dark Knight's vast cave filled with giant coins and a dinosaur. Yet absent for much of this era is Queen's mansion or infamous 'Arrowcave,' with Roy and Ollie clearly identified as living in an inner-city apartment at least until 1945,[36] although references to Queen's status as a socialite or to a 'secret basement' indicated it wasn't his only abode.[37] One of Green Arrow's early recurring villains was Bulls-Eye (a.k.a. Leapo the Clown), a forgettable jester who mirrored Batman's most famous foe, the Joker[38]. Around this time, he also encountered a female burglar named The Cat, who also evokes Batman's feline foe Catwoman.[39] Yet if Green Arrow remained simply a Batman imitator, we would not be discussing him in depth over seven decades later. Even so, the first part of Green Arrow's amalgam origin was undoubtedly influenced by the Batman archetype, whether the prolific writer was conscious of it or not. It would be a noose around the archer's neck for decades, and the character would literally have to change appearance and attitude in the 1960s to be seen as anything other than Batman with a bow.

---

[35] The Arrowcraft debuted in *More Fun Comics* Vol. 1 #78 (Apr 1942). Although Batman may have used a proto Batboat in several earlier adventures, the first official Batboat wouldn't debut until *Detective Comics* Vol. 1 #110 (Apr 1946).

[36] *More Fun Comics* Vol. 1 #104 (July 1945). The Arrow-Cave doesn't actually appear until *World's Finest Comics* Vol. 1 #59 (July 1952), "The Case of the Vanishing Arrow!" Here it appears as an "Arrow Workshop," one that seems to be their building's basement. By "The Spy in The Arrowcave," in *World's Finest Comics* Vol. 1 #112 (Sept 1960), it was a fully-fledged cave. A terrific summary of these changes can be found at http://supermanartists.comics.org, which adds the comment: "By this time, all of the Weisinger / [Jack] Schiff heroes had secret caves of one sort or another."

[37] Wells, J. (1 Oct 2001). Emerald Archers and Boy Bowmen. Retrieved 9 Sept 2015 from http://fanzing.com/mag/fanzing39/feature2.shtml

[38] First appearing in 'The Arrow Meets Bull's-Eye!' from *World's Finest Comics* Vol. 1 #24 (Sept 1946), which was also Papp's first work on Green Arrow after returning from service in Second World War. After only six appearances, he would return for the last time in *Adventure Comics* Vol. 1 #137 (Feb 1949), featuring in a Green Arrow story called "Unhappy Birthday to You," penned by George Kashdan and illustrated by George Papp.

[39] *Adventure Comics* Vol. 1 #104 (May 1946), her only appearance.

The Archer from Sherwood Forest: Green Arrow as Robin Hood

It's no stretch that the other major influence on Green Arrow's origin was Robin Hood, and even Weisinger was claiming this as the primary influence on the character. It's no shock either, with the Errol Flynn vehicle *The Adventures of Robin Hood* becoming one of the highest grossing films at its time of release. By the 1950s, Robin Hood had become his own genre with a surrounding minor industry to match, and Green Arrow was simply capitalizing on that popularity. Yet placing a quiver full of arrows on top of the Batman formula resulted in a mishmash of archery influences, with the equally persistent story of William Tell working its ways into the panels of several Green Arrow stories over the course of the decade.

Green Arrow as part of the Robin Hood myth goes beyond the color of his costume and the anachronistic vigilante spirit. Beach (2000) notes that Green Arrow, while fitting the Batman myth from the outset, also displays many of the same tropes that have made Robin Hood enduring: multiple writers, plucked from the aristocracy, and an outlaw hero who plays by his own rules and is beloved by the people.[40] Beach categorizes the Green Arrow of this era as simply a character with "blond hair and an exceedingly bland face... a bland personality... a campy, entertaining read, but in the long run left Green Arrow a peripheral character." This is only partly true: the colorists of the time made him a brunette more often than not. Despite Green Arrow's similarities to the Robin Hood mythos, the difference lies in his relationship with the law. Like Batman, Green Arrow has a good relationship with the police commissioner of what would become known as Star City,[41] whereas Robin Hood was traditionally at odds with the Sheriff of Nottingham. Much later in the Golden Age Green Arrow's run, "The Return of Robin Hood" spells out this fundamental difference when a misguided group of merry men verbalize this distinction: Robin is an outlaw, while he sees Green Arrow is a friend to the authorities. "Not quite!" protests Green Arrow. "But we're on good terms with a lot of sheriffs..."[42] Robin

---

[40] Beach, S. (2000). Robin Hood and Green Arrow: Outlaw Bowmen in the Modern Urban Landscape. In T. Hahn (Ed.), *Robin Hood in Popular Culture: Violence, Transgression, and Justice*. Cambridge: D.S. Brewer.

[41] Green Arrow's home city is initially identified at Manhattan in *More Fun* #73, and then "a great seaboard city" (*More Fun Comics* Vol. 1 #78, Apr 1942) and the "east coast" (*More Fun Comics* #84, Oct 1942) in later issues.

[42] *Adventure Comics* Vol 1. #171 (Dec 1951).

The Arrowplane, which is actually a car, and its dubious ejection seat in *More Fun Comics* Vol. 1 #73. Art by George Papp. © DC Comics.

Hood, who turns out to be a delusional academic suffering a split personality, nevertheless makes a salient point: "Ho! They are varlets and servile hirelings of petty officials." If Green Arrow was inspired by Robin Hood, then it is an equally misguided inspiration, missing the inherent outsider nature of the legendary archer. The appeal of the outlaw brigand in European culture mirrors the popularity of the Western outlaw in America's heritage, and Green Arrow's connections to that heritage are discussed below. Deprived of his status as an outlaw or outsider, or the swashbuckling appeal of Errol Flynn, Green Arrow was simply a do-gooder with an unlikely array of arrows.

The earliest allusions to famous archers come in the third Green Arrow story from *More Fun Comics*, "Crime College."[43] Not only is Green Arrow explicitly referred to as "Mr. Robin Hood," but he plays a game of "William Tell" by shooting a penny off the villain Penny-Ante's head. Yet by the same token he is also working within the law, with sidekick Speedy busting the tail light of the criminal's getaway car to attract the attention of the proper authorities. In the following story, 'The Secret of the Centuries'[44] – by which time Green Arrow has taken the lead spot in *More Fun Comics* anthology – the setting becomes the "labyrinths of a feudal castle," as Weisinger consciously summons an association between the two vigilantes. In 'The Script Calls for Murder'[45], the Wizard Archers visit the set of *The Adventures of William Tell*, although with Ollie and Roy becoming analogues for legendary archery stuntman Howard Hill, it's undoubtedly a commentary on *The Adventures of Robin Hood*.[46] With Green Arrow and Speedy outclassing any other archer, the message is clear: these heroes are more like Robin Hood than the films.

The notion of a lawful Robin Hood becomes more overt a few months later in a story entitled "Robin Hood's Revenge."[47] After Speedy recklessly takes some leftover Time Pills from a case they've just wrapped up, an ironic early

---

[43] *More Fun Comics* Vol. 1 #75 (Jan 1942).
[44] *More Fun Comics* Vol. 1 #76 (Feb 1942).
[45] *More Fun Comics* Vol. 1 #80 (June 1942).
[46] Howard Hill would later be established as a personal friend of Oliver Queen in Mike Grell's *Green Arrow: The Wonder Year* (1993). In 1953, a decade after the publication of 'The Script Calls for Murder', Errol Flynn would actually attempt to produce *The Story of William Tell*. Production began in Italy, but his failure to complete the picture would ruin Flynn financially.
[47] *More Fun Comics* Vol. 1 #82 (Aug 1942).

indicator of the heroin addiction Green Arrow's young ward would develop in the 1970s[48], the Battling Bowmen end up back in the time of Robin Hood. While not an "imaginary story", it has all the hallmarks of one. "Robin Hood himself! It's like a dream come true!" exclaims Speedy, far too readily dismissing his regular world famous partner. The story rewrites the Robin Hood myth to serve the publishing standards of the day, with Robin revealed to be merely someone who encourages other robbers to give up their stolen goods to the poor. A true hero would never actually break the law, and a series of misadventures briefly sees Green Arrow and Speedy arresting Robin for a murder he was falsely accused of. Of course, the morality of the heroes shifts from issue to issue: their refusal to accept a gold reward ("We never take money for doing what's right") is a rebuke of the previous issue, in which the duo happily took a $10,000 reward from the authorities to save Ollie's own fortune! Even in a pre-Comics Code Authority world, Green Arrow and Speedy's moral superiority beat out even Robin Hood, but only if the story required it that month.

The tables were turned when Green Arrow and Speedy made the more appropriate leap to the pages of *World's Finest Comics* and *Adventure Comics*. 'The Archer from Sherwood Forest' combines elements from the aforementioned Robin Hood stories, as an accident on set of a Robin Hood film causes the star to think he is the legendary outlaw, leading to a series of crimes committed by the "Robber Hood."[49] Less than a year later, writer Otto Binder exploited the trend again in 'A Day in the Life of Robin Hood,'[50] directly posing the question "Which archer is better with a bow... Green Arrow or Robin Hood?" by having them swap places. Papp gets to stretch his artistic boundaries beyond the urban landscape when Green Arrow and Speedy visit London in pursuit of the nefarious Monocle Mike (who "turns his accents on and off like a faucet"). Foreshadowing the kinds of science fiction stories Jack Kirby would tell with the character, Binder's yarn sees two arrows shot on the same spot in Sherwood Forest hundreds of years apart, creating a "momentary contact of the two arrows in relative space and time." Robin and Ollie swap places, although from the reactions of the heroes and their companions, they don't

---

[48] In the Denny O'Neil and Neal Adams classics *Green Lantern* Vol 2 #85 (Aug-Sept 1971) and #86 (Oct-Nov 1971).
[49] *World's Finest Comics* Vol. 1 #33 (Mar-Apr 1948).
[50] *World's Finest Comics* Vol. 1 #40 (May-June 1949).

appear to remember their earlier Time Pill induced encounter, and presumably the reader isn't expected to either.[51] The question of their respective prowess is never settled, as Robin deals with modern guns as readily as Green Arrow and Little John deal with storming a castle to rescue captives. "Robin Hood! Green Arrow!" declares the villainous Black Baron, who sums up the issue nicely. "What's the difference? Ho, ho, ho! They're wizards with the long bow!"

Despite Weisinger's intent to steep Green Arrow's origins in the Robin Hood archetype on a superficial level, the character would take on those tropes in a more meaningful way in later eras. Before that, there would be more Golden and Silver Age stories with Robin Hood or William Tell variations, that kept with a similar theme to their predecessors fantasy scenarios and spiritual doffs of the cap to one of the inspirational forces of the archer. Green Arrow once again stands in for an injured Robin Hood, in the Silver Age "imaginary story" 'The Green Arrow Robin Hood!'[52] Under writer Denny O'Neil and artist Neal Adams, his road adventures with Green Lantern and Black Canary would make him the ultimate anti-authoritarian outsider. Indeed, Adams' redesigned costume with Van Dyke beard and swashbuckling attire in 1969 would summon memories of Robin Hood, and firmly distinguish him from being a watered-down Batman. Mike Grell in the 1980s and early 1990s would take it one step further, with Ollie being an actual fugitive from the law, complete with a band of homeless 'merry men'. Yet in the Golden Age, the Robin Hood persona was simply one of the many pieces that made up the collage of Green Arrow.

A Date with the Law: Green Arrow as a Western

One of the other influences on Green Arrow was the 'cowboy and Indians' craze of the 1940s and 1950s, with Western films and literature still at the height of their popularity. Some of the first Western tales to appear in comics came with National Allied's *New Fun Comics* #1 (Feb 1935), the book that would become *More Fun Comics*, featuring the modern Jack Woods stories and the Old West yarns around Buckskin Jim. Westerns were in the blood of the publisher, and more directly, Weisinger's other co-creation of the day was the

---

[51] In 'A Day in the Life of Robin Hood,' however, only Speedy is left with the memory that Green Arrow and Robin Hood changed places.
[52] *Adventure Comics* Vol. 1 #264 (Sept 1959).

Vigilante, introduced the same month as Green Arrow[53]. Illustrated by Mort Meskin, it was an update of the themes of the classic Western stories, mostly set in New York City. If the Vigilante drew his inspiration from the 'cowboy' side of the equation, swapping out a horse for a motorcycle, Weisinger looked to 'Indian' tropes for Green Arrow and Speedy.

Where the Vigilante would have this connection clear from the beginning, Green Arrow and Speedy would not receive their origin story until well over a year after their debut. There were early signs of their Western leanings, with the 'Adventure of the Bankrupt Heroes' story giving us a straightforward 'good versus evil' morality tale against Crime Incorporated[54], while the setup for the mostly anti-Japanese propaganda in 'Hunting Headlines' sees the heroes riding on horseback in a Western recreation during the centennial celebrations of the Old West community of Boomtown[55]. Yet 'The Birth of the Battling Bowmen' went straight for the 'Indian' motif, in an origin story that steeped both Ollie and Roy in Native American lore, albeit a superficial version of it[56]. Indeed, the Native American characters are rife with the casual cultural racism of the time ("Ugh! White man no use thunder stick on boy!"), but Green Arrow nevertheless draws his first official origin from this environment.

In a story written by Joe Samachson – who later co-created Martian Manhunter with Joe Certa – and illustrated by the wartime series regulars of Cliff Young and inker Steve Brodie (often just billed as 'Cliff and Steve'), we join the character *in medias res* before flashing back to their origin via a series of casual shower scenes that would have made Frederic Wertham look twice[57]. In a version that might be wholly unfamiliar to modern readers, Oliver Queen is involved in archaeological work, and has assembled a vast collection of Native American artifacts for a museum. "There was little about Indian life I hadn't mastered, including archery," he explains, neatly eschewing a need to give any

---

[53] In the *Action Comics* #42 (Nov 1941) story "The Origin of the Vigilante."

[54] *More Fun Comics* #81 (July 1942).

[55] *More Fun Comics* #84 (Oct 1942).

[56] *More Fun Comics* #89 (Mar 1943).

[57] Wertham's book *Seduction of the Innocent* (1954) posited that comic books were dangerous to children, making unsubstantiated suggestions that Batman and Robin were gay partners among other things. The resulting splash led to Wertham being called as an expert witness at the Senate Subcommittee on Juvenile Delinquency. See Sequart's documentary film *Diagram for Delinquents* for a fuller exploration.

more explanation to his archery skills. When his whole collection is burned in Ollie's clumsy attempt to fend off a robbery from Dippy Parker's gang, Oliver heads to the Lost Mesa ("a million miles from nowhere") to start rebuilding his collection. A young Roy Harper has already made a life for himself there, learning archery and living off the land with "old Quoag, my father's Indian servant" following the death of his own father in a plane crash. However, the crooks have followed Oliver to the Lost Mesa, believing he is after a gold mine, and conflict ensues between the three parties.

For a retrospective origin story, 'The Birth of the Battling Bowmen' follows many familiar patterns, but its Native American roots firmly separate Green Arrow from both the Batman and Robin Hood archetypes. In the grand superhero tradition of first meetings, Roy and Ollie initially come into conflict over a misunderstanding, and neither is at their full capacity yet, with Oliver clumsily unable to stealthily blend into his surrounds. It all ends with a shared appreciation of their common skills, despite an uncharacteristically belligerent Ollie ("Shut up, brat! You think I'm enjoying this?"), as the two have to work together to outsmart the criminal element loose in the Lost Mesa. This gives Samachson permission to go wild with winking references to the reader about their future as the world-renowned Wizard Archers, from the first Arrow-Line being used to bridge a gap, to the names inadvertently given to them by criminals: "Golly, that kid's *Speedy*!" remarks one of the hoods, while another warns his colleagues to "Watch out for the big guy! He shoots a mean *Green Arrow*!" However, it doesn't fully escape the Batman formula, as his companion Quoag is shot and killed, orphaning Roy for the second time in less than half a dozen pages, just as Bruce Wayne's ward Dick Grayson was. In a blatant example of co-dependency, the kind that just might lead to a heroin addiction if left unchecked, Roy quickly latches onto Oliver as a mentor. "I liked the way you talked, Oliver," reflects the sidekick. "It sounded real and honest! The way a man should talk!" It's a golden rule of children's literature to 'kill the parents,' allowing the child free reign to have adventures without the guilt of leaving the family behind. Here the purpose is twofold, as it not only justifies the death of the criminals by being crushed under a massive golden idol, but it neatly explains why young Roy Harper both lives and works with the millionaire adult Oliver Queen.

Yet some of the most fundamental aspects of this origin are found in the Western mythos, or at least a limited cultural understanding of the 'Indian' side of the equation. The origin of their costumes attempts to co-opt Native

American practices, with Roy first suggesting that the white-shirted Oliver is standing out in the jungle, despite his own ironically bright-red outfit. Dyeing his clothes green with grass, Oliver doesn't miss the opportunity to remind of both his superior skills and knowledge of Native American practices. "Your grass trick was nothing new to me... I knew all about Indian lore, too. From archery to war paint!" In a telling contrast to the costumes of contemporaries – including the blue and red of both Superman and Wonder Woman – Green Arrow's costume is initially designed to *blend in* rather than stand out. As the story ends with a moral resolution ("You can't run from evil men! You must turn and fight them... as we have, with weapons we understand!"), we are given two final pieces of the origin puzzle that intrinsically tie this Green Arrow to the Native American symbolism. The 'trophy' of this case is Quoag's bow and arrows, which they place in their cabinet with the suggestion that there was more to the origin story, "but that will always be the symbol of our first victory... the victory over ourselves!" More than that, Oliver's millions are literally appropriated from what turns out to be a real cave filled with Native American gold, so in retrospect it is more than a symbolic connection to the indigenous past.

It is a very different tone just three years later when Samachson returned to the theme in 'The Impossible Target', a story that sees Green Arrow head out to the long vanished West to introduce Speedy to Wild Horse, the Native American who "taught me plenty about shooting arrows."[58] Adding another layer to Ollie's origin, specifically how he mastered those archery skills, it also does away with some of the cultural stereotypes that plagued the earlier story. Wild Horse is an erudite "college man," and it's Speedy who makes the cultural gaffs, forcing Green Arrow to call him out for speaking to Wild Horse "as if he were a baby learning to talk." The story concerns Wild Horse returning to his people's homelands, feeling he has failed them because he is unable to display necessary archery skills, a prerequisite for retaining the land. It is soon revealed that developers have been sabotaging Wild Horse in order to take the land for themselves, as Samachson touches ever so briefly on social issues rarely seen in Green Arrow stories of the day. It's not just the story that's more sophisticated either, and Maurice de Burgo (the other wartime fill-in artist) has some clever layouts of an eagle spanning several panels of action, adding a narrative flow

---

[58] *World's Finest Comics* Vol. 1 # 22 (May 1946).

that was absent from some of the other Green Arrow stories of the day. No direct references are made to the previous origin story, but here the symbolic nature of Oliver's connection to Native American archery is made a tangible part of his origin. Almost a decade later, in the less progressive 'The Pictures of Peril', Green Arrow tells a faux reporter (in reality a crook in disguise) that "I was raised in the West, and my nearest neighbour was a family of Sioux Indians. It was Little Otter who first taught me to shoot..."[59] A childhood Oliver invents the first Arrow-Line and Boomerang Arrows, and decides to fight crime because "I might as well do good with my arrows..." It's possible to fit this story in with 'The Birth of the Battling Bowmen,'but if nothing else it proves that continuity was fluid at best during the Golden Age.[60]

Soldier of Victory: Green Arrow as a War Hero

Shortly after the launch of Green Arrow and Speedy in *More Fun Comics*, Weisinger wasted little time in seguing them into *Leading Comics*,[61] and he was the driving force behind the new team called the Seven Soldiers of Victory.[62] While the Wizard Archers rose from backing players to cover stars in *More Fun*, they were always destined to remain secondary characters to Superman and Batman when they transitioned to *Adventure Comics* and *World's Finest*. However, as a member of the Seven Soldiers of Victory, Green Arrow and Speedy not only got to be the big fish in a small pond, but they adopted another arrow in their origin quiver, becoming heroes of war as well. While not overtly a wartime book, at least not in the way that some of the other issues mentioned in this section are, *Leading Comics* fit all the hallmarks of a wartime morale booster. Following the simple themes of good triumphing over evil, superhero comics in particular experienced a boom due to their low cost and portability,

---

[59] *World's Finest Comics* Vol. 1 #82 (May 1956).

[60] Similarly, 'The Origin of Speedy' in *Adventure Comics* Vol. 1 #209 (Feb 1955) rewrites Roy's history. Unfortunately for him, his parents are still killed – this time the result of an explosion caused by his scientist father – and the young Roy is taught archery by Chief Thunderhead. In this version, it's the Chief who not only names him "one of speed", but also directs him to find the world's greatest archer, Green Arrow. It's a complete retcon of 'The Birth of the Battling Bowmen', one that has been largely forgotten in the years since.

[61] *Leading Comics* Vol. 1 #1 (Dec 1941) was released only a month after Green Arrow made his debut in *More Fun Comics*.

[62] Harvey, R. (2005), p. 4.

and the Seven Soldiers of Victory embodied a spirit of cooperation that the average citizen could rally around.

Biographer Harvey also suggest that the creation of the Seven Soldiers had nothing to do with the war at all and despite the rallying cry of the team's name, it was more likely a National trying to capture some of the success of All-American's team book *All-Star Comics*, whose Justice Society of America (JSA) was arguably the world's first super-hero team.[63] Yet where the JSA was filled with heavy-hitters like the Golden Age Flash, Hawkman, Hour-Man, the Spectre, the Sandman, *All-American Comics*' Green Lantern and the Atom, and *More Fun*'s Doctor Fate,[64] the Seven Soldiers drew its members from the anthology comics. Green Arrow and Speedy were from *More Fun Comics*, with the Shining Knight (*Adventure Comics*), the Vigilante (*Action Comics*), the Crimson Avenger (*Detective Comics*), and the Star-Spangled Kid and sidekick Stripesy (*Star-Spangled Comics*) filling out the ranks. The presence of the *Star-Spangled* characters is perhaps the strongest indication of this book's attempt to create some level of patriotism, with co-creator Jerry Siegel the only one "who seemed aware of the Nazi menace across the pond."[65] Indeed, there were few overt storylines that directly called out the war in Europe, and the team spirit mostly extended to the bookend segments in each issue. That was left to the Boy Commandos (in *World's Finest*), Quality Comics' Blackhawks (*Military Comics*), and Timely's *Captain America* and *Young Allies*. For the first half of the fourteen issues of *Leading Comics* that contained Seven Soldier stories, before reverting to funny animal stories in *Leading Comics* #15 (1945), many of the stories sent the five teams off in five different directions usually to battle five villains,[66] five historical conquerors or similar foes. Green Arrow took on unmemorable villains like the Hooper, Professor Merlin (no relation to the rogue Merlyn, who would plague Green Arrow for many years), King Baby-Face and Bill "Porky" Johnson.

Instead, Green Arrow's role as a soldier of war was similar to most of his contemporaries at the publisher. Leaving the European battle to the troops,

---

[63] Harvey, R. (2005), p. 5.

[64] Introduced as a team in *All-Star Comics* Vol. 1 #3 (Winter 1940-1941), almost a year earlier than the Seven Soldiers.

[65] Harvey (2005), p. 6.

[66] Including Professor Merlin, who would pose a return threat for Green Arrow and Speedy in the pages of *More Fun Comics* Vol. 1 #75 (Jan 1942).

Green Arrow and Speedy instead dealt with the home front, often encountering many of the problems that average readers would be acutely aware of. In 'Silks, Spice, Everything Nice', the villains are exploiting the scarcity of the titular materials, and are robbing a charity that is meant to benefit the United Service Organizations (USO).[67] Like many of the other books, which also had similar pleas on the cover, the concluding panel reminds readers "you can salt away Hitler and Hirohito by buying war stamps and bonds." In 'The Weather Prophet', Oliver remarks that the weather astute villain the Timer must have his own access to meteorological equipment as "the weather bureau doesn't give out reports in wartime,"[68] while 'Date with the Law' has crooks targeting a "large shipment of industrial diamonds which are needed for the war industries."[69] Green Arrow and Speedy would defend the home front in a far more overt way in the aforementioned 'Hunting Headlines', an issue that has the Battling Bowmen hanging off a fighter jet amidst caricatures of Japanese soldiers, with the words "Green Arrow and Speedy set *traps* for the *Japs* in a mile-a-minute action story!" emblazoned across the cover.[70]

By the time of publication of 'Hunting Headlines', the US had entered the war following the attack on Pearl Harbor by Japanese forces in December 1941, and there is little in the way of subtlety in the story. The previously mentioned horseback challenge in Boomtown opens the feature, only accepted by the team "because the USO can use the money." As the duo return from their mini adventure, they uncover a Japanese incursion setting out towards American oil fields. As Papp's last issue on the title before he went off to war himself, his typically realistic anatomy gives way for a few panels to caricature. Being good citizens, Green Arrow and Speedy immediately report the insurgence to the military, deferring to them as the 'proper' authority and merely offering suggestions as to the next course of action. In what will no doubt be a shock to modern readers, who have seen Oliver Queen as the outspoken voice of the liberal left since the late 1960s, this Golden Age Green Arrow reacts with the outright racism of propaganda rhetoric. "This, my Asiatic apes," he offers during victorious fisticuffs against the enemy soldiers, "is with the sincere compliments

---

[67] *More Fun Comics* Vol. 1 #91 (May 1943).
[68] *More Fun Comics* Vol. 1 #96 (Mar 1944).
[69] *More Fun Comics* Vol. 1 #99 (Sept 1944).
[70] *More Fun Comics* #84 (Oct 1942).

of all who love America." After tossing them into the water, there is little ambiguity in his next words: "Looking for your squint-eyed little playmates, eh? Hah! You'll probably disgust the fish so much, they'll throw you back." The hand of a Japanese soldier is seen sinking beneath the surface as he drowns screaming, a rough death for any foe even by pre-Comics Code Authority standards. As outrageous as the language and behavior may seem today, Green Arrow was simply another cog in the institutional racism of the day, with President Franklin D. Roosevelt's Executive Order 9066 leading to the forced incarceration of around 120,000 people with Japanese ancestry for the duration of the war, including future *Star Trek* star George Takei. The hero's behavior here is explicitly approved of by the people, with a headline closing the issue that reads "Green Arrow's Exploits Stir Nation."

Despite being a born during wartime and appearing regularly in a group called 'soldiers,' the Golden Age Green Arrow is mostly seen as an active combatant in retrospect. When the war was over, Green Arrow and Speedy battle the nefarious Skylark, banned from U.S. soil during the Second World War for sabotage. In 'The Strange Saga of S.K. Lark,' the heroes chase the winged villain across town, sticking to his ban on a technicality by staying above the ground[71]. However, the villain is caught by landing in an aerial Victory Garden, which reminds readers that "Food is still scarce – Don't let your Victory Garden Die!" as the proud American heroes continued doing their bit for their country. Later still, in 'The Master Arrow,' the pair respond to a museum request to donate one of their arrows that proved the greatest help to them in the past. After considering the Boomerang Arrow and the Incendiary Arrow, Roy adds he'll "vote for our 'V' Arrow, Oliver! V for Victory!"[72] This prompts them to recall a previously untold adventure from the Second World War, when they tackled Nazis trying to smuggle microfilm of stolen plans in planes ("Voz iss? Der Yankee Arrow-Men come?"). Destroying the microfilm with two arrows fired in 'V' pattern, the arrow gets its name and is donated to the museum. In the early 1980s, *All-Star Squadron* - a successor to the *All-Star Comics* of the 1940s - had a Roosevelt sanctioned group consisting of the JSA, Freedom Fighters, and the Seven Soldiers of Victory asked to guard the homeland from sabotage. This retroactive continuity (or "retcon") takes place on Earth-Two, a

---

[71] *Adventure Comics* Vol. 1 #114 (Mar 1947).
[72] *Adventure Comics* Vol. 1 #126 (Mar 1948).

parallel Earth that DC Comics had established by the 1960s in *The Flash*, ultimately allowing writers to bring back many of the Golden Age heroes.[73] As continuity soon massively changed at DC Comics, Green Arrow was written out of these stories.[74] If 'soldier' was ever part of Green Arrow's potpourri origin, it was fleeting and of minor importance to his history. What these issues do illustrate is that Green Arrow was inescapably a character who was born in the 1940s, and was just as readily used as a mouthpiece for nationalistic messages as any of his contemporaries.

The Secret of the Masked Archers: Later Origins and Retellings

Green Arrow has continued to evolve over time and, unlike a number of his peers, survived the transition out of the Golden Age by hiding in the back of *World's Finest Comics* and *Adventure Comics* in the late 1940s and early 1950s. Stories in the late Golden Age begin to focus less on inner-city crime, and more on outlandish villains like Bulls-Eye the clown or Mexican border runners smuggling diamonds. They anticipated a trend in the 1950s that would see a backlash against violent comics. As Weisinger steered Superman into a strange and innovative new direction, Jack Kirby and Ed Herron would help usher Green Arrow into the Silver Age of comic books in 1958, bringing with him a plethora of new trick arrows and a brand new origin story that would stand the test of time. Soon Ollie's 'Indian warrior' would give way to the more familiar tale of a millionaire playboy stranded on a remote island, where he crafted his first green camouflage suit and net arrows[75]. Fighting off pirates to board a ship to get him off the island, it is the framework that would later serve every retelling of the origin story from Mike Grell and Gray Morrow's *Green Arrow: The Wonder Year* (1993) to Andy Diggle and Jock's *Green Arrow: Year One* (2007).

---

[73] The issues involving Green Arrow primarily take place chronologically between *More Fun Comics* Vol. 1 #82-83 (Aug-Sept 1942), along with *World's Finest* Vol. 1 #7 (Sept 1942), placing these stories in the second half of 1942. During this time, Green Arrow and Speedy were actually having comparatively innocent adventures involving Time Pills and Robin Hood in the 12th century. In one of the cases of retconning becoming increasingly complex, the absence of heavy-hitters Superman and Green Lantern from the theatre of war is conveniently explained by Adolf Hitler's possession of the Spear of Destiny, giving him dominion over magically vulnerable heroes.

[74] Following *All-Star Squadron* Vol. 1 #59 (July 1986).

[75] *Adventure Comics* Vol. 1 #256 (Jan 1959).

Yet it is the very different science-fiction direction that Kirby and his contemporaries would add to Green Arrow during this period that will be the focus of the next chapter.

Weisinger would find his place in comic book history as the editor who ushered in the 'weird' period of Superman comics, and his devotion to writing continued with the novel *The Contest*, based on his own fascination with beauty pageants. Under Weisinger as an editor, Papp would illustrate the majority of the Superboy issues from 1958 until leaving the publisher during the DC Writers Purge of 1968, where he and a number of his colleagues would be forced to leave the company after demanding health and retirement benefits.[76] Yet during his tenure, including much of the early work of the Legion of Super-Heroes, he also co-created Superman characters Mon-El and the backwards Bizarro with Robert Bernstein and Otto Binder respectively. More significantly, he became the co-creator of General Zod in 1961, a hero that would be a key villain for Superman in print and film half a century later.[77] His creative worlds would collide in 'Superboy Meets the Young Green Arrow', where Superboy's time monitor reveals the future heroism of a young Oliver Queen, shown as being an incompetent archer during his youth.[78]

As far as modern readers are concerned, the many pieces that make up the origin of this Golden Age Green Arrow no longer exist. By the end of the 1960s, he had a vastly different look and attitude, one that would serve him throughout the 1970s as the voice of reason in a world of 'gods'. In the seminal 1985-1986 event *Crisis on Infinite Earths*, which streamlined DC's complex Multiverse, an aged version of the character is killed by a wave of attacks from the Anti-Monitor's Thunderers. In terms of comic book continuity, the character that came out on the other side was literally a different hero from a different Earth, one that only had the island origin as his official backstory. What emerged during this era was a much darker character written by Mike Grell, designed for the urban vigilante era of the 1980s. In a far more literal sense, the Golden Age stories remain mostly inaccessible to modern readers, with only a handful of key issues receiving the archival reprint treatment. While these

---

[76] Barr, M. (1992). "The Madames & the Girls: The DC Writers Purge of 1968." *Comic Book Artist*, Summer(5), 10-11.
[77] *Adventure Comics* Vol. 1 #283 (Apr 1961).
[78] *Adventure Comics* Vol. 1 #58 (Mar 1959).

stories may not be essential, or in some cases completely antiquated, they remain fundamental to understanding how a second-string character like Green Arrow lasted when audiences began to demand more complex and realistic heroes. From the very beginning, Green Arrow's adaptability was his most enduring feature.

Each of these revivals would still find a new angle for the constantly moving target of Green Arrow, with his origin continually being updated to reflect his place within the tide of history. Yet remnants of this simpler time survive to this day, even if they have weathered the darkening of comics across several decades. Indeed, it has become the butt of jokes in the more recent comics, with even Kevin Smith's Batman commenting decades later in *Green Arrow* Vol. 3 #5 (Aug 2001): "Good Lord, man -- did you ever have an original thought back then?" This Golden Age version still appears in animated series and associated lines of toys, despite the retconning of this history out of existence. The early parallels with Batman continue to be played upon in episodes of the animated series *Batman: The Brave and the Bold* (2008-2011), where a friendly rivalry between Batman and a Golden Age/early Silver Age version of Green Arrow (voiced by James Arnold Taylor) perpetuates over three seasons. Darwyn Cooke's award-winning *DC: The New Frontier* (2004) comic mini-series not only depicts an idealized version of Green Arrow in the bridge between the Golden and Silver Ages of the early 1950s, but spawned a film (2008's *Justice League: New Frontier*) and toy line of the same name. Even when the character is updated, as he is in the ongoing CW television series *Arrow*, he is still taking on aspects of other characters, with the hero becoming a de facto Batman just as he did 70 years earlier. In the third season of *Arrow*, traditional Batman villain Ra's al Ghul (portrayed by Matt Noble) tries to convince Oliver (Stephen Amell) to take over his position as the head of the League of Assassins, as Heir to the Demon[79] with his daughter Nyssa (Katrina Law) offered as a bride. This not only mirrors some of the classic tales of the love affair between Talia al Ghul and her father's consideration of Batman as an heir, but another offer only a few years before of a different Ra's al-Ghul (Liam Neeson) to Bruce Wayne/Batman (Christian Bale) in Christopher Nolan's film *Batman Begins* (2005). Indeed, the first few seasons of the show were very much following the tone of Nolan's Batman films. So seven decades later, Green Arrow is not just under the

---

[79] "The Offer." *Arrow*, season 3. Aired 18 Mar 2015.

shadow of the Bat, but appropriating some of his stories wholesale. Part of this renewed spate of appearances is born purely of nostalgia, casting a glow around the patchwork nature of the origins of the heroes of the Golden Age. It's also recognition that despite the many revolutionary changes to the comics industry over the 75 years since his creation, the basic matter that made up Green Arrow could be moulded to meet any era or medium. While change is a constant for almost all heroes, for Green Arrow it was a birthright.

Prisoner of Dimension Zero: How Jack Kirby's Second Origin Ruined Green Arrow for the Better

Jack Kirby ruined Green Arrow. At least, that's the complaint editor Mort Weisinger and the art department made to fellow editor Jack Schiff in the late 1950s[1]. There are few names in the history of comics as big as Jack Kirby, and while "The King" may not have necessarily cared for the Green Arrow during his handful of issues at his initial stint with DC Comics, his impact on the character remains to this day. If Kirby's unconventional direction distanced him from Weisinger and fellow artists at DC, then his science-fiction Green Arrow may have just ruined the character in the best way possible.

Green Arrow transitioned from the 1940s through to the 1950s not just in spite of his secondary status, but largely because of it. In fact it would be more accurate to say that he *survived* the journey in the pages of *World's Finest Comics* and *Adventure Comics*, and it was unusual for one of the secondary characters to be appearing in two serials as a backup feature. Public interest in

---

[1] Ro, R. (2004). *Tales to Astonish: Jack Kirby, Stan Lee, and the American Comic Book Revolution.* (p. 61) New York: Bloomsbury.

superheroes began to diminish as the post-war 1940s drew to a close, and anthology books like *World's Finest* reflected this with the addition of popular *Western Comics* characters like the Wyoming Kid and the short-lived Tom Sparks, Boy Inventor. Hiding in the last half-dozen pages of *World's Finest* by the mid-1950s, Green Arrow was holding fast to a formula that saw the archer fight a series of one-shot villains with names like Greenface, The Snare, The Blue Lancer, and The Switchman, or have to protect his identity through some convoluted series of events[2]. There were the odd quirky entries like "The Ape with the Human Brain,"[3] or 1952's '1001 Ways to Kill Green Arrow,' in which a mastermind writes a book by the same name and sells it to a group of crooks who are keen to make use of it.[4] Rather than simply disappearing alongside a number of his stablemates, Green Arrow's vanilla flavoring made him a staple next to the more exotic tastes of the moment. However, Oliver Queen was about to literally get shot into the stratosphere under Kirby in a series of stories that went against the grain.

In 1958 and 1959, Kirby worked on 11 separate six-page Green Arrow stories in the pages of *World's Finest* and *Adventure Comics*. They were significant not just for the rarity of Kirby inking his own pencils,[5] but that they took Green Arrow in an entirely new narrative direction. While his contemporaries were being given fresh new takes throughout the 1950s, a period that would be known as the dawn of the Silver Age of comic books, Green Arrow would become a more outlandish version of his existing persona. Under Kirby's influence, alongside writers Dave Wood and Ed Herron, Green Arrow's similarities to Batman were rapidly shed in favour of increasingly specific trick arrows, while Kirby's fascination with the science fiction of the atomic age would take him into space and beyond. More importantly, the run

---

[2] In an almost annual set of similar stories, Oliver Queen has to cover up the fact that he has broken his arm (*World's Finest Comics* Vol. 1 #63, Mar 1953), sprained his ankle (*World's Finest Comics* Vol. 1 #72, Sept 1954), a sprained leg (*World's Finest Comics* Vol. 1 #88, May 1957) or in the case of the ridiculous *Adventure Comics* Vol 1 #172 (Jan 1952), *both* Green Arrow and Speedy had broken their legs under a conveniently fallen log. Each time, the overcomplicated plots saw Green Arrow going to great lengths to protect his secret identity.
[3] *Adventure Comics* Vol. 1 #178 (July 1952)
[4] *Adventure Comics* Vol. 1 #174 (Mar 1952), and reprinted in *The Brave and the Bold* Vol. 1 #117 (Mar 1975).
[5] With the assistance of his wife Rosalind "Roz" Goldstein.

gave us the single most important Green Arrow story in the character's history, crystalizing the hitherto fractured origin[6] into a single origin about a millionaire who found himself stranded on an island, influencing decades of stories and breaking free of the formula that plagued him for decades.

Seduction of the Innocent: The Silver Age Begins

The Golden Age of comics, such as the stories explored in the previous chapter, lasted about 20 years from the late 1930s until the mid-1950s. Comics historians use this term not so much to suggest that these were the best years for comics, but they were certainly the years where many of the archetypes we still associate with caped crusaders come from.[7] The plethora of characters that came out of this period, including Green Arrow, were all about chasing the latest newsstand sensation, whether it was the popular jungle stories, Westerns, romances or licensed comics from Disney. Issues would regularly sell in excess of a million copies each, but by the start of the 1950s shifting tastes saw a rise in horror and crime comics, led notably by EC Comics and their humour publication *Mad* (1952-present) and the notorious *Tales from the Crypt* (1950-1955). Then something unexpected happened.

Comics were drawing the attention of lobby groups, and due to some of the increasingly macabre horror titles on the stands, some of these groups saw them as a corrupting influence on children. While Senator Joe McCarthy led his crusade against the "Red plots" and perils of communism, Republican Senator Robert Hendrickson (and later Democratic Senator Kefauver) pushed the United States Senate Subcommittee on Juvenile Delinquency to take action against the sinister threat of the comic book menace. Coupled with the publication of Frederic Wertham's *Seduction of the Innocent* in 1954, and combined with the bad press that comics were receiving out of the Subcommittee hearing, the comics industry adopted the Comic Book Code of the Comics Code Authority (CCA). A self-regulatory set of rules that specifically targeted depictions of sex and horror, it effectively killed off the three major EC Comics horror titles in the

---

[6] See chapter 1.

[7] Michael Uslan identifies the origin of the "age" terms in *Alter Ego* Vol. 3 #54 (Nov 2005) as coming from the reader Scott Taylor's published comments in the letters column of *Justice League of America* Vol. 1 #42 (Feb 1966): "If you guys keep bringing back the heroes from the [1930s-1940s] Golden Age, people 20 years from now will be calling this decade the Silver Sixties!"

process, including *Crime Suspense Stories* and *The Vault of Horror*. Of particular note in the Code was the rule that "In every instance good shall triumph over evil and the criminal punished for his misdeeds."[8] The superhero comics that had gone out of favour made a comeback, and it's for this reason that the Silver Age (roughly 1956 to the early 1970s) represent the 'second great age of the superhero'. Some heroes from the Golden Age were revived, others were initially pushed to one side, with new versions of those characters born out of science. *Showcase* Vol. 1 #22 (Oct 1959) brought an all-new version of Green Lantern, an intergalactic cop, onto the scene in the form of Hal Jordan, Ollie's future partner and friend. Yet it was the earlier *Showcase* Vol. 1 #4 (Oct 1956), introducing a new character named Barry Allen as The Flash, that is largely cited as the birth of the Silver Age of comic books. Green Arrow wouldn't escape a refresh either, and under Kirby he received an all-new origin for this Silver Age.

The Unmasked Archers: The King Takes on Queen

Despite co-creating Captain America with Joe Simon for Timely Comics during to the Second World War, and practically inventing the romance genre with Simon in the post-War years, Kirby found himself at something of a loose end by the mid-1950s. After pencilling for Atlas Comics (the company that succeeded Timely to become Marvel), he wound up at National/DC freelancing for a 30 month period. During this time, he is said to have created 600 pages worth of material, including co-creating the *Challengers of the Unknown* with writers Dick and Dave Wood[9]. Editor Jack Schiff gave the Green Arrow art assignment to Kirby, to replace original Green Arrow artist George Papp, who was about to begin a decade-long tenure on Superboy[10]. According to Kirby's former production assistant and biographer Mark Evanier (2001), neither the

---

[8] Senate Committee on the Judiciary, Comic Books and Juvenile Delinquency. (1955). Comic book code of 1954 (Interim Report). Retrieved from https://en.wikisource.org/wiki/Comic_book_code_of_1954

[9] In *Showcase* Vol. 1 #6 (Feb 1957).

[10] Papp would get to combine these two characters in "Superboy Meets the Young Green Arrow" from *Adventure Comics* Vol. 1 #258 (Mar 1959). Superboy turns his time monitor to the future and learns of Oliver Queen's identity as the Green Arrow. A adolescent Ollie then joins young Clark Kent's class the following day, but this character has not yet learned how to shoot. Green Arrow fans were treated to a rare two stories in one issue, as this feature was followed by a Green Arrow and Speedy standalone piece, "The Arrow Platoon" by Ed Herron and Lee Elias.

editor nor the artist was particularly excited about the gig, especially after being turned down from *Superboy* in favour of Papp. Yet both Schiff and Kirby had bigger plans for the character:

> Kirby didn't particularly like the character, and, oddly enough, neither did Jack Schiff, Green Arrow's longtime editor. When Kirby suggested revamping the feature so that it might blossom into more than just a back-up strip, Schiff was interested. Kirby's proposal gave it a new and unique science-fiction slant, Schiff liked it and Kirby immediately wrote at least one story that reflected his new ideas.[11]

Yet from the beginning, Kirby was making his mark on the book, and stylistic analyst Marin O'Hearn argues that Kirby not only drew these initial stories, but either wrote "or at least rewrote existing scripts for" *Adventure Comics* Vol. 1 #250 (July 1958) and *World's Finest Comics* Vol. 1 #96 (Sept 1958).[12] Kirby's first issue for the character was the somewhat formulaic 'The Green Arrows of the World' in *Adventure Comics* Vol. 1 #250 (July 1958), with Batman co-creator Bill Finger credited as the writer. At an international crime-fighting convention, the hitherto unknown Green Arrows of the World meet for the first time, bringing Green Arrow and Speedy together with counterparts such as the Ace Archer of Japan, Phantom of France, Spain's Verde Flecha, Archer of the Alps and several others. A fraudulent Bowman of Britain tries to blow them all up with a Big Ben Arrow, but the combined efforts of these Emerald Archers puts the matter to bed. Although frequently compared with the earlier "Batmen of All Nations" story,[13] what we see from Kirby here is his ability to immediately reinvent, taking the stars of literally hundreds of backup stories and giving us almost a dozen variations on the hero in his first Green Arrow story. While the Batmen of All Nations were later seen in various forms, most prominently in the Grant Morrison's *Batman* run, the Green Arrows of the World were never heard from since. It would not, however, be the last Green Arrow counterpart that Kirby would introduce.

---

[11] Evanier, M. (2001). Introduction. In Kirby, J., & Kirby, R. *The Green Arrow By Jack Kirby*. New York, NY: DC Comics.

[12] Morrissey, R. (1997). "A King for a Queen." *The Jack Kirby Collector*, 4(17), 26.

[13] *Detective Comics* Vol. 1 #215 (Jan 1955) by Edmond Hamilton (writer) and Sheldon Moldoff and Charles Paris (artists).

The Mystery of the Giant Arrows: Green Arrow Goes Sci-Fi

Kirby's science-fiction slant made itself known shortly after these initial issues, anticipating his work at Marvel in the 1960s. Former Marvel Editor-in-Chief Marv Wolfman perhaps summed up the shift best: "Back when I was young, Green Arrow... [was] one of the most boring strips around...the strip changed and all of a sudden, giant arrows were falling from space and it was crazy."[14] In 'A Case of the Super Arrows,' written and illustrated by Kirby, the people of the year 3000 AD send a gift back to their heroes, Green Arrow and Speedy, in the form of a canister of futuristic arrows, including ones that freeze and a hypnosis arrow that accidentally stuns them, allowing the gifts to fall into the wrong hands. Kirby's art is fluid, his versions of the archers looking as though they could almost leap out of the panel as they spring into action. Green Arrow himself is phsyically transformed in these early stories so that he is built with all upper body strength, and is a tangibly more *present* character than his Golden Age counterpart. As Speedy comes to the realization that their Super-Arrows have been stolen, his exclamations are almost directed at the reader, with Green Arrow and Speedy facing out of the page. Comic book artist Alan Weiss, who began working for Marvel in the 1970s, best described this era of Kirby's art in the first letter column of *Fantastic Four*: "The guy whose figures all look like they're moving, even when they're standing still."[15] The story concludes with the duo recovering the future arrows, and Green Arrow declaring "I think we'd rather keep them out of circulation for a while." It was almost as if Green Arrow was speaking for Weisinger, who wasn't thrilled about a sci-fi Green Arrow, but Kirby had plans to continue a theme in the very next issue.

In the ambitious two-part story 'The Mystery of the Giant Arrows'/'The Prisoner of Dimension Zero,'[16] Kirby takes us deep into the willing heart of science fiction. It wasn't the first time that Green Arrow had dabbled in the realms of sci-fi. As early as 1949's 'The Unknown Adventure!', writer Otto

---

[14] Buxton, M. (2015, July 17). SDCC: Jack Kirby's Contemporaries Pay Tribute to "The King" Retrieved 30 Sept 2015 from http://comicbookresources.com/article/sdcc-jack-kirbys-contemporaries-pay-tribute-to-the-king

[15] Weiss, A. (2015). A Letter to the King. In *The Marvel Legacy of Jack Kirby, Volume 1*. New York: Marvel. The letter originally appeared in *Fantastic Four* Vol. 1 #3 (Mar 1962).

[16] *Adventure Comics* Vol. 1 #252-253 (Sept-Oct 1958).

Binder took the Battling Bowmen to Mars in one of their first overt sci-fi adventures.[17] However, in that earlier story, Green Arrow's memory is wiped following the adventure, and only a handful of attempts were made to put Green Arrow in a sci-fi scenario after that, including a veiled version of Disney's Tomorrowland in 'The Dangers from Tomorrow,' in which the archers must fight their way through the experimental technology found in the World of Tomorrow expo.[18] Similarly, in 'A Sword, A Rifle and a Bow,' Green Arrow and Speedy travel to the planet Tropicus, where they fight aliens in an arena alongside King Arthur and Daniel Boone. The somewhat silly tale ends as an "imaginary story," with an unconscious Ollie evidently dreaming about the adventure.[19] Kirby wasn't interest in "imaginary" stories, and it's unsurprising that these stories were less disguised in their sci-fi leanings. As Sims (2015) notes, even for issues that also contain stories of Batman's Robin travelling back in time to smash Superboy's prize possessions, and Aquaman fighting dinosaurs with a rainbow, Kirby's Green Arrow stories are comparatively weird.[20] Multi-part stories were unusual in those days, especially for Green Arrow who enjoyed space in two serial titles, but according to Morrissey (1997) "Kirby seemed frustrated by the 6- and 7-page length of Green Arrow's stories, and took full advantage of the extra space."[21] The first part begins with the unusual vision of giant arrows falling out of the sky, a sight that the wizard archers take as a natural fit for their investigative prowess. Sucked into a dimensional portal in the process, in what is probably Green Arrow's first trip through the Multiverse,[22] they find themselves in Dimension Zero. Populated entirely by giants, the source of the arrows is a petulant child with a bow and quiver. However, the far more interesting development is the introduction of Xeen

---

[17] *World's Finest Comics* Vol. 1 #42 (Sept 1949).

[18] World's Finest Comics Vol. 1 #85 (Nov 1956).

[19] *World's Finest Comics* Vol. 1 #52 (June 1951).

[20] Sims, C. (28 July 2015). "Bizarro Back Issues: Green Arrow Meets Xeen Arrow." Retrieved 1 Oct 2015 from http://comicsalliance.com/green-arrow-xeen-arrow/

[21] Morrissey (1997), p. 26.

[22] In 'The Flash of Two Worlds,' from *The Flash* Vol. 1 #123 (Sept 1961), hero Barry Allen visits Earth-2 and his Golden Age counterpart Jay Garrick. Retrospectively, this created the notion of the DC Multiverse, a once infinite number of parallel Earths where heroes and humans were variations of those found on the subsequently named Earth-1. The Golden Age Green Arrow, with his different origin story, was later seen to be a hero of Earth-2.

Arrow, a giant and willowy Multiversal alternate to Green Arrow that our duo follows around on his own crime-fighting adventures. "What an imitation," exclaims Ollie. "He must be at least a mile tall!" Just like Green Arrow, he has a quiver full of giant trick arrows, and it's a jet-powered one that he uses to transport Ollie and Roy back to their home. In no other era do we get to see Green Arrow clinging onto the shoulder of his giant doppelgänger fighting an interdimensional foe. It was the best kind of nuts, and a jolt to the white-bread character, signalling his infinite possibilities.

While not as flashy as his later *Fantastic Four* work, or as world-defining as his New Gods pieces when he returned to DC in the 1970s, it's nevertheless a clear example of Kirby trying to work his ideas into a character, even if editorial had other plans. In *World's Finest Comics* Vol. 1 #97 (Oct 1958), released in the same month as the Xeen Arrow tale, Green Arrow and Speedy give chase to jewel thieves using a large mechanical octopus out of an underwater base. Dave Wood and Ed Herron are often credited as a writer on these two books, but Morrissey (1997) notes that "in all probability Kirby continued to have a hand in the plotting."[23] However, Weisinger was notoriously less than pleased with the changes, as Evanier (2001) later recalls in his introduction to the collected works, and it was Kirby that bore the brunt of Weisinger's gripes:

> Then the arguments started. Others in the office, mainly Weisinger... objected to the makeover. Schiff suggested toning down the new elements, and eventually they were toned down to the point that Kirby felt they were too compromised to make a bit of difference.[24]

There was definitely a little less Kirby in the stories the issues that followed, and with the exception of 'The War That Never Ended' – in which Green Arrow and Speedy crash land on an island with Japanese soldiers who don't realize the Second World War is over[25] – the tales take on a more subdued tone. Instead of aliens and robots, he's tackling Sioux Indians, gangs of robbers with a gimmick, and the reliable formula of someone threatening to unmask the hero. Although Kirby's influence was brief, Hammond (2002) reminds us that his ambition and scope was larger than the book. "Kirby's Green Arrow fought injustice in more exotic, even more cosmic locales," argues Hammond. "Green Arrow expanded from localized Star City action to become a bigger scale influence throughout

---

[23] Morrissey (1997), p.26
[24] Evanier, M. (2001).
[25] *Adventure Comics* Vol. 1 #255 (Dec 1958)

Xeen Arrow appears to carry Green Arrow into a new era. From *Adventure Comics* Vol. 1 #253. Art by Jack Kirby and Roz Kirby. © DC Comics.

the DC Universe. The King, for that brief time, made Green Arrow larger than life."[26]

The Green Arrow's (Second) First Case

It's a little bit ironic that one of Kirby's last stories for Green Arrow was 'The Green Arrow's First Case', a completely new origin story that replaced his Golden Age adventures in the Lost Mesa. Editor Weisinger is often credited for the retcon, and indeed a 1976 reprint explicitly says "Weisinger revamped Green Arrow's and Speedy's histories in January, 1959" without any reference to Kirby at all.[27] The story, appearing in *Adventure Comics* Vol. 1 #256 (Jan 1959) and now usually credited to writer Ed Herron and Kirby, sees Roy and Ollie spot a news report about an expedition happening on Starfish Island. An alarmed Ollie suits up and heads out there via Arrowplane, worried about his secret identity being exposed, telling Roy his origin story in the process. When he was "just Oliver Queen, wealthy playboy, world traveller," he became stranded on the island. Fashioning arrows "after the methods used by Indians" (the only vague reference to any origin that had gone before), Ollie learns archery in order to survive. He crafts not only his first green costume out of leaves, but the Rope Arrow, Drill Arrow, and Net Arrow along the way. During this time, he also recorded his real name and adventures on a cave wall, hence the fear of his identity being exposed. Foiling a plot by boat hijackers, he is rescued and returns home, deciding "in a split-second, that my existence on the island could now serve a useful purpose! When I returned to civilization – I would fight crime with my trick arrows!" In the present day, Green Arrow and Speedy divert explorers with their conveniently appropriate Fake Uranium Arrow. Destroying his cave diary, Ollie's identity remains safe to fight another day.

'The Green Arrow's First Case' is one of the most important Green Arrow stories in his long history. Aside from being the basis of every origin tale that has come since, it's a remarkable piece that wilfully reinvents a well-established character, and a contrast to other Silver Age revisions such as the Flash and Green Lantern, who were replaced by new heroes entirely. Weisinger dismissed the idea that people would care about the retcon of the origin, as it had been

---

[26] Hammond, K. (2002). King Meets Queen. *The Jack Kirby Collector*, 10(34), 12-14.
[27] Green Arrow: A Streamlined Robin Hood. (1976). In D. O'Neil (Ed.), *Secret Origins of the Super DC Heroes* (p. 177). New York: Harmony Books.

16 years since the last full origin story had been told. Speaking of it in 1976, he explained:

> At the time we figured who'd remember?...At the time we weren't involved in the reprinting. The new origin seemed schmaltzier and better, and we used it. We weren't aware that fans kept the comics and they would take you to task... We never got letters. Later, I introduced the letters columns, and it was a new ball game.[28]

Yet fan memory wasn't the only thing Weisinger may have misjudged in his reflections, as this "schmaltzier" story was far more sophisticated than the 1943 'The Birth of the Battling Bowmen' origin.[29] In less than seven pages, Herron and Kirby tell a multi-layered story that gives weight and meaning in ways that their comparatively lightweight Golden Age counterparts never needed. Brownie and Graydon (2015) note that the story provides a utilitarian explanation for his costume, "to camouflage myself while hunting small game". By making Green Arrow's costume a "functional necessity," they argue "it's extraordinary design can be presented as incidental rather than intentional."[30] This element is mirrored in later retellings, most notably Andy Diggle and Jock's *Green Arrow: Year One* (2007), and the anchor chain grease he initially uses as a mask is mirrored in the first season of television's *Arrow* in 2012. However, unlike other versions it is Oliver Queen who definitively chooses the name Green Arrow ("Just call me *The Green Arrow!*"), rather than actively dismissing it. It's possibly one of the few moments where Herron and Kirby allowed themselves some "schmaltz", apart from the inexplicable cave diary, as 'The Green Arrow's First Case' attempts to give the same logic to Ollie's origin as the scientific dousing of The Flash's Barry Allen in chemicals. Following this story, the adventures of the Silver Age Green Arrow had begun.

Artistically, the issue may not have been one of Kirby's greatest triumphs, although the style is unquestionably the work of The King. The square-jawed Oliver Queen looks more like Captain America's Steve Rogers, with his muscle-bound and shirtless physique occupying the first half of the story. It was arguably Kirby's most "traditional" work on the character since he began, perhaps finally bending to the will of Weisinger's demands that the book take

---

[28] Ibid.

[29] *More Fun Comics* #89 (Mar 1943)

[30] Brownie, B., & Graydon, D. (2015). *The Superhero Costume Identity and Disguise in Fact and Fiction* (p. 45). London: Bloomsbury Publishing.

The first of many origin revisions in *Adventure Comics* Vol. 1 #256. Art by Jack Kirby and Roz Kirby. © DC Comics.

on a less radical approach than the places Kirby's instincts were leading him. Regardless, like Kal-El's escape from Krypton, the death of Bruce Wayne's parents, or Peter Parker's encounter with a spider, this basic structure has remained unchanged since. The stories have expanded and become more elaborate, and the references have been updated. In the case of Jeff Lemire and Andre Sorrentino's New 52 run,[31] for example, Ollie's presence on the island is orchestrated by his father. Yet almost 60 years later, all versions of Green Arrow's origin involve a man learning his craft after being stranded on an island, and we have Herron and Kirby to thank for that.

The War That Never Ended: Kirby's Legacy

The Green Arrow team of Dave Wood and Kirby would get a chance to start exploring their science fiction leanings with *Sky Masters of the Space Force*, a syndicated newspaper comic strip that Schiff helped the duo secure. Schiff claimed royalties from the profits of the strip, and while Wood sent Schiff money, Kirby refused to pay, believing Schiff's original percentage was a one-off deal.[32] Schiff not only fired Kirby from *Challengers of the Unknown* for allegedly taking Challengers story conference ideas to Sky Masters, but also successfully sued him for breach of contract. The aftermath of the legal disputes saw Kirby leave National/DC Comics, and return to Atlas Comics. Besides which, by the time Kirby departed Green Arrow, he felt that the new elements he was so keen to introduce had been toned down to the point that they were too compromised to make any further difference.[33]

DC's loss was Atlas's gain, as Kirby would soon start making waves under the banner of Marvel Comics. Kirby put aside some of his old differences with Marvel's Stan Lee, cutting loose on his cosmic concepts by co-creating lasting characters such as The Fantastic Four, The Hulk, the original X-Men, Thor, the Inhumans, Black Panther, and Iron Man to name but a few. His sci-fi would shatter planets as the Fantastic Four faced off against Galactus and the Silver Surfer, although he would ultimately leave Marvel dissatisfied in the early 1970s. His return to DC under editor Carmine Infantino would yield what is arguably his greatest sci-fi epic to date, as he introduced readers to his "Fourth

---

[31] *Green Arrow* Vol. 5 #17-34 (Apr 2013 – Oct 2014)
[32] Evanier, M. (2008). *Kirby: King of Comics* (p. 107). New York: Abrams.
[33] Kirby, J., & Evanier, M. (2011). "Introduction." *The Jack Kirby Omnibus Starring Green Arrow*. New York: DC Comics.

World" along with the trilogy of titles: *New Gods*, *Mister Miracle*, and *The Forever People*. We may never know exactly what a Kirby Green Arrow free from creative interference would have looked like, but they are some early indications of the grand multiversal stories that were waiting to be unleashed from somewhere within his very talented brain, one that flipped between DC, Marvel, film and television, and independent publishers between then and his death in 1994.

Kirby's run did not rapidly change the course of Green Arrow's fate. "They wanted the same Green Arrow strip they'd been doing for years," Kirby later lamented. This is demonstrable in the types of familiar and formulaic stories that immediately dropped following Kirby's departure, including at least the third retelling of Ollie and Roy's 'first' meeting in *Adventure Comics* Vol. 1 #262 (July 1959). Yet Kirby's tenure did ultimately open up the character to a wider variety of stories. Only a year or so after Kirby left DC, more outlandish elements started making their way into the books. There was Ed Herron and Lee Elias' story 'Green Arrow's Alien Ally', in which Green Arrow and Speedy team up with an alien law enforcement officer to beat an alien criminal from the Planet of Two Suns, or the same team's 'Prisoners of the Giant Bubble', where crooks use electronic bubbles to commit crimes.[34] In an era where Supergirl and Krypto the Dog was becoming the norm under Weisinger's Superman line of comics, Arrow got his own family expansion with the Amazing Miss Arrowette, who came equipped with such unfortunate arrows as the Hair Tint Arrow, Hairpin Arrow, Lotion Arrow, Nail File Arrow, Needle and Thread Arrow, Powder Puff Arrow and the Soap Bubble Arrow for good measure. The rogues gallery would expanded with villains the Camouflage King and The Clock King in 1960. With the exception of his long-standing association with Green Lantern in the 1970s and beyond, Green Arrow would rarely have such an overt sci-fi connection in his history. The irony is that the most incongruous issue throughout the brief Kirby run is the one that has had the most lasting influence, with his co-created origin story still forming the basis of mini-series and graphic novels exploring the period decades later. If Weisinger was right, and Kirby "ruined" Green Arrow, then he unquestionably ruined him for the better.

---

[34] In *World's Finest Comics* Vol. 1 #114 (Dec 1960) and *World's Finest Comics* Vol. 1 #109 (Dec 1960), respectively.

Divided – They Fall! Green Arrow as the Conscience of the Gods

Green Arrow is not the only non-powered human member of the hero community. As was the case with his earliest adventures, he follows Batman in that regard. Yet since the late 1960s, Green Arrow and his alter ego Oliver Queen have consistently been the outspoken voice of the liberal left – and all humans, for that matter – as the most powerful beings in the DC Universe came together to form the Justice League of America. His clashes with the conservative Hawkman and the artificial human Red Tornado became a running motif, and his friendship with the intergalactic cop Hal Jordan/Green Lantern saw him tackle the social ills of America head-on. Yet for a character that scarcely had an identity for the first two decades of his existence, what makes Oliver Queen so effective in this role? More importantly, what would it take to break that self-assuredness and for him to turn away from his colleagues?

From starting the decade as a staple supporting player, to the latter part of the 1960s where he would find his voice and new facial hair, Green Arrow's evolution was most pronounced when he joined the Justice League. Throughout the decade he would speak up for underdogs, lose his fortune, and ultimately part ways with the powerful members of the League, foreshadowing his intensely solo adventures of the 1980s. If Green Arrow was metaphorically going through his teenage rebellion, his next step would be to leave the nest. Here we explore Green Arrow's political and physical changes in a decade where the world was growing a little more politically active, with the Emerald Archer mirroring the protest movements that were causing divisions across America.

Starting with the radical changes writer Denny O'Neil made when he identified Green Arrow as the voice of human reason, and continuing through to post-9/11 reactions such as *Identity Crisis* and *Justice League: Cry for Justice*, this mortal in the world of 'gods' would not only become the default conscience of the Justice League, but challenge the very notion of the kinds of 'justice' they were espousing.

Seeds of Rebellion: Green Arrow Joins the Justice League

In the mid-1960s, Green Arrow didn't have a regular feature to call his own. His *Adventure Comics* appearances would come to an end after 15 years, not lasting much beyond Jack Kirby's brief run, eventually shuffling him out of that title to be replaced with the Congorilla. Ironically, or perhaps knowingly on the part of writer Robert Berstein and artist Lee Elias, the final *Adventure Comics* story is about creators commencing publication on a new comic book called 'The Golden Archer'.[1] Green Arrow's regular appearances in *World's Finest Comics* had also dried up by mid-1964, and with the exception of a few one-shot stories, even these were limited to reprints of previous adventures by the time he first exited that title[2]. Yet it was during this time that one of Green Arrow's more important career moves came about in the pages of *Justice League of America*, with Green Arrow one of the first non-foundation members to be let into the club. It was not only Green Arrow's primary outlet throughout much of the 1960s, but it saw his first major steps out of the individual formula stories and into a more team-based effort. Green Arrow finally joined the wider DC Universe in a significant way, but the question remained as to how a character based on aspects of so many other archetypes would fit in with the heavy-hitters of the publishing house.

The Justice League came about when editor Julius Schwartz sought to revive the notion of the Golden Age's Justice Society for the booming Silver Age,

---

[1] *Adventure Comics* Vol. 1 #269 (Feb 1960).

[2] Green Arrow would not appear again regularly in this book until *World's Finest Comics* Vol. 1 #244 (May 1977), where he would enjoy almost five years of back-up stories in this title. As we will discover in Chapter 5, it was a very different character who returned to its pages.

one that had already given birth to renewed versions of Green Lantern and The Flash. Debuting in *The Brave and the Bold* #28 (Mar 1960) under writer Gardner Fox and artist Mike Sekowsky, the team of Superman, Batman, Aquaman, Flash, Green Lantern, Martian Manhunter, and Wonder Woman would rapidly get their own book with the release of *Justice League of America* Vol. 1 #1 (Nov 1960). The original creators stayed with the book for the first eight years of its initial 27 year stand. Green Arrow was the first non-founding member to join the team in *Justice League of America* Vol. 1 #4 (May 1961), having survived the Golden Age and stuck around through sheer force of will into the Silver Age revival of superheroes. It was not his first team, of course, with that honor belonging to the Seven Soldiers of Victory throughout the early 1940s, but this collaboration would be his most lasting. In the historic Silver Age union by writer Fox, 'The Doom of the Star Diamond', Batman moves to add Green Arrow to the roster of the Justice League. Martian Manhunter seconds the motion, but no sooner than Wonder Woman calls for a vote than they get word Ollie has been taken captive by Carthan. The exiled alien hero initially tries to deceive the League into helping him topple a dictator, work they would have gladly done *gratis*. Following the adventure, Green Arrow is formally inducted in the League after breaking his colleagues out of a giant diamond-shaped structure with his own diamond-tipped arrow. Even before he was a fully-fledged member, it was not simply democracy alone that secured Green Arrow a place, but a deed that showed he could act where other more powerful members of the League could not. Later, this 'otherness' and different way of thinking about problems is what causes Green Arrow's departure from the Justice League in 1980.

Green Arrow was given few opportunities to rebel in his earliest Justice League appearances, continuing his *World's Finest* and *Adventure Comics* role of being a supporting player. An exception came in his second appearance with the group in *Justice League of America* #5 (July 1961), when he is falsely accused of betraying the team. Here we see some of the earliest examples of the kinds of speeches he would later become notorious for. "Wait! You call yourselves champions of justice! Is it justice to deny me what any accused person in America enjoys... a fair trial!" His outrage would not last long, as he quickly fell back to being a convenient plot device when a very specific trick arrow was needed. Indeed, he was rarely seen in any of the Justice League stories throughout 1965 and much of 1966, frequently "away on other cases" or simply absent. Perhaps it was simply because like a number of other writers throughout the previous two decades, Fox was struggling to find the hook that made Green Arrow interesting in the context of a super-powered group. Fox must have noticed this around the start of 1966, when Green Arrow comments on the frequent absences in 'The Plague That Struck the Justice League!' "I don't like to complain," Green Arrow notes, "but I'm usually somewhere else when things go bang!"[3] None of that statement would remain true for long, as a new creative team came on board for *Justice League of America*, following a 65 issue stand from Fox and Sekowsky. Yet even in the late Fox/Sekowsky era, seeds of Ollie's growing social conscience could be found. In a story that retrospectively sounds like it was taken out of the 1970s, 'Man, Thy Name is Brother!' sees Oliver offer to help out Snapper Carr with his Brotherhood Week project by investigating why a teen with Apache heritage has dropped out of school, despite high grades. Green Arrow passionately defends the victim of prejudice and misunderstanding, and investigates the crime the boy is accused of. In words that would resound with meaning a year later when Denny O'Neil took over the title, Green Arrow argues "Listen – nobody can help how he was born! Black skin, red skin, white or yellow – are just colors... You're meeting up with prejudice – and you're no exception there!"[4] While he would take on a more overt role as the conscience of the League in the following years, this foreshadows the changes that were to come for the non-powered hero.

From Silver Age to Golden Beard: Degrees of Justice in the Justice League

The popular depiction of Green Arrow as a representation of late 1960s rebellion is almost entirely the creation of Dennis "Denny" O'Neil and artist Neal Adams. Then in his late 20s, O'Neil came over with editor Dick Giordano from Charlton Comics, bringing a fresh attitude to the company and quickly became a favoured writer, and one who would help recraft DC Comics and bring it into a new era. Going to work on *Green Lantern* and *Wonder Woman*, he began his run on the flagship team with *Justice League of America* Vol. 1 #66 (Nov 1968) alongside artist Dick Dillin. He immediately showed an affinity with a character he would later define in his acclaimed *Green Lantern/Green Arrow* run just a few years later. In a debut Justice League story that would later drip with significance, 'Divided — They Fall!' shows the League turning down a job

---

[3] *Justice League of America* Vol. 1 #44 (May 1966).
[4] *Justice League of America* Vol. 1 #57 (Nov 1967).

they deemed to be too trivial. While the powerful members of the League chastise the less godlike members Green Arrow, Batman and the Atom for being more interested in Green Arrow's new "sonic transmitter" arrow, seeds of dissent are sewn. An uncharacteristic exchange takes place as Superman talks down to the trio, telling them to "Save your little gab-fest for later!" The Atom immediately becomes defensive, but the crux of the rift comes when professional hanger-on Snapper Carr brings the League a letter from a college professor requesting the JLA's help in locating a stolen machine. While it was the kind of routine mission that would have been a staple in the hundreds of similar Golden Age scenarios, it's Green Lantern who sums up the feelings of Superman and Wonder Woman: "We can't be bothered with capers that a bush-league private eye could handle without working up a sweat!" In a turning point that is now seen as the birth of the rebellious Green Arrow, he becomes the mouthpiece for the mortal members: "What makes you so almighty certain this *isn't* important! Look, we're sworn to battle injustice - *all* injustice!" Superman, increasingly depicted as a stubborn parent throughout the exchange, replies, "But there are *degrees* of injustice! We can only concern ourselves with *major* breaches of the law!" Green Arrow is furious that they won't help out all those in need, and storms off after breaking a glass, refusing Green Lantern's offer for help. The notion of "degrees of justice" is both a provocative and terrifying statement in the hands of Superman.

This single moment foreshadows not only the so-called "relevant comics" of the 1970s, where social issues would become the focus of Green Arrow and Green Lantern's battles, but some of "gods versus humans" arguments that would become a focus of darker edged comics in the 1980s and beyond. Here the two most 'godlike' characters are confronted with the legitimate anguish of their human friend, and choose to dismiss it. While there is nothing overtly religious about this, it is as if the gods are deaf to the cries of mortals. Yet more directly it's a commentary on governmental structures having a limited understanding of smaller community needs. A telling conversation between Wonder Woman and Superman reveals their private feelings on the matters. "I've often wondered if they don't feel a bit... *inferior!*" ponders Wonder Woman. "I mean, we *do* overshadow them! They're human and we're, well... *more* than human!" Superman dismisses the argument, offering "they shouldn't have stormed off like spoiled kids!" The profound shift represented a new dichotomy within the Justice League, one that drew a definite line between god

From *Justice League of America* Vol. 1 #66. Art by Dick Dillin and Sid Greene. ©
DC Comics.

and mortal to create a new dynamic, rather than any definitive political statement. That would come later. As Levitz (2010) comments, it was a more than a simple plot device:

> It was a jarring transition: Fox's stories were rich in plot but light on characterization. By contrast, O'Neil concentrated less on complex stories and more on giving each hero an individual voice for the first time. Fox's Leaguers were interchangeable; O'Neil's bantered, bickered, fought and joked. Under Fox, they were a team because of their similarities; under O'Neil, they were a team despite their differences.[5]

Significantly for Green Arrow, this was the first indication of his attitude towards social justice that would ultimately see him take Green Lantern on the road to teach him about the 'real world' under O'Neil. In this issue, however, he merely apologizes for "flying off the handle". Nevertheless, the supporting character had finally graduated to something far more important, in providing an increasingly vocal platform for the moral decisions that the Justice League needed to consider.

Green Arrow began to be the center of more of the stories he was present for, including being a cover feature when he was falsely accused of murder a few months later[6]. Ollie's continued changes came in several parts for the character, physically transforming out of his dated Golden Age apparel. Beginning with Batman team-up book *Brave and the Bold* Vol. 1 #85 (Sept 1968) written by Bob Haney, Oliver Queen got a new look for a new age from artist Neal Adams. The artist had a commercial and advertising background, and after turning to comics, would help restore Batman from his camp depiction in the 1960s live action series to something darker and more in line with modern versions of the Dark Knight. His hyper-realistic style, with rippling muscles that were more human than human, was an ideal choice to give physical weight to Oliver Queen's newfound voice. Throwing out the red boots, gloves and a hat that colorists in the 1940s and 1950s were never consistent with anyway, Adams' redesign for Green Arrow was the epitome of the functional modern hero. Green Arrow could not rely on super powers like his companions, and even his would-be companion Black Canary, previously only known for her judo skills, developed her sonic Canary Cry only a few issues after joining the Justice

---

[5] Levitz, P. (2010). *75 Years of DC Comics: The Art of Modern Mythmaking*. Cologne: Taschen.
[6] *Justice League of America* Vol. 1 #69 (Jan 1969).

League[7]. Like the leaf costume he crafted in Kirby's origin story a decade earlier, his new costume would be also come from a place of necessity. The significance of Adams' artistic changes, and the question of whether this recreation can be considered another 'origin' for Green Arrow, will be discussed in detail in the next chapter.

The stories themselves evolved too, and Haney's story highlighted Oliver's internal struggle in this highly politicized issue. While both Batman and Green Arrow race to investigate the assassination of a Senator, their alter egos echo a sense of social responsibility that was highly topical in the late 1960s. Bruce Wayne, a friend of the senator, is sent to fill in his seat and help pass an anti-crime bill. Oliver is at a juncture in his life, trying to decide whether or not he should give up the (new) costume and focus on using his wealth to finance the construction of New Island, a second Gotham City. The matter would be resolved for him in the *Justice League of America* Vol. 1 #75 (Nov 1969) story 'In Each Man There Is a Demon!", where Ollie literally fights his inner demons as they emerge in the form of a green spirit during a session with a psychiatrist. He begins to doubt himself, and is initially unable to take down a jewelry thief due to his own indecision. By the end of the story, Oliver Queen has lost his fortune to the machinations of "corporate fat cats". Unleashed from the burden of money, his energies were free to be channelled into his twin passions in this era: social issues and his growing love for the recently widowed Earth-2 character of Black Canary. He took issue with the assistant mayor of Star City on environmental concerns ("Mister, the Earth is in trouble! Experts say we are killing this world... strangling it with waste..."[8]), jive-talking his way into an arrest. Meanwhile, Canary was initially a Multiversal 'fish out of water', while Oliver was becoming alienated from the rest of the League. He would confess his love to her several times before she was ready to start a new relationship following the death of her husband. He continued to play his role as not just the social conscience, but an impossible mix of youthful rebellion and grumpy old man. Oliver Queen would continue to be a supporting character, but that didn't necessarily mean he would always agree with the group.

---

[7] *Justice League of America* Vol. 1 #75 (Nov 1969).
[8] *Justice League of America* Vol. 1 #78 (Jan 1969).

And Through Him Save a World: Green Arrow as the Lusty, Hot-Tempered Left

The dichotomy between Green Arrow's humanism and the rest of the League's top-down approach to law and order can be seen most clearly in arguably the most prominent collaboration of O'Neil and Adams. Combating sliding sales on the title, O'Neil and Adams sent an electric shock through two characters who were far from the A-League, even if the effects were more about character legacy than sales. In their era-defining 'Hard Traveling Heroes' arc in the pages of *Green Lantern*,[9] Ollie confronts his super-powered Emerald companion Green Lantern with the accumulated angst of ordinary humans. At the start of the run, Green Lantern witnesses tenants roughing up a seemingly respectable man, who turns out to be slumlord Jubal Slade. Green Lantern Hal Jordan summarily applies the law, O'Neil immediately setting him up as a space cop with a right-leaning conservative view of the world. Green Arrow gives Lantern a "guided tour" of the ghetto, and the grey areas of the law. Fresh from losing his fortune, and complete with a cool new look, Green Arrow became the "lusty, hot-tempered anarchist to contrast with the cerebral, sedate model citizen who was Green Lantern."[10] So instead of being defined by his similarities to other characters like Batman, O'Neil's take was to highlight the differences that he represented to the rest of the hero community. In doing so, Ollie became the reminder of a world full of problems that the League had been too busy to tackle.

The heroes are forced to confront the very social issues the League partially dismissed only a few years before, travelling across America to see what the "real" world looks like. In the "No Evil Shall Escape My Sight!" story that kicks off the run,[11] Green Lantern must confront a black man who claims Hal's done more for alien races than he has for "the *black* skins! I want to know... *how come*?!" Lantern is deflated and unable to answer. Later it is Ollie who berates Green Lantern, in his most reprinted speech to date:

---

[9] Originally in *Green Lantern* Vol. 2 #76-89 (Apr 1970 to Apr-May 1972) and *Flash* Vol. 1 #217-219 (Sept 1972 – Jan 1973). It is now reprinted in various editions as *Green Lantern/Green Arrow: Hard Traveling Heroes*.

[10] Wells, J. (2010). "And Through Them Change an Industry." *Back Issue*, 1(45), 39-54.

[11] *Green Lantern* Vol. 2 #76 (Apr 1970).

You call yourself a *hero*! Chum, you don't even qualify as a *man*. You're no more than a puppet... and the *Guardians* pull your strings. Listen... *forget* about chasing around the *galaxy*! And remember *America*. It's a good country... beautiful... fertile... and terribly sick! There are children dying, honest people cowering in fear, disillusioned kids ripping up campuses. On the streets of *Memphis* a good black man died... and in Los Angeles, a good white man fell. Something is *wrong*. Something is killing us all! Some hideous moral cancer is rotting our very souls. And you... sitting on your mudball, preening like a smug tomcat. How *dare* you presume to meddle in the affairs of humanity, when human beings are no more than *statistics* to you and your crew.

This is what makes Ollie unique to this era: an unwavering belief in his own moral correctness, a fatigue in having seen optimistic voices shot down, and the self-granted moral authority to argue with those who can do something about it. Ollie's rage echoes the protests movements that ripped America apart in the late 1960s and early 1970s, which is why these comics were often referred to as an experiment in 'relevancy'. He believes he has the backing of America, or at least the version of it he believes to be true. Ollie is a guardian of sorts, charging himself with protecting the moral compass of the superhero world. As one of the few characters that survived the passage of time from the earliest points in comic book history, he is certainly in a position to make a case for it. Terjesen (2011) identifies Ollie's certainty in philosophical terms, contrasting Hal's moral *rationalism* with Ollie's moral *sentimentalism*, and that the two necessarily complement each other. Green Arrow is there to prompt Green Lantern to "rethink his abstract moral principles" and allow the Guardians an "appreciation for the need to have exceptions to more complicated rules."[12] Green Arrow might have begun as a skilled archer with a host of trick arrows average humans could never hope to see, but it only took O'Neil and Adams a handful of issues to make him one of us.

The pick-up truck journey of self-discovery and broadened horizons is Hal's, it being Green Lantern's titular book after all, but Green Arrow is his perpetually angry Jiminy Cricket. Yet instead of being a tiny voice in the back of Lantern's mind, he was a very vocal point of view in his face whether Lantern wanted it or not. Cut loose from his teenage ward Speedy, his fortune or any of his ties to

---

[12] Terjesen, A. (2011). Hard-Traveling Ethics: Moral Rationalism Versus Moral Sentimentalism. In J. Dryden & M. D. White (Eds.), *Green Lantern and Philosophy: No Evil Shall Escape This Book* (pp. 105-121). Hoboken, NJ: Wiley.

the past, Ollie sets out to educate Hal in the very human "capers that a bush-league private eye could handle". Using his background as a journalist with a keen interest in social activism, O'Neil sought to apply some of what he was witnessing to his Green Lantern stories[13]. It follows in the tradition of the New Journalism O'Neil was reading, and as such shares some DNA with Tom Wolfe and Hunter S. Thompson. At its most basic level, *Green Lantern/Green Arrow* pondered what would happen if a super-hero was put in a real-world setting knowing that he could not solve all the problems of the world. It's a dilemma that writers of many Superman volumes have avoided for obvious reasons, as it leads to natural questions about why the heroes aren't doing more. Keeping a certain amount of safe distance from the actual headlines of the day, O'Neil later remarked that while the book was published in the early 1970s, "the stories belong to the previous decade as much as surely as do Owlsley Acid, the Fillmore, protest marches, draft-card burning, the Johnson Presidency and those innocent, arrogant naifs, the Flower Children."[14] The Hard Traveling Heroes, who also included Black Canary for a number of issues, would be forced to confront racism, the unions, and elements of the "hideous moral cancer" that was crippling America in Green Arrow's eyes. The dream of the 1960s might have died with the realities of the 1970s, but the spirit of rebellion was alive in the hyper-reality of this comic book.

Green Arrow was a representative of the left and kept partly in line with O'Neil's own politics, but it didn't stop the writer from depicting the Emerald Archer as an insufferable jerk at times, and an excessively preachy one at that. So convinced of his own moral correctness, Ollie goes so far as inferring that Hal Jordan's adherence to law is similar to that of Nazi Germany. So the response was to burst Ollie's liberal bubble by giving him something that would challenge his worldview. In what is arguably the other most iconic moment in the run, the Comics Code Authority challenging *Green Lantern* Vol. 2 #85 (Sept 1971) story 'Snowbirds Don't Fly', and its companion 'They Say It'll Kill Me... But They Won't Say When!" in the following issue,[15] shows what happens when Ollie finds out that his ward and estranged partner Roy Harper (a.k.a. Speedy) is addicted to

---

[13] Zimmerman, D. (Aug 1986). Denny O'Neil. *Comics Interview*, 22-37.
[14] In an introduction to *Green Lantern/Green Arrow* Vol. 1 #1 (Oct 1983), reprinting *Green Lantern* Vol. 2 #76 and #77.
[15] *Green Lantern* Vol. 2 #86 (Nov 1971).

heroin. Rather than being a bastion of understanding, he instead slaps Roy and they go their separate ways. "Look... sure, I'm ticked off at the pushers because they prey on weakness," he explains by way of justification for his behaviour. "But that doesn't mean my heart bleeds for junkies. Life is tough for everyone. If you want to claim humanity, you don't crawl into a drugged stupor." The moral compass of the Justice League faltered when it came to matters close to his own family, the irony that his roadside preaching has distracted him from his own role as a father figure, but it is this human flaw that makes Green Arrow even more effective somehow as the League's conscience.

The issues keep the alarmist tone, with Speedy taking on Ollie's role in the second half of the story to lay some truth on his mentor about the folly of a war on drug users. The series is, after all, just as much about Green Arrow's failures as his moral victories. The ultimate ending of the series, following the cancellation of *Green Lantern* due to declining sales, takes place in *Flash* Vol. 1 #217-219 (Sept 1972 to Jan 1973), concluding with "The Fate of an Archer" story. Feeling the weight of the ills of the world, and accidentally killing a boy due to an injured arm, Ollie removes himself from society and enters a monastery[16]. However, he discovers that the life of violence has a way of finding him, rediscovering his unerring aim when both Black Canary and Green Lantern's lives are threatened. "Yeah... I *found* myself out there," he announces. "At least temporarily, I know who *I* am. Sometimes, *Lantern*, I can almost believe in a *happy ending*." Laying in a hospital bed as he gives Canary a blood transfusion, the bittersweet final panel seems anything but happy, indicating that the optimism of the 1960s may have actually given way to cynicism in the 1970s after all. In this instance, the very conscience of the Justice League had his faith tested, and in many ways swapped roles with Lantern by the end of the series.

Where his previous appearances in *Justice League of America* had suggested it, *Green Lantern/Green Arrow* conclusively established Green Arrow's role as a hero with a conscience. After running the gamut of headline topics, O'Neil later explained that they simply ran out of issues to get angry

---

[16] The only incongruous issue at this time is *The Brave and the Bold* Vol. 1 #100 (Mar 1972), written by Bob Haney with art by Jim Aparo. In a move that disappointed O'Neil, Green Arrow is shown wilfully shooting and killing a man in the pursuit of an alleged drug supplier. 'The Fate of an Archer' storyline restored the O'Neil/Adams vision shortly afterwards.

about, although he felt that they had still achieved much of what they set out to do. "We had just about exhausted the list of social causes that any of us was genuinely interested in... The danger would have been 'Cause of the Month Comics,' which would have become boring and banal after a while."[17] The "relevancy" approach may have earned them a following in colleges and the press, winning numerous awards along the way, but it did not translate into sales. Goulart (1986) cites a conversation with editor Julius Schwartz about the sales, asking him how relevance was doing. "'Relevance is dead,' he informed me."[18] It may have been for the time being, but it gave birth to a new Green Arrow in its place. Argumentative, single-minded, and at times confronting the goofiest of villains – not least of which was a little a girl with psychic powers who looked like Richard Nixon[19] – this Green Arrow wasn't just a pastiche but a hero, and a hero with a voice that differed from the rest of his peers. Moore (2003) sees this as an essential element of the *Green Lantern/Green Arrow* run, arguing "that it is through conflict that groups develop political consciousness and become all the more aware of their positions in society."[20] During the run, Hal Jordan begins to doubt not only his own role in the universe, but question the very authority that mandates him his power. As early as *Green Lantern* Vol. 2 #77 (June 1970), he was declaring "Green Arrow has made me think that maybe *authority* isn't always *right* – and I don't know what is just." By the end of the run, in *Green Lantern* Vol. 2 #89 (Apr 1972), the two come into conflict over the actions of an environmentalist protester sabotaging Ferris Aircrafts. Lantern's ultimate decision is to defy that authority following the death of the saboteur. As his sometimes girlfriend Carol Ferris declares that "I suppose progress must *always* claim victims!", Green Lantern steels himself and blows up the aircraft that the protester was metaphorically "crucified" on. Adopting some of Ollie's cocky bravado, he coolly declares "Send me a *bill!*" as he walks away. Green Arrow's moral bullheadedness may not win him any fans in the League, or among some of the readers, but the conflict he creates with his

---

[17] Brodsky, B., & Kevin, H. (Feb 1998). "Denny O'Neil: Writer on the Storm!" *Comic Book Marketplace* (56).

[18] Goulart, R. (1986). *Ron Goulart's Great History of Comic Books* (p. 297). Chicago: Contemporary Books.

[19] *Green Lantern* Vol. 2 #83 (May 1971).

[20] Moore, J. T. (2003). "The Education of Green Lantern: Culture and Ideology." *The Journal of American Culture* (26), 263–278.

From *Green Lantern* Vol. 2 #76. Art by Neal Adams and Frank Giacoia. © DC Comics.

wilful points of difference allow Hal / the Justice League to grow and learn more about the nature of humanity.

A Different Way of Looking at Things

Green Arrow's principled ways ultimately led him away from the Justice League, which was a particularly bold move for a fellow who had only just returned to back-up stories in the pages of *World's Finest Comics*. As the 1970s came to a close, Green Arrow was no longer co-leading a title with Green Lantern, but he continued to be uniquely positioned as the antithesis of the increasingly galactic focused League. In 'Testing of a Hero!' Oliver Queen sponsors potential recruit Black Lightning to join the League[21]. The two had teamed up several months before in the *World's Finest Comics* Vol. 1 #256 (May 1979) story 'Encounter With a Dark Avenger,' sharing an acknowledgement that they would work together again. Green Arrow made good on that exchange when the League were looking for a new recruit. "He's just what we need, troops," he argues. "Cool, smart – and black!" The Flash surprisingly accuses Ollie of tokenism, claiming "That's not how we make decisions in the League. I never thought you would suggest we take in a *token black*." The Flash then goes one step further in his accusations: "I think your judgment is warped! You're trying so hard to be Mister Liberal – you don't think straight anymore!" The reaction could very well be one of writer Gerry Conway, paring back some of the occasionally one-note socialism Green Arrow had begun to display throughout the 1970s, although the Flash's reaction - partly defended by Ollie's hard traveling pal Hal Jordan – is also typical of the reaction unwitting prejudice has when confronted. In the following issue, Green Arrow accuses the League of messing with Black Lightning's test to enter the JLA, Conway hinting that Ollie would not stay in the League ranks for long.

Ollie's first proper departure from the Justice League was a logical progression of this evolving character. Following an encounter with a demonically possessed villain of the week, Ollie yearns for the good old days and the "simple villains we used to fight." Fellow Justice Leaguer Red Tornado is the first to suggest that "Green Arrow does not share the general relief. I fear that there is trouble brewing with our friend, the bowman."[22] His suspicions are

---

[21] *Justice League of America* Vol. 1 #173 (Dec 1979).
[22] *Justice League of America* Vol. 1 #180 (July 1980).

founded the following month, when Ollie's "different way of looking at things" ultimately leads him to quit the Justice League in *Justice League of America* Vol. 1 #181 (Aug 1980). In another Gerry Conway story, 'The Stellar Crimes of the Star-Tsar!' Ollie realizes that his way of seeing the world is just too far removed from the rest of the Justice League. Following his powerless way of defeating their enemy, and the temporary hospitalization of Black Canary, he records his resignation into a tape recorder in a beautifully poignant moment.

> Smog! I used a Smog Arrow to wipe out the Star-Tsar! Pretty simple, huh? But you guys never *thought* of it. That's just one of the reasons I've made up my mind to *quit the Justice League.* Face it, we've got different ways of looking at things. I'm not placing blame. I'm not saying it's your fault or my fault. Once, the League was *right* for me. Now... I'm not so *sure*. So that's it. I've gotta go see how Dinah's doing. The docs say she'll be *okay*, but she needs her rest. So do I. I'll miss you guys. *All* of you. We had some *times*, didn't we? Goodbye.

With a single tear and the click of a tape, Green Arrow leaves the League and doesn't return to the publication for almost two years. Whether consciously or not, Conway brings Green Arrow's initial involvement with the Justice League full circle with this issue: it was his "different ways of looking at things" that earned him a place in the League, and a similar stunt with a trick arrow that led to the decision to leave it. It also partly foreshadows the importance of the Ollie/Dinah relationship, placing her well-being above his own need to be part of the gang, a relationship that will later lead the pseudo-pacifist liberal down a path where he will deliberately take a human life[23]. Here we see just how far Ollie has come in the 20 years since he first joined the League, graduating not only from supporting character to central conscience, but willing to walk away from the League when they choose to ignore his protestations. It also speaks volumes about a group of heroes who were willing to let their conscience go over these differences, rather than embrace them as a growing organization. These rifts telegraphed the darker direction comics were heading in the 1980s, the consequences of which a new generation of writers would mine decades later.

---

[23] During Mike Grell's *The Longbow Hunters*, discussed in detail in Chapter 7.

Identity Crisis, *Crisis of Conscience*, and *Justice League: Cry for Justice*

One of the strongest contemporary examples of Green Arrow's role as the conscience of the Justice League is *Identity Crisis.* By the time writer Brad Meltzer launched the controversial seven-issue mini-series in 2004, with Rags Morales as the principal artist, Oliver Queen had undergone a significant amount of change. The rifts of the early 1980s gave way to the DC's line-wide reboot with *Crisis on Infinite Earths*, and Mike Grell's subsequent run turned Green Arrow into a darker urban hunter, completely divorced from the rest of the DC Universe. Indeed, the darkening path was only resolved with Oliver Queen's death in a 1995 issue of the comic[24], and his subsequent resurrection under writer Kevin Smith in 2001[25]. Meltzer himself followed Smith in rebuilding the character for modern audiences in his arc 'The Archer's Quest'[26]. Green Arrow wasn't alone in having been resurrected by this stage, joining Superman and a temporarily disabled Batman in coming back from the 'dead' to reclaim their mantles from successors, legacy characters, and pretenders. From the start, Meltzer's *Identity Crisis* is already a consciously revisionist view of DC history, filtered through a remembered version of DC's Silver Age characters and then subverting their pasts further. As we have seen, the rifts were always there, but Meltzer gives us reasons to understand why it all didn't fall apart earlier.

Following the suspicious death of Sue Dibny, the wife of Elongated Man, the whole superhero community investigates. Green Arrow is forced to reveal to the current Flash (Wally West) and Green Lantern (Kyle Rayner) that the villain Doctor Light once raped Sue, and the League of that era wiped his memory and altered his personality using the sorceress Zatanna. Throughout the course of the investigation, it's further unveiled that it was not the only time that the League had done so, primarily to keep their civilian identities secret. The bombshell moment comes when it is discovered that Batman also had his mind altered for objecting to the actions. Curiously, where Wally West is outraged at this perceived betrayal by his own mentors, Green Arrow tacitly stood by them. "You think Dr. Destiny forgot the time he invaded our dreams?"

---

[24] *Green Arrow* Vol. 2 #101 (Oct 1995).
[25] *Green Arrow* Vol. 3 #1 (Apr 2001).
[26] *Green Arrow* Vol. 3 #16-22 (Oct 2002 – May 2003).

argues Green Arrow, defending the League's past actions. "It didn't just happen by itself. We *made* it happen. And we were okay with it..."[27] Here, Green Arrow might be defending a position his former self would probably have been opposed to, but like the narrative itself, it's filtered through the lens of memory and the perspective of an ageing revolutionary. Green Arrow is no less of a radical than he was in the 1970s and 1980s, but now as a father to multiple children[28], he now understands the importance of family. "You don't just wear the mask for yourself," he concedes. "You do it for your wife, your parents, even for your children."[29] Here he is not just the conscience of the gods, but bearing the moral weight of their decisions as well. He may have agreed to go along with the group, but this was fully in keeping with Green Arrow having the interests of individuals at heart. Batman has the luxury of not remembering the incident, or at least claiming plausible deniability, but it is Green Arrow who must explain it to the next generation of heroes. Decades after walking away from the League, being martyred and resurrected in the intervening years, he still bears the weight of their sins.[30]

While *Identity Crisis* is ostensibly about superhero identity and the importance of its protection, not to mention the violent impact violent lives have on those close to the heroes, the implications of Meltzer's story run much deeper than that. As a post-9/11 reaction to the state of domestic security in the United States, *Identity Crisis* parallels Marvel's goliath *Civil War* event, a divisive split in the Marvel Universe that took well over 100 issues to resolve. In particular, both books are reactions to the real world 2001 US Patriot Act, a significant extension of the powers of governmental organizations and bodies that fall under the auspices of Homeland Security, allowing what opponents believe to be a sacrifice of individual liberties in the name of 'freedom'. Where *Civil War* takes the more literal route of having costumed heroes divided over a

---

[27] *Identity Crisis* #3 (Oct 2004).

[28] In the intervening years, it is revealed that Oliver Queen fathered children with the assassin Shado (discussed in Chapter 7), and has another son named Connor Hawke who briefly took over as Green Arrow during Ollie's "death" (discussed in Chapter 8). He is, of course, the de facto father figure to both Roy Harper and Mia Dearden, the two characters to officially be known as his sidekick Speedy.

[29] *Identity Crisis* #6 (Jan 2005).

[30] In Chapter 9, we discuss the weight of Ollie's Catholic guilt alongside Kevin Smith's exploration of religion and resurrection.

new law requiring them to register their identities to a central body following a large-scale tragedy, *Identity Crisis* unpacks the moral ambiguity around sacrificing personal freedoms for the greater good.

This thread culminates in the 'Crisis of Conscience' arc,[31] and later the *Cry For Justice* event, where the "fall" of Green Arrow results from him losing his moral authority. In the latter 7-issue mini-series by writer James Robinson,[32] the villain Prometheus tests the heroes, including ripping the arm off Red Arrow, the then current alias of the sidekick formerly known as Speedy. Green Arrow's home turf of Star City is partially destroyed, killing Red Arrow's daughter Lian in the process. Green Arrow tracks down Prometheus without the aid of the Justice League, shooting him with an arrow in the head and killing him instantly. When the other Leaguers discover this and confront him, he surrenders himself to the city authorities, and his then wife Black Canary returns her ring and ends the marriage. The city is more forgiving, finding him not guilty but nevertheless exiling him to the mysterious forest in the center of town. Green Arrow had turned his back on the Justice League in the past, but here they do the same to him when he at last puts his own desire for revenge above the collective need for justice. Green Arrow is the conscience of the gods, but as is far too common when dealing with extremes, his more powerful friends can be frequently wrong, while he only has to falter once.[33]

Continuing the Fight

Most of the depictions of Green Arrow since the late 1960s have referred to his moral core, and until the reboot of the DC Universe following 2011's *Flashpoint* event – immediately following his exile in the forest - a clear line of evolution could be drawn from his Silver Age origins to his moral fall and redemption. As a mortal in the world of 'gods', Green Arrow's unabashed confidence is not just an interesting character trait but a necessity in order to fight alongside them. Being a supporting character in this case meant

---

[31] *JLA* Vol. 1 #115 - #119 (Aug-Nov 2005).

[32] *Justice League: Cry for Justice* #1 (Sept 2009 - Apr 2010).

[33] Although this was not the first time Green Arrow had killed. He had accidentally done so during *Green Lantern/Green Arrow*, forcing him into a monastery to atone for his sins. Similarly, when he deliberately took a life in *Green Arrow: The Longbow Hunters* #2 (Sept 1987) in order to save Black Canary, he spends time in therapy dealing with the aftermath.

supporting the moral health of the League as well as their missions. He wasn't a morale booster for the Justice League, which was the job of professional sidekick and comic relief Snapper Carr, but someone the League could also turn to during a crisis of conscience.

The perfect example of this interrelationship actually comes from outside the comics, in the retro-inspired version of the character depicted in the *Justice League Unlimited* animated television series. In the first episode of that series, 'Initiation', Green Arrow becomes the first new hero shown to join the ranks of the Justice League. Beamed aboard the orbital Watchtower, he confesses his own insecurities about his place amongst more powerful heroes. "Come on. I don't belong up here — fighting aliens and monsters and super villains. I just help the little guy."[34] Just like his comic book counterpart in 1968, he was worried that the League was focused too much on the big picture to fit in someone with his Earth-bound focus. It's Batman, his fellow mortal member of the League, who ultimately counters with an argument O'Neil had made half a century earlier: "Someone like you will keep us honest." The story comes full circle the following year, in an episode entitled 'Divided We Fall', a clear tribute to the first O'Neil story on *Justice League of America*. In that episode, Superman announces his intentions to disband the League. Green Arrow once again acts as the voice of the average person, who now firmly believes that the Justice League has purpose for all the people of world:

> You remember what we did yesterday? We saved the world, again. You don't think that has any value? Well, think again, pal! The Justice League goes on, with or without you... But if you're quitting because it's easier than continuing the fight, then you're not the heroes we all thought you were. The world needs the Justice League, and the Justice League needs you, Superman.[35]

In a singular passionate speech, the kind that could have been written by O'Neil 40 years earlier, Green Arrow not only asserts why it is important for the Justice League to consider the rights of the individual, and why the world needs the Justice League, but why the Justice League needs Green Arrow.

---

[34] "Initiation." *Justice League Unlimited*, season 1. Aired 31 July 2004.
[35] "Divided We Fall." *Justice League Unlimited*, season 2. Aired 16 July 2005.

More Than Real: The Art of Neal Adams on the Hard Traveling Road to Relevancy

"Stop!" proclaims the cover to the first issue of the Hard Traveling Heroes storyline. "This is the NEW *Green Lantern/Green Arrow*!" A convincingly muscled Green Lantern takes the Oath that recharges his power ring: "*In brightest day, in blackest night, no evil shall escape my sight!*" The shaft of one of Green Arrow's titular weapons shatters his comrade's lantern as Arrow coolly declares "Never again." We don't know what rift has caused these two emerald warriors to spar, or why Green Arrow is determined to stop Lantern from preventing the escape of evil from his sight. This is how Neal Adams visually opens the team-up that defined an era, practically paring back the two heroes to line art against a glowing green background that bathes the both of them. It is such a showstopper of a cover that the audience scarcely needs reminding that this is the new *Green Lantern/Green Arrow*. Thematically and visually, truer words had never been printed, especially in an era where the art and artists in the comic book industry would begin to put their own stamps on the house styles.

So much has been written on the importance of the initial *Green Lantern/Green Arrow*[1] issues in terms of their approach to "relevancy" and establishing Green Arrow as the conscience of the DC Universe. Indeed, this was largely the subject of the previous chapter of this book. Denny O'Neil's voice is a fundamental one in the development of the modern version of the Green Arrow character, giving Oliver Queen the final pieces of character building that were needed to transport him from supporting player to a star member of the Justice League capable of at least co-leading a monthly book. Yet this wouldn't have been possible without first changing the public's perception of the character from the bland and generic costume to something more in line with a modern superhero. When Neal Adams redesigned Green Arrow in the late 1960s, the character that emerged wore the functional outfit of an archer. It visually conveyed the weight this new version of the character would yield, putting to rest a Golden Age look that was still very much part of the 1940s. This moment is so pivotal in the history of Green Arrow, it could be argued that Adams didn't simply redesign Green Arrow but (re)create him. Just as George Papp is responsible for the visual aesthetic of the first two decades of Green Arrow's existence, Adams would pave the way for the next 20 years and beyond. With this in mind, it is only appropriate that *Moving Target* also takes its own thematic shift, and focus primarily on the visuals of Green Arrow in this turning point of an era.

Following an argument that Adams himself has made for a number of years, here the role Adams had in the *third* origin of Green Arrow is examined, with Adams the creator of a fit-for-purpose version of the hero[2]. By dissecting his commercially inspired approach to character design, a look at the visual language of *Green Lantern/Green Arrow* aims to explore the realism of the seminal work in terms of its artistic style, rather than simply the headlines it sought to respond to. If O'Neil was the journalist reporting on the ills of America in the 1960s and 1970s, then Adams was his wartime photographer, opening up the hidden truths of the DC Universe by laying its heroes bare.

---

[1] While *Green Lantern/Green Arrow* was the cover title, specific issues and numbers will be referred to by their more technical attribution of *Green Lantern* Vol. 2.

[2] The first two being his Golden Age origin story, and the Jack Kirby illustrated piece in 1958, covered in Chapters 1 and 2 of this volume respectively.

The hard-traveling heroes unite on the cover of *Green Lantern* Vol. 2 #76. Art by Neal Adams. © DC Comics.

Defining a style: Neal Adams before Green Arrow

Born on Governors Island, New York on 14 June 1941, just a few short months before Green Arrow's debut comic hit the stands, Adams graduated from the vocational School of Industrial Art high school in Manhattan (later called the High School of Art and Design), following fellow alumni such as Carmine Infantino, Joe Orlando, Alex Toth, John Romita, and Dick Giordano. This is one of those biographical details that finds its way into all standard works about Adams, included here as an early indicator of the art-driven outlook he had towards character creation over his career in and out of comics. Along with his commercial work, it was where he would have learned a fundamental grasp of anatomy and realism that would be his trademark on the comic book industry, an influence that echoes into the modern notion of a 'house style' as well.

Understanding what Adams brought to comics is easier when one looks at his earlier work as a young artist. Finding a comics industry that was notoriously difficult to break into, and being turned down by DC in the late 1950s, he took work where he could get it, including several pieces in *Archie's Joke Book Magazine*, where he very much worked to a formula already set by previous house artists. Where we start to see a more familiar Adams style emerge is in some of the commercial pieces he did as a freelancer for the Johnstone and Cushing agency in New York, which went for a domestic market in special purpose comic books and strips for advertisers. Melodramatic pieces where a housewife declares "I can't go on living this way!", with perfectly proportioned couples in the foreground, show the seeds of Adams style. There's far more of a direct line-through to *Green Lantern/Green Arrow*'s look with his subsequent *Chip Martin, College Reporter* advertising strips for AT&T and the *Flash Farrell* pieces for Goodyear. The Chip Martin pieces in particular, such as a 1966 strip called "Project Gemini," showcase an artist skilled in portraying photo accurate humans of all ages, engaged in the everyday activities of their jobs at the spacecraft center in Houston. The attention to background detail, as well as individual lines and creases on faces, would mark his later work on Batman and Green Arrow.

When Adams did manage to start making a living from comic books, he was one of the few people to successfully straddle the line between freelancing at both Marvel and DC, a virtually unheard of prospect prior to this. What's striking about Adams work coming into comics is how self-assured it is from the start. In Warren Publishing's *Creepy* Vol. 1 #14 (Apr 1967), in a short story called

'Curse of the Vampire,' he illustrates the Archie Goodwin script with all the foreboding and tilted shots of a Hammer Horror film. Panels rarely stick to the straight lines of the traditional grid, a girl runs out of a panel entirely, and a pair of eyes floats without the need of borders at all. It's almost a portfolio of his available styles. He'll zoom in on dramatic close-ups, fearful faces half in shadows. In other panels, the passing of time is signified by three different phases of art, from the fully finished to the half-sketched figure in the foreground. It's a technique he would employ on his later Green Arrow work. Earlier at DC, on *Our Army at War* or the Elongated Man in *Detective Comics,* he was far more restrained in panelling, but the heightened emotions of the characters remained. Where we really start to see his styles combine were with the character of Deadman in *Strange Adventures* Vol. 1 #207-216 (Dec 1967 - Feb 1969). Here characters occupied large parts of the page's real estate to bawl their eyes out, while comics style stories *within* the existing narrative relay flashbacks in a black-and-white photocopy style. At other times, stunning multi-panel pans gave a fluidity and illusion of movement that utilized the uniqueness of the comic medium. For this he won a special Alley Award in 1969, given "for the new perspective and dynamic vibrance he has brought to the field of comic art."

Two collaborations would set the course of the near future in comics: freelancing at both Marvel with Roy Thomas on *X-Men* and *Avengers*, and at DC Comics with Dennis O'Neil on *Batman* and *Detective Comics*. The former saw him work with some of Marvel's most iconic characters and storylines, including the creation of the mutant Havoc and a run on *The Avengers* "Kree-Skrull War" arc that resonates in comic storylines to this day. He would collaborate with O'Neil at both publishers for the first time on *Uncanny X-Men* #65 (Mar 1969) and *Detective Comics* #395 (Jan 1970) respectively, commencing a run on the latter that would revive Batman for DC. In the wake of the camp 1960s *Batman* TV series, the characters Ra's al Ghul, Man-Bat and a far more menacing Joker were all introduced by the duo to shift the perception of the character from Caped Crusader to Dark Knight. The culmination of his work could not have been more symbolically represented than on cover of their first *Detective Comics* collaboration, with a mistress of the night straight out of Warren Publishing offering Batman "immorality – or instant death." Thanks to the hyper-realistically muscled and heavily shadowed Batman that Adams concocted, it was the former that both were destined for.

The Senator's Been Shot! Adams and the (Re)Creation of a Hero

Green Arrow's new look literally came at the audience arrow-first, challenging the reader to defy the revolution. In one of the most daring redesigns of a character, readers got their first look at Green Arrow on the cover of *The Brave and the Bold* Vol. 1 #85 (Sept 1969) without so much as a banner declaring a "Exciting new look!" or a "You've never seen Green Arrow like this before!" There was no easy transition for Green Arrow's new look, and initially no explanation for the radical makeover. Instead, the Bob Haney penned story declares itself early, with an Adams cover that not only has a dynamic use of perspective, increasingly larger figures charging towards the heroes Batman and Green Arrow from the background, but also a costume for the latter that instantly marked him as a more mature hero capable of standing toe-to-toe with the darker Dark Knight that Adams had also helped usher into existence.

On the cover of the team-up tale, 'The Senator's Been Shot!', Green Arrow looks angry and determined, and far from the affable supportive type that he had been for the previous 27 years of his existence. As Batman holds the titular senator while looking over his shoulder at the oncoming crooks, Green Arrow has his new compact collapsible bow drawn and ready to fire in the direction of the reader. If "Batman and Green Arrow" were not emblazoned in fonts three times the size of the book's official title, audiences in 1969 may have scarcely recognized the scowling bearded man who (artistically at least) cast a shadow over Batman, his new green boots seemingly using the issue's title to balance himself for the next shot. It's a shock to the system, as the familiar and good-natured hero had been a fixture of DC's stable almost since the inception of the brand, travelling through the decades as a back-up player. He was as much a part of the institution as Superman, Wonder Woman, and Batman, and unlike contemporaries the Flash and Green Lantern, he had survived the 1950s and most of the 1960s without any lasting changes. Now the red pixie boots and gloves were gone, replaced with the functional outfit of an athletic archer, and this older-looking hero seemed willing to fight anyone that had a problem with it. The cover tells us that the senator has been shot: did the Green Arrow with his weapon drawn have something to do with it? It was unlikely, but we knew for certain that he would have something to say about it, especially given the groundwork Denny O'Neil had laid out in *Justice League of America*, giving Ollie a penchant for lengthy speeches. The oft-reprinted *The Brave and the Bold Vol. 1 #85* remains a cover that doesn't so much invite the reader inside, but throws down the gauntlet and calls out the audience to find out more about this exciting new Robin Hood type.[3]

Discussed briefly in the previous chapter, the design was not simply based on aesthetics but also aimed to mature the character. The issue is one of Green Arrow's first overt forays into political matters, following Ollie's business deals over a city-wide development application that dovetails with Bruce Wayne's personal interest in the Anti-Crime Bill before the Senate. As both heroes grapple with the idea of whether they can do more good in or out of costume, Oliver makes his only direct commentary on the new threads, and in the process subtly indicates to the audience that this was a soft reboot for the character. "My other identity... as Green Arrow," he muses to himself. "I'd almost forgotten it! It's been some time... like something from another life... I haven't even gotten any use out of this new costume I had made up!" Writer Haney's implication is that this was a reset point for a character caught between two professions, businessman and vigilante, for some time. For the Green Arrow part of the equation, argues writer and historian Mike Carlin, Adams was making the visual point that the hero would be "something tougher and more important to the world."[4] Dispensing with almost everything but the color, Green Arrow's revived costume would keep some semblance of the pointed archer's cap, replacing the simple shirt and pants and red boots/gloves with something that meant business. With this version, Adams pushed the evolution of Green Arrow past the surface level.[5] His maturity was signified by a Van Dyke beard framing a much sterner face, further distinguishing him from the clean-cut heroes at the top of the food chain. The costume itself was modern, utilitarian and swashbuckling. A cross between a pirate and a professional archer, the criss-cross pattern on the chest and the leather arm bracers showed a character who meant business. "I designed a new costume

---

[3] Curiously, Neal Adams' original unpublished cover to *The Brave and the Bold* Vol. 1 #85 was a very different entity. Adams depicts Batman and Green Arrow lying on twin couches on either side of the shocked psychiatrist son of the titular senator, as they simultaneously pull of their masks to reveal their respective identities. The unused cover is classic Adams, albeit nowhere near as dynamic as the final product.

[4] Sheffer, R. (Ed). (2007) "The Green Arrow: Legend of the Emerald Archer." On *Smallville: The Complete Sixth Season* [Blu-ray]. Burbank: Warner.

[5] Cowsill, A. (2010). *DC Comics Year By Year: A Visual Chronicle*. New York: DK Publishing.

A new Green Arrow for a new generation in *Brave and the Bold* Vol. 1 #85. Art by Neal Adams and Dick Giordano. © DC Comics.

for a character who was truly an archer rather than some guy putting on an archer's costume," Adams explained to the *New York Post* years later. "You see that glove, for example, on his hand. It's really a protective glove for the inside of the arm, for when you put a bow there — you have to let it go so you need something in there."[6] Taking a combination of the Robin Hood concept that Mort Weisinger and George Papp had originally saddled Green Arrow with, Adams' version also borrowed actor Errol Flynn's beard and adventurous appeal, and after almost three decades delivered on a part of his origin pastiche that his Golden Age counterpart only played around the edges of. Even the three-part quiver had a practical function, recalled Adams in 2016, so that it "would bend with the body as you turned... so he could have room for all those arrows."[7]

While the *Brave and the Bold* issue tended towards some of the soap opera melodramatics that were creeping into comics at the time, including the internal angst that would be physically manifested when Ollie had to fight a darker version of himself in a contemporaneous Justice League story,[8] it highlighted Adams' skills as an artist and the possibilities of what a fully functional archer could do. Breaking the traditional boxed-in structure of panels, a building explosion early in the issue arrives in an irregular shaped panel that actually juts into other panels on the page to emphasise the magnitude of the blast. Later in the piece, Adams shows us a single panel made up of three fluid actions of Green Arrow drawing, cocking, and firing an arrow, the kind of movement that had previously felt static on page. Modern readers may not spot the significance of this, but this was a character that had traditionally had most panel space occupied by explanations of his various trick arrows, with the depiction of their firing often just an afterthought. It was a change so dynamic, in fact, that editor Murry Boltinoff wrote an explanation to readers in the letters column of that issue, one that was accompanied by biographical notes from Adams' wife:

---

[6] Greenfield, D. (22 Aug 2013). Gotham Post: The Neal Adams Interviews – Brave and Bold #85. Retrieved 21 Oct 2015 from http://nypost.com/2013/08/22/gotham-post-the-neal-adams-interviews-brave-and-bold-85/

[7] Neal Adams, personal interview, 8 Feb 2016. See elsewhere in this book for the full transcript.

[8] *Justice League of America* Vol. 1 #75 (Nov 1969).

Readers... may be startled by the Ace Archer's appearance here. Things have happened to him. Because of a climactic upheaval in his personal life, Green Arrow's costume, facial appearance and behavior pattern (to use the head-shrinker's phrase) were affected. Not only does space forbid us to explore and explain this vital development, but rather than be redundant, we direct your attention to the details as delineated in a forthcoming issue of *Justice League of America*.[9]

One can only imagine what readers would have thought of suddenness of the physical changes to Green Arrow, especially those that had been following his adventures for a while, or perhaps his supporting stature in the DC Universe once again allowed him to slip under the wire. We do have the letters columns of the day to reflect upon, including an M.D. Kelly who joined a very Green Arrow-centric JLA Mail Room that month when wrote into *Justice League of America* to suggest that "the outward manifestation of his new search from within, that is, his stylish golden beard and mustache and contrasting uniform gave him a distinguished yet commonly dignified appearance."[10] With a public mandate of approval for Green Arrow's new look and attitude, he found himself hitting the road and bringing a more realistic art movement with him as well.

In the Heart of America: *Green Lantern/Green Arrow* and making comic art history

Due to the manner in which Green Arrow's new costume was introduced, Adams can be said to have *created* the Green Arrow we now know. Speaking with *Print Magazine* decades later, Adams is on record with journalist Petit as feeling responsible for the creation of Green Arrow. "I took Green Arrow, who was a copy of Batman, and turned him into his own independent-type character that you never saw before. So in effect I created Green Arrow, yet I'm stuck with the fact that I recreated Green Arrow."[11] Denny O'Neil is undoubtedly responsible for much of Green Arrow's voice, having established a tone of dissent over several years in the pages of *Justice League of America*. The relationship between writer and artist is a symbiotic one, the cool new form of Green Arrow feeding his fledgling function as the League's conscience, one that

---

[9] *The Brave and the Bold* Vol. 1 #85 (Sept 1969).

[10] In the back-matter of *Justice League of America* Vol 1 #79 (Mar 1970).

[11] Petit, Z. (22 Sept 2014). "Stubborn, Aggressive, Positive: An Interview with Neal Adams." Retrieved 2 Nov 2015 from http://www.printmag.com/article/stubborn-aggressive-positive-an-interview-with-neal-adams/

necessitated something weightier than a Golden Age costume to give that voice legitimacy. Author and critic Douglas Wolk argues that nobody was doing anything like Adams at the time, his "pumped-up sort of photorealism" was full of the heightened close-ups, warts-and-all, and realistic anatomy that was mostly absent from comics prior to Adams, at least not at DC.[12] Coupling O'Neil's different 'grass roots' approach to his Emerald Allies, taking Green Lantern and Green Arrow on a road trip to see the 'real' America, Adams rose to the challenge and found a different way of presenting that world to an unsuspecting audience.

Adams' flourishes inform the tone of the book from the first story, "No Evil Shall Escape My Sight" in *Green Lantern* Vol. 2 #76 (Apr 1970), taking over from a decade of stories by artist Gil Kane. Like O'Neil (replacing writer John Broome), he was brought on board under editors Carmine Infantino and Julius Schwartz as one of DC's new young guns intended to revive the flagging sales on the Silver Age hero. Almost a decade before Frank Miller's Daredevil for Marvel, the villain of the month Jubal Slade is bathed in an orange light that would similarly bathe Miller's version of the crime boss Kingpin. Action shots of Green Arrow firing make good on the promise of fluid motion Adams signalled in *The Brave and the Bold*, and a series of tight panels convey a rapid-fire sequence to the action. Adams added shadows and the graininess of photography to his close-ups of the character, a staple throughout the run, resulting in what often appeared to be a black diamond mask over Ollie's eyes. Adams knew the power of the eyes, which is why he so often focused on them in dramatic close-ups, and Green Arrow's new facial coverings were ripe for (melo)dramatic flourishes. In the epilogue, the scene in which Green Lantern must confront his apparent lack of caring for the impoverished, Adams uses his intimate touches to facial expression to make them three of the most iconic panels in comic book history. O'Neil attributes the power of the aforementioned 'black skins' scene to Adams, saying that his script directions requested a "great face," with O'Neil adding "he certainly gave me a great face."[13] Adams invested a career's worth of technique into that face, not needing a photographic reference to respond to O'Neil's request. "I put the

---

[12] Wolk, D. (2007). Reading Comics: How Graphic Novels Work and What They Mean (p. 51). Cambridge, MA: Da Capo Press.
[13] Brodsky & Kevin, H. (1998).

world on his face, I put the care of the world on his face, because I studied that," he later recalled. "So when you see that face – and you have to say, some of the things he said were a little uncomfortable... when you look at that face, you go 'Oh my god' and it doesn't feel as uncomfortable."[14] The nearly photographic rendering of the face is powerful, the "great face" reprinted so many times in the following decades not simply because of the political message and reminder of the comic book world's diversity, but because such a strong and very real representation of a human being stood in contrast with the hyper-masculinity on the other pages of the book.

Adams was continually pushing the boundaries of what was seen as traditional comic book art, applying his commercial art techniques in a way that would earn him international praise. The use of photomontage and similar pop-art influences in his comic art didn't lessen the accuracy by juxtaposition; rather they only served to heighten the sense of realism. In 1972, international design magazine *Graphis* ran a special issue dedicated to "The Art of the Comic Strip". Pierre Couperie makes a special mention of Adams' relationship to modern art in this article, noting "Neal Adams remains the master of narrative technique, juggling incessantly with his pictures, he often achieves remarkable effects."[15] While an issue of *Strange Adventures* was used as an example there, the remark could just as easily apply to his *Green Lantern/Green Arrow* work. In *Green Lantern* Vol. 2 #78 (July 1970), Black Canary is the focus. As she tries to break away from the influence of a cult leader in the vein of Charles Manson, Canary comes to the realization that she is in love with Ollie in the process. Adams dominates the page with a thin outline of her face framing a montage of inserts representing memories, eschewing with panel borders altogether. Later in the same issue, Adams uses three consecutive panels to show Canary wordlessly coming to a decision. Similarly, in 'Death Be My Destiny!' from *Green Lantern* Vol. 2 #81 (Dec 1970), Green Lantern stands at a crossroads. To illustrate this, Lantern's head and shoulders hang fully formed at the top of the page, detached from the rest of his body. Taking it one step further, Adams fills Lantern's body with images from the swirling void of the universe, visually

---

[14] Neal Adams, personal interview, 8 Feb 2016. Again, more of this conversation can be found elsewhere in this book.

[15] Couperie, P. (1972). Echoes of Modern Art in the Comic Strip. *Graphis*, 28(159), 14-25.

connecting the character with something larger than himself, but also artistically suggesting that his head and his body are not in the same place. The characters were larger than life, and Adams was ensuring that their inner struggles were just as vividly visualized as their physical fights.

Adams' experimentations drew their influence from pop culture and established art techniques that were already common in his advenrtising work. O'Neil and Adams were part of the same movement that produced outsider films such as the similarly themed *Easy Rider* (1969), and visual cues for the series were taken from the Black Panther movement, Charles Manson, Alfred Hitchcock films (including a crafty 'cameo' from the director at one point), and a crucifixion scene that graced the cover of *Green Lantern* Vol. 2 #89 (Apr-May 1972) that was as subtle as a sledgehammer in its Biblical allusions.[16] The strangest of these is in "And a Child Shall Destroy Them!" from *Green Lantern* Vol. 2 #83 (May 1971), featuring a little girl with psychokinetic powers under the control of a devilish older man. The latter is depicted by Adams as the then current US Vice President Spiro Agnew, while the little girl bizarrely bears a striking resemblance to President Richard Nixon. Meanwhile, artistic influences weren't just limited to cultural parody. Photomontage was becoming popular again in the 1960s, around the same time that the neo-Dadaists were once again getting their scissors and glue out, and the memorable cover for *Green Lantern* Vol. 2 #84 (May 1971) is unmistakably an example of this art movement. A heavily restrained Green Lantern and Green Arrow are on a platform surrounded by an angry mob. The video screens behind them show the same black and white photo of the villain of the month, "Wilbur Palm" (a.k.a. Black Hand). The photo, often mistakenly cited as being artist Carmine Infantino, was actually another member of the DC Comics family, Marc Iglesias, Vice President of DC Comics. Adams experiments refused to yield solely to the 'realist' model that he had laid down himself, with trippy drug sequences featuring a cartoonish and distended construct of Green Lantern looming over Roy Harper, soon to be revealed as a junkie.

The two drug issues are arguably some of Adams' most daring pieces of work, not simply because they dealt with heroin addiction and social consequence in an era when the Comics Code Authority expressly forbade

---

[16] Kronenberg, M. (Dec 2010). "The Headlines Behind *Green Lantern/Green Arrow*." *Back Issue* (45), 55-58.

mentioning drugs. As discussed in the previous chapter, Green Arrow discovers his ward Roy Harper/Speedy is addicted to heroin in the "Snowbirds Don't Fly" storyline. Over at Marvel, Stan Lee and former *Green Lantern* artist Gil Kane beat O'Neil and Adams to the punch by a few weeks, making history with the first mainstream comics story under the Code to speak out against drugs in 'Green Goblin Reborn!'[17] Yet where Lee and Kane's story presented the superficial cliché of someone popping pills and believing they could fly, the bold cover of *Green Lantern* Vol 2 #85 (Sept 1971) claims to have "The shocking truth about drugs!" The Adams cover would go far to convince a potential reader of this, and newsstand customers were greeted with Green Arrow's estranged partner Speedy clutching his arm, as his full kit of powder, a needle and a spoon sit on the table before him. If there was any mistaking his activities, an unsupportive Green Arrow declares "My ward is a junkie!" Inside, the story doesn't quite match up to the titillating cover – or as Grant Morrison calls it, "as eye-poppingly melodramatic as any Reefer Madness cult movie poster"[18] – but the follow-up issue makes good on this. The cover of *Green Lantern* Vol 2 #86 (Nov 1971) is a striking montage of photorealistic faces, everyday humans like us afflicted by the 'scourge' of drugs. A giant syringe occupies the middle ground, as a comparatively dwarfed Green Arrow carries the unconscious Roy Harper to safety. The language is inflammatory ("More deadly that the atom bomb!"), but not as much as the literal first page hit of an enraged Green Arrow smacking Roy across the face. Pages later, Roy's friend finds Speedy's gear, and because he "don't need *food*... don't need *girls* – just ol' Mama Spike into the *mainline*!", he overdoses. Adams shows another man leaning over his fallen friend, the figures highlighted only by Dick Giordano's striking inks. A psychedelic swirl surrounds the duo as one of them comes to the font-enlarging realization that "He overdosed! He's... *dead*!" As sensationalist as it might be, the gut-punch moment remains a highlight of Adams' art.

Speaking of punches, Adams had a more direct influence on the end of this story than originally intended by O'Neil. The original script saw Speedy and Green Arrow peaceably walking off together after he had beaten the habit by

---

[17] *The Amazing Spider-Man* Vol. 1 #96-98 (May-July 1971).

[18] Morrison, G. (2012). *Supergods: What Masked Vigilantes, Miraculous Mutants, and a Sun God from Smallville Can Teach Us About Being Human*. New York: Spiegel & Grau.

himself, except that Adams felt that Green Arrow had to learn some kind of lesson after unceremoniously forcing Speedy into giving up heroin cold turkey. So Adams added the last few pages, with Speedy returning Green Arrow's punch so he could share "a very small piece of the pain I've just gone through these last few days." Despite O'Neil's disagreement, who felt that the artist's ending said that violence was the solution, Schwartz agreed with Adams and published his version of the ending. So in a very real way, the final impact of this controversial drugs storyline belongs to Adams.[19]

Behind The Panels: A Close-Up Look at 'What Can One Man Do?'

Throughout this period, Green Arrow's artistic changes mirrored his personal growth. The focus artistically was initially on the flashier Green Lantern, but that didn't last long either. As the co-star of Green Lantern's book, Ollie was merely guiding Green Lantern through the wilderness and introducing him to a side of humanity that was perhaps far more interesting to Neal Adams from an artistic point of view. That said, Adams is still responsible for Green Arrow's modern appearance, and there are key moments when Adams' illustrations aid in defining that character. In *Green Lantern* Vol. 2 #87 (Dec 1971), the issue that introduced the first black Green Lantern John Stewart, contains a back-up story by Elliot S. Maggin that focuses entirely on Green Arrow[20], and more specifically the man underneath the mask. In the tale 'What Can One Man Do?,' Oliver looks back over his life in trying to decide whether he should run for mayor. While the story may be thematically similar to the Adams' pencilled *Brave and the Bold #85*, with Ollie once again at a crossroads in deciding which persona can do the most good for the world, 'What Can One Man Do?' is distinguished by being an art-driven story with some very deliberate choices that distinguish it from its contemporaries. Here we take a

---

[19] Adams tells this entire story in the interview found in this book.

[20] The story, the first of Maggin's stories to be published in a comic, was written by the author as a term paper at college. Despite receiving a B-plus, he sent it to Carmine Infantino at DC Comics, who in turn gave it to Julie Schwartz. After showing it to Neal Adams, he said that he would illustrate it. Maggin would go on to write a series of Green Arrow back-up stories in *Action Comics* through the 1970s. Thanks to Schwartz, his name would be frequently stylized as Elliot S! Maggin, with an exclamation point after the "S."

closer look at this 13-page story, dissecting Adams' approach to the most Green Arrow centric tale of the *Green Lantern/Green Arrow* run.

Following a feature story on Green Lantern and his new colleague John Stewart, the first page of 'What Can One Man Do?' seems quaint by comparison. Even the 'Green Arrow' titles at the top of the page are reminiscent of the logo design used in the late 1940s and 1950s for the character's back-up stories. This first page is very traditional in many ways, with four thin horizontal panels showing the transformation of Green Arrow from his Golden Age costume to the modern 1970s depiction as Ollie reflects on his life behind the mask. This is what makes the second page, ostensibly the title/credits page, a visual shock to the system. Setting the tone for Adams' artistic approach on this issue and much of his work in the era, this second page does away with panel borders altogether. Holding the art at arm's length, there is a fair bit of visual noise from a design point of view. There's so much going on for a page that also utilizes white space so judiciously. The top of the page is occupied with green tinted sketches of the various aspects of Oliver Queen's life, from the domestic Ollie to the outspoken action brawler. Yet the real focus of the page is the centerpiece image, showing Ollie and his alter-ego Green Arrow standing back to back, their bodies forming a kind of doorway or arch. Adams has filled the space in between with an image of an inner-city street and a small black child descending some stairs onto the streets. We will find out his identity later, but it's worth noting that it is Green Arrow himself acting as the panel for the page. On closer inspection, the two faces he wears could be an angel and a devil on each shoulder. All of this can be garnered visually, with Maggin's descriptive introduction discreetly off to the side in the case of both pages.

The next few pages follow a more standard approach to layout, although they both pack a lot of information into a limited space. On Adams' third page there are five panels laid out in a grid, comprising of four squares with a wider horizontal panel in the lower third. Even here Adams has trouble staying within the lines, with the middle two panels broken open by Green Arrow's bow, the angle of the right hand square slightly elongated to accommodate the archer pulling back his bowstring, as if the page itself was straining with the might of his masculinity. Maggin dramatically sums up the transition from an average man reading his mail to Green Arrow swinging into action. "It's a kind of rush that comes over one when one sees a man transform himself into something

From *Green Lantern* Vol. 2 #87. Art by Neal Adams and Dick Giordano. © DC Comics.

that is *more* than man... Envied – admired – respected – not a *man* at all... but a *legend!*" In five quick shots, Adams takes us from Oliver Queen "the man" to Green Arrow "the legend", creating a sense of movement by breaking down his page into five simple actions. Oliver is still and pondering his mail. A close-up of his legs in a swift movement as he exits civilian life. A torso shot in costume of Ollie arming himself with a bow, complete with heroic backdrop. A panel straining shot of firing a bow. Finally, a wide panel as the "legend" swings above the crowd of onlookers. It's the kind of cinematic fast-cutting techniques later popularized by the likes of Edgar Wright (*Shaun of the Dead*, TV's *Spaced*) or Sam Raimi's *Evil Dead* series, but here we see it in its original language of sequential art. So it's curious that the page following it is less visually interesting, and perhaps this is because it breaks away from Ollie/Green Arrow almost altogether. Feeling for all the world like one of Adams' commercial *Chip Martin, College Reporter* advertising strips for AT&T, the first two images are of a pair of businessmen in "an office uptown," discussing prospects for the new mayoral candidate. The cinematic leanings still remain: as the men finish their conversation in "voice over", Adams 'pans' his lens from left to right across three small vertical panels, each panel pushing in closer on a boy playing with his dog in a train yard, until at last the archer is revealed to be standing behind him.

From the fifth page onwards, Maggin and Adams' story becomes even more art-driven. Laid out in what is more or less a six-panel grid, it's virtually a reverse of the third page, as here we see the hero transform back into the man. Even out of the costume, there's a strong display of masculinity, perhaps even more so than in costume. Literally stripping off his costume and putting on his civilian clothes, Oliver Queen is the epitome of the 1970s Burt Reynolds manliness, right down to the hairy chest that Adams' Batman also sported during this era. However, instead of returning to a state of still contemplation that he'd enjoyed in his civilian life only a few pages before, his moment is interrupted by the ringing of a phone. The panel reads like an insert, with the phone placed in the foreground to make it the subject of the scene. Ollie's expression as he answers says it all, with his trademark Adams scowl incredulous at the idea of someone wanting him to run for mayor. The flipside on page six divides the area into eight panels, cleverly split by the phone cord Ollie is using to call his various super friends for opinions. Each of them are deliberately placed in their civilian identities, as he contacts Dinah (Black Canary), Bruce (Batman), Hal (Green Lantern), and Clark (Superman) for similarly negative responses. Depicting them in their civilian clothes puts Ollie on the same footing as his colleagues, but as the archer – still showing off his hairy chest thanks to an unbuttoned shirt – moves up the hero food chain, his body language changes too. He stands assertively when talking to Dinah, faces Bruce's panel as equals, takes a casual knee with his friend Hal, and finally sits slumped in the back recesses of the frame with Clark. In this way, the phone cord makes the panels mirror images that reflect back various aspects of Ollie.

As readers turn the page, the color choice is the first thing that jumps out on the seventh page of the story, as the narrative cuts straight back into action. The page is filled with earthy colors, and aside from Green Arrow's contrasting costume, they are the reds, oranges, and browns of the inner city at dusk. Once again firing an arrow and launching himself via a zip-line into the air, Adams takes a half-page square and divides it into three dynamic panel shapes. Each panel shape points towards the top right corner of the square, drawing the eye and by extension the action in that direction. We follow the action up and to the right, almost feeling the need to pitch ourselves forward with the momentum. The action continues onto the next page where Ollie is airborne, Adams using the perspective of anybody who might be on the street looking up to frame Green Arrow from underneath. Two panels later, Green Arrow lands in a crouching position on those streets, and the color scheme changes to blues and greys almost immediately. The panels get smaller and more claustrophobic as Green Arrow finds himself in the midst of a riot on a hot day, a motif Adams carries over to the ninth page. Here he finally encounters the small boy teased back on the title page, and color choice becomes important again. The boy wears a red shirt, and seeing them together can't help but conjure up memories of Speedy, who only a few issues before grew up quickly thanks to his heroin addiction. Any protective instincts Ollie might have are put into high gear when the boy is shot in the chaos, his 'Adams eyes' going wide while Green Arrow is seen in profile helplessly on the side of the panel. The physical layout of this tenth page actually mirrors the fourth page of the story (two horizontal, three parallel vertical panels), and as the boy falls to the ground in the second horizontal panel, the background color drains away. Instead of a cinematic pan in the lower third, Adams gives us three quick shots that apply a similar amount of distance to the earlier page's mirror. In the first, the crowd threatens to swallow up Green Arrow as he fights his way out of it. A low-angled shot of him loading the boy into an ambulance leaves the reader in a place of vulnerability. An aerial shot of the same ambulance driving away creates distance between the audience and the object, as Adams did back in the train yard, making us feel as equally helpless as the hero.

In the final two pages of the story proper, prior to a bookend epilogue, Adams turns his lens solely on the fragile hero. The eleventh is the most cinematic of the pages in the issue, with five horizontal panels stacked on top of each other. Ollie's position as relative to the other actors in the scene remains in a similar spot for the whole page, so it feels like the scene is either changing around him or Adams is slowly pushing his "camera" in for a close-up. Set to a passage of Ernest Hemmingway's *A Farewell to Arms*, the attending doctor wordlessly delivers the news that the boy has died. We don't need to hear it: the line riddled expression on the doctor's face says it all. On the next page, three small panels are filled with long to mid-distance shots of Green Arrow. In each, Adams has positioned the archer relative to street and car lights so that he is always halfway between light and shadow, reflecting his emotional state as well. Finally, the archer breaks: a half page extreme close-up on Ollie's face. We see his eyes clearly through his diamond mask, not just the white shapes that typically fill the space. Whether conscious or not, here near the end of this *Green Lantern/Green Arrow* run, Adams visually recalls the angry and accusatory man on the streets, giving Maggin the same "great face" he gave O'Neil, only this time for Green Arrow. Tears stream down his face, and he is at once the hero and the man, with an overwhelming sense of failure at being either. In the slightly incongruous epilogue, one that returns to more standard panelling of six square panels, Ollie (still in costume) visits Dinah, both of them in a similar half-light to the archer on the previous page, Giordano's rich shadows moodily setting the scene. It's Dinah out of costume that comforts Ollie, now tenderly supportive as she leaves him in solitude. Just as the book started, Ollie is alone with his thoughts again, laying down to rest as he accepts his roles as man, "legend," and potential mayoral candidate.[21]

---

[21] In a case of swings and roundabouts, there's an odd parallel to Gil Kane's art in *The Amazing Spider-Man* Vol. 1 #122 (July 1973), in which Mary Jane comforts Peter Parker after the death of Gwen Stacy. Kane was, as mentioned, Adams' predecessor on *Green Lantern*.

The Fate of the Archer: The Legacy of Neal Adams and *Green Lantern/Green Arrow*

From the iconic covers, drawing inspiration from photo montage and pop art, to the interiors that both beatified and lampooned public figures, Adams in this period didn't just influence the direction of Green Arrow, but the future of comic book artistry. By emphasizing Green Arrow's humanity, both at conflict with and an essential part of his 1970s hyper-masculinity, Adams' art physically made him the hero that writers O'Neil and Maggin were crafting him to be. Between his *Green Lantern/Green Arrow* work and the original redesign in *The Brave and the Bold*, Adams can be said to be largely responsible for the third major "origin" of Green Arrow.

The Adams legacy remained strong after he departed the title. Following the cancellation of *Green Lantern* at the end of this run, signalled by a full-page ad redirecting readers to continue the story as a back-up in *The Flash*, Adams continued to work in the comics industry for a few years, including uncredited work on the first intercompany superhero crossover between Marvel and DC in *Superman vs. The Amazing Spider-Man* #1 (Jan 1976). Before returning to commercial work with his own company, Continuity Associates, he tackled another classic piece of social relevancy in *Superman Vs. Muhammad Ali*[22]. The Adams design would remain with the character until 1987, when Mike Grell recrafted the character as a mature urban hunter in the wake of DC Comics' line-wide reboot and *Crisis on Infinite Earths*. Yet even Adams has a hand in this story, Grell frequently citing Adams' work on *Green Lantern/Green Arrow* as the reason that he got into the comic book industry. Indeed, when O'Neil revived the *Green Lantern/Green Arrow* stories after a four year hiatus in *Green Lantern* Vol. 2 #90 (Sept 1976), it was Grell who initially took over as the artist[23]. It wasn't just the characters that changed either, but the form as well. In 1972, the Paperback Library released two small 160-page softcover reprints of the stories in black and white, designed for mass market consumption, more than a decade before trade paperback collections would become popularized in the direct and mass markets. Socially relevant art required a socially acceptable form of reading the 'funnybooks', and the discreet covers and compact size made them portable, readily available, and virtually indistinguishable from the

---

[22] Officially numbered *All-New Collectors' Edition* Vol. 1 #C-56 (Apr 1978).

[23] Discussed in detail in Chapter 7.

other hard traveling novels that could be found on the spinner racks of malls and airports across America. In 1983, the run was collected with new introductions as a 7-issue mini-series titled *Green Lantern/Green Arrow*, and has since been reprinted in multiple deluxe editions.

When Kevin Smith resurrected Oliver Queen following a six year absence from comics, it was the Neal Adams design that he and artists Phil Hester and Ande Parks chose to return to. He sought to instantly caption the memory of "better times," and give unfamiliar readers a shorthand (re)introduction to the outspoken liberal with complicated feelings. Adams' design was evocative of all of those things, and just like the panels in the best Adams Green Arrow stories, Hester and Parks conveyed this without having to say a word. "Green Arrow's look for me is basically the Neal Adams look," Hester recalled. "There was never any real consideration given to changing his costume."[24] Both O'Neil and Adams were certainly guilty of some melodramatic flairs in their 1970s run, taking the series away from just being action-oriented and also focusing on the emotional core of the characters. Having followed Jack Kirby in recrafting the Green Arrow from the plainest of 1940s Robin Hood designs, Adams found the intricate lines and details of Green Arrow's face to make him more human than human, and more masculine than any superman.

---

[24] Phil Hester, personal interview, 26 Feb 2016. The full transcript is in this book.

Neal Adams Interview

Neal Adams is no stranger to fans of the Emerald Archer, especially if they've already read Chapters 3 and 4 of this book. Inducted into the Will Eisner Comic Book Hall of Fame in 1998, and the Harvey Awards' Jack Kirby Hall of Fame in 1999, the comic book and commercial artist helped usher in the modern house style for DC Comics and Marvel in the 1960s and 1970s. In 1968, he gave Green Arrow a much-needed new visual origin and, with writer Denny O'Neil, helped revamp the character as a loud-mouthed liberal scrapper for the so-called "relevant comics" of the *Green Lantern/Green Arrow* series of the 1970s. The look and attitude persisted well into the 21st century.

The following conversation occurred late in the evening of 8 February 2016, when an emailed interview request from the author in Sydney, Australia to Mr. Adams was immediately met with "NOW is good." What followed were several hours on the phone talking about politics, comics, art, the industry and a lot of Green Arrow.

RICHARD GRAY: If we could start a little bit before Green Arrow, start at the very beginning of your career as it were. You found a comic book industry that was difficult to break into in the late 1950s.

NEAL ADAMS: I would say impossible. Well, there's nobody that's my age, either five years my junior or five years my senior. I mean, I don't have contemporaries in the comic book business. You couldn't get in. The only people that are near my age did something else first. In other words, people like Denny O'Neil was a newspaper writer. Jim Steranko, was somewhere near my age I guess, was a magician, he was not a comic book artist. He didn't intend to be a comic book artist. There's no one in the industry... in a ten year period or more, maybe a fourteen year period but certainly a big period – I don't have people that are my contemporaries. Anybody that would have been my contemporary gave up and did something else. It just doesn't exist. From 1953 to 1963? Nobody. Really, really strange business.

When I came to show my stuff, they turned me away and told me they were going to be out of business in a year. 'Kid, forget it – we're going to be out of business in a year. Don't waste your time. Find something else for yourself to do; we are not going to be here in a year.' And that was not just from one guy. I got that from Joe Simon, Jack Kirby's partner. I got that from DC Comics. We're not hiring. DC Comics were turning down all the people that worked for EC Comics. Al Williamson, Alex Toth, name them. Wally Wood. Jack Davis. Jack Davis became a commercial artist, did cartoons for commercials. Wally Wood became a spot illustrator doing various spy illustrations for various strange magazines, science fiction magazines and things like that. He wasn't doing comic books. The only time he got into comic books was to meet Jack Kirby when Jack Kirby was doing *Challengers of the Unknown*, but he was an inker. Wally Wood. DC Comics kept their steady guys, and turned away everybody else. Alex Toth went off to California to do *The Flintstones*. [Laughs] It was a dead time, and I come up in the middle of that out of high school thinking that I wanted to be a comic book artist. Oh, there was a mistake.

RG: So you found yourself doing other things. You found yourself doing a lot of commercial work as I understand it.

NA: Well, I did Archie Comics, because they let me, because they felt sorry for me. Because Joe Simon and his partner Jack Kirby had to turn me down because they didn't want me to ruin my life. The Archie guys let me do Archie joke pages which I wrote, drew, lettered and inked. So there's a whole series of Archie joke pages that I stole from Junior Scholastic Magazine, of course. The source of all jokes. Then I did backgrounds for a comic strip that was a failure. Then I did comic books for advertising, or comics for advertising which actually paid more money than regular comic books. I mean, I would do a page of comics for advertising and I would get $200 a page, and at DC Comics the most they paid was $50. I would do pages for the telephone company,[25] "Chip Martin: College Reporter," and they would pay me $300 a page, and then later on $400 a page. I was being paid six times as much as regular comic book artists doing comics for advertising. So I was very protective, and I was very aggressive and competitive, and I got very, very good doing this kind of work, because I had to be very good. Anybody could walk along and do advertising comics for this company called Johnston and Cushing, but who could do it well? So I found a place to do comics that wasn't regular comics.

Then I get a syndicated strip by the time I was 20 years old. So those two years between the time I graduated high school and 20 years old, I had a career, a whole career. I was an illustrator; I did... anything that would come along. By the time I got to DC Comics, and I had done that strip for three and a half years, I was a finished comics illustrator. Comics illustrator and regular illustrator. I was a painter, I could do any kind of graphics, I could do anything. When I showed up at DC Comics, for the second time, I was a finished artist, and they had no idea who I was. They didn't know I did a comics strip based on the *Ben Casey* TV series, and it appeared in the *World Telegram & Sun*, which is a New York newspaper. They had no idea who that was or what that did. Comic book

---

[25] AT&T, specifically.

people were so isolated, so protected, so ghettoized that they had no idea about the outside world. They had no idea about rates, they had no idea about rights, no idea about contracts, they had no idea about anything. They were ready to go out of business, waiting for the axe to fall. It was like cavemen. They wore regular clothes. They were like Cro-Magnons, they were like Neanderthals. Do you guys know anything? Do you write a contract? You write a statement on the back of a check that takes the places of a contract. Well, a statement on the back of a check doesn't take the place of a contract, don't you know that? Even the smallest advertising agency in the world does a purchase order. You don't even have a purchase order. You people are primitive gorillas. Of course, you couldn't say that too much out loud, because that would shock them to their knees. They wouldn't know what to say. You print on toilet paper. You print on presses that Ben Franklin invented. The same presses that Ben Franklin used, you use. You do letterpress printing, and you print on toilet paper. It is the worst printing in the world. It was really weird, I got to tell you.

RG: So I've looked at some of those Ben Casey pieces that you did, and Goodyear, AT & T and even the stuff that you did with *Creepy*, around the same time that you were doing some of the early DC work...

NA: Pretty good stuff, huh? [Laughs]

RG: It's pretty amazing stuff! And it strikes me that you've got a lot of that photorealism that you would use in Batman and Green Arrow much later is all present there.

NA: You have to remember that I was out there, when I was doing the strip, I was among illustrators. I was among artists who were applying their trade in the illustration field. People who would take photographs for reference, who would trace photographs, who would render from photographs. Who would find reference; really find reference, unlike comic book artists who couldn't even reference a tree. I would find reference for what I did. So if you saw backgrounds for Ben Casey, and somebody walking through a park, that would be an actual park there. If I did paintings, I would take photographs of myself and other people and I would illustrate from those photographs. So I was doing illustrative work, not that I could easily afford it. At the rates that DC, *Creepy*, *Eerie* and *Vampirella* paid, I was shooting myself in the foot, because they only paid $40 and $50 a page. I could go to an advertising agency and do a panel, two inches by three inches, and I could do 20 of them in an evening. I couldn't do 20 pages in an evening, that would be totally insane. That divergence between doing that comic book work that you see and comic strip work that you see, and doing work for advertising agencies, is ten-to-one. On the other hand, advertising agencies just flush the stuff down the toilet. You would never see it, it didn't matter, it would never reach the public. On the other hand, they paid well. I was able to put my kids through school, I was able to *have* kids. I was able to get married and have kids, put them through school. My kids don't have loans out for their tuition, because I was able to pay for their schooling through college. Imagine doing $50 a page and being able to do that?

So what I brought to comic books? People don't know this, but every day that I worked on comic books, half of that day I worked on advertising. There are people in advertising who know me as Neal, the guy who does storyboards. They don't know me as the guy who did comic books. The guys that I did comic books for had no idea I did advertising, why would they? So I made more money doing advertising by far than I did doing comic books. On the other hand, I fell in love with comic books. I gained a reputation doing comic books. There's different things you get for what you're doing. I had to make a decision, when I was doing the *Eerie* and *Vampirella* stuff, and I did some work for DC. Then advertising work started to pick up, and I had to make a decision. Am I going to do these crazy comic book things, do I like it that much to give up all that time to do it? I thought, yeah: if I can change the industry. If I can change the business somehow, from the inside out, then I could stay. But it had to change, everything had to change. So I made that decision. It seemed like an odd decision to some people, but not to me.

RG: That sounds like a good jumping-off point to bring us up to Green Arrow. Prior to your design of Green Arrow, the character had been around for over 20 years. Did you have any impression of the character before you came onto him?

NA: Sure, I read DC Comics. I knew just like everybody, well maybe not everybody, that he was an imitation Batman as we all knew. Why they did him, I have no idea. I guess it was just another weapon. They decided as a backup feature, remember it was just a backup feature, just like Tom Tomorrow and the other characters that were backup features at DC Comics. It was basically just so that the people who did the first story didn't have to do all those pages. You'd get somebody else to do the six pages in the back. So they came up with – I don't even know who did it, George Papp? Somebody like that – came up with an imitation Batman. They did Green Arrow, who by the way was a serial in the movies. *The Green Archer*, which I suspect was the derivation of Green Arrow. Then they had Speedy, and the Arrowcar with those spring-loaded seats that would fire you up to the third floor and then smash you against the wall like peanut butter. It was pretty much an imitation of Batman; very little effort was made to do stories that were worthwhile. It was basically fill-in. Until Jack Kirby did it. For us fans out there watching the stuff, 'what the hell is this?' Jack Kirby with the thin lines, he did a very different style, it's very strange. But Arrow gets pulled into another dimension, he just did great stuff. 'Holy cow, what the hell is this?' So for that time that Jack Kirby did it, it was blow-aways. Totally blew me away. But that ended. I think Jack Kirby after that must've done *Challengers of the Unknown*, and then he got Wally Wood to work on it and that was wonderful.

But the Green Arrow essentially fell into disrepair, and when Murray Boltinoff, my editor on *Brave & the Bold*, told me they wanted to do Green Arrow, I said no! It's not a character. They said we're supposed to do [it]. I said, I'll change it, if I can change it. So Murray said 'yeah, you can change it.' So he had Bob Haney write a script, that implied or described Green Arrow getting a new costume. It was Green Arrow by himself, not Green Arrow and Speedy, which made things a little easier. He focused on him being rich and stuff. So that was my open door, that was great. Now I could change Green Arrow, but what would I change it into? I thought anything I do to change him would still make him an imitation of Batman, unless I make him an imitation of Robin Hood. So I made him a direct imitation of Robin Hood. I took the onus of Batman off of him, and blatantly. I made him into a modern day Robin Hood. So those people who didn't know he was an imitation Batman had no idea that I was tricking them into thinking he was an imitation Robin Hood. So I deflected that bad view, and turned him into a modern day Robin Hood which is perfectly logical and sensible.

Then I was able to design a costume that was reminiscent of Robin Hood. It got rather corrupted as time went by, and is still rather corrupted in weird and wonderful ways. For example, he's got a hood on. If you ever put a hood on and try to turn left, it's hard to see. You really have to twist around to be able to look out from under that hood. Not a good idea, yet that stuck. The bad thing was, when other people took it over they did weird things, because they want to change them. There are people who did Green Arrow who knew very little about archery. I grew up on Coney Island, or part of my life was on Coney Island. I worked the rides, and I also worked the archery range. I learned a lot about archery, and it's one of the things that made what I did with Green Arrow so much fun for me, and made it at least partially authentic. There's things that you should do, and one of the things I did was, you know those gloves that he wears that go all the way up to his biceps? Well the idea of those gloves was that, when you do archery, you want to have an arm guard for your forearm. You don't want to stiffen your arm until it snaps forward. You don't want to snap your elbow forward, because you will hit your arm with that strength. But assuming you know how to hold the bow properly, every once in a while you can hit your arm with that bowstring, and the stronger the bow, the worse that hurts. So you want to have an arm guard. Traditionally, in modern archery, there's an arm guard. I didn't want to have an arm guard, but if I could have a glove that acted as an arm guard, I could then pull it all the way up to the bicep. But if I pull it all the way up to the bicep, and it was a leather glove which it needed to be, then the arm would get hot. So why don't I do this? Why don't I air-condition the glove by cutting three holes as you go up the glove, one in particular at the elbow so the elbow has flexibility, so you can bend the elbow without pulling on this leather which tends to become stiff. So that would be the air-conditioning, so air could get to the glove without it being overheated, and you would have your whole forearm protected, and it would also help in fighting.

Then I designed a three-part quiver that goes on the back, so that the three-part quiver would bend with the body as you turned. The three-part quiver would have this flexible thing between the three parts. So he could have room for all those arrows, including if he wanted to pull out the Boxing Glove Arrow, which seems to be the butt of everybody's humor. But he could have quite a variety of arrows if he could have them in a quiver that went all the way across his back. It couldn't be one part, because that would be like carrying a giant plank on your back. Of course, I gave him the Robin Hood hat, which in modern days I will admit is pretty stupid. I was thinking today that maybe they could switch it to a Tyrolean hat, that Germans wear, and is worn in some parts of the world. It might be a good replacement. Hood? No. When I saw the hood appear, I thought "thank god there are no archers reading this book." Anybody who wears a hood knows that if you get approached from the left-hand side, you're going to get socked before you know what the hell is going on. So I made him into Robin Hood, clearly and obviously. The idea from my point of view is that Robin Hood is a great character, how do you take advantage of that without doing Robin Hood? Well, you make him a modern day Robin Hood. The guy exists in comic books, he goes around with a bow and arrow, why not turn him into Robin Hood? So that was my thinking at the time. Apparently, everybody on Earth that read comic books loved it, and then they didn't know what to do with it. We got this great character, but we don't know what to do with it. So they started to plant him around in Justice League, they did *some* things with him.

Of course, then I volunteered to do *Green Lantern*, because Gil Kane had left *Green Lantern* and they were handing it out to various artists including Jack Sparling. Of course, my office in DC Comics at that time, where I was doing covers for them, was very close to Julie [Julius] Schwartz's office, and you could hear him bemoan the fate of *Green Lantern*, and they're going to cancel it. They're going to cancel the book. So I went into Julie Schwartz's office, and because I was such a big fan of Gil Kane, I said "Can I do a couple of issues before you cancel the book?" And of course he kicked me out of his office. Later on, I asked him enough times that he said, "Ok, we'll do that." But he had a plan, and apparently in editorial they were responding to the fact that people love Green Arrow in that one story, and wanted to see him. Why not put Green Arrow in there with Green Lantern? That might otherwise seem like a stupid idea. Not that Julie Schwartz hasn't had stupid ideas that have worked. *Superman Vs. Muhammad Ali* is one. So I talked to Denny O'Neil, they talked about what they could do with it, and sure enough Denny was at that time very political. Very big liberal, he's very vocal on his liberal attitude about a lot of things. He's an Irish writer, you know? Just one of those guys. So it was perfect for him. It was perfect for me, because I was one of those quiet liberals that would actually go out and do things. Instead of rant and rave, I would actually change things. [Laughs] So I was perfect to do it, because I quietly went about my task of insulting the Vice President of the United States, and doing all the stuff with joy and fun and good will. So anyway, it was a great combination, because Denny was a good raving liberal, and I was a good quiet liberal and so we started to do this thing, and it was very different from any other comic book that was out there.

Of course, the key *was* Green Arrow. He was the best and the worst of characters. He was a pain in the ass, and caused lots of trouble, and crawled right up Green Lantern's ass, but he did it in a good way [Laughs], and got him to stop – and taught him a few lessons. So it was a romp. I don't think it could ever come up to what it was, of course, now it's a TV show. That's its next highlife. Those guys seem to be trying to do, as much as they can, Denny and I's Green Arrow. I mean, within certain boundaries.

RG: Well, I was going to ask you about that later actually. But the [*Arrow*] TV series has been running for a few years now, and it feels like there's a lot of Neal Adams and Denny O'Neil in the DNA.

NA: We call it the Neal Adams show. [Laughs] I don't know how we can call it anything else. The Neal Adams and Denny O'Neil show. But they've got a lot of Deadman in there, and I did an awful lot of Deadman. I did most of the writing on *Deadman*. They've got Nanda Parbat, and they've got the Lazarus Pit, Ra's Al-Ghul and the League of Assassins that I created for *Deadman*. They just seem to be romping through our stuff, and having a good time doing it.

I can tell you this, a small story. I was at the San Diego convention after the first season of *Arrow*, and these people came up to my table and I was signing and chatting with folks. He introduced himself, the one guy at the lead of these other two people, introduced himself as the head writer of the Green Arrow show. Or the "Arrow" show as it was called then. I say, "Hey, cool, that's very cool." So we chatted for a little bit and he said, "I just wondered what you thought of the show." I said, "Ok so basically you want me to bullshit you and tell you that you're doing a great job." He said, "No, no, no, I really want to know what you think." I said, "I don't think you want to know what I really think, I think you just want me to say nice things, and I'll be glad to do that." He says, "No, no, I really want to know what you think." I said, "Ok, fine. First of all, Green Arrow doesn't shoot arrows into the hearts of people and kill them. You see, that's sort of the anti-Green Arrow. That's what he shouldn't be doing, because he's not a hero if he does that. He's a murderer... That's why he has all those trick arrows, see? To avoid killing people! So he said "Next season, you got to watch it next season, because we're going to stop that." I said, "Really? You're not going to kill people? That's good, good for you." He said "Is there anything else?" "Yeah, you could put a smile on his face once in a while. I mean, what the hell is that? Is it Dour-man? I mean, put a smile on his face." And the guy was taken a little bit aback by that, and said, "OK, I guess we didn't think about that." But he said, "There's other things you're going to want to see... there's other people going to be showing up in the show that you know." I said, "Oh really?" He said, "You got to keep your eye on the show."

So anyway, we opened a little correspondence, so I kind of write back and forth to him, relative to the show and the characterization and stuff. Not that he listens to me. For all I know, he puts the notes in his back pocket and thinks about them, and that would be fine. I do see little bits and pieces where he's paying a little bit of attention. But he is not loathe to go borrow from *Green*

Lantern/Green Arrow, and from Batman. I mean, I would say the reason we call it the Neal Adams show [Laughs], not just because of *Green Lantern/Green Arrow* – and they haven't even gotten into Green Lantern yet. Think about that. That's going to happen, you know, they'd be stupid if they didn't. I can see a whole season of that. But they're clearly getting in Batman, with Ra's Al-Ghul and the League of Assassins and all that, and the whole nine yards. And they know it, and they talk about it. I mean, I don't know if you pay attention to the Internet, but they did an interview, the writers did an interview, and the focus was that swordfight on the top of the mountain with Arrow and Ra's Al-Ghul. First of all, the way they promoted it was as "the next episode is going to be the swordfight on the top of the mountain." Basically, everybody's got their shirts off and they're fighting with swords. Hello? Green Arrow, fighting with swords. I think he's a bow and arrow guy, isn't he? And why did he take his shirt off, he didn't have to take his shirt off to fight – well, that's what they *did in Batman*. So they're on this show, and they say "Well, of course we stole that, what did you think? The only thing was that we're in Vancouver and we didn't have a desert. Otherwise, we'd be having the swordfight in the desert, but we're having it on the top of a mountain."

I think it's funny... "No, no, we just took it!" They were very, very open about, and very joyful about it. I think that was great. And let me just say that, they do it with joy. You can't fault them for that. A lot of people are clandestine, they steal my stuff all the time but kind of hide it. These guys are just out there... "You got anything else? We'll take it. We're just having a good time." And they are – they are having the damnedest time.

RG: Speaking of that era, I don't think we can have this discussion without going back to *Green Lantern/Green Arrow*'s first issue – issue #76. And there is graininess in some of the photographic style of your art. You focus on faces a lot. You've said, O'Neil asked you to give him a "great face" during the infamous "black skins" speech. Did you draw on any actual inspiration? You mentioned before that you drew on some photographic influences.

NA: I do, but in particular, he did ask. The old woman in the hallway is a direct swipe from a photograph. But the black guy on the roof? No. When I was in high school, one of the assignments was to do a pencil render, and it didn't matter what it was. Because I had to advance quickly, because I had to make a living quickly when I left high school, I didn't have a choice. I couldn't have gone to college, there was no money in my family, we were poor. So I had to be good. If I took on any assignment, I would make it the best thing in the world.

So in this particular one, I found a photo of a black guy – African theme *from National Geographic* or something – and I really, really, really rendered it. But I spent two weeks doing it. I'm sure it didn't take all of the two weeks, but one of the things I learned while I was doing it was the difference between...different types of people around the world. I've made that kind of a focus of what I do – of faces, and people. So that piece is probably one of the best pieces I did in high school, but it was a jumping off point for me to understand faces, and not just Anglo faces, but also black faces, and Asian faces. So I'm very angry at artists who don't learn these things, and when I say angry, I really am angry, because it's all around you. You can't miss it. There's people and photographs and stuff you can do. If you're too stupid to learn it, you don't deserve to pick up a pencil from my point of view. These things are there to learn.

So for me to do that face was like breathing. I didn't want a pretty face. At that time, we were doing "Black is Beautiful" and there was a lot of "Black is Beautiful." And of course black is beautiful, it's very, very important to understand that. But it's also very important to understand that black is old – just like white and Spanish, and Asian – and it's young, and it's a pretty girl, and it's a mean guy, all these various things. So if I'm called upon to do this old sympathetic black guy, I'm not going to do a pretty black guy, because it doesn't make any sense. I'm going to do a kind of an ugly, you know? I don't mean "ugly ugly," but ugly in the sense that he's old. As you get older, you get uglier, it's just too bad. That's how it works. Beautiful model gets older, she gets uglier. It's just *life*. So I put the world on his face, I put the care of the world on his face, because I studied that. So when you see that face – and you have to say, some of the things he said were a little uncomfortable, the people with the purple skin... what he was saying was uncomfortable – when you look at that face, you go "Oh my god" and it doesn't feel as uncomfortable. I've had black people say "why does he say that shit?" but everybody looked at that face, and coming out of that face, you're just going to listen and you're going to feel. Imagine how that affected a cross-section of comic book readers around the world? You look at that face, and you read those previous pages, and you've been reading comic books for whatever and bam, you hit those six or seven pages. Maybe five pages, it's a very short little segment. You hit that old guy, and it's very emotional. But that came from high school, and rendering that face, that... African face and learning from that. This is different, I got to find some other old faces and other shit to learn from. This is like the lesson, we're drawing *people*.

From *Green Lantern* Vol. 2 #76. Art by Neal Adams and Frank Giacoia. © DC Comics.

We forget sometimes, it's not just guys with muscles. We're comic books: comic books are drawings of naked guys with lines on their bodies. *Really*. Naked, muscular guys with lines on their bodies. Isn't that what comic books are? When do we get to the faces? When do we get to the people underneath it? And that's what I had learned outside of comic books, I brought that into comic books. All of that was in my mind, I didn't have to find a photo for that. It was already in my head.

RG: The places where you did find photos, you were experimenting with photomontage as well, particularly on the covers.

NA: Believe me. *Believe* me, I wasn't experimenting. I had learned it in advertising. The difference was, if you go back and look at the old EC Comics, they were doing all that stuff. When EC Comics got shot down – with Bill Gaines going to Congress and testifying like a fucking idiot, and the country turning on comic books — we were doing drop outs, and we were doing color photo montages. Jack Kirby did photo montages. Everybody did that stuff. I was just an artisan, a professional artisan, who was out there and knew what was going on. I didn't hardly experiment at all, I knew what was going on. Of course, I was amongst a sea of Neanderthals who didn't know what was going on. So if I said I wanted to do a drop out here in a color, I want to drop this out. How about we do a moiré pattern of a pencil drawing. 'A moiré pattern?' How about we do a steel engraving pattern of a pencil drawing? 'A steel engraving pattern, you can't get that.' No you can, guys. You have a Photostat machine over there. All you have to do is buy halftone patterns in regular halftone, a moiré pattern, a mosaic pattern, a steel engraving pattern. You can buy them, they come in packages of five. Just buy them, and I'll give you a pencil drawing, and you'll shoot a photograph of it, and it will appear as a pattern. You can do a picture of a city. You can do a high-con. 'A high-con, what's that? You give me a photograph of a city, and it's going to come out grey.' No, no it's not. You just make it high-contrast on your Photostat machine, you see. 'No, Neal, you're crazy. What are you talking about, you're out of your mind. Oh gee, it works. OK, we'll try it.' It was like teaching gorillas, that's all it was. Out there in the real world, we do it all the time. It's regular stuff. Study artists, study graphic designers, study magazines. Read magazines! See that? Look at different artists, it's there. I'm not coming in and making it up. I'm not Edison. Everybody does it. So I never did anything new, I was knowledgeable. I knew shit, but it wasn't an experiment. I didn't have to. It was done by other people *50 years before I did it*. So yeah, I experiment in that I twisted their arms and made them come up with the goods in a production room at DC Comics. And everybody went, 'Ooh, Neal's inventing new colors.' No I'm not, there's no new colors to invent. Guys, really, no. 'How did he do that? All those lines in the background with the character screaming, he did all those tiny lines.' No he didn't, that's a steel engraving of a pencil drawing.

RG: Speaking of reading magazines, I found an article on you from 1972 in *Graphis* magazine. They referred to you as saying, rather than experimenting, they talk about you "juggling incessantly with your pictures." Would you say that's a more accurate description?

NA: "Juggling with pictures." People say shit like that. I don't know why they say that. I'll tell you what I did. One of the contributions that I made, if you can call it a contribution, was that when I came into comic books, I experimented at Warren, with *Creepy* and *Eerie*. When you do syndicated strips, or you do commercial advertising, you have to be pretty straight-laced. Even commercial comic books have to be pretty standard stuff. But when I did *Creepy*, and *Eerie* and *Vampirella*, each one of those stories was an experiment in storytelling. Each one was different. Each one had a different concept. Each one had a different design. One might be done 100% in pencil, one might have 100% Zipatone and line, one was done in wash and mixed media, one was done in magic marker. Then I did one story that every page was a compositional difference. It was the guy that starts as an old man, and he gets to be a young man, and then he sucks the blood of a vampire and he dies or whatever. Every page of that story is a different compositional experiment. One of them is if you took a page and blew it up, and cut edges off the page, so they were thrown away and you had only what was left in the middle. Another page was a mirror image on the left-hand side to the right-hand side. Another page was only horizontal panels of all the same size. Another page was no borders, it had six panels but no borders on the page. So every page was a compositional challenge, which I consider to be part of what you do with a comic book, you ought to.

So I'm at DC Comics, and I noted for years that since comic book pages were done twice up – or two times the size that they were printed – that it led to a certain kind of thinking. Now when I started at DC Comics, they were doing pages 150% up, they weren't twice up. 150% up means that you had a smaller page. I noted, having been constrained by the comic strip I had done, the Ben Casey comic strip – because they had very hard constraints on the daily strips and on the Sunday strips. This panel would drop out and wouldn't exist, so you had to write it around that panel. In some newspapers, the top tier of panels was removed, so they can't exist as part of the story, so they had to be extra. So when I'm doing comic books, there's no rules, you get a page. So what I see in the way that comic books are done, because the pages used to be so big, that the artist could not look at the page as a whole. He could only look at the panel he is drawing, and look at the next panel, and the next panel. It's like when you are looking at your desk right in front of you, if you put your hand up right in front of your face... but it's a little hard while you are looking at your hand to look six or eight inches to your left or to your right, because you are just looking at your hand. So you don't see the whole page. If you were to take your hand and move it about a foot and a half away, you see all around your hand, you hand becomes much smaller. You see all the area around your hand, just like you see the whole page when you have a smaller page.

So you can actually design the layout of the page, rather than layout one panel, then layout another a panel, in this kind of boring panel, panel, panel, panel. You can choose how segmented and regimented it is, how crazy it is. So the layout of the page can contribute to your storytelling. Or if it's chaotic, if your layouts are chaotic, you can put that in your panel layout. If your page is shattering, you can put that in your panel layout. If it's dull and boring, you can put that in your panel layout. If it's progressive, you can put that in your panel layout. You can take all of these things you normally put in the panel, which was very limiting, and put it in your page layout and suddenly you're telling the story with you panels, your balloons and your page layout. You can have your balloons track through the page in a flow, an eye flow that allows you to read them more easily. Or you can put them in such a way that you have to go back and forth, and back and forth, and back and forth through the page. You can make the eye of the reader see the balloons, and see the action; in a different way than they *think* they're reading it. You can fool them. In other words, you can make them read it the way you want them to read it by your layout and design. So what I did was, I started to layout pages for those reasons. So you did get what seemed like erratic pages. Then other people would imitate me, but they would put in the erraticism without putting in the thinking. So you would read one of my books, and it would seem very erratic and the panels were different shapes, but you would read them and pace your reading according to what I'm making you read. But then someone else would try it, and it was just chaos, because they weren't understanding the concept of using the page as a layout. So what those people were commenting on, was something that wasn't true. [Laughs]

No, that's what art critics do. "Oh, Mr. Adams was thinking of how to upset the mind of the reader and throw all this about." Artists never think that shit.
RG: That's what I spend half my time doing. [Laughs]
NA: I did a story called "Thrill Kill" for Warren,[26] and some guy did an article on "Thrill Kill" and he analyzed every page, in a page long or two pages long of writing, because of concepts that were in the pages. All I could do was read it in wonder, and think 'Did I do that? Did I think that? My god, really. This guy's a genius.' These thoughts are vagrant and fly through your mind, and you try it. One of the things that I'm proudest of, and this is a very, very personal thing, is

---

[26] Written by Jim Stenstrum, and published in *Creepy* Vol. 1 #75 (Nov 1975).

that I'm willing to commit to a stupid idea. Because these thoughts will fly through your mind, and you'll go 'ah, I'll do it, see what happens.' It's an experimentation, and I love that. As long as you don't experiment too much and make the reader crazy, then you can do some new and different things. So you have the opportunity to do that, because stupid ideas will always fly through your mind.

RG: One of the ideas that you had during the *Green Lantern/Green Arrow* run was during the infamous drug issue. The ending, of course, was changed several times and you've mentioned previously because you redrew those pages.

NA: The drug issue I didn't redraw the pages, I added the pages... There are times people will say I changed Denny O'Neil's stuff. I never changed Denny O'Neil's stuff, because from my point of view the writer does his job, and I do my job, so I would never change Denny O'Neil's stuff. I would have to go through the editor to do that, wouldn't I? You don't do that. However, I had made suggestions to other writers in the past, like [Bob] Haney. "Can I do a new Green Arrow? Can you make him new because I can't do it this way." But even then, I would never make changes. I would have somebody maybe come through a window, rather than come through a door. But I would never change the script, and that was true all the way through *Green Lantern/Green Arrow*.

But since I initiated that *Green Lantern/Green Arrow* story by doing the first cover and handing it into Julie Schwartz, who promptly dropped it on his desk and said, 'We'll never do this cover. Why are you doing this? Are you just causing trouble?' Of course, I said no I think we should be doing this, but I know the Comics Code [Authority] will reject it. That's not the point; the point is we should be doing it. I don't go against the Comics Code, I agree with the Comics Code. As long as they have the rules, we stick by the rules. I get it, I'm fine. But we have to do this, even if it makes change in the Comics Code, we have to do it. 'Neal, not only will this cover never be printed, I will never pay you for it.' But I left it with Julie; he said 'take it away.' I said; no just let me leave it on your desk. I showed it to various people around DC, I horrified everybody. You can imagine, with that cover - you've got the fixings for a heroin addict sitting right there on the table - terrified everybody. Really, just dropped it. 'Don't let me touch this because I think it's burning my fingers.' Anyway, over at Marvel Comics, Stan Lee decided he would have somebody pop some pills, I think it

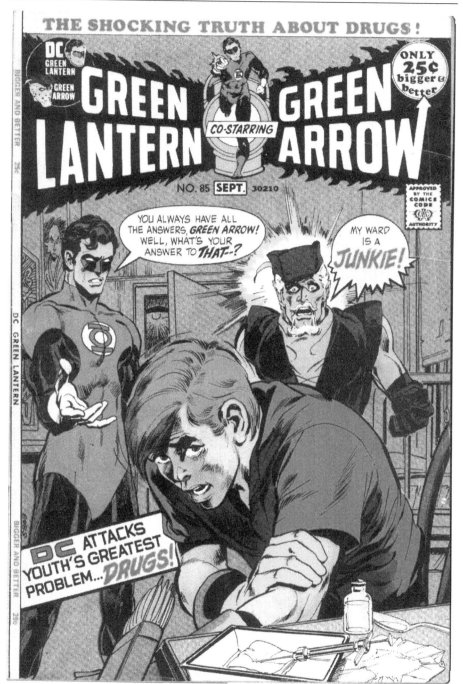

The controversial cover of *Green Lantern* Vol. 2 #85. Art by Neal Adams. © DC Comics.

was Harry Osborne, and walk off a roof or something.[27] Now, I know a little bit about drug addiction. Generally, if you "pop some pills" it generally had to do with what pills you're "popping." Generally, you go and sit in the corner really quietly. [Laughs] Don't go near windows or doors, it's not a good thing. Maybe it happens. Maybe somebody did, and Stan read an article about someone who popped some pills and ran off a roof, I don't know. I'm guessing that's Stan's relationship with drug addiction. He read that article and decided to do that.

Denny O'Neil and I have a different perspective, because both of us were asked to come up with a comic book that would be against drug addiction for the state of New York. Maybe it was the city of New York, I'm not sure. Both of us went to Phoenix Houses, which are drug addiction centers, and both of us spent several days talking with the various people at the Phoenix Houses, and learning a little bit about drug addiction. And in some cases, learning a lot about drug addiction, and some of the myths and some of the stupid things that people believe. I was also the head of our local committee for our drug addiction center up in the Bronx. I was the chairman, and since we were very next door to the drug addiction center, I spent some very cold evenings tracking down drug addicts and taking them home to the center while they were drooling, and crap is coming out of their noses. Getting them settled back into the drug center at four o'clock in the morning. So I was pretty familiar with drug addiction and the other shit that happened. So we both did outlines of what the comic book would be. The City of New York did not like our outlines, either one of us, because we did imply that drug addiction was a community problem, it wasn't just the kids. It takes a society to involve the kids in other things to do, and not to just blame them for being junkies and punishing them. That's probably the opposite of the right direction. Anyway, we were not sympathetic to the government's point of view, so they cancelled the deal. Anyway, so I was left with that, and I thought we've got to do that in our regular comic books. Screw this. So I did that cover. So I did that cover, and if you look at the fixings on the table, you know I know something about drug addiction, because *that's* the fixings.

So when Stan was going to do that cover, I was talking to Johnny Romita — because I would periodically go over and talk to the guys at Marvel — and

---

[27] In the "Green Goblin Reborn!" storyline from *The Amazing Spider-Man* Vol. 1 #96-98 (May-July 1971).

Johnny had done that book. I said, "What are you going to do?" He said, "Well, the Comics Code rejected it." I said, "Is Stan going to change it?" He said no. He said he went to his uncle, who was the publisher, and asked if he could run the book without a Comics Code seal. His uncle said, "Sure, go ahead." Really? So a week later I go back, and I corner Johnny and said, "what happened with that Spider-Man cover?" He said nothing. Nothing happened. Nothing. I said, "Nobody sent any letters? Nobody noticed the seal wasn't on it?" "No, nobody noticed the seal wasn't on it, we heard nothing. Nobody *cares*." So I go back to DC Comics, and they're in an uproar. They're like, "what the hell's going on? Damn Stan Lee, he's scooped us." And they had that cover sitting there for a couple of months. They could have done something, they could have scooped Stan, but no they didn't do it. So anyway, since the Comics Code Authority was really established by the publishers, it had nothing to do with the public or any of the government, it was a self-regulating agency. They could call a meeting of the Comics Code Authority any time they wanted to. So they did within a couple of days, and within a week, the Comics Code was changed, it was stripped of its seriousness and it became a toothless thing. My editor Julie said, "OK, Denny's going to write a script, and we're going to do that thing." I said, "Are you going to use the cover?" He said yeah. I said, "Are you going to pay me for it?" "*Yes, Neal. Now get the hell out of my office.*" So that became the basis of that story.

Now, if you look at that cover, you could hand that cover to any writer and say do that story. You understand what I mean? The story is in the cover. However the story goes, whether it's a junkie salesman or whatever it is, that cover explains what it's going to be. Speedy becomes the junkie. Period. So Julie decided it would be a two-parter. Julie and Denny and I decided it would be a two-parter. So in the middle of it, on the second book, Green Arrow slaps the shit out of Speedy. Right on the first page. So then Denny finishes the story, and at the end of the story there's Speedy and Green Arrow and Dinah Drake standing at the gravesite. So Green Arrow says, "So what's going on with you?" And the kid says, "Well, I'm OK, with the help of some friends." And I read it, and I went to Denny and said, "Denny, we just did two whole books here. You can't end it like that. Something has to happen. We need something to happen here, this is not an ending." So then he explained to me the rhythm of the story and all this other stuff, all this writer shit, and I really tried to get him to change it and he didn't. He said, "No, it's fine" and moved on. So I went to Julie Schwartz, but before I went to Julie Schwartz I wrote two pages, those last two pages. I went to Julie, and I said, "Julie, I went to talk to Denny, and Denny felt the story was fine the way it was. I really don't agree. I've just spent the last month and a half doing two whole books, and I'm working up to the ending and this is anti-climactic. Nothing's happened here. We need an ending... I just wrote out this sample piece, an ending. And I'd like to suggest that it or some version of it be used as an ending." He read it, and he said "OK, do it." I said "Hold on a second, I'm not going to do it, because Denny just turned me down." He said "Go ahead and do it on my authority." I said, "Julie, you have to go to Denny. You have to convince Denny that's it OK, or some version of this... because... you're the editor. You can't screw me with my writer, because that would be a bad thing." He said, "OK, I will talk to Denny and I will give him a copy of this and it will be fine. Go on, because Denny's working on other stuff"... Do you think he told him? No. Maybe he did, because Denny went and said "What the hell is this?" and Julie had to explain it, but I never heard anything from Denny. I could tell from his attitude that he was pissed off. But it needed it, those last two pages. I took the proper channels... Julie agreed with me 100% and made the editorial decision. I was able to go ahead and do it... Now I have never confronted Julie, and never confronted Denny because I'm accepting the word of other people. But that story did need it. Have you read those last few pages?

RG: Absolutely. Many times.

NA: Well, enough said. I don't think it needs any more explanation than that. It had to be there. It just doesn't work without it. After two books, you need that kind of ending.

RG: We've spoken a lot about Denny O'Neil, but there was another writer on that series, even if it was for one short story, which was Elliot S. Maggin, who did his first script in the back pages of one of those. It concentrates very much on the difference between Ollie the man and Green Arrow the hero. From an artist's perspective, is there much difference in the approach you take?

NA: Not really. I mean, you have to understand in those days, I was introducing DC Comics to the concept of new people, and the way I got to do - and the way I had so much power to do it - was that I would agree to draw the story. So the temptation of having me draw the story was enough to convince the editor to let a new writer write a story, you see. So Elliot came to me and had me read the story and get my input. Of course, it was a good story. So in effect, it was presented to Julie with my approval and that I would draw it. So Julie accepted it. The same thing happened, I think, with Len Wein and Marv Wolfman... When I tell you that they were repressed at DC Comics, they had a habit of ten years of not accepting new people. To get new people in there, talented people, was almost impossible. They would hide out in my room. You know, I had a room and I had an overhead projector. We'd turn the lights out; guys would come in... and hide out. Then I would say, "I've got this artist here. Bernie Wrightson. His name is Bernie Wrightson. He can draw. Want to use him?" It was weird. It was like the Underground Railroad. Then we would stay late at night, and everyone would leave, and we'd be the only people in the place. We would either argue, and carry on and bullshit and laugh, go to the coffee room and get coffee. Or we would go to the hallway to the accounting department and play gorilla. I kind of liked playing gorilla. Certain guys wouldn't play gorilla. Howard Chaykin didn't want to play gorilla. Len Wein would. It's a really simple game, you see. Since it's pitch dark [Laughs], certain guys would go into the accounting department and they would hide out. The person who is 'it' would try and find them before they were spotted, or before you could jump on them and wrestle them to the floor. Like a gorilla. It's a stupid game, but it's fun late at night. Of course the accounting department didn't like it very much.

RG: Well, that was the culture of DC then. But you've of course come back very recently, in fact.

NA: Yeah, but we can't play gorilla.

RG: But you did get to do a cover for DC. You got to do a flip on your original Green Lantern cover.

NA: They were kind of looking for stuff for me to do. Because they're terrified that maybe *Batman: Odyssey* really wasn't written well. Which [laughs] maybe it wasn't written well because those idiots on the Internet said so. Let me give you a little bit of history real quick. It was Frank Miller that got me back into DC Comics. Partially, and I wanted him to, because the advertising business had collapsed. The advertising agency had taken everything in-house, and studios like mine were too expensive. So, basically I told everyone I'm going to come back to comics when things get better. And things are better. They really are quite a bit better. They pay a lot more money. Anyway, so it was through Frank Miller that I got to do a story, and Frank Miller was going to dialogue it but he got very busy, so I dialogued the story. It was *Batman: Odyssey*. But the world had changed, and I was not really aware of the world changing. You would think I'd be smart enough, but you know sometimes the smartest people can be the stupidest people. So the book started to come, and I started to get criticism on the Internet for the books. 'I read the first *Batman: Odyssey* and I didn't understand what was going on. So it's a piece of crap. I don't understand why is

Neal writing?' I'm sorry, it's going to be a 12-issue mini-series and you expect to know the story in the first chapter? You pick up a Stephen King novel and read the first chapter and you know what the story is going to be about, is that the deal? But I didn't say that. I just asked editorial. I said, 'Guys, I'm being attacked by the Internet, and I feel like I should be answering them.' They said, 'Don't do that, you don't want to get into it. That's a bad idea.' It was stupid of me not to respond, I just let these guys go. Now I did a terrific graphic novel. I've written comic books forever, whether it was doing advertising comic books, wrote most of *Superman Vs. Muhammad Ali* when Denny O'Neil dropped out. I did most of the *Deadman* stories. I did three Spectre stories. I plotted at Marvel, from beginning to end. Except people just recognize me as the artist. The truth is that I'm a really good storyteller, and beyond that I write really well. Anything I've written has been received very well. I mean, I just translated a *Blacksad* into an American idiom, and I just got an award for it.

RG: And by the way, can I thank you for that? It's absolutely one of my favorite books of all time.

NA: Good, except for the first one where the writing was terrible. Not the writing, the translation. The writing is quite good, I'm sure, if you get someone to transliterate it. And I've been asking them if I can do it. Because you can't really read it.

Anyway, so they talked me out of it. Now, I have a science site. If anybody attacks me on the science site, I am hammer and tongs. I will go after them, and I will tear them a new asshole. I don't put up with that. I did not make that mental jump from responding on the science site to responding to these idiots. Now I have one of the best comic collections out there, *Batman: Odyssey*, and the word is that it's not written well. How did that happen? Because I let it happen. I didn't adjust to the new world. So now I have to live this down. I'm doing *Superman: Coming of the Supermen*, and they're paranoid over there at DC so they're helping me with the writing. Because now they're counting on me. 'We're behind you this time Neal, just like we weren't behind you when we were doing [New] 52 and you were doing *Batman: Odyssey*, so we weren't paying any attention. So now we're pumping it, and now we're pushing it. So we're having a little back and forth here. A little shoving match.

But in the middle of this, because I had finished the pencils on *Batman: Odyssey* and I was essentially inking and needed something else to do, they call me up and said 'Neal, how would you like to do 25 covers of a legendary comic book artist's covers revisited?' I said well, who's this legendary comic book artist. They said 'You.' [Laughs] I said that's a really stupid idea. They said, you would take a cover and you would change the characters. So instead of having Superman throw Batman off a building, you would have Wonder Woman throw Superman off a building. Something like that... They said, we'll get different inkers to ink each one. I said, ok this sounds stupid enough to be good. So it ended up being something like 28 covers. First they started to give them to inkers, so just inkers were interested. Suddenly, the pencillers, the artists came out of the woodwork and said 'We're going to get to ink Neal? I want to do one too.' So the pencillers, really popular pencillers - Walt Simonson, P. Craig Russell, Frank Miller, Jim Lee, Kevin Nolan's done three - are all inking the covers. So you're not only getting the quote "legendary Neal Adams" doing different versions, but you're getting the inking by all these different guys including Brian Bolland. It's become this massive experiment. How does this guy look on top of Neal? How is he going to repress himself, or how is he going to break loose. And it's been great, it's been kick-ass. Even Frank Miller tried really, really hard to do Neal Adams, but he didn't. He did it in his style, but it looks like an original drawing. He didn't change it and make it weird... My son Josh did one, he did the drug cover. It's fantastic. It occurred to me in the middle of it, I could have done 52 of those things. There's enough legendary covers. We only did one Deadman cover, we could have done them all. They're all legendary, if you use that word. I know, because they keep giving me mint-condition copies to sign at these conventions. But it's a crazy thing.

RG: I should say that speaking of legendary covers, I'm sure you're aware that the original art for the *Green Lantern/Green Arrow* cover sold for over $440,000 recently.

NA: Yes, well it sold for $440,000 but a percentage of that was the auction house percentage. So it's three-hundred and something thousand dollars. You may or may not be aware of this, but I got a percentage of that sale.

RG: Well, keeping that in mind, what would the 2016 Neal Adams say to his 1970 counterpart given that knowledge?

NA: He would have said, everything you did was right, Neal - and you win. [Laughs] On the other hand, he would have said "why the fuck did you let somebody steal that cover?" You have to understand that I was fighting for the return of original art, I was fighting for royalties. I was doing a lot of fighting, but quietly - with a smile. Unfortunately, if you're the guy who wears the white hat and you stand for truth, justice and the American way, you can't go in the drawers and steal your own artwork and take it home. You have to leave it there for other people to steal. Because if they catch you, then suddenly they have something on you. So you have to be 100%. You can't have a crack. There can't be anything wrong. You can't have clay feet, because they'll get you, and I don't have clay feet. I will never lie, I will never do a wrong thing, and I will always stand up for the things I believe in because I know the problem you run into if you do. And I don't really have any. It's a thing you learn. I learned from being poor and in a really bad neighborhood. It's not the worst, I wasn't really very white trashy, but I certainly grew up in that kind of environment, so I know about it. I know what weakness does.

RG: Before I let you go, it's been a number of years since you've dealt with the character on an ongoing basis. Do you feel that if you returned to a character like Green Arrow, would you have a completely different perspective on him?

NA: I don't think so. I think I established the character. It's one thing to establish a character and to have him have other experiences, and the question that you have to ask is do those other experiences change him? With everything that they're doing with the character in the TV show and in the comic books, I don't really think his basic character has changed. I still don't see him smiling enough. I would have him smiling more. Outside of that, if I did it, I would have him smile more. I like the Errol Flynn, 'you're smiling at the wrong time, pal. We're in trouble here.' That's his attitude, and I think there are people who miss that. So if I did it, I would put that back in. Other than that, no. We all kind of know him by now. Hell, he's got a TV show.

Nothing but a Man: The Rebuilding of Green Arrow as an Everyday Hero

Due in no small part to the work of Denny O'Neil and Neal Adams, Green Arrow had been re-crafted in the 1960s and early 1970s as the radical voice of the liberal left. The problem facing creators in the remainder of the decade was what to do with this hot-headed crusader for social rights now that DC Comics had effectively abandoned its experiment in relevancy. His membership in the expanding Justice League of America meant he had to at least appear monthly, and as an outspoken know-it-all, provided a foil for the more conservative leaning characters like Hawkman. In a 1978 reader poll, Green Arrow and his partner Black Canary ranked at number five and six on a list of popular characters, beating out top tier characters like Wonder Woman.[1] However, his profile outside the League would take him in a very different direction, as the chili-eating, loud-talking womanizer most remember him as.

From 1972 to 1986, Green Arrow returned to his life of vigilantism in back-up stories in the pages of *Action Comics*, once again hit the road with Hal Jordan in a revived *Green Lantern/Green Arrow* under a different creative team, found

---

[1] As reported in *Justice League of America* Vol. 1 #151 (Feb 1978).

a temporary home in *World's Finest Comics* and *Detective Comics*, and ultimately secured his first solo mini-series after 40 continuous years of publication. In many ways, there are parallels between these two decades of stories and Green Arrow's first 20 years of publication. Where O'Neil claimed to have found a blank slate when he took up the mantle in 1968, albeit one that was overburdened with a mishmash of archer tropes,[2] he left behind a character that was ripe for a similarly fresh approach. As such, writers from this period – primarily Elliot S. Maggin, Gerry Conway, and Joey Cavalieri - experimented with the types of stories they could tell, replacing the Green Arrow/Speedy team with the dynamic duo of Green Arrow and Black Canary, one where the archer wasn't always the one in charge.

This era is often overlooked in Green Arrow's history, sitting as it is between the highly acclaimed *Green Lantern/Green Arrow* run and the beginning of his first solo runs under Mike W. Barr and Mike Grell respectively in the 1980s. However, a top-level overview of this period can be found in Jim Kingman's excellent 2013 article 'The Ballad of Ollie and Dinah' in *Back Issue!*, which certainly helped inform certain elements of the analysis in this chapter[3]. However, this piece aims to expand upon Kingman's summary, examining key aspects of Green Arrow's character that were present in this era. It was a tumultuous time for DC Comics, as the publisher responded to Marvel's dominance with 57 new titles from 1975 to 1978 under the banner of the 'DC Explosion,' raising the cover price of many of the titles. However, in 1978 DC adopted a new distribution strategy, partly blaming poor sales from the blizzard conditions of the winter of 1977 to 1978 and the rising cost of paper stock. The subsequent 'DC Implosion,' as it was named by the comics media, resulted in the cancellation of 17 titles, several full-time staff being laid off, and their 50 cents for 25 page model reduced to 40 cents for a 17-page story format[4]. The consolidation of the printing line to present a more appealing incentive for purchase to consumers most likely came from the Warner Communications mothership, and it also meant that the likelihood of a new Green Arrow title being launched in this period was slim. On the flip side, it did mean that DC

---

[2] As discussed in Chapter 1.
[3] Kingman, J. (2013). The Ballad of Ollie and Dinah. *Back Issue!* (64), 10-21.
[4] "The DC Implosion: DC Adopts New Distribution Strategy, Cuts Line by 40%." (1978). *The Comics Journal*, (41), 5-7. Retrieved 25 Feb 2016 from http://tcj.com

books had regular creative teams, and sustained thematic runs of Green Arrow and Black Canary stories emerged in this time.[5]

If the Golden Age Green Arrow was a patchwork of the popular Robin Hood, Batman, Western, and wartime stories, then the 1970s and early 1980s can be classified as an experiment in different archetypes. Having lost his fortune, he was the everyman, a hero of the people who shared their everyday struggles. He was a partner and lover to Black Canary, one of the most complex relationships in the history of the comic book medium. He was a cosmic adventurer thanks to his association with Green Lantern and the Justice League, a mantle that didn't always sit well with the archer. He was a political actor, literally trying to take up office as the character's politics changed over the course of a decade.

The Wrong Side of the Tracks: Green Arrow as an Everyman Hero

> Yesiree, I'm a regular man of a thousand faces!... Provided each of those thousand faces has a yellow beard![6]

With the start of Green Arrow's solo adventures following the O'Neil/Adams run, the stories became increasingly about Oliver Queen's everyday struggles rather than social relevancy or super heroics. Marvel is typically seen as the kings of the everyman hero – that is, an ordinary person the audience can relate to, placed in extraordinary circumstances – and the emergence of the down-on-his-luck Peter Parker/Spider-Man in 1962 created a lasting character that is just as popular for his human failings as his superhuman abilities. As comic book critic and historian Peter Sanderson puts it, this is because Spider-Man is "beset as much by the banal miseries of everyday existence as by the grotesque supervillains who embody the forces arrayed against him."[7] Green Arrow during this period, or more accurately Oliver Queen, was a character who struggled to keep the two distinct aspects of his life in check. During this time, he would often find that his dedication to the pursuit of street justice either contributed to those "banal miseries," such as being able to afford the rent, but those scenarios would just as readily present opportunities to solve some of his everyday problems.

---

[5] "Post-Implosion Fill-In Fallout" (1978). *The Comics Journal*, (43), 13. Retrieved 25 Feb 2016 from http://tcj.com.

[6] *World's Finest Comics* Vol. 1 #281 (July 1982).

[7] Sanderson, P. (1996). *Marvel Universe*. New York: H.N. Abrams.

When we re-join Green Arrow in 'The Headline Maker', the first of his new back-up stories in *Action Comics* Vol. 1 #421 (Feb 1973), written by Elliot S. Maggin and illustrated by Sal Amendola and Dick Giordano, there are several marked differences to his previous set of supporting stories. With the Adams designed threads, the character is a full-on action hero, swinging into the scene to save patrons from a burning theatre and sporting trick arrows again. More significantly, Ollie is unemployed, and after helping his now established girlfriend Dinah Lance/Black Canary set up her Pretty Bird Flower Shop in Star City, he becomes inspired to be a public relations agent and drum up customers for her business. It's the first of several odd jobs that Ollie will tackle during this period, including newspaper columnist and mayoral candidate, setting him up as the same kind of freelancer living from one pay check to the next that worked as a motif for Peter Parker before him. During this period, Ollie typically set out to promote someone (in 'The Candy Kitchen Caper' it's a fudge shop, while in 'The Plot to Kill Black Canary!', he promotes Trump Motorcycles by loaning out Black Canary's talents before asking her permission[8]), but he was distracted by a case that would either inadvertently promote the business or lead him into a solution for his personal dilemmas. The stories are mostly lightweight in a way that recalls some of the simpler problems of the Golden Age, especially when compared with the social relevance of O'Neil/Adams stories, or even Maggin's own contribution to *Green Lantern/Green Arrow*. Nevertheless, they touch on issues that are important to a slightly older generation of readers, and more specifically, Maggin himself. After all, Ollie's speech patterns were modelled after Maggin's own "New York wiseass," a fact he plays upon in the Multiversal meet-up of the writer and his character in the meta-story 'Where On Earth Am I?' in which various DC characters meet their Earth-Prime creators, including Julius Schwartz and a rampaging Cary Bates[9]. So thanks in no small part to a writer with an affinity to his proxy avatar, the Green Arrow stories of this era became less about the giant social ills of the world and more about personal crises.

These stories demonstrate why it is important to keep heroes grounded if they are to remain believable in an increasingly cynical world. The O'Neil/Adams stories represented the death of the ideals of the 1960s, and

---

[8] In *Action Comics* Vol. 1 #424 (June 1973) and #428 (Oct 1973), respectively.
[9] *Justice League of America* Vol. 1 #123 (Oct 1975).

Green Arrow in the 1970s was about life finding a way regardless. Early in Maggin's run, Ollie encounters a businessman named Osborne. "I remember that I'd be a lot like Osborne when I inherited *my* father's estate," he muses. "And that a punk... had stolen my own fortune and broken my dreams."[10] By the time we get to 1977's 'Slings & Arrows,' the Tony Isabella penned script admits "The days when Oliver Queen got around by Arrow-Plane are long gone."[11] Maggin chose to ignore the incongruous *The Brave and the Bold* Vol. 1 #106 (Apr 1973), in which Ollie is the last man standing for a ten million dollar inheritance. Instead, in the aforementioned 'The Candy Kitchen Caper' he "has to *walk* home... because he hasn't the price of a *taxi*... or even a *bus!*" Echoing the hunger pangs of college students across the country, a few issues later Ollie admits he had "practically become a vegetarian just to save money." This is still a core actor in the DC Universe, a member of the Justice League of America, but one living between pay checks like his audience. Almost 40 years before Marvel's card carrying Avenger and Green Arrow analogue faced similar problems under Matt Fraction and David Aja's *Hawkeye*, Oliver Queen was demonstrating to audiences that the less glamourous side of super heroics was just as engaging as his vast array of trick arrows.

Many of the greatest challenges Green Arrow faces as the everyman hero are in his civilian identity, and not necessarily in costume. As we will explore later in this chapter, a large focus of this era was on the interpersonal relationship between Dinah and Ollie. Yet the everyman hero is now developmentally in his 30s or thereabouts, and while he isn't necessarily willing to take life too seriously, he is exploring new job opportunities and taking them seriously in his own way. One of those jobs is as an editorial columnist for the Daily Star, one of the major newspapers in Star City[12]. His inflammatory columns would earn him the ire of mobsters and public officials alike, but his dual role as Green Arrow would just as often gather the evidence needed to support his otherwise outlandish rants. Writer Mike W. Barr explores this line between those two personalities starting with the aptly named 'The Archer or the Man?' story in *World's Finest Comics* Vol. 1 #274 (Dec 1981). Just as he did

---

[10] *Action Comics* Vol. 1 #426 (Aug 1973).

[11] *World's Finest Comics* Vol. 1 #244 (May 1977).

[12] In *World's Finest Comics* Vol. 1 #258 (Sept 1979), discussed in more detail later in this chapter.

when departing the Justice League, Ollie leaves Dinah a recording explaining why he is on his way out of town. In the arc, Oliver Queen is asked to give up the source for a group of drug pushers he took down. In the 24 hours the judge gives him to reveal the "stoolie", he revisits the island where "Green Arrow was born". Rather than give up his integrity, something he sees as a "nothing...or *everything!*" prospect, he chooses to give up the Green Arrow persona. "Before I was an archer," he muses to Dinah, "I was a *man!*" If Ollie is the Justice League's conscience, Black Canary is Green Arrow's. "Men like you are bound by their ethics," she assures him, "driven by your *conscience*... and sustained by your *love*..." In a story that does not conclude until *World's Finest Comics* Vol. 1 #277 (Mar 1982), Ollie elects to go to jail, released when Green Arrow is framed for murder. While it's a kind of protagonist-centered morality that has us believe it is Ollie's choice that is the correct one here, in the context of Oliver Queen being an everyman hero, major turning points nevertheless hinge on this otherwise average guy *due* to his costumed persona.

One of the most attractive things about Green Arrow throughout his history is that writers have continually found moments in his complex backstory that are worth mining for more emotional impact, showcasing a willingness to deal with the consequences of his actions and not simply stay stuck in the 'villain of the week' rut that plagued his fellow second-stringers. Two of the most poignant moments in Ollie's recent history were the ways that he handled (or failed to handle) the revelation of his ward Speedy's drug addiction[13], and the accidental death of a criminal at his hands[14]. Both of these stories are revisited during this era by Maggin. 'Young Man with a Drum' smacks of an era of comics trying to consciously appeal to hipper young audiences, introducing us to a rock band called Great Frog[15]. Attempting to track down a gang trading in stolen goods, Ollie discovers Roy Harper/Speedy is the drummer with the band. Found talking to Green Arrow, Roy knocks Ollie out cold, but they ultimately work together to bring the gang to justice. However, not one to tie their relationship up in a neat bow, especially after the emotional resolution O'Neil/Adams had reached a few years earlier, Roy declines additional help from Ollie. "I still need to be a loner for a while! Got to sort things out... get my head together! You can

---

[13] *Green Lantern* Vol. 2 #85-86 (Sept-Nov 1971).
[14] *Flash* Vol. 1 #217 (Sept 1971).
[15] *Action Comics* Vol. 1 #436 (June 1974).

dig that, can't you?" Ollie can dig it, with Maggin signalling that his hero is in a similar headspace. Yet the biggest circle is closed towards the end of his *World's Finest* run in a story by Mike W. Barr and Gil Kane, who were by then regularly creating stories for the character. Mrs. Hollinger, the mother of the street rat he accidentally killed back in *Flash* Vol. 1 #217 (Sept 1971) manipulates Green Arrow into a confrontation with regular rogue Slingshot, switching out one of his trick arrows so that he kills instead of wounding his enemy. In the end, Ollie is wise to the scheme and easily outwits them both, but in the face of Mrs. Hollinger's hatred, he indicates to Dinah that he has learned something from his stint in a monastery: "I *know* a little bit about hatred. And I know that if you hate *long* enough, *hard* enough... the only thing you wind up hating is *yourself*." As the everyman, Ollie's musings allow readers to put ourselves in the archer's position, and rest assured that there is a light at the end of the tunnel.

The Plot to Woo Black Canary: Green Arrow as *Archie* for Adults

> Two lovers, one a woman born on a parallel Earth, sworn to fight crime with her martial skills and sonic cry – the other a super-skilled bowman, once a millionaire, now a defender of the poor and underprivileged: they are – Green Arrow and Black Canary.[16]

From the beginning of their relationship, Green Arrow and Black Canary have been treated as equals, even if their published existence is very different. Black Canary's canonicity and history is a complex one, and it could readily fill its own volume. Created in 1947 by Robert Kanigher and Carmine Infantino for *Flash Comics* Vol. 1 #86 (Aug 1947), alterations to her retroactive continuity (or "retcons") meant that the Black Canary we talk about in this era began with *Justice League of America* Vol. 1 #75 (Nov 1969). Black Canary joined the Justice League after one of the annual Crisis events, crossing dimensions from Earth-2 to Earth-1 following the death of her husband, Larry Lance. In the process, she gained a superhuman sonic 'Canary Cry.' In the latter part of this era, DC adjusted its continuity to establish that *this* Black Canary was in fact the daughter of her Golden Age counterpart, explaining how a character active since the 1940s had not aged. *Justice League of America* Vol. 1 #220 (Nov 1983) explains that the original Black Canary had died not long after her husband, but infused her already super-powered daughter with her own memories and sent

---

[16] *World's Finest Comics* Vol. 1 #248 (Jan 1978), as well as subsequent appearances where the characters are featured as co-leads.

her to Earth-One. All of this has been rendered void by subsequent line-wide reboots, and readers were unaware of the retcon prior to 1983, but it is sufficient to note that both Green Arrow and Black Canary had long and complex changes to their backstory, and their fledgling romance would be treated with equivalent maturity.

One of the more unique aspects of the Ollie/Dinah romance is that it follows a more realistic model of an adult relationship. "They found comfort in each other despite their differences," writes Kingman (2013) "and a relationship formed, a loving one, yet tumultuous."[17] During the O'Neil years, both in *Green Lantern* and *Justice League of America*, their friendship was confined to some flirting, with Ollie the one that helps Dinah control and come to terms with her fledgling powers. As early as *Justice League of America* Vol. 1 #79 (Mar 1970), only a few short months after Black Canary joined the League, Ollie confesses his love for Dinah, who is simply not ready at this stage to form a relationship after the death of her husband. Two issues later, Dinah is missing Green Arrow while he is on the hard traveling road with Hal, and gets taken in by a Charles Manson cult figure when she heads out to find him. Green Arrow kisses her for the first time in an attempt to deprogram her, and in a beautiful multi-panel montage from Neal Adams, we witness her slowly coming to terms with her feelings for Ollie[18]. Throughout the early run, Ollie becomes overly protective of Dinah, flying into a jealous rage when another man pays her attention or she is in any kind of trouble. His sometimes patronizing attitude belied the liberal beliefs he espoused, with Ollie often dismissing super heroics as work not fit for a woman, although Dinah would have none of his bluster. In the aforementioned 'The Plot to Kill Black Canary', she calls out Ollie for being "Mr. Domineering Male". They physically fight, with Dinah's high level of judo skill frequently besting Ollie. The latter accurately guesses that they are fighting about something else, and Dinah admits that she "thinks" she loves him. This is not, contrary to convention, the start of happily ever after. Instead, Ollie suggests something else: "Do you want to talk about it?" he asks her, immediately positioning this as the start of one of DC's most realistic couples. It was not a conversation that ended quickly.

---

[17] Kingman, J. (2013).
[18] *Green Lantern* Vol. 2 #78 (July 1970).

Here was a couple that we got to watch fall in love, and much later grow into middle-age together[19]. Mike Grell, the writer largely responsible for that middle-aged coupling in the 1980s and 1990s, later spoke of the couple as a whole entity: "I think Ollie and Dinah together are better than either of them apart. The problem with relationships in comics is that a lot of the writers don't seem to understand how to do a story where people are functioning as a couple without marrying them off."[20] Yet Maggin and subsequent writers understood that the key to this relationship was not just the tension between the two of them, but their casual love for each other as well. Ollie's increasingly ridiculous jealous tantrums were balanced with a playful banter the two of them shared. In Steve Englehart's script for "No World Escapes the Manhunters" from *Justice League of America* Vol. 1 #141 (Apr 1977), in which Green Arrow and Black Canary come to the aid of friend and comrade Green Lantern, Ollie is impressed with her fighting moves. "Well *bust* my chops, woman! You can still surprise me!" As antiquated as his sentiments might be, it showcases some genuine affection between the characters. It's hard not to smile, after all, when Green Arrow cheesily contributes "That was the lady I love!" after a particularly deadly move from his partner. This wasn't a case of Lois Lane attempting to trick Superman into falling for her every week, as she frequently did throughout the 1940s and 1950s. It went unsaid, at least in these initial issues, but this was a couple in comics that was *involved* with each other, emotionally and physically. There were undoubtedly some silly stories in the mix, such as the one in *Action Comics* Vol. 1 #434 (Apr 1974) where Maggin gives us a DC spin on the Archie Comics formula. "All I did was innocently walk into my office and got caught between two steam-rolling women," laments the archer in 'Zatanna's Double Identity!' With Zatanna under a spell that has her believing she is Black Canary, her arrival and sudden amorous affection towards Ollie flips the script and has Dinah storming off in a jealous rage for a change. It's all well that ends well in a story even the editor notes was "contrived" in the panel descriptions, with Ollie the Archie Andrews to Black Canary and Zatanna's Betty and Veronica (or

---

[19] In Mike Grell's 1987 mini-series *The Longbow Hunters* and subsequent ongoing series, the duo aged in real time. They fought, argued about children and their adventurous lifestyle, came back together and sometimes strayed from each other. This is discussed in detail in Chapter 7.

[20] Mike Grell, personal interview, 29 Mar 2015. Available at *Behind the Panels* [podcast]. Retrieved from http://behindthepanels.net

maybe Sabrina in the case of the magical character), yet Maggin and his contemporaries never left us in any doubt that these two loved each other. In one of future *Green Arrow* writer Mike Grell's first stories as writer and artist for DC, he places Dinah in jeopardy while an emotional Green Arrow desperately searches for her. It not only foreshadows a pivotal story that Grell would tell in *The Longbow Hunters*, but also that even the mighty Black Canary could still be used as a damsel in distress when the plot called for it.

When the Green Arrow back-up feature in *Action Comics* ended in 1976, the subsequent *World's Finest* stories aimed to put the pair on a more equal footing. As early as the 'Nutty Kid' trilogy in the last of the *Action Comics* appearances, what had once been a 'Green Arrow' adventure was now being listed as "Green Arrow/Black Canary," making it clear that these characters were co-leads in the same way "Green Lantern/Green Arrow" had been under Denny O'Neil and Neal Adams. While both characters still enjoyed their regular appearances in *Justice League of America*, and Ollie got back half of the marquee in the revived *Green Lantern/Green Arrow* run[21], both would enjoy their own features in *World's Finest*. Starting with *World's Finest* Vol. 1 #244 (May 1977), Black Canary got her own feature. 'Rainbows of Doom', written by Jack C. Harris and gorgeously illustrated by the art team of Michael Netzer and Terry Austin, dynamically highlights Black Canary as an independent character. Green Arrow cameos, but Dinah sums up their relationship best by defining their differences. "I love the big lug, but *boy*, can he be *bull-headed*!" Chasing the Rainbow Archer, an otherwise throwaway villain last seen in the 1950s[22], the story continues in 'Slings and Arrows', where the same art team shifts the focus to Green Arrow. The pattern continued like this for a time, sometimes appearing in individual but connected stories, teaming up as co-leads or operating separately. It gave both characters the opportunity to grow into something more than supporting players, but also highlighted exactly why they were able to work as a couple in the first place. Green Arrow and Black Canary are a couple not in spite of their differences, but because of them. They would fight and make up just as quickly, but as fully formed individuals in their own

---

[21] Starting with *Green Lantern* Vol. 2 #90 (Sept 1976) through to #122 (Nov 1979), and discussed later in this chapter. There is also a section on Mike Grell's art in Chapter 7.

[22] In *Adventure Comics* Vol. 1 #246 (Mar 1958), in a formulaic story from Ed Herron and George Papp.

right, they had something to offer each other, as well as something refreshing to show readers that might have thought comic book romance was standing still in Archie's Riverdale high school.

While the conscious 'relevancy' aspect of the books were no longer the focus of the stories, through Ollie and Dinah's relationship various writers were able to explore feminism and the independence of Black Canary. Although Green Arrow often poked fun at 'women's liberation', it was still *on* the agenda. Dinah increasingly sought a more fulfilling career, including some work as a fashion designer, a topic she frequently came into conflict with Ollie over. While just as regularly creating an adolescent (or Freudian) wet-dream by having the character fight a wolf man in a towel or near nudity[23], or being captured and tied up every other issue, Dinah's fierce independence ran throughout all of her appearances. Indeed, Gerry Conway's narrative in *World's Finest* Vol. 1 #246 (Sept 1977) introduces her as "a woman in transition, caught between her love for a certain *Emerald Archer*, and her desire for *independence*." The story of Green Arrow during this period was also one of Black Canary discovering that the two ideas weren't mutually exclusive, a lesson the stubborn Ollie took more than one argument to come to terms with. In *Justice League of America* Vol. 1 #151 (Feb 1978), Black Canary protests the bachelor party the League is throwing Ray Palmer/The Atom: "Anything that segregates men and women isn't harmless! It may be tradition... but it makes me mad." In the same issue, she defiantly rebuffs the help of the reluctant League, independently tackling a crisis. A telling exchange between Ollie and Dinah sees the archer apologize for a mouth that "moves faster than my *mind*," confessing that he has a lot to learn about women. The touching scene sees them come to a kind of understanding, although only a month later, in the pages of O'Neil's *Green Lantern* Vol. 2 #102 (Mar 1978) Dinah notes that they are still having these arguments and that they "shouldn't see each other for a while – until we get our feelings sorted out!" Dinah is finally able to articulate the cause of their rift in the anniversary issue of *World's Finest* Vol. 1 #250 (May 1978). Picking up on a thread that had been running for years in the various comics, she explains that after her departure from Earth-2, she gravitated to Ollie because he seemed "strong, someone self-contained":

---

[23] As was the case in Gerry Conway and Sal Amendola's *World's Finest Comics* Vol. 1 #247 (Nov 1977) story "Requiem of Rage."

Lately it seems like I'm being *smothered* by your love... There's so much of you... and so little of me. [...] I do love you Ollie, but you've been *too* good for me. You've helped me when I should have helped *myself* – and that's *bad*. For us both! I told you I wanted a *more meaningful career* – something more fulfilling than running a *flower shop* when I wasn't chasing around the world as the *Black Canary*. You thought I wanted more *money*, and you offered to *help me – again*. That's why I exploded. It was the *wrong* thing... at the *wrong* time.

It was by no means the last time that "Star City's answer to the Dynamite Duo"[24] of Barbara Gordon (Batgirl) and Dick Grayson (Robin) would argue. Like the contemporary Han Solo and Leia Organa from the *Star Wars* series playing out in cinemas during this era, their arguments helped peel back some of the character layers and got to the heart of what made each tick. They were a fighting duo that also fought with each other, fiercely maintaining their independence while working out where their Venn diagrams intersected. They supported each other as much as they did their teammates. What Maggin, Conway and O'Neil did more than anything in this era was give them both a rounded character base, and a realistic love story unlike any other in the DC mainstream.

Sign Up and See the Universe! Green Arrow as a Hard Traveling Action Hero

In the 1973 *Super Friends* animated series episode 'Gulliver's Gigantic Goof,' the Green Arrow (voiced by Norman Alden) responds to an SOS message at game warden headquarters in "Bornego", located somewhere in Africa, claiming giant ants are attacking nature photographers. Spouting catchphrases like "Great flaming arrows!" and "By Robin Hood's bow!" his television fame was short lived, not appearing on TV again until 2004's *Justice League Unlimited*. The appearance of an action-oriented Green Arrow is somewhat incongruous, and despite a handful of trick arrows, it shows very little of the loud-mouthed liberal persona that had emerged in the previous decade. The earlier O'Neil and Adams run had made Green Arrow 'relevant' in the late 1960s and early 1970s, and his role within the Justice League was to act as the group's conscience, so the return of the *Green Lantern/Green Arrow* run in 1976 marked his positioning as an action hero. It was an era, after all, that introduced one of Green Arrow's most enduring rogues: Count Vertigo.

---

[24] As described in *Justice League of America* Vol. 1 # 154 (May 1978).

While Green Arrow's *Action Comics* appearances were naturally more action-oriented, as we have seen they also ironically concentrated on showcasing the more personal side of Ollie and Dinah's relationship. Running concurrently with this *World's Finest Comics* arcs was the return of *Green Lantern* after a four year absence, beginning with *Green Lantern* Vol. 2 #90 (Sept 1976). It was an odd move for DC, given that the previous series had effectively been cancelled due to poor sales despite massive critical acclaim. It wasn't rebooted and renumbered, and *Green Lantern/Green Arrow* simply continued as though the friends were off on a new adventure. The return was heralded with a big logo on the cover proclaiming "At last... the return of the greatest comic of them all!", although this second series would not be as well received. Written by Denny O'Neil, art duties would go to the then up-and-coming artist Mike Grell, with Adams transitioning back into the world of commercial art. The first issue, affectionately titled 'Those Who Worship Evil's Might' in reference to both the Lantern oath and the debut issue of the original run,[25] doesn't bother giving us a reason as to why Green Lantern is re-teaming with his friend Green Arrow, and even Ollie points out the obvious fact that Hal doesn't really need him on his missions. Hal has an improved power ring, and the initial story serves mostly to introduce a new element to the Lantern mythology. The point of difference comes from Ollie at the end of the issue, who knowingly observes "There's usually a moral at the end of our sessions together!" Even O'Neil is acknowledging the shift in tone here.

Despite being written by O'Neil, most of the stories in this revived run were far less issues-oriented and focused more on placing the duo in consciously adventurous scenarios. It was a difficult balance for the Everyman hero, who comments in *Green Lantern* Vol. 2 #91 (Nov 1976) that it's "hard to hold a steady job when you're busy chasing crooks." Even so, O'Neil managed to find ways to expand the "hideous moral cancer" that was destroying America in the previous series to global issues, and in the same story lands the duo on a planet that is similar to medieval England, complete with the Robin Hood scenario of a sinister Prince Yaun attempting to seize power from his brother Richard Stoutarm before he returns from war. Never one to remain quiet, Ollie takes the opportunity to criticize the locals for their treatment of women and the impoverished. The disparity between rich and poor are highlighted in *Green*

---

[25] "No Evil Shall Escape My Sight!" in *Green Lantern* Vol. 2 #76 (Apr 1970).

Lantern Vol. 2 #93 (Mar 1977) around Carol Ferris' world, an issue which is ostensibly about Hal investigating a spacecraft that is kidnapping Earth's impoverished citizens. A year later, Green Arrow joins a protest march in *Green Lantern* Vol. 2 #104 (Mar 1977), the same issue that he argues with Green Lantern over his inaction due to restrictions placed by the Guardians. It necessarily recalls the earlier arguments from the first run, but without the immediacy of the political climate that surrounded the 'relevant' books.

As Green Arrow's partnership with Black Canary began to grow, the types of stories that O'Neil could tell with Green Lantern and Green Arrow were limited by the very different paths they were taking elsewhere. As Green Lantern's mythology expanded, Green Arrow had less of a place as a co-lead in Green Lantern's book. The two-part story that spanned *Green Lantern* Vol. 2 #96 and #97 (Sept-Oct 1977) literally has Green Arrow and Black Canary sitting next to the bed of the ill Lantern Katma Tui, while in *Green Lantern* Vol. 2 #107 (Aug 1978), the couple are scarcely in an issue that mostly concerns Hal. Indeed, the issue introduces a new back-up feature, 'Tales of the Green Lantern Corps' to highlight the expanding Green Lantern mythology even further. Pulling on various elements of Green Arrow's origin, *Green Lantern* Vol 1 #110 (Nov 1978) sees Hal and Ollie take on Western personas on a distant planet, with Green Lantern as a Clint Eastwood style cowboy, and Green Arrow taking on the 'Indian' motif he often played with in the 1940s and 1950s[26]. Apart from the patently silly nature of the story, Ollie only heads into space on the flimsy premise that he was fighting with Dinah, further indicating that space was not his natural habitat. Green Arrow describes his role best in *Green Lantern* Vol 2 #112 (Jan 1979), dismissively stating "I'm just a low-class brawler." The rift in the formula, which eventually ended less than a year later in *Green Lantern* Vol. 2 #122 (Nov 1979) was conscious of its own tensions. In *Green Lantern* Vol. 2 #114 (Mar 1979), Hal's civilian identity as a truck driver is pushed to the limits when he is put into a scenario straight out of the 1953 Henri-Georges Clouzot film, *The Wages of Fear*, or the more likely influence of William Freidkin's 1977 US remake, *Sorcerer*. Hal is forced to drive a truck of dangerous explosive materials, while Green Arrow's expected rant about the "greed heads" Hal is working for is met with aggression. "Sometimes your self-righteousness gives me a *pain!* Go polish your halo elsewhere!" Which is exactly what Ollie did a

---

[26] See Chapter 1.

few months later, returning to a series of back-up features in *World's Finest* and *Justice League of America*. The split was sudden as well, ending with an argument between Ollie and Hal, as the latter declines Green Arrow's help on a space-bound mission. "You saying I can't cut it?" demands the stubborn archer. "If that's how you want to hear it..." replies the pragmatic space cop, although the message was clear that there was no room for the Everyman in space anymore.[27]

Nevertheless, the number of Green Arrow's rogues grew significantly in this era, with the return of some older villains and the introduction of some classic ones. We are told that killed archer and assassin Merlyn was known to Ollie before his first appearance to readers in *Justice League of America* Vol. 1 #94 (Nov 1971), setting the stage for a character who plagued the Green Arrow for much of the 21st century. Count Vertigo first appeared in the Black Canary story "The Vertigo Version" in *World's Finest Comics* Vol. 1 #251 (July 1978), establishing the misguided villain with a discombobulating "Vertigo effect" that would literally turn the page upside-down and sideways to disorient the reader as well. Much of the credit for the impact of this character, who would soon serve as one of Green Arrow's primary antagonists in his first solo series in the early 1980s, goes to artist Trevor Von Eeden. The artist co-created Black Lightning for DC the year before, and brought the unique style to the pages of *World's Finest* as a complete antithesis of the hyper-realistic art of Neal Adams.[28] The character solidified a few issues later, when the comics took Green Arrow across the world to "Vlatava" in *World's Finest Comics* #270-273 (Aug-Nov 1981) in a three-part epic that was a sure sign Green Arrow was outgrowing back-up features. There were some clear indulgences, including Auntie Gravity, an elderly woman who develops anti-gravity telekinetic power after exposure to pollutants,[29] or the musically themed Anton Allegro (who has it in for both Oliver Queen and Green Arrow).[30] For reasons that perhaps only writer Paul Kupperberg can explain, the silly Silver Age villain The Clock King was revived after an 18-year hiatus for *World's Finest Comics* Vol. 1 #257 (July 1979). Without as many relevant windmills to tilt at, these action scenarios

---

[27] *Green Lantern* Vol. 2 #123 (Dec 1979).
[28] Von Eeden's style, particularly his work on the Green Arrow Vol. 1 (1983) mini-series, is discussed in depth in the next chapter.
[29] *World's Finest Comics* Vol. 1 #261 (Mar 1980) and #262 (May 1980).
[30] *Justice League of America* Vol. 1 #163 (Feb 1979).

Art is radically turned on its head in *World's Finest* Comics Vol. 1 #251. Art by Trevor Von Eeden and Vince Colletta. © DC Comics.

replaced relevancy-driven plots for the hero. If Black Canary represented all the things that Ollie was now fighting for, the new set of villains gave the outspoken action hero something to be against in the absence of social ills to fight.

"Vote 1" for Oliver Queen: Green Arrow as a Politician

Back in *Green Lantern* Vol. 2 #87 (Dec 1971), Maggin's first published story 'What Can One Man Do?' introduced the notion of Oliver Queen running for mayor. The amazing debut, examined from an artistic point of view in the previous chapter, was described by then Green Lantern editor Julius Schwartz with the highest of praise.

> I've been a comix editor for over 27 years and never... have I ever come across a 'first-time' script... that can come within a light-year of equaling 'What Can One Man Do?' in professional slickness and comix know-how. ... Indeed, to equalize this thrilling experience, I must go back three decades when, as a literary agent, I sold the very first story of a young Ray Bradbury![31]

The story sees Oliver Queen trying to balance the two aspects of his life and decide which was more useful to the world, concluding with the hero deciding that he would run for mayor. Unfortunately, with the cancellation of the *Green Lantern/Green Arrow* series only two issues later, the thread was dropped for the time being, at least until Maggin began to tug on the edges of it during this period. Prior to the campaign proper, Maggin slipped in a reference to Ollie's mayoral consideration in *World's Finest Comics* #210 (Mar 1972), unfortunately undoing some of his own work by having Ollie deciding that he will not run for mayor at this stage. It freed up the archer to concentrate on his relationship with Dinah and his adventures with Hal. It was from those issues that Maggin was given the opportunity to continue the storyline, with the 'Beware the Blazing Inferno' secondary feature in *Green Lantern* Vol. 2 #100 (Jan 1978) not only reintroducing Speedy's band Great Frog, but Star City's Mayor Major, who has worked out Ollie's (barely) secret identity, and requests that he runs for mayor. Ollie agrees to run, justifying his position to Dinah by contextualizing it within all the changes he'd gone through over the years: "Listen, lady – so far I've survived wealth, substitute parenthood, and membership in the freaking

---

[31] Wells, J. (2010). "And Through Them Change an Industry." *Back Issue*, 1(45), 39-54.

Justice League – give me a little *time*… and maybe we'll see how great a man I *really* am!"

Ollie's intention to run for mayor might seem like something of a conflict with his personality up until that point. He had shifted away from being tight with the Star City Police Commissioner during the Golden Age, and showed significant distrust towards authority figures during the O'Neil/Adams run. These contradictions in his character are voiced in *Green Lantern* Vol. 2 #103 (Apr 1978), also written by O'Neil, when Green Arrow becomes frustrated with the actions of politicians, and the United Nations in particular, over their inability to deal with an alien asylum crisis. In what is otherwise a mostly action-based issue for the archer, his disgust with the politicians almost makes him reconsider his decision to run for mayor. "Hmm… maybe I should duck out of my mayoralty race before *I* wind up like them." The throwaway line speaks volumes about the character at the time. Here Ollie is as highly principled as ever, never missing a beat to express his true feelings on a matter, yet his willingness to walk away so quickly from something he has been musing about for a long time also speaks to his adolescent maturity. If any further evidence of this is needed, Ollie launches himself into the cold void of space without protection in the same issue, a problematic action for a potential publicly elected official.

The ultimate resolution of the first 'Ollie for Mayor' arc comes from Maggin in *World's Finest Comics* Vol. 1 #255 (Mar 1979) in a story entitled 'Nothing But a Man'. As the title would imply, it closes out the narrative that began with the question 'What Can One Man Do?' first posed in 1971. Running against Ralph Halstead, Ollie is given a boost by having Dinah as his campaign manager, campaign contributions from Bruce Wayne, and endorsements from his fellow heroes, including Congresswoman Barbara 'Batgirl' Gordon. However, Ollie's distrust of public office is confirmed when he is abducted by thugs working for Star City crime boss Thaddeus Cable, who attempts to bribe Ollie. To his dismay, Ollie also discovers that his friend and mentor, the incumbent Mayor Jack Major, has been corrupt for over two decades. The elections appear to be rigged, and Ralph Halstead wins the vote. However, when Clark Kent phones Ollie at home to let him know that his investigations could prove corruption and his actual victory pending an investigation, Dinah tells Clark that he shouldn't pursue the story. "If you give a *damn* about your *friend*… you'll go on the TV and say he *lost*… He's safer on the streets as Green Arrow than as Ollie Queen. And

I'd *hate* for him to have to become the kind of man poor *Jack Major* had to." Ollie remains disillusioned, and decides not to run for mayor anymore, while Dinah remains "strong enough to *keep* her secret *forever*." Maggin neatly ties together several strands at once in the process, dovetailing the dedicated and caring relationship that Ollie and Dinah share with the struggles Ollie has experienced in trying to find an identity. Having mocked her desires for exploring other career paths, and Dinah's sense of being smothered by Ollie's love, here *she* takes the career choice away from him, while simultaneously dedicating herself to keeping a lifetime secret *for* him.

O'Neil and Adams showcased the death of the dream of the 1960s in their *Green Lantern/Green Arrow* run. Here, with the defeat of the everyman hero trying to do his best as "nothing but a man", Maggin deftly represents the death of the American Dream as well. More pointedly, just as O'Neil's journalistic research informed his stories, Maggin's tale comes from his own journey. Speaking with journalist and science fiction author Jayme Lynn Blaschke (2001), he talks of stepping away from the politics and reflecting on his "personal fortunes" in an objective way. In the time between 'What Can One Man Do?' and 'Nothing But a Man', he'd gone from "inspired amateur" to a professional writer. Oliver Queen's transition reflected Maggin's own.

> I think that, with Green Arrow as my personal Everyman, that was what I was expressing in 'Nothing But a Man.' It was my last Green Arrow story, and I intended it to be. When I wrote the first one, I was a junior in college in the middle of an election of my own. I was running for President of the Student Council. As it happens, I won. Or so I learned about six months later. A friend who was an officer of the Student Council at Brandeis was apparently funnelling money into some personal expenses, and it was his judgment that he would be found out if I were elected. So he contrived to get someone he considered more malleable elected — without that person's participation...[32]

Maggin's intention was to have Ollie win the election, but reflected that the "upper echelons" of DC weren't ready for that kind of move in one of their heroes. Ollie wouldn't actually achieve his goal of becoming mayor of Star City until 2006. Writer Judd Winick not only replenished Ollie's vast fortune in the wake of a city-wide crisis, but installed him as the elected mayor as well.

---

[32] Blaschke, J. (Nov 2001). Interview: Elliot S! Maggin. Retrieved 19 Nov 2015, from https://web.archive.org/web/20030923135436/http://www.greenarrowfansite.co m/

Winick's run, as we will explore in Chapter 10, was also fundamental in restoring large amount of 'relevancy' to Green Arrow's narratives, showing that just like political careers, everything comes in cycles. In the end, Gerry Conway directly answered Maggin's question in *World's Finest Comics* Vol. 1 #258 (Sept 1979), during the aforementioned stint as a newspaper columnist. "Losing made me realize... who am I kidding? One man can't change the world. So I'm back where I started, playing Robin Hood." The pull-quote from his column, and the title of the story, answers Maggin's question of what one man can do: "One Man Can Cry."

Detectives and Dark Knights: Green Arrow in Transition During the Reagan Era

When Green Arrow debuted in the pages of *Detective Comics* in 1982 in the last of his back-up features, the personas of the action hero and the political actor were combined. The two-fisted brawler of a bowman went up against some patently ridiculous villains at this time, from the goat-headed Printer's Devil, a card wielding Death Dealer, and a resurrected monk named Barricade, who was effectively a skeleton in a suit of armor. The quiver would expand with the Feedback and Cryonic arrows, returning the character to the same serialized fun of the 1940s and 1950s. It was also an era that was happy to add some levity, some of the last the character would see in the lead-up to a decade filled with darkness. The *Detective Comics* run spanned several important touchstones in comics, including Alan Moore and Dave Gibbons' deconstruction of the superhero genre in *Watchmen*. During the *Crisis on Infinite Earths* event, the Golden Age Green Arrow symbolically (and literally) died as the Multiverse collapsed. Towards the end of the *Detective Comics* issues, Frank Miller, Klaus Janson and Lynn Varley's *Batman: The Dark Knight Returns* was published. Miller's Oliver Queen is older and missing an arm from an implied run-in with Superman, yet he is still formidable with a bow, and has evidently been working against "the system" in his own way over the years, not least of which is the sinking of a nuclear submarine. Miller's Ollie is the antithesis of the military industrial complex of the 1980s, and writer Joey Cavalieri's Green Arrow in *Detective Comics* is a bit of an anachronism by comparison.

With the exception of two notable issues written by superstar Alan Moore, and one written by the otherwise unknown Dean R. Traven,[33] Green Arrow's final back-up series would be almost entirely scripted by Cavalieri. It was a series that saw the typically left-aligned hero standing alone against a tide of crime on the gritty streets of President Ronald Reagan's America. It wasn't until 1984 that Black Canary would regularly reunite with him as a partner in crime, enjoying some of her own solo success as one of DC's leading lights in a new costume. Personal issues and idealistic crusades gave way to cybercrime, shady government operations and the disparity between the rich and the working class. Running amazing parallels with the reaction to ultra-conservativism and distrust of government that populates alternative media 30 years later, it all served to foreshadow not only Green Arrow's much darker turn under writer and artist Mike Grell in the late 1980s (discussed in Chapter 7), but of the tone comics in general were taking in this era. Across the 45 appearances that Green Arrow made in the pages of *Detective Comics* between issue #521 (Dec 1982) and #567 (Oct 1986), there are strikingly similar themes to a post-9/11 world. Urban street artist Ozone has familial connections to Z.Z.Z., a government science agency developing weaponry that's tested on Star City's subway, continuing a thread of untrustworthy shadow governments[34]. In a three-part story set around the paramilitary villain Survivalist, in *Detective Comics* Vol. 1 #530-532 (Sept-Nov 1983), extreme rightists and Afghan terrorists are the focus. The constant in the middle of this is the self-described "working stiff" of Oliver Queen, who is described by his colleagues as "so Sixties." Even in the 1970s, Ollie was a throwback to the hippie movement, so here Cavalieri was hurtling his already antiquated idealist at some modern windmills. Cavalieri's Ollie is naïve and idealistic, despite his vocal bluster, and his regular opposition to (and fights with) pieces of technology was at odds with the major industry around personal computers booming in the decade, but consistent with one perception that the machines were "taking over." As an extension of his everyman persona, Ollie here is filibustering the system as long as it takes, using both of his personas to make sure *someone* listens.

---

[33] "Believe Everything I Hear," illustrated by Green Arrow regular Trevor Von Eeden, appeared in *Detective Comics* Vol. 1 #558 (Jan 1986). There are no indications of any other contributions by the mysterious Dean R. Traven to the comic book world.

[34] In *Detective Comics* Vol. 1 #527-529 (June 1983 - Aug 1983).

Green Arrow's appearances in this era aren't as heavy-handedly political as the O'Neil years, nor are they about political action in the same way as Maggin's "Oliver Queen for mayor" arc. This is not to say that they aren't politicized, and the multi-part stories allowed for the creative teams to play with ideas beyond the "villain of the week," even if Cavalieri's first rogue in this series was Hi-Tek, an early cybercriminal who ultimately turned out to be a 14-year-old boy and future ally[35]. Yet Cavalieri very quickly segues into the three-part 'Mob Rule!', running in *Detective Comics* Vol. 1 #523 (Feb 1983) through to #525 (Apr 1983). As the story begins, the sanitation, firemen, and transit workers of Star City are on strike. It immediately sets up a contrast between the entitled rich and the working class, the former disparaging the legitimate claims for improved working conditions from the latter. It all turns out to be the machinations of a costumed mobster calling himself Machiavelli, setting up a literal interpretation of the power-based *realpolitik* the 16th-century Italian prince's name is associated with. "Criminals will run this city's courts," he declares in a secret meeting of mobsters, positing that they will run the city better than the current politicians. "We'll provide asylum for fugitives from justice... and keep the rackets thriving. In short, this city will turn a profit... probably for the first time." It may not have been as consciously "relevant" as the comics of the 1970s, but they were far from apolitical at a time when street violence, protests and economic downturn filled the newspapers. Only two years earlier, the August 1981 strike of over 12,000 members of the Professional Air Traffic Controllers resulted in Reagan terminating jobs with the net effect that "polarized our politics in ways that prevent us from addressing the root of our economic troubles: the continuing stagnation of incomes despite rising corporate profits and worker productivity."[36] Machiavelli is not a direct analogue for Reagan in this case, although comparisons between the two figures have been made, but the villain nevertheless represented Reagan's

---

[35] In *Detective Comics* Vol. 1 #521-522 (Dec 1982 - Jan 1983), and more than likely a reaction to the popular mistrust of the computing boom and films such as *Tron*. Video games were increasingly being advertised in DC Comics at this time, and Apple's "1984" campaign (originally screened in 1983) reflected a grass-roots desire for people to have more control of their techology.

[36] McCartin, J. (2 Aug 2011). The Strike That Busted Unions. Retrieved 1 Dec 2015, from http://www.nytimes.com/2011/08/03/opinion/reagan-vs-patco-the-strike-that-busted-unions.html

assertion of power over the working class by undermining their authentic industrial actions.

Writer Alan Moore, who as a freelance writer for Marvel UK, *Warrior* magazine and 2000AD in the early parts of the 1980s, brought his own political views to the world of Green Arrow too. He had begun to express his thorough disgust with the Thatcherite Conservative government in his native U.K. through his early pieces for *V for Vendetta* in *Warrior* around 1982, in which a lone anarchist in a Guy Fawkes mask aims to bring down the fascist British government. At DC, Moore had been hired by editor Len Wein to revive *The Saga of the Swamp Thing* for the publisher, where he would introduce characters such as John Constantine, later the star of *Hellblazer*. The creator found himself in high demand at DC, and Wein was in a "bit of a jam" on the Green Arrow stories for the month. Assigning Moore to write a two-part story for the character allowed the publisher to keep Green Arrow visible until they could spin him off into another mini-series or an ongoing.[37] 'The Night Olympics', spanning *Detective Comics* Vol. 1 #549-550 (Apr-May 1985) is a reflection of the view that the hot-button topic of urban crime had become as much of a spectator 'sport' as the quadrennial event. It begins in typical Moore humor, a mock-sporting commentary on a street rat Green Arrow is chasing: "The first event was the four-hundred meter dash with television set and first-stage drug withdrawal." His Green Arrow is self-aware, and gradually becoming the kind of urban vigilante that was required in the face of Reagan's 1980s. The archer confronts the runner, asking him if he would "prefer the *quiet* moral instruction or the *noisy* moral instruction?" It's not only a nice nod to the sometimes on-the-nose rants of the Battling Bowman, but it sets the tone for the darkly comic, fists-first Green Arrow. He and Canary lament the "Darwinism" of "gradually weeding out all the just-plain-average goons, gradually improving the strain." Proving his point, another archer manages to hit Black Canary, declaring "My name's Pete Lomax. I'm just an ordinary person." Taunting Green Arrow from above, the archer eventually gets the shot and fires a well-aimed barrage of near misses at the wannabe villain, who collapses in their wake. "You were *right*, bird-lady," Ollie expresses out loud. "They don't make 'em like they *used* to."

---

[37] Moore, A. (2006). *DC Universe: The Stories of Alan Moore*. (p. 51). New York: DC Comics.

The simple story, heightened with some street-level poetry thanks to Moore's detailed scripting, is otherwise fairly typical of the era. Throughout the story, we see a dichotomy between two criminals: the initial runner has "super-hero psych-outs" at the mere sight of a costumed figure, while the main antagonist is constantly demanding proof of Green Arrow's prowess throughout the two issues. Like Reagan or Machiavelli with the unions, the hero's response is a blatant display of power, under which the would-be villain crumbles. The story is also notable for the artwork of Klaus Janson, already well-established at delivering the gritty urban streets in Frank Miller's *Daredevil* for Marvel throughout the early 1980s. Like Moore, Janson was transitioning between projects with his inks on Miller's *Batman: The Dark Knight Returns* still several months away. The book starts out with a visually lighter tone, from the visibly agitated runner's double-takes to Canary's loving looks at her "tall, blond, and socially concerned" man. Yet from the first appearance of Lomax, Janson's mastery of shadows comes to the foreground, stalking the hero like a mohawked Batman. Drawing inspiration from the rooftops of Manhattan and his own photographic reference, Janson later commented that the experience allowed him to gain confidence, and played to his strengths. "Moore's script proved an excellent tutorial in pacing and scene-setting. Knowing my work, he kept things on rooftops and in the dark, letting me play with light and shadow."[38] Green Arrow's final confrontation with Lomax is panelled as cinematically as a Sergio Leone film, with five thin horizontal panels of almost identical layout showing the foes aiming and firing at each other, almost entirely in silhouette. It reads like the corners of a flip-book, and you can almost imagine cutting out each panel to create an animation. 'The Night Olympics' is nowhere close to the brutality seen in contemporaries such as Marvel's Punisher or DC's own increasingly violent reimagined version of the Vigilante, let alone the darker urban hunter Green Arrow would become only two years later under Mike Grell. Yet it is a prime example of the flag going up signalling a change of direction for a character that began the decade as an everyman with relationship problems, and ended it as an urban vigilante.

---

[38] Moore, A. (2006), p. 51

Winner and Still Champion: Green Arrow on the Road to Going Solo

One of the most important developments that came out of this period for Green Arrow was the commissioning of the first Green Arrow mini-series in 1983 by writer Mike W. Barr and Trevor Von Eeden, and acting as a kind of extension to his *Detective Comics* appearances, one that ultimately paved the way for his first ongoing series that began in 1987 under Mike Grell. Both of these will be examined in detail in the two chapters following, but neither would have been possible without the fundamental groundwork done on the character during this transitional period. While it is not a perfect mirror, it was an era for Green Arrow that served as a bookend for a character that had been finding his way since 1941. While the backup features may have been frustrating for those readers who craved a longer format magazine featuring Green Arrow, this was arguably the last time that a group of writers and artists were allowed the luxury of experimenting with aspects of the character in such a free reign environment, as Grell's ongoing series was the start of more distinct periods for the archer, and longer sustained stretches for individual creative teams. Nevertheless, aspects of this period left their mark on almost every era of Green Arrow that followed. Grell's gritty urban hunter continued the notion of Ollie as an everyman, working alongside his life partner Dinah in a new flower shop in Seattle. Under Judd Winick, the 'One Year Later' storyline of 2006 actually sees Oliver Queen as the newly installed mayor of Star City, fighting as both the vigilante and the legitimate face of the broken city. Indeed, television's *Arrow* made Ollie's electoral campaign one of the focuses of its fourth season. Then after almost four decades of courtship, breakups, breakdowns, and even a death, Ollie and Dinah finally tied the knot in the *Green Arrow and Black Canary Wedding Special* Vol. 1 #1 (Nov 2007). By this stage, their relationship was so much a part of DC culture that it was touted as a miniature event, even if the wedding night didn't go according to plan.[39] So on one hand, while Ollie could have been seen as lost in the wilderness for this fourteen year period and effectively DC's most popular 'homeless' hero, it is a character-defining era that set up the second half of Green Arrow's fictional life.

---

[39] More on that event, and Judd Winick's run more generally, in Chapter 10.

Boisterous Mischief: Green Arrow's Murder Mystery on the High Seas

If Oliver Queen could have sent a letter to his editors on Earth-Prime, he would have undoubtedly blasted them about the injustice of going 42 years without his own series. After all, the previously unknown *Amethyst: Princess of Gemworld* was granted a titular 12-part maxi-series only months after her introduction, and the Battling Bowman had clocked in well over 600 appearances by the early 1980s. In 1983, Green Arrow shot straight out of the backup pages and into his own series at long last – for a few months at least.

"The New DC is on the move" was the marketing push behind a slew of new titles that were being added to the publisher's line up at the time. For Green Arrow, DC saw it as an opportunity to finally get some wider recognition beyond the back-up pages of *World's Finest Comics* and *Detective Comics* that had been his bread and butter for the better part of the decade. "50 against 1? I've got 'em outnumbered?" was emblazoned across the top of the promotional poster for a four-issue *Green Arrow* mini-series, with the Emerald Archer standing in front of a target as numerous guns opened fire. Returning fire with a barrage of arrows, the copy exclaims "Hard-hitting, high-spirited adventure from Mike W. Barr, Trevor Von Eeden and Dick Giordano." Using the same artwork for the cover of the debut issue, DC was positioning the archer as an action hero for his first solo outing, testing the water for an ongoing series. Yet the actual product they delivered turned out to be a cleverly rendered murder mystery that faithfully maintained Oliver Queen as an everyman hero. What remains most innovative about this incongruous series in Green Arrow's history is the power of the art, with Von Eeden and Giordano taking a leading role in the development of the character.

Mike W. Barr came to DC in the mid-1970s, and made his professional debut with the eight-page story 'The Magical Mystery Mirror' in *Detective Comics* Vol.1 #444 (Jan 1975). While he would write for both DC and Marvel, Barr took on editorial roles at DC from 1981, including *Legion of Super-Heroes*, *The Flash* and *World's Finest Comics*. In the latter, he'd also write a number of Green Arrow stories (as highlighted in the previous chapter of this book), several of which were illustrated by Von Eeden. The artist, born in Guyana and moving to New York at the age of 11, was studying medicine at Columbia University when he came to DC, impressing editor Jack C. Harris[1]. During the 1970s, Von Eeden was a rising star and had co-created Black Lightning with writer Tony Isabella to be DC's first African-American superhero to receive his own series. For Green Arrow fans, Von Eeden made his mark as early as 1977, as the artist on the *World's Finest Comics'* Black Canary and Green Arrow serials under Gerry Conway, with whom he (and inker Vince Colletta) would co-create the roguish Count Vertigo. His artwork would have been a jolt to monthly readers, playing with conventions of reality and defying the hyper-realism that pervaded the house style of the time. Take, for example, his debut of Vertigo in *World's Finest Comics* Vol. 1 #251 (July 1978), showcasing the villain's abilities by literally flipping the art upside-down and sideways. The eighth page of that story is an M.C. Escher inspired nightmare as various sized figures of Black Canary and Vertigo face off on a single-page panel that is best described as a twisted board game. Yet this was only the tip of the iceberg compared to what he would bring to the first *Green Arrow* mini-series in 1983.

As with the examination of Neal Adams in Chapter 4, here we turn to the art as a means of exploring the evolution of Green Arrow over the course of his history. While Von Eeden did not "recreate" the Emerald Archer in the same way that Adams did, Von Eeden took the solid foundations set down in the

[1] From "DC Profiles #10: Trevor Von Eeden" in *Superman* Vol. 1 #313 (July 1977).

1970s and began experimenting with them in ways that influenced the character and his villains for decades.

All My Sins Remembered

Barr and Von Eeden's *Green Arrow* mini-series, or simply *Green Arrow* for convenience, followed a series of increasingly lengthy and layered pieces the pair had worked on in the years leading up to its release. The stories were frequently multi-part, sometimes stretching across three or four issues, craving a longer format to cut loose in. The slogan across the top of the first issue, "The Battling Bowman in his own magazine *at last!*" is an exalted sigh of relief as much as it is an advertising slogan. *Green Arrow* is an extension of the *World's Finest* and *Detective Comics* appearances, firmly re-establishing the idea of Oliver Queen as the urban everyman, living in an inner-city apartment, and trying to make ends meet. Memories come flooding back when he is invited to the reading of a will from recently deceased friend Abigail 'Abby' Horton, and he suddenly becomes the beneficiary of $34 million and a controlling interest in Horton's company. With this narrative stroke, it already becomes a story touching on what makes the man, testing whether his resolve for the 'little guy' sticks with the (temporary) restoration of his fortune. We get the answer fairly quickly, as Ollie is not content to rest on his laurels, but rather uncover the truth about his friend's death and how the oil industry was involved. It's what reviewer Russel Freund calls a "murder mystery, a whodunit in super type drag."[2] Injecting a healthy dose of Agatha Christie into the Green Arrow persona was a new twist on a character once considered to be a Batman clone, one that Colin Smith marks in 2012 as "a notable and successful attempt to re-frame the cape'n'chest-insignia comic for a somewhat older and more literate audience."[3] Yet more than anything it was a faithful continuation of the work Elliot S. Maggin, Gerry Conway and Barr himself had already done in crafting Green Arrow as a working class hero, allowing themselves the luxury of space after telling stories in the cramped formula of the back-ups.

---

[2] Freund, R. (1984). "Four Mini-Series: An Optimist's Report." *The Comics Journal* (89), 55-60.

[3] Smith, C. (19 June 2012). "On *Green Arrow*, by Mike W. Barr and Trevor Von Eeden (1983)." Retrieved 8 Nov 2015 from http://sequart.org/magazine/12646/the-year-in-comics-24-green-arrow-by-mike-w-barr-trevor-von-eeden-1983/

Von Eeden establishes this point of difference on the third page of *Green Arrow* Vol. 1 #1 (May 1983) with a full-page heroic splash shot of Green Arrow, Giordano's inks heavily shadowing the figure in a way we had rarely seen on the character before. Bathed from the back in a powerful street light, Green Arrow is every bit the star of his own book. Neal Adams made a modern hero out of a Golden Age hodgepodge, but Von Eeden and Giordano shade him for the 1980s, a stylish mix of noir with a healthy throwback to the groovier parts of 1970s version of the archer. Von Eeden gets the chance to actually reframe some of Ollie's past with his own pencil strokes in this first issue. Within a single panel, Von Eeden morphs the contemporary Ollie's head back to his beardless bachelor days before his time on the island, allowing Von Eeden to put his own stamp on an origin story that had previously been illustrated by such prominent artists as Jack Kirby and Mike Grell, in *Adventure Comics* Vol. 1 #256 (Jan 1959) and *DC Super-Stars* Vol. 1 #17 (Dec 1977) respectively.[4] In just three short pages, Barr and Von Eeden recap Ollie's transition from spoiled rich kid to Star City's hero through to the loss of his fortune. The time on the island itself is an elegant five-panel retelling of Kirby's seven pages of artwork, borrowing the trappings of Kirby's style – and keeping the goofy leaf costume and hat that the archer crafted in exile – but Von Eeden adds his own distinctive stamps as well. With heavy silhouettes of trees and long grass, inked black by Giordano, framing Oliver crafting his first bow and catching the smugglers, it's almost as if Von Eeden was hiding just out of sight to record the events. It's actually amazing to see the first three decades of Green Arrow comics covered in four floating newspaper fragments, but an indicator of how Von Eeden's best work is expressed through these disjointed puzzle pieces of imagery.

One of Von Eeden's strengths in this series is guiding the reader through Barr's narrative at a controlled visual pace. While he will give Count Vertigo a spotlight later in the series, Von Eeden uses panel layouts to disorient the reader and to emulate Ollie's experience. After inheriting the money, an attempt is made on Ollie's life by trying to blow him up. The subsequent page showcases the aftermath, a scattering of a handful of irregularly shaped panels

---

[4] The *DC Super-Stars* origin was written by Dennis O'Neil and illustrated by Mike Grell. The artist would contribute to the origin story again in *The Longbow Hunters* mini-series in 1987 as writer and artist, write the "Sometimes a Fool Notion" origin story in *Secret Origins* Vol. 2 #38 (Mar 1989) and finally again as a writer in the 1993 mini-series *Green Arrow: The Wonder Year*. See Chapter 7 for more on these.

strewn across the page, as if the explosion has rattled the panels out of their grid. The images tumble towards the bottom of the page, leading the reader in a particular direction. Pages later, those huge shadows re-emerge to dwarf figures (including Ollie) in the long corridors of the Horton Chemicals Building, a visual indicator of Ollie being at odds with big business. Like Adams before him, Von Eeden doesn't feel the need to adhere to the panel grid structure, except where it suits the pace. Freund describes his style as though he "draws as if each page were a single panel, a panel to be subdivided by subordinate images."[5] This becomes increasingly evident in *Green Arrow* Vol. 1 #2 (June 1983), where a contemplative moment on the fourth page is presented as a loose borderless panel, and sepia-toned sets of smaller shapes recap the previous issue. The sixth and eighth pages of the same issue follow similar layouts to the ones Freund described, and in both cases an object enters the page in the upper left corner that appears to spill all the other objects onto that layout. In the case of the former, it's a car speeding on the page as though it has burst through the page borders, bringing us straight into Ollie's renewed lifestyle of wealth, and a montage of him setting up an arrow-making workbench in his new apartment. The following handful of pages are more tightly controlled, using smaller panels to quicken the pace through a wealth of exposition, showing Ollie either battling his computer or a rapid-fire series of interview questions with suspects in Abby's death. The next time we see Von Eeden cut loose is to pull the ground out from under us and Green Arrow alike, with the reintroduction of a character he co-created: Count Vertigo.

Von Eeden's previous work on Vertigo had pushed the limits of what could be artistically achieved in an eight-page story in the late 1970s, but the "feature length" version of Vertigo would play out in widescreen. Influenced by Alex Toth, a DC comics artist in the 1940s and an animator for Hanna-Barbera from the 1960s, Von Eeden admired art that "seemed to come straight from the artist's subconscious... imagination made visible."[6] This is what Von Eeden gave us in final six pages of the second issue, as the Vertigo effect takes hold of our emerald-clad hero. Green Arrow's foe up until that moment is jilted heir Ted Horton Jr., who had just taken a shot at Oliver Queen. Against bright pink

---

[5] Freund (1984), p. 56.
[6] Fiffe, M. (2009). "The Trevor Von Eeden Interview." The Comics Journal (298), 82-108.

From *Green Arrow* Vol. 1 #2. Art by Trevor Von Eeden and Dick Giordano. © DC Comics.

psychedelic waves and a green and blue anguished face, Horton comes barrel-rolling across the page, once again bursting out of the top left. A giant white silhouette of Green Arrow occupies the lower third of the page, as a smaller version of the archer goes tumbling into a mental abyss. All the while, Von Eeden's Vertigo stands resolutely still, albeit horizontal, in the lower left corner, simply stating "Greetings, Green Arrow!" His calm against the chaos he is causing is soon demonstrated across one of Von Eeden's greatest layouts, a two-page spread that occupies the 19th and 20th pages of the issue. Consisting of four large vertical panels divided by white space, the splash pages show what appears to be a "giant" Vertigo casually lounging on a rock and spanning all four panels. Around him are floating images of Green Arrow firing wildly, the hero's disembodied head floating upside-down, or abstractly holding onto a piece of debris. It's more like reading a Steve Ditko piece from Marvel's 1960s *Strange Tales* featuring Doctor Strange, and yet still entirely within the organic version of the Green Arrow universe of this era. We are wholly inside Von Eeden's world by this point in the issue, but just as he has us there he slams the reader back into a sense of reality by following his two-page featured piece with another full-page close-up of Ollie's angry face, Giordano's inks clearly defining the edges of the determined bowman, marking the literal redrawing of the lines in this battle of the wills. On the penultimate page of the issue, Von Eeden turns those artistic tricks back on the rogue, as Ollie ricochets an arrow precisely off the point that will do the most damage to Vertigo. In this case those "subordinate images" once again begin to coalesce into normalcy, visually indicating that Ollie is regaining control of the fight. As Vertigo is hit, a close-up of his face occupies the lower part of the page, and his bloodshot eyes turn to rose-tinted target shapes to show the tables of unreality have turned. As the issue closes out, it's an evenly spaced set of thin panels that show Ollie observing Horton's lifeless body and the surreally colored sunset. The reader gets a chance to breathe, back on familiar territory, allowing their brain to reset for another adventure.

For all the convention-breaking in the sophomore issue, Von Eeden and Barr are telling an Agatha Christie style mystery at its heart, and the comparative restraint of the next two issues is reflective of this. Smith is partly right when he notes "the quality of the work of both artists declines somewhat as the series progresses, with every sign of looming deadline crises, the pages in *Green Arrow* are never less than intriguing and telling." The aforementioned inky silhouettes remain a theme throughout the four issues, sometimes bordering an image, and at other times either jet black or pure white trees or figures will occupy the foreground, dwarfing the human actors on the page. Following the thrilling opening pages of *Green Arrow* Vol. 1 #3 (July 1983), in which a series of panels decreasing in size show the hero archer torturing Vertigo with a game of "William Tell," Green Arrow gets back to the business of investigating Abby's death. As such, it's the contrasting chiaroscuro lighting of *noir* that Von Eeden yields effectively throughout this chapter. As Ollie scours his available sources for information, his unsuccessful meeting with the CIA is appropriately shown entirely in blackened silhouettes, indicative of the amount of information he actually gets out of them. At the Horton board room meeting, it's all canted Dutch angles, subjective point of view shots and smoke trails, because it's not *noir* unless everyone is smoking at each other. Even Ollie smokes in this issue; as he plays the part of the anti-hero millionaire as a rouse, Von Eeden, Giordano and colorist Tom Ziuko effectively under-lighting Ollie's face in an contrasted orange glow as he lights up a cigar with money. The only time Von Eeden uses his montage style pages in this third chapter is for a splash of Ollie's social antics, convincing the world that he is a spoiled lout. It's immediately back to the shadows after this, culminating in an art-led action sequence that spans four pages, in which Ollie and CIA Agent Jones fight unseen attackers. The entire sequence is depicted with the faceless attackers in the foreground, their forms simply colored a high-contrast black, mimicking the backlighting of the style. The faces of the attackers are actually unimportant in this section, as it's more about Von Eeden and Giordano leading a tightly controlled action scene. It's actually unfair to call it an emulation of *noir*, as that would imply something inauthentic. This *is* comics *noir*, with the artist doing things that can only be achieved in comic book form, even if the language of film just as readily applies here.

The final chapter of the saga is somewhat incongruous with the rest of mini-series. This was pre-*The Dark Knight Returns* and *Watchmen*, and the darkness could only be taken so far before being dragged back into the daytime. With the lights turned back on, Barr shifts the setting from the darkened alleys of Star City to the high seas, with Von Eeden still immediately making it his own. The opening shot of a ship making its way across four small panels moves from a wide establishing shot to an extreme close-up of the rear of the boat, creating the illusion of movement. Yet the distinguishing features of the final issue begin with the title page. "Look, up in the sky! It's a bird! It's a plane! It's… Green Arrow!" declares the hero, as he and Black Canary parachute into the scene, the red and yellow lines of the tracer bullets criss-crossing the entire page giving the shot an energy that sets it apart from the moodiness of the previous outing. Yet Von Eeden also has the unenviable task of making Cap'n Lash a menacing villain in his first and thankfully last appearance, with Green Arrow facing the pantomime pirate throwback in his quest to chase down the narrative MacGuffin of a viable substitute for petroleum. With his Errol Flynn moustache, purple headband, puffy shirt, bright blue cavalier boots and trusty whip, it's not one of Von Eeden's finest hours, although it's hard to imagine what possessed Barr to introduce a flamboyant swashbuckler three-quarters of the way through a murder mystery, complete with a fight amidst the sails. About the nicest thing that can be said about Lash is the way Von Eeden depicts the fight, at one point using five elongated panels that all stretch to a single point on the page as a way of adding a fluid sense of movement to the motion of the whips and arrows of this outrageous misfortune.

With the obligatory action spectacle out of the way, all that is left is the resolution of the mystery, and Von Eeden once again envelops his characters in heavy shadows. In the absence of Ollie gathering all of the suspects together in a single room, Von Eeden gathers them all together in a single page, as the inky-black figure of Green Arrow makes his way towards his intended quarry. Once again, on the nineteenth page of the final issue, the silhouette of Green Arrow enters from a darkened doorway in the upper-left corner of the page. A tumble of close-ups, off-angle renderings of figures and claustrophobic panels are designed in line with the genre, all intended to create a *mise-en-scene* that unsettles the reader in the same way the earlier explosion did.[7] Discovering his chief suspect apparently dead from a gun wound to the head, the revelation of the femme fatale completes the *noir* archetypes, and naturally she appears in a half-light amidst a tendril of gun smoke. Green Arrow becomes a passive observer as the last scenes play out, the femme fatale revealing her reasons behind the murders. It turns out to be Cynthia "Cindy" Horton Sinclair, the daughter of Abby and ex-flame of Oliver Queen, adding an additional personal sting for the archer. Von Eeden's abstract panel placement heightens the tension during this reveal, as a single gunshot we are meant to believe is intended for Ollie goes off. Over the page, three close-ups of Cindy's face show that she has been shot in the forehead, each panel slowly unleashing an inch more blood dripping from the wound. Her late husband, who Cindy had believed dead moments before, managed to get out one last shot at the woman who betrayed him. With everybody who knows Ollie's identity dead and the mystery solved, and Abby's fortune turned over to Abby's brother Maxwell Stein, Barr wastes no more time in wrapping the story up, leaving Oliver as he began: broke and in shadow, bathed in an indeterminate glow, while raising a glass to his dear departed friend Abigail Horton.

"We'll Never See Your Like Again... and We're All the Poorer for It!"

While Trevor Von Eeden's work on this series isn't highlighted nearly enough, it can be seen a progenitor of the art-led storytelling that would become more commonplace a decade after Von Eeden's primary work at DC. Von Eeden would stay in the Green Arrow universe for a while, at least tangentially through the 1991 and 1993 Black Canary series, even if he didn't find the character particularly interesting[8]. At DC, he would find fans on his

---

[7] Janey, P., & Lowell, P. (1996). "Some Visual Motifs of Film Noir." In *Film Noir Reader* (pp. 65-75). New York: Limelight.
[8] Fiffe (2009).

work for the Batman family, and later at Marvel on Power Man and Iron Fist and the independent The Original Johnson, a biographical piece on boxer Jack Johnson. When artist Andrea Sorrentino took on Green Arrow under writer Jeff Lemire in 2013, his discombobulating approach to the reimagined Vertigo had more than a little bit of Von Eeden in its DNA. Even if the storytelling techniques were very different in the 30 years that separated the two runs, Von Eeden and Sorrentino share a virtual link of creating environments that draw the reader in by altering the expected landscape. They require the reader to engage with the material in a physical fashion, whether it is turning the page upside-down or simply react to the claustrophobic darkness of the *noir* corridors.

None of this is to discount the work of Mike W. Barr, who built on a solid foundation that he, Gerry Conway, Elliot S. Maggin and Joey Cavalieri had created in the everyman hero of Green Arrow. Setting up Green Arrow at odds with big business doesn't seem too radical now, but in 1983 it was positively counter-culture to stand against 'Big Oil' in a mainstream comic. The introduction of the character of Abby Horton, as an older friend and confidant to Ollie prior to his being stranded on that fateful island, not only gives the archer a different kind of relationship with a woman to the intense romantic one with Black Canary, but it allows Barr to reframe the entire Green Arrow history within this more personalized context. Through Abby, we glimpse what Oliver Queen's life might have been like before he learned the way of the bow, something few of the other origin stories explore in any depth, with her influence and companionship bringing out the inherent good in the errant playboy. Through his friendship with Abby, the main thrust of the series is achieved, continuing to distinguish him from the rest of the DC Universe as a human being first, and a costumed adventurer second.

The *Green Arrow* mini-series might always remain a curiosity, given that it is entirely self-contained and with the exception of the pre-existing heroes like Black Canary, none of these characters appeared beyond this series. The events are not reflected in the concurrent series of *Detective Comics*, predominantly written by Joey Cavalieri, but its legacy was far more lasting than that. In the letters column of *Green Arrow* Vol. 1 #3, readers are told "If sales of this mini-series go through the roof, we won't be able to afford *not* to give Ollie his own book." While DC's plans for the line took a major shift with the universe-shattering *Crisis on Infinite Earths* anniversary event in 1985, the publisher would make good on that promise in 1987 with Mike Grell's mini-series *The Longbow Hunters* followed immediately by an ongoing series that ran from

1988 through to 1998. Von Eeden contributed to that run on *Green Arrow* Vol. 2 #25 (Oct 1989) and *Green Arrow Annual* Vol. 2 #5 (1992), but what his art on this *Green Arrow* mini-series proved was that it was possible to create a piece of work filled with artistic experimentation alongside a showcase of the more human side of a costumed superhero. Indeed, it was the entire *modus operandi* of *The Longbow Hunters*, where Grell's art was just as important as his writing in the prestige format storytelling. Nevertheless, *Green Arrow* remains a bubble in time as the archer transitioned between his Silver Age swashbuckling and his darker post-Crisis persona.

What Can One Man Do? Mike Grell and the Era of the Urban Hunter

What can one man do?

The question was posed by Elliot S. Maggin during the *Green Lantern/Green Arrow* run of the 1970s, in a back-up story that saw a superhero deal with a race riot and respond with the very real world solution of running for mayor.[1] While Maggin explored the notion, writer and artist Mike Grell's run on *Green Arrow* allowed audiences to examine the answer at length. Grell also defined the modern version of the character during his seven-year tenure on the book by breaking all the rules. Focusing on alter ego Oliver Queen as the man behind the mask, and creating a version of the hero that would stand as distinct from his contemporaries, he influenced subsequent writers for decades, forming the basis of the *Arrow* television series almost 30 years after his seminal work began. In his first ongoing series after almost 50 years as a DC hero, Green Arrow would take a frank look at sex, drugs, love, governmental corruption, and urban decay. He would also do it without the aid of the Justice League or his

---

[1] *Green Lantern* Vol 2 #87 (Nov 1971).

"super friends." With Grell at the helm, Green Arrow transitioned into a darker and grittier vigilante.

Green Arrow would become the urban hunter.

Mike W. Barr and Trevor Von Eeden's 1983 *Green Arrow* mini-series had been a commercial and critical success. It proved it was possible to repurpose an existing character for a more modern and literate audience, argues Colin Smith, maintaining his position as an everyman hero behind the mask without diminishing his heroics.[2] By the late 1980s, Green Arrow had parted with his Golden Age persona, literally being killed off alongside countless others in DC's *Crisis on Infinite Earths* (1985) event (or *Crisis* for short), an unprecedented hard reboot of the entire 50 years of the publisher's comic book continuity. Frank Miller and Lynn Varley's *Batman: The Dark Knight Returns* (1986) and Alan Moore and Dave Gibbons' *Watchmen* (1986) had sent lightning bolts through the industry, reimagining classic heroes as more complex and tinted mirrors of their Golden and Silver Age counterparts, ushering in the "Modern Age" (or as some call it, the "Dark Age") of comic books.

It wasn't just the tone of the books that was changing either, but the voices behind them as well. New independent companies such as Eclipse Comics, First Comics, and Pacific Comics saw a creator-driven era where creators Howard Chaykin (*American Flagg!*), Mike Baron and Steve Rude (*Nexus*), and John Ostrander (*GrimJack*), emerged, and old guard legends like Jack Kirby were being enticed back into comics by Pacific with the relatively new notion that creators would own their work.[3] Art Spiegelman began publishing his *Maus* as a serial (1980-1991) in the avant-garde comics anthology *Raw*, depicting his father's tale as a Holocaust survivor, a story that gave legitimacy to the medium when it won the Pulitzer Prize in 1992. Other new independent publishers like Fantagraphics and Dark Horse Comics made their mark, the latter producing almost a dozen new titles in its first year, pushing DC and Marvel even further towards experimentation. While Grell was already established as a fan-favourite voice in the 1970s, it was out of this environment that he would put

---

[2] Smith, Colin. (2012, June 19). "On *Green Arrow*, by Mike W. Barr and Trevor Von Eeden (1983)." Retrieved 25 Aug 2015 from http://sequart.org/magazine/12646/on-green-arrow-by-mike-w-barr-trevor-von-eeden-1983/

[3] Jack Kirby returns to comics with Cosmic Hero. (1981). *The Comics Journal*, (65), 23. Retrieved 26 Aug 2015 from http://tcj.com

his stamp on one of DC's oldest secondary characters. DC's *Crisis* would become Oliver Queen's mid-life crisis. Yet if the Emerald Archer was to survive in this brave new world, and prove that he finally had what it took to lead a book rather than just be a supporting character, the "one man" would have to do it without the aid for the rest of the DC Universe. He would not simply become an urban vigilante in the vein of Marvel's Punisher, but instead he would be something more "attainable," as scholars Scully and Moorman suggest. "Green Arrow gave Americans a more easy-going vigilante, suggesting that you do not have to be brooding or conflicted to carry out justice."[4] Over the course of his seven-year run, Grell would take the liberal-left crusader and fashion him into a more accessible, mature, and most importantly, a *human* version of the vigilante archetype.

For the purposes of a thorough analysis of Grell's major themes and influences, a series of major periods have been selected. Firstly, it is impossible to begin this discussion without a critical look at *Green Arrow: The Longbow Hunters*, the three-issue prestige format mini-series that formed the precursor to an ongoing run and set the tone for the urban hunter. The immediate consequences of that series were felt in the long-running *Green Arrow* Vol. 2, particularly in the arcs "Here There Be Dragons" (*Green Arrow* Vol. 2 #9-12), "Blood of the Dragon" (*Green Arrow* Vol. 2 #21-24), and "The Black Arrow Saga" (*Green Arrow* Vol. 2 #35-38), a series of annual thematic sequels to *The Longbow Hunters*, ones that turn the table on the most contentious issues in that seminal mini-series. Falling within these arcs are those smaller pieces that typify the vigilante / urban hunter persona of the decade, with "The Trial of Oliver Queen" (*Green Arrow* Vol. 2, #19-20) getting to the heart of the "law versus justice" debate. Finally, *Green Arrow: The Wonder Year*, another retelling of Green Arrow's origin, sees Grell rewrite Green Arrow's origin in such a way that would make sense within his modern take on the character.

Origins of a Hunter: The Ballad of Two Mikes

The mainstream comics industry was going through its own shifts. Grant Morrison argues that *Green Lantern/Green Arrow* ushered in the Dark Age almost a decade earlier: "It was all here: the photo-realistic artwork, the social

---

[4] Scully, T. and Moorman, K. (2014), The Rise of Vigilantism in 1980 Comics: Reasons and Outcomes. *The Journal of Popular Culture*, 47: 634–653.

and political awareness, the super-hero divided into agent of the Establishment or rebel anarchist."[5] It's a description that could just as readily apply to the industry itself, with the old guard being phased into the new. Long running war comics such as *Sgt. Rock*, *G.I. Combat*, and *Weird War Tales* were brought to a close, while leading Marvel creators like Marv Wolfman and George Pérez made the jump to DC, where they would make comics history on *The New Teen Titans* and *Crisis on Infinite Earths*. Following *Crisis*, new and existing creators found themselves in an environment where they felt more free to scratch behind the panels and see if there was anything new that could be done with characters that were, in some cases, half a century old. Readers in turn were being enticed back to comics with the publisher's marketing slogan "The DC Universe will never be the same." Looking to capture both the emerging youth market, as well as cater to the aging population that made up their existing reader base, mainstream comics would look to people who were making a mark outside of the big two publishers. Comic book voices used to the freedom of independent publishing were storming the castle, and those same creators were being encouraged to turn their eyes to DC's extensive catalogue.

Speaking about his earliest days in the industry, Grell recalls that "Green Arrow is the reason I got into comics. He's my favourite character, and always has been. Even from the time when I was a kid."[6] Grell's strong sense of politics, military background and dedication to his art style served him well in the shifting comics industry of the 1970s. His art earned him a legion of fans, but his own background and political leanings would find their way into the character of Green Arrow. During his U.S. Air Force service in Asia, Grell met a cartoonist who told him the profession works "two or three days a week, and make a million bucks a year." He was also inspired by Neal Adams' work on *Green Lantern/Green Arrow* to take the Famous Artists School correspondence course in cartooning, and once he was out of the Air Force, he enrolled in the Chicago Academy of Fine Art. His first job in the comics industry was working for Dale Messick (the pseudonym of Dalia Messick) on the *Brenda Starr* comic strip in 1972. After moving to New York in 1973, Grell got his first job with DC Comics,

---

[5] Morrison, G. (2012). *Supergods: What Masked Vigilantes, Miraculous Mutants, and a Sun God from Smallville Can Teach Us About Being Human*. New York: Spiegel & Grau.

[6] Mike Grell, personal interview, 29 Mar 2015. Available at *Behind the Panels* [podcast]. Retrieved from http://behindthepanels.net. Full transcript in this book.

almost immediately making a splash at the publisher. When asked about this, Grell explained that after going to the New York Comic Art Convention in 1973, he literally walked into editor Julius Schwartz's office with his portfolio, and walked out with his first assignment.[7]

As the highly in-demand commodity of both a penciller and inker, Grell worked on several stories for Aquaman in the pages of *Adventure Comics*, covers for *Wonder Woman*, and an Elliot S. Maggin story in the launch of *The Batman Family* #1 (Sep-Oct 1975). During this period, Grell worked on Green Arrow for the first time in *Action Comics* Vol. 1 #440 (Oct 1974) in a story called 'Little Dog Lost!' Maggin's script is a simple affair, as Oliver and his partner Dinah/Black Canary get involved in a smuggling operation after picking up a mysterious dog that turns out to be Superman's Krypto. It is a mostly forgettable tale, but Grell's art is the standout. Just a few issues later, a reader commented that Grell "came closer than anyone else has to the Neal Adams Green Arrow. Mike is one of the few people who can do a decent job on GA's beard."[8] He wasn't wrong: Grell's Green Arrow was peppered with nods to Adams, albeit modifying some of the photorealistic close-ups and exchanging them for Grell's brand of fluid action and lithe movements. It's an issue that opens with Green Arrow flying in on a jetpack, a feat he sadly rarely repeats these days[9], and maintains that graceful movement for Black Canary as well. Over the course of the next few issues, Grell began to carve out something more distinct. 'The Black Canary is Dead!'[10] thematically foreshadows the pivotal moment Grell would develop in detail over a decade later in *The Longbow Hunters*, with Canary captured and Ollie desperately on the hunt for her. The tight paneling on the close-ups of Green Arrow's anguished face was an early indicator of the kind of visually heightened language Grell would use in *The Longbow Hunters*, where entire splash pages would be dedicated to reaction shots and close-ups of eyes.

---

[7] Grell relates this story in detail the personal interview transcribed in the back of this volume.

[8] Letters column in *Action Comics* Vol. 1 #444 (Feb 1975).

[9] Grell would strap Ollie into a jetpack again in *Green Arrow* Vol. 2 #50 (Aug 1991) in order to rescue Dinah and some hostages from Seattle's Space Needle. Its whereabouts are currently unknown.

[10] Also in *Action Comics* Vol 1. #444.

Grell proved himself as a triple threat by adding writer to his list of credits, at first in the *Action Comics* back-up stories with Maggin,[11] and later in the creation of The Warlord.[12] Grell's *The Warlord* began its life as a series called the *Savage Empire* that Grell was trying to sell as part of his portfolio when he was first trying to break into comics, about an archeologist catapulted back in time to Atlantis. With a title and a location change, Grell would rework this concept once he had his foot in the door at DC, now about an Air Force pilot named Travis Morgan who crash lands in a hidden savage tropical world named Skartaris. As a lone hunter in a literal kill-or-be-killed jungle, Morgan is the prototype for Grell's later version of Oliver Queen as an urban hunter[13]. There's an element of pure male fantasy to *The Warlord*, with Morgan rescuing the lightly clad savage woman Tara in the first issue. She teaches him about survival in the wild lands, and he tries valiantly to educate the woman in the complex civilized notions of "gravity" and "compasses." Amidst psychedelic visions of Greek inspired goat-man Satyrs, dinosaurs and rival warriors, we are constantly reminded that "The only law is the law of the jungle. The strong prey upon the weak...and they are, in turn, preyed upon by the stronger." This line would echo darker sentiments in Grell's *Green Arrow: The Longbow Hunters* #1 (Aug 1987) almost twelve years later, by which stage he had refined it to: "It's a myth that predators prey only on the weak. Mostly, it's a question of odds."

Grell illustrated Green Arrow in a more permanent way when he took over art duties on the revived *Green Lantern/Green Arrow* run in 1976, starting with *Green Lantern* Vol. 2 #90 (Sept 1976), as O'Neil picked up the numbering where he left off after a four-year hiatus. Artist Neal Adams did not return, his output for DC and Marvel at that stage limited to individual issues while he concentrated on other media and advertising. Grell was quick to jump at the opportunity to work on one of the titles that had inspired him. "I was fortunate

---

[11] *Action Comics* Vol 1. #444-445.

[12] The Warlord originally appeared in the oddly named *1st Issue Special* #8 (Nov 1975).

[13] Apart from the thematic similarities, elements of *The Warlord* would later be incorporated into his ongoing Green Arrow run. The characters share an uncanny resemblance and beard, although the inspiration was not Queen but Grell himself, as was evidenced by a meta cameo from the creator in *The Warlord* #35 (July 1980). (The characters would also share a panel in *Green Arrow* #27 in the late 1980s, satisfying a long-running joke amongst fans).

that I was in the office the day that O'Neil decided that he was going to bring it back," he recently explained. "I heard the rumor in the hallway, and went straight to his office and said 'Ok, who do I have to kill?' That was, sort of, the culmination of my initial goal, to be able to work on that book."[14] Green Arrow under O'Neil/Adams was the last kicks of the hippie movement, a (r)evolutionary liberal who talked loud and travelled hard. Yet the new stories in the revived series took a dramatic shift from the "relevance" comics of the 1970s, shooting Green Lantern back into outer space where the character rightfully belonged. From the sublime to the ridiculous, the low point was perhaps the appearance of Itty, a sentient alien plant that Hal Jordan kept as a pet. However, there were a few gems in this series, including the two-part 'Lure of an Assassin'/'Terminal for a Tragedy'[15], in which Grell depicts Ollie with his trademark beard shaved clean, while the character employs some rarely seen detective skills for a spot of undercover government work while Lantern is out with the flu. The second run of *Green Lantern/Green Arrow* has not been reprinted in trade to date, which is indicative of their standing. Grell remained on the book until issue #100, where a short run from Alex Saviuk (later known for his seven-year run on Marvel's *Web of Spider-Man*) began. When Grell returned to the character in the 1980s, he would ensure that his take on Green Arrow would be something far more memorable.

The solidification of Green Arrow's place at DC in the 1980s is a tale of two Mikes: the now legendary and influential run of Mike Grell will forever associate his name with the character, but returning DC editor Mike Gold was also fundamental in the creation of the urban hunter character as well. Gold's career as group editor at DC Comics saw him oversee books such as *The Shadow*, *The Question*, *Action Comics Weekly*, and *Hawkworld*. Yet it would be their work together on a character that DC had barely given a masthead to in over 40 years that would arguably define them both going forward. In 1983, Gold co-founded First Comics, where he published and edited the likes of Howard Chaykin's *American Flagg*, Jim Starlin's *Dreadstar* and Mike Grell's *Jon Sable Freelance*.[16]

---

[14] Mike Grell, personal interview, 29 Mar 2015.

[15] *Green Lantern* Vol. 2 #94-95 (May-July 1977).

[16] If the idea of Grell as a cowboy in the comics industry needed any more weight, it can be found in the story Gold tells about a meeting he had with First's attorney and Grell, in which the latter went fishing in his bag for his favorite pen to sign the contracts, and placed a .45 calibre gun on the table. It was during this exchange that

Gold's return to DC in 1986 began a second major run of titles for the editor, and the ability to influence a number of these superstar writers back to the DC roster. Meanwhile, Grell had also been away from DC Comics for almost a decade, making waves during the 1980s while writing the likes of *Jon Sable Freelance*, *Starslayer* and the Tarzan comic strips for various independent publishers. Chatting with UK's *Speakeasy* in April 1987,[17] shortly before the release of *Green Arrow: The Longbow Hunters*, Grell spoke about Gold's unique hook on the character that drew him back. Not interested in Batman, after his own dark transformation at the hands of Frank Miller in *Batman: The Dark Knight Returns*, it was Gold who suggested Green Arrow to the creator. "Mike described what he had in mind for the character – an 'urban hunter.' That got me hooked, and more or less provided the springboard for my approach to the character."

The Longbow Hunters and the Urban Vigilante

"First *Dark Knight*. Now... *Green Arrow: The Long Bow Hunters!*"

That's how DC Comics led their own press for *Green Arrow: The Longbow Hunters* in the August 1987 *DC Releases* newsletter,[18] published in May of that year, highlighting the relatively new prestige format that had made Frank Miller's work stand out as a distinct art form. That the company was giving the Emerald Archer the same treatment as Batman was indicative that at long last, Green Arrow was being taking seriously and "presented in a way that will take your breath away." Grell, much like Miller, came onto the project as both a writer and an artist. Following DC's 1985/1986 *Crisis*, in theory any DC character could be anything they wanted to be. Even Superman was rebooted the previous year in John Byrne's *Man of Steel* mini-series, similarly modernizing the hero's origin. Yet the connection was not simply one of formatting, with *The Longbow Hunters* tapping into the same themes of street justice, corruption, and inner-city decay that Miller and Alan Moore explored throughout the

---

Grell chose to ask the pertinent contractual questions, and as the editor tells it, Grell "came out ahead on a few contractual points." From Gold, M. (1989). Introduction. In Grell, M. (1989). *Green Arrow: The Longbow Hunters* (pp. 3-7). New York, NY: DC Comics.

[17] Slings & The Arrow: Grell on the Return of the Emerald Archer. (Apr 1987). Speakeasy, 10-11.

[18] *DC Releases* Vol. 1 #39 (Aug 1987).

decade. However, in order to combat this oppressive system, Green Arrow had to become someone else. He had to become something else: the urban hunter.

Vigilantes in comics were hardly a new concept. After all, the very notion of Batman's 1939 origin comes from a character growing up seeking justice after witnessing the murder of his parents as a child. Throughout the 1970s, heroes were turning away and questioning the institutions that they once defended. Even Captain America became disillusioned with the U.S. government in 1974-75 after discovering that someone (hinted to be none other than Richard Nixon) was the head of a terrorist organization, and he became Nomad, the vigilante "without a country" - albeit for only a handful of issues.[19] Frank Miller might have taken Daredevil into the dark heart of New York in the early 1980s, but he never crossed the line into killing. That was for anti-heroes like The Punisher, introduced as a villain in the pages of *The Amazing Spider-Man* in 1974, who frequently came to physical blows with Daredevil and Spider-Man over The Punisher's choice to murder those he decreed guilty of crimes against the city. The heroes and anti-heroes would just as readily team-up, showing the contrast between their styles of justice, most notably in Miller's own run with Daredevil and The Punisher in *Daredevil* #181-184 (Apr–July 1982). In 1983, DC Comics responded with their own version of the character with Marv Wolfman and George Pérez's update of the Vigilante, supplanting the 1940s DC Western hero with his own brand of street justice. Scully and Moorman point out that by hunting down criminals who escaped prosecution, he would also frequently struggle with the morality of his actions.[20]

Urban decay and crime was the flavor of the 1980s. It wasn't just in the comics and movies (like the popular *Death Wish* series) either, with actual US crime rates on the rise throughout the decade. Steven Levitt references the rise of the crack cocaine market and its rapid expansion from 1985, leading to violent crime as gangs battled for dominance of distribution of this cheap but powerful drug on the streets[21]. The public hysteria around crack may have been somewhat exaggerated, perhaps as journalists Levine and Reinarman suggest,

---

[19] *Captain America* Vol. 1 #180-183.

[20] Scully and Moorman. (2014), p. 645.

[21] Levitt, Steven D. (2004). "Understanding Why Crime Fell in the 1990s: Four Factors that Explain the Decline and Six that Do Not." 18 (1). pp. 163-190. Retrieved 20 June 2015.

to divert "the nation's attention and resources from more serious problems."[22] This was, after all, an era where television screens were filled with a series of *The Thrill Can Kill* PSAs. Clint Eastwood, Ally Sheedy, Bette Midler, and the unlikely squeaky voice of Pee Wee Herman's moral authority warned of the "cute little vial" that contained the "glamour drug of the 80s" that wasn't worth dying for.[23] Grell's Green Arrow is a reflection of the media reports of urban crime. With storylines that were ripped straight from the newspapers, Grell combined elements of actual unsolved Seattle murders with the Iran-Contra affair. The significance of taking this approach with a character such as Green Arrow was precisely *because* his history had been that of a stable secondary character. Grell would actively work to put Ollie in a situation where he was forced to become a different kind of character that suited the times.

With *The Longbow Hunters*, Grell adopts Gold's notion of an "urban hunter" philosophy almost immediately, shifting the action from the fictional Star City to the very real Seattle. This shift was a suggestion of Gold's, not just due to their familiarity with the area, but its underused status in the DC Universe and proximity to the Canadian border would allow for an expansion of stories into a completely different location.[24] Super powers and other heroes simply don't exist in this world, or if they do then Grell isn't interested in them. While a killer stalks the streets of Seattle, a second archer with a vendetta is targeting rich old men. *The Longbow Hunters* is very much an indicator of the perceived dangers that living in a major built-up city represented in the 1980s, just as Batman and Green Arrow represented protectors of new urban landscapes of the 1940s. Green Arrow was not immune to the dark ink that had crept into comic book cities during the decade, from Frank Miller's visions of New York and Gotham in *Daredevil* and *Batman: Year One*, to the "extended gutters" of "accumulated filth of all their sex and murder" in Moore's *Watchmen*. Just as Grell's Warlord was a singular figure in the actual savage jungle, Grell's Seattle was no less of a wild hotbed of lawlessness, with everybody in it either predator or prey in the food chain. Grell's Green Arrow is an aging white hunter, an anachronism that sees the world for what it is.

---

[22] Levine, H. G., & Reinarman, C. (4 Jan 1987). "The Monkey on the Public's Back." *Newsday* (Ideas Section), 1-10.
[23] Eastwood, C (12 Feb 2012). "Clint Eastwood: The Thrill Can Kill PSA" [video file]. Retrieved from https://youtube.com/watch?v=SskPBwn4eg4
[24] Gold, M. (1989), p. 6.

From an establishing shot of the iconic Space Needle, Grell informs us "The hunters are dying." The first issue of *The Longbow Hunters*, appropriately and simply titled 'The Hunters', opens at night in the Pike Place Public Market, a waterfront tourist center known to anybody who has been near Seattle. The stylized realism of Grell's art is coupled with painted finishes from Julia Lacquement and meticulously detailed backgrounds by assistant Lurene Haines. Robbed of the daylight and the familiar fish flinging frolics of the local retailers, it's a dark and foreboding place, lit only by the transformative "Public Market Center" sign that gives off a red glow with an undercurrent of sex and seediness. The quintessential eightiesness of it is punctuated by the presence of punks and street toughs, sporting the cut-off denim vests, mohawk hairstyles, and distinctive Devo robot sunglasses of the era. Grell's contention is that the hunters of old, maybe the very same that he created in *The Warlord*, had given way to "a system of barter," by which he visually indicates prostitution. Through the eyes of a killer, there is a remembered flash of a nearly nude woman, before Grell splatters the two-page spread with the blood of the Seattle Slasher's eighteenth victim. A newspaper report on the prostitute's slaying segues to Ollie's face as he rips the newspaper from the windows of the Sherwood Florist, a shop that he and Dinah – now a fully fledged couple – have just purchased. It's a literal castle in the heart of Seattle, with "his," "hers," and "ours" spaces firmly foreshadowing the individual and communal aspects of these heroes going forward. Yet as soon as we are introduced to this domestic bliss, it is literally shattered by someone hurtling through the window, ostensibly on crack.

Grell takes the story one step further, smashing through the golden and silver sheens of Ollie's past as well, with a neat flashback to Ollie's pre-*Crisis* life, as he reflects with Dinah on his past exploits. In one of the few moments that references a continuity other than Grell's, or indeed anything of Queen's past life (including the only mention of the name "Green Arrow" beyond the cover), a painting of Robin Hood prompts him to comment that those "Old days of glory are gone for good," adding to Dinah "We'll never have those days back again, will we?" Yet at the same time, Grell gives us his first retelling of Green Arrow's origin, flashing back to his time on the island. "I learned to kill," he remarks, suggesting that those "old days of glory" were already tainted. It's here that Grell's skills as an artist come to the fore, using innovative layouts, such as the framing of flashbacks within the loose borders of an arrowhead. Grell's importance as an artist in the Green Arrow legacy can't be overlooked.

Some contemporaneous reviews were vitriolic in their analysis of his art, including *The Comic Journal*'s Rob Rodi, who saw him as an "off-Broadway [Neal] Adams," and thought he "may be the one cartoonist alive whose work would be improved by a Macintosh."[25] Yet it's those flourishes that make Grell's art stand the test of time, with critics now referring to it as "extraordinary and realistic artwork, with sophisticated coloring by Julia Laquement."[26] Grell's cinematic artistic leanings and clever layouts are forebears to the work of writer Jeff Lemire and artist Andrea Sorrentino decades later.[27] More importantly, Grell created the iconic hooded look still used, or at least visually referenced, 30 years later, on page and screen.

So while the violence might be the thing that is often spoken about in crafting Grell's realism, and in fact it forms the basis of much of this chapter, the far more fundamental and basic fact is one that Grell establishes *visually* early in the series: Ollie is getting older. "Of course he is," you might think, but over four decades since the creation of Superman, almost all comic book characters existed in a floating timeline that ignored aging, a way of abstracting comic book events from their real world markers, unconsciously and continually rebooting the date of their origin to fit the needs of the current generation.[28] At the start of *The Longbow Hunters*, Oliver Queen is now 43 and old enough to be a grandfather to former ward Roy Harper's child. He and Dinah Lance/Black Canary settle into their new city with very ordinary day jobs at the Sherwood Florist. The choice of age was no coincidence either, as 1987 was pushing closer to the 50th anniversary of Green Arrow's debut in *More Fun Comics* #73 (Nov 1941). Indeed, Grell himself was hitting a milestone 40th birthday around the time the first issue of *The Longbow Hunters* went to the presses. "I felt that it was essential to age the characters as you go along," Grell explains when questioned about this element, "because it sets them firmly in the real world... We all have our heroes, and as different as our heroes are from ourselves, it's

---

[25] Rodi, R. (1988). Prestige, Schmestige. *The Comics Journal* (119), 32-34.

[26] Raiteri, S. (2013). Green Arrow: The Longbow Hunters. *Library Journal*, 138(4), 65.

[27] *Green Arrow* Vol. 5 #17-34 (Apr 2013 - Oct 2014).

[28] There are naturally exceptions to this, including 2000AD's *Judge Dredd*, whose characters have been aging in real time since its debut in 1977. The subsequent *Hellblazer*, a contemporary with Grell's ongoing *Green Arrow* series, also saw hero John Constantine age with every passing issue.

the similarities that make us love them so much."[29] Ollie's birthday became an annual tradition throughout Grell's run, typically marked by an appearance from Shado, a Japanese assassin introduced later in this first issue of *The Longbow Hunters*.

Another sign of the growing realism of Green Arrow was the levels of intimacy on display in this first issue. We see the couple goofing around in their new home as any newly committed couple might, albeit punctuated by another graphic display of the Seattle Slayer's latest kill. Dinah uses her Black Canary costume for the purposes of foreplay, the last time we will see her in the garb for several years. In a rare moment for comics at the time, we also see the couple in a semi-nude post-coital embrace in bed. It isn't the near-nudity of both of these characters that gives the scene its intimacy, but rather how emotionally exposed they are in honestly discussing the future of their relationship. Grell sets up the notion that Ollie's biological clock is ticking, with the Emerald Archer finally wanting to marry and have children with Dinah. Her point blank refusal to do so, because she "won't make orphans" in their dangerous life, coincides with a back-to-basics approach for the Green Arrow. Dinah also notes the changing nature of the "hunter" in Grell's gritty world. "There's a different breed on the streets these days," she analyzes. "They're not hunters... they're *predators*." It's a conversation that serves as a catalyst not only for her own foray into breaking up a drug cartel, following up a lead from the girl who broke their window earlier, but Oliver's return to the streets as a vigilante. It is also worth noting that here Dinah is exercising a choice that will be brutally taken away from her later in the series.

"Some hunt the hunters," Grell reminds us as the newly suited Oliver Queen steps out into the streets for the first time in a new hood and costume, the first new look for the character since the classic Neal Adams redesign in 1969. He has abandoned the outlandish trick arrows and his traditional garb, adopting a now more utilitarian hood that was appropriate for Seattle's weather. Editor Gold later explained away the lack of trick arrows as a post-*Crisis* revision, but still effectively maintaining Ed Herron and Jack Kirby's 1959 origin story.[30] Gold argued "one of the purposes of *The Longbow Hunters* was to establish Green Arrow as a man who neither needed nor wanted to rely upon

---

[29] Mike Grell, personal interview, 29 Mar 2015.
[30] *Adventure Comics* Vol. 1 #256 (Jan 1959).

The casual intimacy of *Green Arrow: The Longbow Hunters* #1. Art by Mike Grell and Lurene Haines. © DC Comics.

gimmick arrows, so we conveniently 'forgot' this story element."[31] Yet even with the more "serious" outfit, the ridiculousness of a costumed hero running around the slate grey Seattle in a bright green outfit is patently obvious. We go with it as readers because it's the form, the thin green line between fact and the heightened fiction of comic book realms. The common problem with basing heroes in increasingly realistic situations is that, as Grant Morrison has pointed out so eloquently, they aren't real.[32] Even so, the superficial laughs that go with spotting the goateed, green-hooded vigilante in the alleys of the Pacific Northwest, especially as contrasted with the punks and street toughs that litter the panels, are quickly punctured by an arrow through the hand and ear lobes of some would be predators. Grell's suggestions in the panels that follow echo a theme that has followed Green Arrow throughout much of his career, as some witnesses remember him as a green devil, dripping with fiery vengeance, while the kindly elderly victims see him as an Errol Flynn inspired Robin Hood. Both of these are true at this stage for Grell's Green Arrow, and it is the subsequent events of *The Longbow Hunters* that begin to push him towards the former.

The most enduring development of the first issue of *The Longbow Hunters* is the introduction of the aforementioned Shado, the only true rival to Dinah for the title of Ollie's spiritual counterpart. While Dinah is pursuing leads on her crack cocaine case, Ollie concentrates on the Seattle Slasher, with the added complication of another archer picking off a seemingly disconnected group of men throughout the city. Ollie's roughing-up of the streets leads to the abandoned Seattle Underground, where Vietnam War veteran known as the "Tunnel Rat" is revealed to be the killer. Ollie surmises that "They tripped a switch somewhere inside him... trouble is... they forgot to turn him *off*." It might be the first direct bit of politicization of the series, and a theme that Grell would later return to, but certainly not the last mention of a government using its pawns anonymously. However, in this issue it is the assassin Shado who manages to get to the Slasher first, skewering him and a nearby elderly motorist. As the cycle of violence continues with a pimp killing one of his own sex workers over money, Ollie is left with "only more questions." It's curious to note that here the vigilante is robbed of any kind of justice, not even having any evidence to suggest that his target was the real killer. Grell draws a parallel to

---

[31] Letters column of *Green Arrow* Vol. 2 #2 (Mar 1988).
[32] Morrison, p. 56.

this in the final issue of *The Longbow Hunters*, where he similarly robs Dinah of her own sense of justice. At this point, the identity of the other archer is a mystery to both Oliver and the readers, but that is about to change with the reveal of Shado.

The second prestige issue, titled "Dragon Hunt," marks an initial tonal shift for the book. With both Shado and the shadowy men who hired her revealed, Grell takes a moment to explore both of their origins. Shado is not simply another deranged killer, like the Seattle Slasher, but rather she is something more of an instrument of vengeance. She is the daughter of a Yakuza agent incarcerated during the Second World War, where a group of American soldiers forced him to reveal the location of major collection of Yakuza gold. After killing himself in atonement, Shado's lot in life is one of revenge against those who dishonoured her father, and by extension the Yakuza. She is literally marked with an intricate tattoo of a dragon signifying her blood debt. The surviving soldiers, now the powerful merchants of an empire that spans legal and illicit activities, are in fact her intended targets and the Seattle Slasher was merely an opportunity killing. It signifies her immediately as someone with a sense of honor, not simply a kindred spirit to Oliver Queen but a fellow hunter. If Grell's Green Arrow is now the same kind of urban hunter/protector of Seattle that Daredevil is to Frank Miller's Hell's Kitchen, then Shado is his Elektra. The latter, argues Lindsay (2013), "was a strong lead who could not only hold her own with Matt [Murdock] but could potentially subjugate him."[33] This is almost doubly true for Shado, who would quite literally subjugate Ollie in order to have a child by him in a later arc of the ongoing series.[34] Grell's art style shifts to reflect this, even more influenced by Eastern artistic pencil work to reflect the dominance of Shado's arc in this chapter, with Lacquement's finishes and Haines's realistic backgrounds disappearing in lieu of light pastel brush strokes, a stark contrast with the noisy Seattle that Grell literally covers with exaggerated lyrics from background music.

The tonal shift of the second issue extends beyond just the Japanese influenced artistic leanings, changing Ollie himself. "He's usually a little more

---

[33] Lindsay, Ryan. *Blind Dates and Broken Hearts: The Tragic Loves of Matthew Murdock*. Edwardsville, Illinois: Sequart Organization, 2013.
[34] In the "Here There Be Dragons" and "Blood of the Dragon" arcs of *Green Arrow* Vol. 2 #9-12 and #21-24, respectively.

left of center," quipped former Dark Horse and DC editor Bob Schreck in the 2007 documentary *The Green Arrow: Legend of the Emerald Archer*. "But if you look at the Mike Grell run, he started leaning a little more to the right."[35] Grell himself didn't necessarily see Ollie's politics aligning with his own: "My politics tend to be conservative, but I see Oliver Queen as a moderate humanist."[36] The introduction of Mr. Magnor, one of the aforementioned powerful businessmen, is also the first time that the Iran-Contra affair – in which senior officials in the Reagan Administration had secretly sold arms to the embargoed Iran – is explicitly mentioned. "Ever since the Iran Arms fiasco," quips Mr. Osborne, another of the powerful group, "they've been looking at us closer than my proctologist." Grell boldly rips his story from the headlines, as drug cartels, urban crime, governmental conspiracy, and "the AIDS scare" are all mentioned in rapid succession. It's as if Grell was cataloguing the fears of Middle America in the form of sequential art, and by doing so illustrating exactly what it is 'one man' is facing, be it Oliver Queen or an audience who can connect with these fears. Green Arrow is evolving, from a person who sought refuge in a monastery after accidentally killing a boy[37] in the 1970s to someone who would deliberately kill. It's something of a vigilante cliché about the little guy who is pushed too far, and Grell shows his libertarian leanings by portraying a system that is hamstrung from positive activity. The Iran-Contra references and a black ops mission that goes wrong expose the illegitimacy of a government that doesn't have the people in mind, while on a smaller scale a police force presented with Ollie's evidence is unable or simply unwilling to do anything. An interrogation of street punks shows the increasing frustrations of Green Arrow, who breaks the fingers of a perp trying to take an elderly woman's handbag. "Hey, you ain't allowed to do stuff like this," the perp protests, appealing to an authority he's already disrespecting. "I heard you're s'posed to be a *good guy*." Ollie acts tough around these low-level street rats, but a confrontation with Shado immediately afterwards exposes him as still a predominantly "good guy". Facing off on a rooftop, as all good rivals do, Shado correctly assesses that Ollie "doesn't have the eyes of a killer," swiftly besting the hero, killing her intended

---

[35] Sheffer, R.(Ed). "The Green Arrow: Legend of the Emerald Archer." On *Smallville: The Complete Sixth Season* [Blu-ray]. Burbank: Warner Bros., 2007.
[36] Boney, A. (Oct 2006). "Mike Grell on Green Arrow." *Back Issue* (18), 35-45.
[37] In *Flash* Vol. 1 #217-219 (Sept 1972 - Jan 1973).

target, and leaving Ollie feeling old and alone on his birthday. Shado is right, of course, as Ollie is not a killer – at least not yet. Like many of the vigilantes of the era, the final push would have to be closer to home. This, as they say, would be personal.

One of the most shocking elements of the second issue of *The Longbow Hunters* remains the brutal treatment of Dinah / Black Canary at the hands of her kidnappers. Many subsequent pieces on this moment have suggested that Dinah was raped by her attackers, a sight that not only resulted in Oliver killing the perpetrator without hesitation but resulted in the loss of her "Canary Cry" powers. Like the similarly ambiguous scene of the aftermath of The Joker's assault on Batgirl / Barbara Gordon and her father the following year in Alan Moore and Brian Bolland's *Batman: The Killing Joke* (1988), it's a notion that is perpetuated decades later. In Will Brooker's analysis of Frank Miller's *The Dark Knight Returns*, he not only dismisses *The Longbow Hunters* as being "the most notorious example of mismanaged 'maturity' and 'dark revisionism,'" but cites "the implied rape and graphically depicted violation of his female partner."[38] Brooker isn't alone in this assumption, and it hardly seems to matter to the argument that Dinah is never assaulted on panel, and nor was it Grell's intention to imply that a sexual assault had occurred. Instead, it could be argued that this is one of the few examples where comic book brutality that is afforded the opportunity of real world consequences.

After Green Arrow closes in on his prey at a warehouse, we witness the aftermath of what would appear to be the brutal torture of Black Canary for information. "I can gut you like a fish, with one stroke," threatens her captor. "Or I can make you last a couple of hours." The language *is* suggestive, particularly as the attacker offers his companion "a little of this while she's still got a face." Green Arrow, without pausing, bursts into the warehouse and kills the first attacker with an arrow to the chest, shooting the second perp through the leg, witnessing the latter inadvertently set himself on fire. With scant regard for the man he has just shot or any other danger presented, Green Arrow immediately unties Canary, and carries her out of the building. It is Shado who shoots a third attacker through the eye, as the two archers share a silent exchange of understanding, foreshadowing their meeting and eventual

---

[38] Brooker, W. (2007). "The Best Batman Story: *The Dark Knight Returns*." In A. McKee (Ed.), *Beautiful Things in Popular Culture*. Malden, MA: Wiley-Blackwell.

relationship in the issues that follow. As the warehouse explodes behind them, Dinah rouses long enough to apologise for missing Ollie's birthday. It's a heartbreaking moment as Shado makes her exit, but the very existence of the scenes also goes a long way in reinforcing the idea that women were being disproportionately used as victimised plot devices. At least it would, if Grell had left it there.

Grell sought to use the scene as a motivator for the character, which does present some issues in and of itself. In a 2006 "director's commentary", Grell attempts to give some further context to this. "I set out to create a situation that would change Ollie from the avowed pacifist to a man capable of killing if it's justified. There's a transition in one panel from the easy-going Errol Flynn Robin Hood to a man capable of killing coldly and violently."[39] Dinah is never actually shown being hit or attacked on panel, and the reader remembering her rape is perhaps explained by her near-nudity and the overall brutality of the scene. While Brooker and similar analyses are based on a misreading of the text, it still doesn't escape the fact that it is part of a cycle of violence against women in comics as a plot device to motivate the vigilante into action.[40] Indeed, it should hardly matter what the extent of Dinah's injuries are, physical or otherwise, when discussing their troubling implications. Yet those implications are precisely what distinguishes The Longbow Hunters from its contemporaries. In Frank Miller's The Dark Knight Returns, violence is a way of life that actually revitalizes the Batman. Miller's staging of violence in that book is operatic, escalating a war of the streets to an almost literal clash of the titans as the Dark Knight takes on Superman. This act against Dinah in Grell's book was treated like a real incidence of violence. However, these costumed heroes

---

[39] Grell, M. (30 Oct 2006). "Green Arrow: The Longbow Hunters 'Director's Commentary.'" Retrieved 7 Aug 2015 from http://web.archive.org/web/20061030025853/http://www.mikegrell.com/mikegrell/feature-longbow.jsp

[40] In 1999, writer Gail Simone and some of her contemporaries would develop a website and list of female characters that had been "killed, raped, depowered, crippled, turned evil, maimed, tortured, contracted a disease or had other life-derailing tragedies befall her" as a plot device. Named Women in Refrigerators, in response to the violent death of Kyle Rayner's girlfriend in Green Lantern #54 (1994), it sought to analyse why female characters were disproportionately used in this way. Black Canary is listed as being "tortured, made infertile, depowered" by the list. http://lby3.com/wir/women.html

The turning point for a hero in *Green Arrow: The Longbow Hunters* #2. Art by Mike Grell and Lurene Haines. © DC Comics.

try and deal with it the same way that we regular mortals would: through conversation and therapy. "When I did the monthly book, I made a point of raising that," Grell responded when asked about the violence of Green Arrow in a 2000 interview, referring to *Green Arrow* Vol. 2 #2 (Mar 1988), in which Dinah discusses the incident with her therapist Dr. Annie Green. When Dinah's in therapy, she uses the phrase "People say 'well, at least you weren't raped' as if that's the worst thing that could happen."[41] So even if the original scene still had enough content to suggest sexual assault - which despite Grell's intent it is still easy to reasonably infer that Dinah was being at least threatened with such an assault - the ramifications of those actions were still being felt years later, demonstrating a remarkable devotion to the theme of consequences. Indeed, it wasn't until *Green Arrow* Vol 2. #59 (Apr 1992), almost five years later, that Black Canary would officially suit up again.[42] By this stage, Oliver had his own instance of torture to contend with when he was rescued by Dinah (in a variant costume) after being strung up in similarly bloody scene during *Green Arrow* Vol. 2 #32 (May 1990). Indeed, during the 'Here There Be Dragons' and 'Blood of the Dragon' arcs discussed later in this chapter, it is inferred that Oliver himself has been raped, as assassin Shado conceives a child with Oliver while he is delirious from pain and medications.

None of this diminishes the implied sexualization and systemic misogyny in a darkening comic book medium, yet this singular incident not only defined the course of the third and final chapter of *The Longbow Hunters*, 'Tracking Snow,' but also the nature of Oliver and Dinah's relationship for at least the next seven years. In the short term, Dinah is removed from the action and confined to a hospital bed, leaving Oliver to deal with revenge and closing the case, and this certainly smacks of more than a little 'white knighthood.' Oliver's nightmarish recap of the previous issue does not end with Grell's dragon filled two-page spread, with the physical and mental impact of the event lasting well into Grell's subsequent ongoing series. During Shado and Ollie's final meeting in *The Longbow Hunters*, she notes how he is no longer the same person. "They've changed," she observes, referring to his eyes again, "as you have. You can never

---

[41] Cooke, J., & Knutson, J. (2005). Mike Grell, Freelance. In J. Cooke (Ed.), *Comic Book Artist Collection* (Vol. 3, p. 218). Raleigh: TwoMorrows.
[42] With the exception of using the outfit to flirt with Oliver in *Green Arrow* Vol 2. #34 (July 1990).

go back. Nor can I." It binds Shado and Ollie together in a way that plays out over the better part of the next decade, and much later in Ollie's run he remarks that he was never able to find an inner peace after this. In the ongoing series, the couple doesn't simply wind up in therapy for a single issue, but rather Grell would go to great lengths to keep that reality in check. Dinah's inability to use her sonic Canary Cry might be a conceit of Grell's adherence to his "no capes, no powers" policy, but it also robbed Dinah of one of her defining features. She would later be unable to have the children that she initially *chose* not to have, robbing her of any choice in the matter, and with Ollie's preemptive revenge on the business cartel, it would also rob her of her own justice[43], just as Ollie was denied it in the first issue. Yet when the roles are reversed in "Broken Arrow" (*Green Arrow* Vol. 2 #33, June 1990), Ollie confesses he is angry over the very notion that Dinah got to his torturers before he could ("I have a *right*, damn it! I have a right to some *measure* of *justice!*"). There he is finally forced to confront this denial of Dinah's justice in *The Longbow Hunters*, along with the *choice* he made to take a life.

Ollie confronts Magnor about the use of funds from Iranian arms deals to fund Nicaraguan Contras, just as the real-world Iran-Contra story played out only months prior to the publication of *The Longbow Hunters*. Set against Lacquement and Haines's phenomenal snow-capped backgrounds of Mt. Rainier, it is Shado who tips off Ollie as to the location of the place she intends to kill Magnor, and Ollie in turn stops hired sniper and mercenary Eddie Fyers from taking out Shado. At first it seems Magnor has escaped and *everyone* is denied their just desserts. Ollie attempts to frame Magnor for the murder of the drug supplier, but Shado kills him with a single arrow. Left with the drug money, Oliver Queen's fortune is restored, although what we are left with is far from the free-wheeling outspoken liberal of the 1970s and early 1980s. If *Crisis on Infinite Earths* killed the Golden Age Green Arrow, then *The Longbow Hunters* drove the nails into the coffin for his Silver and Bronze Age persona.

Green Arrow: The Longbow Hunters remains a groundbreaking piece of comic book literature and art of the 20th century, not only reinventing a

---

[43] As suggested by "Lost Voice: How The Canary Lost Her Cry" (10 Dec 2014). Retrieved 24 July 2015 from https://thegothamrogue.wordpress.com/2014/12/10/lost-voice-how-the-canary-lost-her-cry/

hitherto undervalued character but also giving him a validity and authenticity that few of his contemporaries have ever received. More than this, *The Longbow Hunters* is an example of a radical redefinition of a character, who had once shown what one man can do through words, but was now doing it with actions. Nominated for "Best Finite Series" at the 1988 Will Eisner Comic Industry Awards, alongside the bold and experimental work of Frank Miller and Bill Sienkiewicz's *Elektra Assassin*, it lost out to another groundbreaking piece of work: Alan Moore and Dave Gibbons' incomparable *Watchmen*. In three extended issues, Green Arrow finally grew up and earned the right to his own ongoing series, one that would initially last for eleven years. Indeed, the legacy was confirmed in 2012, when it served as the inspiration for the TV series *Arrow*, with the producers wisely giving a nod to the creator in the naming of the unseen Starling City Judge Grell. More immediately, it was popular enough to commission an ongoing comic book, largely written by Grell, which would run for the next 11 years.

Green Arrow by Any Other Name: Right Makes Might

Off the back of the success of *The Longbow Hunters*, DC wasted no time in green-lighting the first solo ongoing adventures of Green Arrow. House ads appearing in DC Comics at the time touted the ongoing series as being part of DC's "New Format" of high quality titles that included Grant Morrison's *Animal Man*, and bore a Comics Code Authority defying "Suggested for Mature Readers" label that would also be seen on the covers of *The Question*, and Steve Bissette and Alan Moore's *Swamp Thing*.[44] As part of DC's mature readers line, Grell could freely deal with issues of a frank and adult nature, including Dinah and Ollie's shared trauma from *The Longbow Hunters*. Written by Grell, with initial artists Ed Hannigan, Dick Giordano, and Julia Lacquement returning as the colorist, Grell's 80-issue stand, plus several annuals and a handful of

---

[44] DC Comics Inc. (1986). DC Comics Publishes Comic Book Editorial Standards [Press release]. Retrieved 22 Jan 2016 from http://jimshooter.com/. On 5 Dec 1986, DC Comics issued a press release proclaiming that "comics are no longer strictly for kids" and the intention to include "For Universal Readership" or "Suggested for Mature Readers" readership indicators on all regularly published comics. "Many of the titles published today are written for an older, more sophisticated audience," explained the release.

mini-series, would veer Green Arrow even further to the right as he traveled down the dark and often violent path of urban vigilantism.

Green Arrow Vol 2. #1 (Feb 1988) picks up almost immediately after the events of Grell's mini-series. Rather than simply throwing the newly revived character back into the DC Universe, Grell chose to maintain Ollie's segregation from the super powers of the "outside" world. The writer jokingly called his closed environment the "Grellverse" or "Earth Grell",[45] one where no other super-heroes appear to exist but the ones he created. Indeed, such was Grell's devotion to the idea of steeping Green Arrow in a world without capes, that the only time the name "Green Arrow" is mentioned in his entire seven-year run is in the first issue of *The Longbow Hunters*, and even then only in flashback scenes.[46] That name, after all, was only ever an amalgam of Fawcett Comics' *Golden Arrow* and Edgar Wallace's *The Green Archer*, intended to evoke Robin Hood, and Grell wanted no signs of tights and red booties in an urban environment. Black Canary was without her sonic scream, a result of the aforementioned trauma of the mini-series, but this was not fully explained until the back-matter of *Green Arrow Annual* Vol. 1 #2 (July 1989): "Dinah lost her ability to generate sonic cries when the extra ligaments in her throat which gave her this power were permanently damaged when she underwent torture at the hands of a sadistic criminal." This wouldn't quell debate over the nature of Dinah's torture, but it did explain why her innate powers were missing for the entirety of Grell's run. Even when other established heroes showed up, such as Hal Jordan in *Green Arrow* Vol. 2 #20 (July 1989), they did so out of costume. At the other extreme, the similar-looking Warlord/Travis Morgan arrived without any mention of the realm of Skartaris in *Green Arrow* Vol. 2 #28 (Jan 1990). Even towards the end of the run, during the anniversary *Green Arrow* Vol. 2 #75 (June 1993), it was as if Grell was consciously taunting audiences with an ungainly costume for Roy Harper/Arsenal during his brief cameo.

---

[45] Renaud, J. (29 Jan 2009). "Mike Grell returns to *The Warlord*." Retrieved 18 Aug 2015, from http://comicbookresources.com/?page=article&id=19757

[46] Cronin, B. (10 Apr 2008). "Comic Book Urban Legends Revealed #150 - Comics Should Be Good!" Retrieved 8 Aug 2015 from http://goodcomics.comicbookresources.com/2008/04/10/comic-book-urban-legends-revealed-150/

From the first issue of the ongoing *Green Arrow* series, simply titled 'Hunter's Moon,' Grell establishes three fundamental truths about this incarnation of the character. Firstly, the concept of the urban hunter was there to stay. "The quarry has changed, but the hunt is the same," he explains in narration. Secondly, and more importantly, the character is being pushed further to the right of center, and the path *The Longbow Hunters* set him upon is one that he will be increasingly unable to return from. Running down some familiar looking punks, with Hannigan's pencils a variation on the generic punks that Grell stylized in the previous mini-series, the titular hero comments, "You know, just when I started to think there's hope for mankind... I run into guys like you, and my faith in human nature is restored." This is the same character who just over a decade earlier gave an impassionate speech to Green Lantern about "the other half," about "honest people cowering in fear" and the "hideous moral cancer rotting our very souls." He didn't simply accuse Green Lantern of being Nazi adjacent, but stuck it to the immortal Guardians of Oa too.[47] The liberal left crusader was giving way to something more politically right. Oliver not only threatens to kill a suspect with an arrow through the heart, but is also asked by the end of the issue: "Are you still a good guy?" It's a question that Grell poses of Ollie for the remainder of the run. Thirdly, Grell takes immediate steps to address the trauma both Oliver and Dinah suffered during *The Longbow Hunters*.

Grell doesn't leave Dinah/Black Canary as simply a victim throughout these stories. In this very first issue, the two have trouble being intimate with each other, with Dinah finding herself unable to be touched even by Oliver. "We can face it together," reassures Oliver, before the two seek out the aforementioned therapist, which conveniently ties in with the criminal they are tracking in this two part story as well. Dinah speaks to the "helplessness... not being able to fight back." By *Green Arrow* Vol. 2 #3 (Apr 1988), Dinah is able to reclaim some of her own power when she beats up some crooks out on the streets, and shortly afterwards she and Oliver can be together again sexually. In a scene that mirrors the intimacy of similar moments in *The Longbow Hunters*, Dinah says "thank you for being patient" to Oliver. Yet her "power" is not fully restored: she is without her cry, or indeed her costume for another 50 (or so) issues.

---

[47] In the classic *Green Lantern* Vol. 2 #76 (Apr 1970).

Oliver's internal angst isn't one that was so readily fixable. Even as an entirely new persona, Green Arrow continued to be a moving target.

Here There Be Dragons

. While the first handful of issues in this ongoing series spent their time establishing a thematic follow-up to *The Longbow Hunters* – continuing Ollie's inner turmoil over killing, and facing off with the soon to be recurring character of mercenary Eddie Fyers – 'Here There Be Dragons' (*Green Arrow* Vol. 2 #9-12) was the first legitimate sequel to the series. "Here There Be Dragons" opens with a literal seasonal change, with Ollie and Dinah enjoying the sun of springtime, even if Ollie has yet to deal with the trauma of the last year. Pausing at a shop window, Dinah asks Oliver "Do you ever think of her?", and his rapid response betrays that he has turned his mind to Shado. The conversation between the couple at the start of *Green Arrow* Vol. 2 #9 (Oct 1988) is the first time the duo haven't been completely open with each other, a stark contrast with the intimacy one year earlier in *The Longbow Hunters*. Every time Ollie opens his mouth to speak, the word "Lie" appears in a captain box next to his dialogue. This changes when Ollie finally admits something that has been obvious to readers since the fateful shooting in *The Longbow Hunters*. "I'll tell you one thing," he confesses to Dinah. "If I could turn back the clock... I'd kill that bastard all over again." To punctuate the point, artists Ed Hannigan, Dick Giordano and Frank McLaughlin (along with *The Longbow Hunters* colorist Julia Lacquement) recreate Grell's dragon filled two-page spread from the mini-series, along with key moments from that prestige series. It's a change of pace for an incongruous issue that focuses mostly on Shado, complete with the same minimalist artwork and backgrounds that characterized her appearances in the previous outing. Hannigan doesn't go for the same flair as Grell, but his delicate figures emphasize the grace and elegance of Shado's brand of archery. Further, the use of Shado brings a renewed focus for Grell, after sending Ollie in search of a space-born virus (*Green Arrow* Vol. 2 #3, Apr 1988) and, in one of the most cringeworthy moments in Green Arrow history, commandeering a sled full of dogs in the Alaskan Iditarod (*Green Arrow* Vol. 2 #8, Sept 1988). 'Here There Be Dragons' is about the hunter being unleashed again.

The plot for this arc isn't a massive leap forward from *The Longbow Hunters*, nor does it aim to be. Once again, Grell makes Oliver's birthday the flagpole to mark the passing of time in Green Arrow's universe. As Ollie puts it in *Green Arrow* Vol. 2 #10 (Nov 1988), it's "a reminder of my own mortality, and the insidious encroachment of middle age, all in one swell foop." Heading to the zoo with Dinah, they find themselves tailed by the CIA's Greg Osborne and the very familiar Eddie Fyers. Trying to ensure the economic stability of the Philippines, Osborne seeks Ollie's help in tracking the location of treasure buried during the Second World War. With the Yakuza also on the trail, it turns out that Shado conveniently stole the map to the gold, and Ollie is once again tasked by a government operative to fix a problem that isn't of his own making. The added incentive is twofold: Osborne has not only discovered the open secret of Ollie's identity, but has blackmailed the hero as well. In another case of Grell leaving no consequence unturned, Osborne threatens to turn Oliver in for avoiding tax on the "inheritance" he received in the final issue of *The Longbow Hunters*. Indeed, Ollie was outed by his own charity, a $100,000 donation to an inner-city youth center to help eradicate gang crime, identifying him as a modern-day Robin Hood. Here Ollie faces an undeniable truth, and not for the last time either: no good deed goes unpunished[48]. A series of such incidents make him rethink his position as a vigilante, culminating in the undermentioned "The Trial of Oliver Queen."

This choice of whether to continue pitching in with the whims of various government operatives marks the start of a significant turning point in the history of the character. Lampert (2007) argues that Ollie must face the choice of being a one-man war against crime on the streets, or saddle with the government in a truce that goes against some of his more liberal instincts. "Oliver Queen succumbs to the same dilemma faced by every post-deconstruction superhero... Either crypto-fascist super-cop, or crypto-fascist criminal; either way, the political choice is clear."[49] Ollie's choice is actually less clear than that, as he is not out for the cold-blooded vengeance of The Punisher, and his attitude towards authority figures was well established by the adventures he had with Green Lantern under Denny O'Neil in the 1960s and 1970s. His attempts at dealing with the taking of a life is his motivation throughout the majority of this run, and Grell will often use the repeated

---

[48] Grell plays with that notion again after this arc in the "Moving Target" two-parter of *Green Arrow* Vol. 2 #14-15, where Ollie becomes the target for assassination after he stops a domestic violence situation, helps change a flat tire, and even rescues a cat from a tree!

[49] Lampert, M. (12 Aug 2007). "The Fate of an Archer!" Retrieved 14 Aug 2015 from http://sequart.org/magazine/20018/the-fate-of-an-archer/

nightmarish dragon imagery and Dinah's torture as a meme during those times of crisis of conscience. "Hanging Dinah from a forklift, and putting her through all that, was a necessary step in the evolution of Oliver Queen," Grell responded when asked about writing this kind of lone warrior character. "To get him away from the ultra-liberal, goody two-shoes, 'I will never take another life' attitude that Denny had."[50] This sums up the direction and evolution of Green Arrow under Grell, as incrementally (and sometimes dramatically) shifting him away from liberal crusader to the persona of an everyman hunter. Grell's own identical looking creation, The Warlord, decries the loss of American "tradition" and "values" during his time in Skartaris[51]. The tension with the government would come to a head much later in *Green Arrow* Vol. 2 #39 (Nov 1990). After being set-up by the government again, Ollie confronts sitting U.S. President George H.W. Bush during an Air Force One invite:

> They picked a loyal American... a guy who had bought the whole god-and-country line of crap... A man who thought this still stood for something... despite the fact that it's been spit on, burned and dragged through the dirt... I believed in it. You tell me... How am I supposed to forget that? Kiss my ass... *Sir*!

Taken on balance, while Ollie was leaning increasingly towards the right during Grell's run, this is a speech that would not have been entirely out of place during O'Neil's tenure. It's also followed by a year-long period in which Ollie wanders the wilderness looking for answers, evoking memories of some of those 'Hard Traveling Heroes' days. The target had moved, but the core remained the same.

The penultimate chapter of 'Here There Be Dragons' (*Green Arrow* Vol. 2 #11, Dec 1988) has a seismic event as powerful as Dinah's torture in *The Longbow Hunters*, although we won't realize this for some time. In retrospect, all of the signs were there. Oliver accepts Osborne's brief, against Dinah's wishes, and heads to Hawaii. There, her fears are realized as the hooded Green Arrow is promptly shot through the chest by a waiting Shado. Grell's repeated nightmarish symbolism of the dragon, coupled with a stylized flashback to Dinah's conversation about not wanting to make orphans, make it clear on repeat readings. Yet during this hallucination, in which Ollie is near-death and under the influence of heavy sedatives, Shado conceives a child with him. These

---

[50] Mike Grell, personal interview, 29 Mar 2015.
[51] *Green Arrow* Vol. 2 #28 (Jan 1990).

facts do not become apparent until a year later, and Oliver himself is not aware until at least the conclusion of 'The Hunt for Red Dragon' in *Green Arrow* Vol. 2 #66 (Sept 1992). Yet consider for a moment the implications of this: Oliver Queen, the Green Arrow, was *raped* by one of his anti-villains to conceive a child.[52] The rest of the issue literally pales compared to that fact, with the bold artistic choice of using nothing but blue outlines on a white background for several pages at a time to represent much of the backstory. Indeed, much of this issue is a recap of past events, with some otherwise platonic romance gradually blossoming between the spiritual partners. In his relationship with Dinah, the choice to have children was taken away from the couple by external forces. With Shado, he became a father without so much as consent or consciousness.

The Trial of Oliver Queen

As comics became darker throughout the latter half of the 1980s, it was only a matter of time before the media took notice. The 'Here There be Dragons' arc ends with a violent case of just desserts, signalled by the duo of Oliver and Shado standing on top of a literal pile of distended bodies on the cover of *Green Arrow* Vol. 2 #12 (Jan 1989). While Rodi (1988) criticized the frequent conversations about human feelings and other concepts allegedly foreign to comic book readers,[53] here Grell stands back to let loose the art team of Hannigan, Giordano, McLaughlin, and Lacquement on an unbroken nine-page wordless action sequence. The tightly paneled pages are stylish, matching the look and feel of a 1980s action film. Ollie increases his kill-count by several bodies, certifying his transformation from that "ultra-liberal, goody two-shoes" to a no-nonsense urban vigilante. Back in *Green Arrow* Vol. 2 #2 (Mar 1988), Seattle cop Lieutenant Jim Cameron, who serves as the antithesis to Batman's Jim Gordon, tells Ollie: "I don't care who you are -- you keep messing in police business, and sooner or later you're going to cross the line." Before that could actually happen for the character in a significant way, a number of readers had

---

[52] Grant Morrison would indirectly mirror this storyline to some extent almost two decades later in *Batman* Vol. 1 #656 (Oct 2006), when a retconned storyline unveiled that Talia al Ghul had raped Batman as part of a "depraved eugenics experiment", also conceiving a son and heir to the hero.

[53] Rodi, R. (1988), p. 33.

already identified a line of good taste that they felt Grell and DC Comics had crossed in their "suggested for mature readers" line of books.

Outrage began at least a year before in response to the violence in *The Longbow Hunters*. *The Ottowa Citizen* (1988) reported that a Canadian autoworker was "mad as hell" to discover his 12-year-old reading a comic where "the heroine is shown dangling by her wrists, clad only in a shirt torn open to reveal her breasts with blood coursing down her torso and legs," referring of course to the torture of Dinah in that series. [54] The publicity resulted in a seizure of various adult oriented comics, including *The Longbow Hunters*, by Ottowa police from local stores in February 1988, although it was determined that no charges could be filed under Ottowa law.[55] This mini-hysteria, perhaps rivaled only by Frederic Wertham's (1954) inflammatory *The Seduction of the Innocent* and subsequent United States Senate Subcommittee on Juvenile Delinquency, reached fever pitch when *The New York Times* and *Time Magazine* published articles in the same month on the growing darkness in comics. "Green Arrow depicts a woman whose eyes have been plucked out by vultures," ran *The New York Times*, referring to a two-issue arc called 'Seattle & Die' in *Green Arrow* Vol. 2 #15 and #16. In the same article, distributor John Davis cites the subsequent arc 'The Horseman,' in which a stripper is crucified, as being "graphic enough in its execution that many would consider it pornography."[56] Comics critic Fiore (1989) also called out the "the sleazy bloodletting" off the issue, naming it the "worst example out of the current crop." Rather unfairly, Fiore added that the "big slaughter scene is a two-page spread that looks more like a bedsheet pattern," and then in a somewhat confused defense of comic book violence, pessimistically concluded that "America's majority culture is a wreck in progress, and the only thing to do now is bail out."[57] This intense criticism targets only a handful of issues, and the

---

[54] Kids' comics take violent turn; father outraged by scenes of rape, racism and brutality. (16 Feb 1988). *The Ottawa Citizen*. Retrieved from http://search.proquest.com/docview/239115533?accountid=12763

[55] Catron, M. Canada Seizure. (1988). The Comics Journal, (121), 8-9. Retrieved 10 Aug 2015, from http://tcj.com

[56] Queenan, K. (30 Apr 1989). Drawing on the Dark Side. *The New York Times*. Retrieved 9 Aug 2015 from http://nytimes.com

[57] Fiore, R. Funnybook Roulette. (1988). The Comics Journal, (130), 60-62. Retrieved 10 Aug 2015 from http://tcj.com

letter columns for the next few issues were filled with passionate arguments on both sides of the debate. Gold deftly handled the mailbox influx, tacitly encouraging the discussion in the aptly named *Sherwood Forum*.

Perhaps it was this public trial by media that Grell had rattling around in his head when he sat down to write "The Trial of Oliver Queen,"[58] as it feels for all the world like a response to these criticisms. The issue opens not on Oliver Queen, but on 30-year veteran cop Egan and his new young partner Stankowsky. After lecturing the rookie cop on the dangers of bringing a baton to a knife fight, the duo respond to a dispatch alert of "two armed individuals", with Egan cautioning his partner to "observe...then act." Ollie, of course, also responds to the incident in costume, and when one of the suspects opens fire and hits Egan, Ollie launches an arrow straight into the suspect's chest. However, the initial shots turn out to be paintballs from a pellet gun, and the suspects are just kids playing KAOS (or Killing As Organized Sport). The boy survives, but Oliver Queen is brought forward to testify in the resulting police inquest. As it is an inquest, the judge is unable to charge Ollie, but unleashes a scathing criticism of vigilantism, as artist Hannigan shows Ollie metaphorically shrinking into the floorboards. Perhaps this is Grell's interpretation of the weight of public criticism on his own work, or simply a timely response to the public hysteria. Turning to alcohol, Ollie wanders the streets drunk, ranting about the world as he sees it. "Just some drunk. I'll have you know I'm doing my duty as a responsible citizen," he argues, choosing to do nothing about some tire thieves by the side of the road. "See, every instinct tells me that I should kick your asses and teach you a lesson before you graduate to the big time. But no, that wouldn't be responsible. Be a good boy, Ollie. Sit! Stay! Bend over! Zap! You're Dead! Join the club." It's another example of the vigilante butting up against an overly bureaucratic system, one he sees as heavy on rules without corresponding responsibilities, only the difference this time is that the hero's response is directed entirely inward.

The second part of this saga is typical of Grell's mix of politics, melodrama, and occasionally goofy humor. After a brief interlude with Egan and Stankowsky, the issue opens with a touch of the latter, as Ollie's nightmarish recap of the previous chapter gives way to being face-to-face with a curious prairie dog. In "The Trial of Oliver Queen, Part 2," Grell apes the format of an

---

[58] *Green Arrow* Vol. 2 #19-20 (June-July 1989).

O'Neil story to reverse the roles of Lantern and Arrow, as Hal Jordan appears out of uniform. Camping out miles from the city, Hal is angered by Ollie's efforts to opt-out of his vigilantism, especially "after all the self-righteous crap you've laid on *me* over the years." Ollie lashes out, and after a three-page wordless fist-fight, Hannigan's art recalls Neal Adams as Ollie grabs Jordan by the shirt to yell at him some more, even if the scene ends with the two hugging. Back in the city, Egan is shot in a moment of hesitation, later telling a re-costumed Oliver Queen that he'll be "taking early retirement after all." Ollie's choice, as it turns out, has been made. Once again, Ollie takes aim at the notion of institutional inefficacy. "If the courts were more concerned with justice than 'law'", he tells Egan, "there would be no use for men like me." As Egan dies, Ollie pulls his alter ego's green hood back up, concluding that for those people who slip through the cracks of the court system, "the answer is people like me." While it won't be the last time that Ollie butts heads with authority, here is he choosing to neither quit nor work within the existing structures. Maybe the choice was clear after all, with Grell's Ollie conclusively taking on the role of outsider everyman cop for a broken system.

Blood of the Dragon

The "Blood of The Dragon" (*Green Arrow* Vol. 2 #21-24, Aug – Sept 1989) immediately follows "The Trial of Oliver Queen," and despite a change of artist with Dan Jurgens – who had previously worked with Grell on *The Warlord* and the aforementioned 'The Horseman' arc – Grell returns us to a sense of the familiar right away. Jurgens' two-page spread that reintroduces Shado could not be more different from the issues that preceded it, with the assassin/warrior breastfeeding her newborn baby against a tranquil Japanese setting. We do not yet know the lineage of the child, but as the series progresses we can make a few educated guesses. The subtitle of the issue is "Uchiokoshi," the Romanization of the Japanese word for the "raising" or the "elevation of the bow" in archery, the point just before the arrow is drawn. In this story, Ollie is once again manipulated by a third party into reuniting with Shado, whose child is kidnapped by the Yakuza so that she will carry out an assassination on an unnamed party. Grell uses the symbolism of the bow's traditional stages of firing to represent Ollie's journey throughout this arc.

There are two important developments that come out of 'Blood of the Dragon.' The first is the idea of Oliver Queen as a father, something Grell had been playing with ever since the first issue of *The Longbow Hunters*. Ollie speaks of his desire to have a son as "the biggest obstacle between Dinah and me for years," adding that "People like me don't have children... we are children," echoing that conversation with Dinah. As he continually argues that Shado's father has a right to know about the child, it becomes patently obvious to everyone but Ollie that he is the father, especially by the arc's final page, as Shado enigmatically suggests that the baby "has his father's eyes" as Ollie walks away. Yet neither Grell nor DC was willing to admit the apparent rape and/or infidelity that led to the child, at least overtly, for another few years. The other major shift here is the use of guns, with Shado pushed to use firearms in the pursuit of her child, causing the observation that Shado and Ollie could be friends or lovers were it not for a few key differences. The divide is accentuated an issue later, where Ollie uses a gun for the first time in the series out of necessity, calling it a "whispering death" and commenting on the impersonal nature of the killing, as he mows down Yakuza in numbers that would make The Punisher blush. Yet when given the option, Ollie rejects holding onto the gun, throwing it down and picking up his arrow again. The hero is still serving his penance, and elects for a weapon that requires a *deliberate* choice in taking a life.

Following the theme of choice, Ollie tries to work within the bounds of the law by visiting the U.S. Embassy in Japan, and warning them of the imminent assassination. Inevitably, this only confirms the power of the men pulling the strings behind the curtains, literally shrouded in shadow for the majority of their appearances, suggesting Grell's view of an opaque government. Indeed, these men are implicated in every major event from the John F. Kennedy assassination to US/Cuba relations. The system has exposed itself again as broken and corrupted, so Ollie takes it upon himself to rescue Shado's child via brute interrogation, preventing the murder of the targeted Russian President Mikhail Gorbachev. Even so, an epilogue reveals that it was all in vain, with the death of Gorbachev's security advisor enough to bring the world "back from the brink of peace" and complete the plan of strengthening the defense industry contracts of the shadow players. With the status quo restored and a default win chalked up for the bad guys, this coda is appropriately called "Zanshin," the stage in martial arts or Zen archery in which things return to their natural position.

Cronin (2010) cites 'Blood of the Dragon' as one of the "greatest Green Arrow stories ever told"[59]. While definitive lists are often tricky with characters that have experienced almost eight decades worth of adventures, 'Blood of the Dragon' is certainly one of the most representative stories of Grell's era of the urban hunter. It's a sometimes cynical dissection of governmental corruption, coupled with a hero that increasingly found himself on the wrong side of the law, even if it was on the right side of 'justice.' If Grell is giving us an answer to the question 'What can one man do?', the answer was increasingly leading us to believe that very little could be done within the confines of the existing legal system.

The Black Arrow Saga

The first 34 issues of Grell's *Green Arrow* form a thematic arc that directly follows the events of *The Longbow Hunters*. With "The Black Arrow Saga," a four-issue story beginning with a fifth prelude issue in *Green Arrow* Vol. 2 #34 (July 1990), Grell aimed to take the series in a slightly different direction and introduced a new character that changed the course of the Dinah/Ollie relationship. Yet in many ways, it also brought to a close many of the themes that were planted as early as the initial prestige series, and of course brings both Shado and Eddie Fyers back into Ollie and Dinah's lives. In the rare prelude issue for an annual event, "The Black Arrow Saga" begins in the springtime, just as "Here There Be Dragons" did several years before. Continuing parallels with *The Longbow Hunters*, much of this prelude concerns Ollie and Dinah attempting to have children. Dinah's catalyst was Ollie's near-death in the previous arc, and her feelings about having Oliver's offspring have been radically altered by his torture and the thought of losing him without having any part of him left behind. After a fair amount of sex, both in and out of costume, Oliver decides it is time to get back on the streets. He butts heads again with the authorities, as Lt. Cameron berates him for ruining a drug bust that was years in the making. He's approached by Eddie Fyers, now apparently working with the DEA, who offers Ollie a way of getting revenge on the people that hurt him. After being sent to Panama, Oliver realizes Fyers has actually framed him

---

[59] Cronin, B. (2010, May 25). "The Greatest Green Arrow Stories Ever Told!" Retrieved 18 Aug 2015 from http://goodcomics.comicbookresources.com/2010/05/25/the-greatest-green-arrow-stories-ever-told/

A truth goes unspoken in *Green Arrow* Vol. 2 #24. Art by Dan Jurgens, Dick Giordano, and Frank McLaughlin. © DC Comics.

when the tracking device he thought he was planting turns out to be an explosive intent on disrupting trade in the Panama Canal.

"The Black Arrow Saga" conclusively turns the tables on two lingering threads that stretch back to Grell's first issues. While Ollie is in Panama, Dinah discovers that she can't have children due to the injuries she sustained in *The Longbow Hunters*, once again robbing her of the choice that she has only just come to make. At the moment Ollie finds out about this, he is arrested by the FBI for treason, ultimately putting him on the run from the authorities and on the wrong side of the law. This is the second thread that Grell had been dangling, concerning Ollie's choice of whether to play by the rule of the law or fully accept his role as an anti-authoritarian cop. Yet as Dinah is careful to point out later in the arc, the idea of Oliver being treasonous is ridiculous. Here Grell has constructed a dichotomy by which Ollie cannot be both hero and loyal to the law. Arguing with his court-appointed attorney in *Green Arrow* Vol. 2 #35 (Aug 1990), he maintains that he won't plead guilty "just to save all that trouble." He brushed up against it in "The Trial of Oliver Queen," but he is now completely on the wrong side of the law. Disappearing into the Seattle Underground, he embraces his role as the urban hunter by becoming the urban *hunted*.

With "The Black Arrow Saga," the extent of Grell's closed world is also fully realized. In place of the rest of the DC Universe, Grell had developed his own repertory company of players to fill out Oliver's world. Apart from the obvious regulars of Dinah and Lt. Cameron, this had been mostly confined to recurring characters such as Fyers and Shado. This event not only brought them all together, but introduced a new recurring player to the company, and her presence is a surprising jolt. Street kid Marianne - a spiritual forerunner to the second Speedy, Mia Dearden, a few decades later - dreams that she is a princess forced to live undercover on the streets. Through her escapist lens of a fairy tale narrative that she writes in a diary, fugitive Ollie comes into her world as the "troll prince". Beach (2000) argues that this fully embraces the idea of Green Arrow being a modern Robin Hood as a hunted outlaw.[60] Even the crooks describe him later in the arc, in *Green Arrow* Vol. 2 #38 (Oct 1990), as a "*highly*

---

[60] Beach, S. (2000). Robin Hood and Green Arrow: Outlaw Bowmen in the Modern Urban Landscape. In T. Hahn (Ed.), *Robin Hood in Popular Culture: Violence, Transgression, and Justice*. Cambridge: D.S. Brewer.

visible, reactionary, known to step outside the technical bounds of the law. Champion of lost causes. Tilter of windmills." Like Robin Hood, Ollie is forced to adopt a disguise – in this case, shaving off his iconic beard and hair – almost as if the Green Arrow who existed prior to this moment was incapable of deliberately defying the law in this manner. Just as Robin Hood used his knowledge of Sherwood Forest to hide from the law, Ollie disappears into Seattle. "This is still my town," he asserts in *Green Arrow* Vol. 2 #37 (Sept 1990). The introduction of Marianne, an obvious close namesake of Robin's Marian, turns his repertory company into a band of Merry Men. Grell literally adapts this idea a few years later, when Marianne leads him into the world of the homeless, and Ollie and his new "band" help solve the case of the Seattle "Smasher" serial killer (*Green Arrow* Vol. 2 #67-68, Oct-Nov 1990).

Shado and Dinah had always been the two driving emotional forces in Ollie's life – at least throughout Grell's run – and while they crossed paths in *The Longbow Hunters*, Shado had remained a source of abstract jealousy to Dinah. Despite this, it is the assassin that Dinah calls when Oliver is on the run, even if it goes against her better judgment. "Every time you come into his life," Dinah concedes in *Green Arrow* Vol. 2 #37 (Sept 1990), "you change him in some way." In Shado's son, Dinah sees something that Ollie could not, recognizing her lover's offspring and painfully acknowledging that it is "something else I can never share." Shado acknowledges this to her, something *she* could not do with Oliver, but also effectively admits to having raped Oliver while he was delirious, her rationale not far from Dinah's own reasons for attempting to have a child with Ollie. "I took a part of him. It was wrong, but it's the only thing of him I will ever have," confesses the assassin. On this point, Dinah and Shado come to some painful point of self-realization, Shado also revealing that she knows Ollie will never love her the way he loves Dinah. Shado almost becomes a tragic figure now, albeit one that has assured Oliver's legacy via an assault.

One final thing that had a massive question mark hanging over it since *The Longbow Hunters* was whether killing someone made Oliver a "murderer." His body count certainly rose over the subsequent three years, as the media was happy to point out. Dinah begins to answer that question in the penultimate issue of the arc: "Oliver has learned to kill, but he's not a murderer... yet." After a standoff between Fyers, Shado, and Ollie in the final chapter, Shado (acting on Dinah's behalf) stops Ollie from killing as a way of "getting back" his former life: "Do not *destroy* it by becoming a *murderer*." Later in the issue, with the real agents that set both him and Fyers up exposed, Ollie is given the opportunity to take his revenge on Reggie Mandell, the drug lord that he has been looking to get even with. Ollie argues he will shoot him for all the pain his drugs have caused, but Reggie replies bluntly, "Bullshit, man! It's for *revenge* and nothing else." Realising he is right, Ollie walks away from Mandell to return to his own life. It is Fyers who answers the question for the audience when Ollie is out of earshot. "Congratulations. You're not a cold-blood murderer... yet," he declares ominously. "Thank God I am," he quips as he shoots Mandell[61].For all Ollie's violence, Fyers crosses the line that Grell's Green Arrow can't, at least not yet.

"The Black Arrow Saga" is not the end of Grell's run by a long shot, and it certainly isn't the last we see of Oliver Queen, Dinah, Shado, or Eddie Fyers. Yet it does conclude a story that Grell spent three years telling. In *The Longbow Hunters*, he took a character known for being a left-wing liberal and gave him an impossible choice, forcing his hand into taking a life. By the end of this arc, Grell showed that it was possible to plumb the depths of darkness in the real world with a fictional character, giving each of his actions consequences that would reverberate not simply in the next issue, but years down the track as well.

New Dogs, Auld Acquaintances

Oliver Queen once again hits the road following his aforementioned confrontation with US President H.W. Bush in *Green Arrow* Vol. 2 #39 (Nov 1990), and embarks on a journey around the world, taking in Ireland and an extended stay in Africa, that wouldn't see him return to Seattle until *Green Arrow* Vol. 2 #50 (Aug 1991) almost a year later. Highlights of the run include a spirit quest with a Native American in the wilderness, in a rare issue illustrated by Grell himself[62]. It was the first in the main run that he had both written and penciled since *The Longbow Hunters*, with the exception of *Green Arrow Annual* Vol. 1 #5 (1992), and it's lyrical exploration of the nature of the hunter and his connection with the Earth remains a poignant moment.

There is a sense of the familiar in the back half of Grell's run, with individual stories such as the hunt for a radioactive isotope in the two-parter 'And Not a Drop To Drink' (*Green Arrow* Vol. 2 #57-58, Feb-Mar 1992) recalling one of

---

[61] *Green Arrow* Vol. 2 #38 (Oct 1990).
[62] *Green Arrow* Vol. 2 #40 (Dec 1990).

Grell's first adventures in 'The Champions' (*Green Arrow* Vol. 2 #3-4, Apr-May 1988). The last full Shado saga, 'The Hunt for Red Dragon' (in *Green Arrow* Vol. 2 #63-66) feels like a necessity rather than being driven by the character building that was typical of the earlier arcs discussed here, and it results in what Morrison (2001) rightly calls a take on Richard Connell's *The Most Dangerous Game* (1924)[63], as Shado and Ollie are forced to survive on an island under the threat of explosive collars. It's not that these stories were lacking in political drive or messages, and if anything they became more topical, but perhaps it was that Grell's closed world was in need of a fresh injection of external characters from the DC Universe. Case in point, some of the stories didn't even focus on Ollie and Dinah anymore: 'Vengeance Is Mine' (*Green Arrow* Vol. 2 #55, Dec 1991) is mostly about Lt. Cameron, and the two-part 'Sign of the Times'/'Pitchforks & Torches' (*Green Arrow* Vol. 2 #61-62, May-June 1992) see the heroic duo take a back seat to a very Denny O'Neil-esque story about a conscientious objector to the military draft.

Grell's saga would reach its emotional apex during an overwrought anniversary issue in *Green Arrow* Vol. 2 #75 (June 1993) that not only reunites Ollie and his former ward Roy Harper (a.k.a. Speedy / Arsenal), but has Marianne confess her love to Oliver as well. The resulting kiss creates a rift between him and Dinah that is irreparable, especially after Oliver consciously cheats on Dinah with Marianne the following issue, something he never chose to do with Shado. Oliver's actions lead him to a closer association with Eddie Fyers, who is now on the run for his own life, and they wind up working for the Mossad this time around. By the penultimate issue of Grell's run, county Sheriff Ned Mannix also lays out in no uncertain terms that Ollie's notion of "justice" at the end of pointy arrow is no longer welcome. "It may serve justice, but the law gets left behind... the law has to work to protect all the people... even from vigilantes." The now estranged Dinah is increasingly disgusted by his actions, particularly working with Fyers, and tells him their relationship is over in no uncertain terms: "We had a good run... while it lasted. It just didn't last." Grell might as well be speaking directly to his readers here.

In Grell's final issue, *Green Arrow* Vol. 2 #80 (Nov 1993), Ollie bids farewell to Marianne as well, while she reminds him that Dinah won't take him back. "I

---

[63] Morrison, M. (1 Oct 2001). "Green Arrow Reading Guide." Retrieved 20 Aug 2015 from http://fanzing.com/mag/fanzing39/feature1.shtml

know," he admits regretfully. "But I still love her." A series of comics that began with an intimate and loving couple at the height of their sex life now ends in heartbreak. Having "settled for tilting at windmills," and fully embracing the consequences of his choices and actions, Oliver Queen is alone in the dark at the end of Mike Grell's run. Maybe this is the final point at which the circle inevitably closes for the urban hunter, showing us that while the everyman could stand up to the biggest of windmills, he could not have a foot in each camp for long. Indeed, Ollie and Dinah wouldn't reunite in a significant way until Kevin Smith's 'Quiver' in 2001[64], by which stage the character had been restored to a pre-*Crisis* interpretation.

The Wonder Year

Every creator that has worked extensively with Green Arrow since Jack Kirby has put a mark on the character's origin story, and Mike Grell was no exception. While he gave us a brief origin recap during *The Longbow Hunters*, conveniently ignoring the outlandish elements that didn't meet his darker post-*Crisis* world, he initially expanded on it during the 'Sometimes a Fool Notion' story in *Secret Origins* Vol. 2 #38 (Mar 1989). It's an issue of contrasts, with Grell's lead story grounding the origin into something that fit more in line with his "Suggested for Mature Readers" line of comics. Ollie's exploits on Starfish Island are brief, where he captures two marijuana growers, suggesting that reports of his dismantling of a criminal empire were the exaggeration of the media. Back at home in Star City, it is the media that dubs him "Green Arrow" – one of the rare times that Grell indulged in using that term throughout any of his series – and hopes that the name won't stick. "I'm going to have to work on that one," Ollie declares, but it would be surprising if that wasn't Grell making an in-joke with readers and editors. By contrast, Elliot S. Maggin's Speedy origin story in the same issue ('The Kid That Couldn't Shoot Straight') is far more traditional, complete with the Arrowcar gimmick, pushing Grell's Green Arrow even further away from the rest of the DC Universe.

The four-issue mini-series *Green Arrow: The Wonder Year* (Feb-May 1993), with art by Gray Morrow, follows the *Secret Origins* story, giving Grell an expanded opportunity to rewrite Green Arrow's origin story within the context of his "Grellverse". Despite this, it's a surprisingly lighter story involving radical

---

[64] In the renumbered *Green Arrow* Vol. 3.

student groups of the 1960s and 1970s. Very little time is spent exploring Ollie's time on the island, except in flashbacks that directly recall *Secret Origins* and that handful of panels from *The Longbow Hunters*. As alluded to in Grell's previous works, this version of Ollie is friends with *The Adventures of Robin Hood* stunt archer Howard Hill, and his first outfit is a hired fancy dress costume paying tribute to this. Once again, his fledgling hero efforts see the media dub him "Green Arrow" much to his chagrin – he wanted the name "Shaft". Yet the primary focus of the narrative is a faked assassination attempt on a would-be presidential candidate involving one of Ollie's old flames, making it a highly personal story for the hero, all the while following Oliver's first attempts to become a hero in an increasingly dark city.

Released towards the end of Grell's run, *The Wonder Year* initially appears slightly incongruous with the rest of his work. Yet beneath the surface are the same politics that undercut the rest of Grell's stories. When Ollie is reunited with his radicalist college crush Brianna, immediately guessing his secret identity, she argues that he has lost his hopefulness. Ollie counters that Brianna, now living as Kelli Harris and the girlfriend of a Congressman, and her contemporaries no longer felt threatened by the Vietnam War so they had given up on the fight. Once again we see Grell's dichotomy of one person tackling "environmental and urban problems" through writing and legitimate legal organizations, while Ollie (as Brianna sees it) is simply "wearing a funny costume and trying to fight evil single handed"[65]. As Grell was given free rein to do what he wanted with the character post-*Crisis*, we can rightfully extrapolate that this is Grell's vision of what *his* Green Arrow would have been up to in the 1960s and 1970s in a world without other super-heroes, although this is certainly isn't that far from the type of character who would travel across the United States with Hal Jordan/Green Lantern. *The Wonder Year* throws the timing of the Denny O'Neil chronology out, somewhat tempering it with the cynicism of the 1980s, especially the knowledge that the government was behind some radical bombings attributed to protest groups in the 1960s.

Yet *The Wonder Year* also retains the spirit of protest, and artist Gray Morrow's work on the issue helps recall Neal Adams defining work from the 1970s. Morrow had begun his career almost 40 years prior to *The Wonder Year*, and his legendary status comes from being one of the artists on the fledgling

---

[65] *Green Arrow: The Wonder Year* Vol. 1 #2 (Mar 1993).

issues of Warren Publishing's *Eerie* and *Creepy* comics of the 1960s, just like Adams. In the second issue of the series, he uses similarly photorealistic images of John F. Kenndey, Robert Kennedy, and Martin Luther King Jr. to talk about how the dream died in America. It's a clear visual reference to that oft-reprinted scene from *Green Lantern* Vol. 2 #76 (Apr 1970) where Ollie anguishes over "the streets of Memphis" where "a good black man died... and in Los Angeles, a good white man fell." This can be read as a prelude to *The Longbow Hunters*, where its tragic ending – which sees Brianna kill herself after her actions indirectly lead to the congressman's assassination – serve as a somber foreshadowing of Oliver's massive amounts of loss by the end of Grell's main run.

The Wonder Year remains an interesting anomaly; an attempt at an official origin story almost seven years after the character was rebooted post-*Crisis*. It's also an example of a very late 1980s / early 1990s origin story of a character who, by his own admission, takes up vigilantism out of boredom. "God knows I haven't got anything better to do," he quips. This is Grell giving Green Arrow fans from pre-*The Longbow Hunters* exactly what they want: an outspoken semi-liberal complete with trick arrows. The rest of Grell's run was completely on his own terms. By comparison, the Grell-penned *Shado: The Song of the Dragon* mini-series (Jan-Apr 1992) saw Grell's original creation return to Japan to help a Second World War veteran close off some unfinished business with the Yakuza. It features Green Arrow in flashback, but is intended to fill in a few of the puzzle pieces around the mysterious Shado. Taken together, they form bookended farewell letters to a world that Grell single-mindedly shaped over the better part of a decade.

What One Man Did: The Legacy of the Urban Hunter

When Mike Grell left the series after issue #80, DC rapidly restored Green Arrow to their wider continuity. Yet the constantly moving target that is Green Arrow underwent an irreversible change in the seven years that Grell wrote the character. Under Grell, the character of Green Arrow didn't simply become an urban hunter, and he certainly didn't become the extreme version of a vigilante that some of his contemporaries were either. A relatively average middle-aged and middle-class guy with liberal attitudes in the 1960s and 1970s, his sense of natural justice was one that happened to come with deadly accurate skill with a longbow, along with a willingness to kill that came from being pushed too far within an impotent system. While he suffered trauma, and his extended family suffered too, he was neither the victim nor the oppressed. Throughout Grell's run, he would rip his stories straight from the headlines, tackling homophobic violence ('Gauntlet'), drugs and gang violence ('The Canary is a Bird of Prey'), governmental corruption (*The Longbow Hunters*), human trafficking, environmental disaster (in the Exxon Valdez inspired 'Coyote Tears'), animal poaching ('Round the Horn'), anti-war protests ('Sign of the Times'), homelessness ('Bum Rap'), and racism. His adventures didn't necessarily solve the problem every time, but provided at least small relief for the people he could rescue and a platform for the issues to be discussed. He was a costumed example of what one man could do, or as Scully and Moorman suggest, that anyone could be a vigilante.[66] As a direct result of *The Longbow Hunters*, that 'one man' could be anybody with the right kind of motivation.

If the 1970s tapped into the notion that the voice of the average person was the most important way to enact change, with Green Arrow literally protesting the actions of the authority figure Green Lantern, then Grell was suggesting that words alone were no longer sufficient against the weight of a broken system. "Grell did for Green Arrow in the late 1980s what Denny O'Neil and Neil Adams did for the character in the 1970s," argues Boney (2006). "Grell not only redefined Oliver (Green Arrow) Queen's look and personality, but also made the character relevant to his time."[67] That time, was one of a culture of fear, where drugs, urban crime, and governmental corruption were part of a media maelstrom that kept Middle America vigilant. Green Arrow was not a right-wing extremist, as might be suggested by some of the language around his actions in this era, but rather someone taking up what he saw as a just cause. Yet once the character started down this road, it would be difficult for him to ultimately return from it, with Grell's eventual successor Chuck Dixon left with the task of marrying this Green Arrow with the role of mentor, crusader and eventually, martyr. After all, that 'one man' could only give so much without major sacrifice.

What would have happened to Grell's version of Oliver Queen is something that we can only guess at, given his fate at DC Comics over next few years. In the 1994 crossover event *Zero Hour*, the Green Arrow that was firmly re-established within the DC Universe was forced to kill his best friend Hal Jordan /

---

[66] Scully and Moorman (2014), p. 648.
[67] Boney (2006), p. 35.

Green Lantern when the latter was possessed by the entity known as Parallax. Of all the death he had directly or inadvertently caused in Grell's era, this was the killing blow to his mental well-being. Under Chuck Dixon, he would discover he had a son, only to heroically sacrifice himself the following issue when he was trapped in an exploding plane over Superman's Metropolis, leaving the mantle to his kung-fu Buddhist offspring, Connor Hawke. When DC restored the character under writer Kevin Smith in 2001, it was a pre-Grell attitude and body, doing away with the darkness conclusively. When asked about what he would do with the characters today, Grell is certain where both Oliver and Dinah would reside:

> I would love to go back and do Oliver Queen, *The Longbow Hunters* version 30 years later. Okay, not 30 because technically speaking he'd be 75... I would love to go back and do Ollie and Dinah, and pick up not necessarily where I left off, but down the road... This is what their life has been, and I would have them still together with no problem at all, and I think the readers would be ripe for it.[68]

In the vast Multiverse that is DC Comics, it's possible to imagine Ollie and Dinah still working out their problems in whatever city they still call home, happily isolated from the rest of the world and doing whatever one *couple* could do to make a difference.

---

[68] Mike Grell, personal interview, 29 Mar 2015.

Mike Grell Interview

Writer and artist Mike Grell's history with Green Arrow goes back to the 1970s, when he collaborated with Elliot S. Maggin on a short piece in Action Comics Vol. 1 #440 (Oct 1974), teaming the Emerald Archer up with Black Canary and Superman's dog, Krypto. As Mike tells it, it was a case of being in the right place at the right time that landed him the gig as the successor to Neal Adams on *Green Lantern/Green Arrow* in 1976. By the late 1980s, a series of successes at DC Comics and in the growing independent market let Grell to be attracted back to the publisher for a gritty "urban hunter" take on the character. When the TV show that his run partly inspired launched its own comic book line, Grell provided art duties on several covers and interiors.

This interview took place at Emerald City Comic-Con in Seattle on 20 March 2015, the very city that Grell's Oliver Queen called home, as Grell continued to sketch several requests for reproductions of his classic works.

RICHARD GRAY: I'm sitting here in Seattle, at a booth surrounded by Green Arrow prints and sketches. Did you still think you would be so intensely involved with the character, and indeed return to the character, all these decades later?

MIKE GRELL: I didn't expect it at first, but I have to say, Green Arrow is the reason why I got into comics. He's my favourite character, and always has been, even from the time when I was a kid. The idea that I was able to get the gig to be lucky enough to reintroduce the Green Lantern/Green Arrow series when it came back. I was fortunate that I was in the office the day that Denny O'Neill decided that he was going to bring it back. I heard the rumour in the hallway, and went straight to his office and said 'Ok, who do I have to kill?' That was, sort of, the culmination of my initial goal, to be able to work on that book.

Then as years went by, and I moved onto other companies, and had left Green Arrow well behind, I got a phone call from my friend and editor from First Comics, his name was Mike Gold. We did [*Jon*] *Sable [Freelance]* together, and Mike had just started up at DC Comics, and he phoned me up and said 'Look, is there anything over here you'd like to do, any character you like well enough to bury the hatchet and come back to DC. My first reaction was to say that I always felt that I did such a crappy job on Batman that I'd like another whack at it. *But* I had just spoken to Frank Miller the week before, and Frank was just beginning to write *The Dark Knight* [*Returns*]. I said, you know when Frank's done with The Dark Knight, you can put a period at the end of the Batman stories for the next 20 years. Turns out, I'm off by ten years in comics so far. Mike Gold said 'Think about this: Green Arrow as an urban hunter.' And I went yup, that's it. Those six words were what I based everything from *The Longbow Hunters* on through the Green Arrow series. To be at the latter end of my career and be right back where I started – it's great. It's great. Like going home.

RG: The urban hunter aspect has been a huge part of the TV series, do you see any parallels between what you're writing now, and have you evolved the concept at all when you go back to looking at the stuff you do for television [tie-ins]? Do you draw on unused ideas from those days?

MG: Well, unfortunately I don't have any input on the series at all, with the exception of that 'Wanted' poster they use every week. I drew that, and apart from the inspiration that my work on Green Arrow presented to the creators of the show, I really can't claim any credit for it. Except to say, I'm the guy who gave him the hood.

RG: With the exception of *The Longbow Hunters*, we haven't had any of your run in reprints until this year. Is it finally a relief to see those coming out in trades?

MG: Yeah, especially since I get a check. [Laughs] I think it's a case of what goes around comes around, and eventually people will remember that was good and popular back in the day and go 'We haven't printed this for a long time.' They're doing the Legion of Super-Heroes, gradually doing all of the Green Arrow, which is pretty good. I wish they would do a hardcover version of *The Longbow Hunters*. Just because I'd love to have that hanging on my bookshelf.

RG: Would something like one of those oversized art books be appropriate?

MG: It would if they could run down all the artwork. I don't have any of it anymore.

RG: The other character I've noticed you still having a huge connection with people, and you've returned to him over the years of course, is Warlord. Simular in his hirsuteness, of course, but where did that character come from?

MG: It was based upon a comic strip I was trying to sell at the time I broke into comics called the Savage Empire. Savage Empire was about an archaeologist who's catapulted back through time and winds up back in Atlantis before it sank. Unfortunately at that time period, nobody was buying anything resembling an adventure comic strip. So I went out to New York, and I was pretty dismayed because I couldn't even get an appointment to speak to one of the newspaper editors. They were just not interested at all.

There was a comic convention going on, New York Comic-Con 1973[69], where I met several people from DC Comics including Irv Novick, who was drawing Batman at the time, Alan Ashman, who was the editorial assistant for Joe Kubert. Those guys looked at my portfolio and told me in no uncertain terms to get my carcass up to Julie [Julius] Schwartz's office and talk to him, which I did. I walked in with my prepared encyclopaedia salesman speech, that goes "Good afternoon, Mr. Schwartz, could I introduce you in this deluxe 37 volume set of Encyclopaedia Britannica complete with annual yearbook and calendar?" And if you get interrupted anywhere along the line, you have to go back to "Good afternoon Mr. Schwartz." That's exactly how far I got. "Good afternoon, Mr. Schwartz." And Julie says "What the hell makes you think you can draw comics?" I unzipped my portfolio, dropped it on his desk and said "Take a look and you tell me." Julie called Joe Orlando in from next door, they put their heads together, and I walked out half an hour later with my first script in my hand. My first assignment.

Now while I was at that convention in New York, Saul Harrison – who was then the president of the company and reviewing portfolios – and I left him a copy of my portfolio with Savage Empire in it, and went off and forgot about it. About five years later, the mail slot opens up and in comes this package from DC Comics. I didn't remember sending them anything that size. So I open it up, and there's my portfolio. *Savage Empire*. It was attached to a form letter rejected saying "Thank you very much for your submission. Unfortunately, it does not meet our current publishing needs." Which is funny, because with a name change and a locale change, they had been publishing it for five years under the title *The Warlord*, and at the moment it was their top selling book.

RG: You've said in the past that characters like Jon Sable are where you feel most comfortable, where you fit. Those down to Earth sort of guys who aren't necessarily superheroes, but they are in extraordinary circumstances. Is this the kind of character you still enjoy working with?

MG: I still do. I try to focus on the character over the action. The action is important, but the characterization is really primary. You can build, for instance, one of my favourite bad examples is the Rambo movies. *First Blood*: great story, great development of the character. You're introduced to him, he's different at

---

[69] New York Comic Art Convention 1973, held at the Commodore Hotel from July 4-8.

the end than he was at the beginning. Then comes *Rambo II*. *Rambo II* is all about shoot-'em-up-bang-bang. But it was fun, I'll give it that. It was successful, and it was fun. Then comes *Rambo III*, where they throw out all the characterization, all the motivation, all the things that make a good story, and just decided "watch us blow stuff up." And that's what it was. My other favourite bad example is *Ocean's 11* versus *12* and *13*. *Ocean's 11*, they introduce all the characters. *12* they figure, ah you've already seen *Ocean's 11* or you wouldn't even be here, right? So character development lagged quite a bit behind. *Ocean's 13*, no character development at all, it's just a heist movie, and not a very good one at that.

I tend to focus more on the characters, and get inside them so the audience will care more about that. When I did *Sable*, the standard for the industry was: page one, introduce the hero. Page two, introduce the hero's family. Page three, the hero's family gets killed. Page four through ninety-five, revenge. So with the Sable story, it is a revenge story, but I took several issues before I got around to actually knocking off his family. When I did, I felt like I was actually killing my own family. I had people write to me, going "I can't believe you did that." Well, it's necessary for the development of the character.

Just like in *The Longbow Hunters*, hanging Dinah from a forklift, and putting her through all that, was a necessary step in the evolution of Oliver Queen. To get him away from the ultra-liberal, goody two-shoes, "I will never take another life" attitude that Denny had, Denny O'Neil had, when he was writing it. There was a whole storyline when Oliver Queen accidentally kills a guy, and goes off and becomes a monk. Goes to a monastery, withdraws from society more or less.[70] I thought no, in order to do the kinds of stories I wanted to do, set in the real world where bad things happen to good people, I needed to take the character through a change. So I put him into a position where people could relate, because if something like that happened to someone they love, they at least want to think that they would probably do the same thing. React the same way. It had to be dramatic, *traumatic*, to make him turn away from everything that he had been espousing for so long, I guess, and make him a cold, hard killer. Even at that, I didn't pass it off. I didn't make it like "Okay, he kills a guy, next episode forget all about it." That incident affected him and his relationship with Dinah. Early on in *The Longbow Hunters*, I established that they had a great

---

[70] In *Flash* Vol. 1 #217-219.

sex life. But all of a sudden after this incident, she can't stand to be touched. Even by somebody that she loves. Not only did that affect her, but it affected him, even if he denied it. He was in denial for a long time, but I did a metaphorical stepping off a cliff: you can't un-jump, right?

RG: One of the things I loved about that run is that relationship between Dinah and Ollie. They even go to therapy at one point to work out those issues. I found that to be a particular real depiction of a couple, not just a couple of superheroes, but a couple. Not to compare them too much, but the current take from DC is to keep couples as far apart from each other as possible. Do you think there's something necessary about his relationship with Dinah to make that character work? Or do you think he works better or worse as a solo character?

MG: I think Ollie and Dinah together are better than either of them apart. The problem with relationships in comics is that a lot of the writers don't seem to understand how to do a story where people are functioning as a couple without marrying them off. They feel compelled to marry them off. That's the death-knell. One of two things happens: either the wife immediately gets pregnant, or is killed off, or something happens. When they married Ollie and Dinah in the regular series, I thought this will never last. That book will be gone in a year. And I was off by about six months. I was being maybe a little overly charitable.

It happened on several television series in the US. There was one called *Moonlighting* with Bruce Willis and Cybill Shepherd. They had a great dynamic relationship until they married them off. The end. They get married, they struggled through one more season where the only thing they can think to do is now they've got to have a baby. That's about it. *Magnum P.I.,* they did the same thing.

RG: They actually killed him off one season.

MG: *Remington Steel,* you know. Nothing else to do. We're out of ideas. We surrender, let's marry them off.

RG: Just returning briefly to Sable. There was a series, of course, which you've spoken largely about over the years, but there was more recent talk of a film that you were involved with. Is that still progressing, or is that in development hell?

MG: Unfortunately, the wheels of the Hollywood machine not only turn slowly, sometimes they just don't turn at all. There's been constant interest. I have a director who wants to do it, I have a star who wants to do it. That's two points of a trio that you need. Now I need a guy to write the check. It seems to be a little on the difficult side to put that final bit of the equation together, but yes, hope does spring eternal and eventually it will get done I'm sure. I've written a screenplay, worked on it with a director, and we've fine-tuned it over the years in several different variations of it, and it's pretty tight. It's pretty good. It's not the same as what you read in the comic books, and it's not the same as what you read in the novel, although it does draw from both of them. I just didn't want to take the readers to that well too many times, so that 'we know how this goes, right?' If the movie gets done, they'll be in for a surprise, because it's not the same.

RG: What are you working on at the moment?

MG: I just finished a Tarzan story for Dark Horse called "The Gods of Opar," which I both wrote and drew. My old friend and cohort, Mark Ryan, who is one of the stars of *Robin of Sherwood*, the television series, he played Nasir. He does the voices of Bumbleebee, Jetfire, and Lockdown in the *Transformers* movies. He recently appeared as Mr. Gates on *Black Sails*, the pirate show from Michael Bay, and we did a project together that fell afoul of publishers who ran out of money before we even got the third issue finished. It's called *The Pilgrim*, and we are resurrecting *The Pilgrim*. It's coming out in the Fall [2015]. It's going to be released through an outfit called Strick 9 Studios.

RG: You've worked on established characters, and created your own original characters. Is there someone you've always wanted to play with and never had the chance?

MG: Captain America.

RG: What is it that appeals about Cap?

MG: One of the first comic books I ever saw was my dad's World War II copy of *Captain America*. It may still be in a box up in the attic, I'll have to go and look. It appeals to me. My take on Captain America would be different from what's being done currently. I would want to focus on the harsh contrast of a man from World War II era waking up Rumpelstiltskin in the 21st century, and explore the difference between the two eras. The entire outlook and attitude of the American way of life.

Not blowing smoke here, but it's one of the things I love about Australia.[71] I grew up in the 1950s, and when I was in Australia in the 80s and 90s, I found Australia and Australians to be very much like America was in the 50s. If you

---

[71] The interviewer is from Australia.

were a stranger in town, you weren't a stranger for long. If you needed help, someone was always willing to lend you a hand. One of my pals drove across [the Nullabor], he started in Sydney and wound up in Perth. Somewhere along the line in the middle of nowhere, his car broke down with his wife and brand new baby on board. Just at the point where they are wondering what happens next, over the hill comes an old Volkswagen bus painted with peace symbols and flowers, driven by some transplanted hippie. The guy pulled over. Before he got back to the car, he got out his toolbox. That guy's wife sat and gave Tracey and the baby cool drinks while the husband repaired the car, he got back in and away they went. Don't tell me there are no such thing as angels. He might be a leftover hippie someone transplanted from Haight-Ashbury, or San Francisco, or wherever it came from, it was loaded with angels that day. You don't see that anymore. It used to be that way in the US. When I was a kid, I could hitchhike anywhere I wanted to go. It was not only safe, but an acceptable means of transportation. People would stop and pick up a kid on the side of the road. 'Where are you going?' 'I'm going to the lake.' 'Hop in, we'll save you three miles of walking.' And we never thought anything about it. Nowadays, even to the driver you're taking your life in your hands by even picking somebody up, let alone trying to hitchhike down the road. The world has changed, times has changed. I don't know where we're going from here.

If you ever saw the movie or read the book *No Country for Old Men*, that's really the point of the sheriff's character. That he's lived through that change, and at the end of it he's realized that he's got to get out because this is no country for old men. Hopefully, we'll find some way to get our soul back. And that's what I would do with Captain America.

RG: That sounds wonderful. Of course, you have dealt with other Marvel characters in the past. You did Iron Man once upon a time. I think you were saying that was something where you very much took that attitude of pulling him back to his simplest level.

MG: Yes. The suit had become so powerful. Tony Stark himself had turned into Arnold Schwarzenegger. I thought that was wrong. The suit had essentially made him Superman. There had been some great Superman stories told, but it was hard to get emotionally invested in someone who can't be harmed. I put back the inherent weakness where he has to recharge his batteries every 24 hours or he could die, and I also added in another aspect that in a time of crisis he could use his heart energy to run the suit at the risk, knowing that he could die. So then it becomes personal sacrifice. I wanted to turn the focus away from the suit and focus on the man inside the suit. Which is why when they announced the Iron Man movie, I was trepidatious. I thought the Hulk movie was like watching a video game, and not a very good one. I was afraid that they'd do that with Iron Man, but they stayed inside the suit. Even when they did the action scenes, they cut to the close-up of Robert Downey Jr. They never let you forget that there was a man inside that suit. One of my approaches was I saw that the suit was the armor that protected him from the dangers on the outside, but it also isolated him from the rest humanity, from the world. I made that part of my stories, trying to get back to the man inside the iron as much as possible.

RG: A couple of things that struck me when you were talking about *No Country for Old Men*, and the notion of coming back to a character years later. It was something you almost did with *The Longbow Hunters* in many ways, it was about returning to an older version of it, and Ollie coming to that realization himself. Would you ever envisage returning to the character, beyond the tie-in comics you're doing now with *Arrow*? Returning to character like that and seeing how age has affected him, how the changing times have affected him?

MG: I would love to go back and do Oliver Queen, *The Longbow Hunters* version, 30 years later. Okay, not 30 because technically speaking he'd be 75. I felt that it was essential to age the characters as you go along, because it sets them firmly in the real world with the rest of us. Now, we all have our heroes, and as different as our heroes are from ourselves, it's the similarities that make us love them so much. I would love to go back and do Ollie and Dinah, and pick up not necessarily where I left off, but down the road. Here they are down the road. This is what their life has been, and I would have them still together with no problem at all, and I think the readers would be ripe for it.

Green Arrow is Dead, Long Live Green Arrow: Chuck Dixon and a Hero's Legacy

Green Arrow could not escape the superhero death toll of the 1990s.

It was a radical time for costumed crusaders, with record breaking sales and a new generation of legacy characters. Coming off the back of the darker leanings of the 1980s, Mike Grell's departure from the Green Arrow monthly book coincided with a major sea-change in the comic book industry. *Teenage Mutant Ninja Turtles* creators Kevin Eastman and Peter Laird had made millions off the so-called 'black and white boom' of the 1980s and 1990s. By 1991, comic book creators were being showcased like MTV rock stars, including artist Rob Liefeld appearing in a Levi's 501 button fly jeans commercial directed by Spike Lee. It's difficult to wrap one's head around decades later, but this was an era where comic books sold in the millions. Marvel's *X-Men* Vol. 2 #1 (Oct 1991), created by Chris Claremont and Jim Lee, sold a standing record of 8.1 million copies across its variant covers, with *X-Force* Vol. 1 #1 (Marvel Comics, Aug 1991), from Fabian Nicieza and Liefeld selling another 5 million copies that same year. This peaked in 1993, often called the "most successful year in comics industry history" outside of the Golden Age, with 11,000 retailers selling tens of millions of comics a month due to the rampaging speculator market[1]. The mad scramble to own a No. 1 issue as an investment, and the corresponding publisher response of rebooting and relaunching their heroes to cater to these demands, "almost ruined comics forever" according to Sims (2012)[2].

Sudden shake-ups of the status quo helped these sales, aimed at reflecting the ideals of their Generation-X creators and readers. Often aided by the massive mainstream media publicity surrounding events including DC's 'Death of Superman', issues such as the black-bagged *Superman* Vol. 2 #75 (Jan 1993) shipped between 2.5 and 3 million copies. Marvel flipped the script on Spider-Man with an elongated event that purported Peter Parker was actually the clone of the original wall-crawler in the "Clone Saga." Comic book artist Kyle Rayner replaced clean-cut military man Hal Jordan as the Green Lantern. Billionaire Bruce Wayne was briefly broken by Bane and the armoured Jean-Paul Valley used his killer instincts as the interim Batman. Four different Supermen, including an angsty teen clone, vied for his throne during the Man of Steel's absence. Yet in the middle of the maelstrom of sales and renewals, writer Kelley Puckett introduced the character of Connor Hawke, who would eventually be revealed to be Oliver Queen's son and successor. The antithesis of his father and innocent in the ways of the world, Connor also represents something of a curious island in the middle of a decade filled with in-your-face reboots of characters that were over half a century old. As a spiritually focused fledgling hero with an Eastern flair, sexually ambiguous and of mixed Asian, African and European heritage, Connor represents not only the opposite number to Ollie's 'angry white middle-aged male', but the third part of a classically infused heroic journey. Connor Hawke is not simply another one of DC's legacy characters, but a symbol of the kind of rebirth required after the darkness of the previous decade. Indeed, this five-year period can be divided into three distinct stages: the hero at the crossroads, the hero descending into darkness and death, and the rise of a new hero's journey in his place.

---

[1] Miller, J. (n.d.). Comic Book Sales for 1993. Retrieved 14 Dec 2015 from http://comichron.com/monthlycomicssales/1993.html

[2] Sims, C. (2012, July 27). Ask Chris #115: What's Up With The '90s? Retrieved 14 Dec 2015 from http://comicsalliance.com/ask-chris-115-whats-up-with-the-90s/

"Ah, Seattle... I Hardly Knew Thee": A Hero at the *Crossroads*

Mike Grell had spent the better part of the previous decade keeping Green Arrow away from the rest of the DC Universe, a "no capes / no powers" policy isolating Ollie and Dinah in Seattle. Yet with their break-up and the departure of Grell from the series, DC wasted no time in restoring Green Arrow to the wider universe. The restoration actually begins outside of Green Arrow's own title, in *Green Lantern* Vol. 3 #47 (Nov 1993), with the angry faces of Green Lantern and Green Arrow challenging the reader. "They're back!" proclaims the Scott Kollins cover, while Green Arrow scowls "You got a *problem* with that?" As Hal Jordan mourns the destruction of his native Coast City, following the devastating fallout from the aforementioned 'Reign of the Superman!' crossover[3], it's a different kind of anger that Ollie displays than the self-righteousness of the Denny O'Neil/Neal Adams run that this issue necessarily asks us to recall. "You needed me to tell you what was right for you," argues Ollie to Hal, retconning their symbiotic relationship, at least in his own mind. "You didn't even know what you believed in." After confronting aliens with Green Lantern, a pair of generic toughs named Shrapnel and Nuklon fight it out over a mutual love interest in Seattle in *Green Arrow* Vol. 2 #81 (Dec 1993), the start of the 10-part 'Crossroads' arc. Showing the self-reflection he would repeatedly demonstrate in this era, Ollie reluctantly quips "If I do this, I'm *outta* here... back in the superhero game... and it's really *over*." Shocking Lt. Cameron, the detective who actively worked against Green Arrow throughout the Grell era, Ollie turns his back on Seattle and hits the road solo.

"Crossroads" wasn't merely a representation of a hero at a turning point; it was at times much uglier. On the surface, editor Scott Peterson calls it a "bridge between the Mike Grell era and the Kelley Puckett" era:

> Basically, it's the story of Oliver Queen at a crucial moment in his life. He's forty-something years old, he's lost the only woman he's ever truly loved, and he's a super-hero because... well, just because... He hits the road to see if he can find some reason to continue doing what he does. 'Crossroads' is the story of what he finds along the way.[4]

---

[3] Specifically in *Superman* Vol. 2 #80 (Aug 1993), setting up the events of the Emerald Twilight arc in *Green Lantern* Vol. 3 #48-50 (Jan-Mar 1994) and the "Zero Hour" event.

[4] In the "Sherwood Forum" back-matter for *Green Arrow* Vol. 2 #86.

That "Kelly Puckett era" would only last three issues when it eventually rolled around, leaving 'Crossroads' as something of a grim anomaly that pre-empted the descent of a hero. Like a twisted version of the O'Neil / Adams "Hard Traveling Heroes" stories, Ollie wanders America to find something much darker and sinister than the 'real' people he encountered under Adams. This is indirectly addressed In *Green Arrow* Vol. 2 #87 (June 1994) when Ollie eulogises a lost America after encountering extreme (and somewhat clichéd) poverty in New Orleans: "America used to mean *working* for something of your own and being happy with it – not the freedom to just *screw* people just to get more." This is an Ollie who no longer believes in the inherent good in people, his own hardships filtering his experiences through the cynical nodes of his brain. Writers Kevin Dooley, Doug Moench, Chuck Dixon and Alan Grant have Ollie encounter increasingly action-based scenarios in the capital cities of the United States. In his first stop in San Francisco, during *Green Arrow* Vol. 2 #82 (Jan 1994) he encounters an extreme version of himself in the obviously-named Rival, a vigilante who is also abusive to his wife and child. Dooley makes a literal break with the Grell era by having Ollie's longbow smashed, only to be replaced with a new compound bow. His journeys take him to Los Angeles, Las Vegas, Dallas, New Orleans, New York City and Gotham, fighting cookie-cutter Yakuza henchmen and villains like the low-fat yogurt queen, Deidre Dallas. Making no secret of DC's attempts to reintegrate Green Arrow into their wider universe, he also encounters Catwoman, Huntress, and the newer version of the Justice League along the way. Despite this deliberate attempt at distance, the arc also consciously apes one of Grell's stories by having an eye-patched Ollie mistaken for Deathstroke in the two-part *Green Arrow* Vol. 2 #84-85 (Mar-Apr 1994), just as Warlord was thought to be Ollie back in Seattle.

The 'Hard Traveling Heroes' were not the only stories recalled, with Dooley posing the question "what can one lone bowman do anymore?" in *Green Arrow* Vol. 2 #88 (July 1994). Echoing the question posed, and answered, by Elliot S. Maggin[5], the archer self-assesses and finds he is lacking a clear identity. Full-tilt action sequences, as the archer leaps from windows and a helicopter with a gun in hand, were the subject of a debate that raged in the 'Sherwood Forum' letters column. Most were concerned with Ollie's decisions to willingly kill. Not helping matters is the cover to the aforementioned *Green Arrow* Vol. 2 #84,

---

[5] Discussed at length in chapter 5.

featuring the hero menacingly toting a pair of pistols, and outright firing a machine gun in a stark conflict with his previous philosophy against firearms. In the leftover mindset of the 1980s, and the blockbuster one of the 1990s, Ollie's choice between fascist-vigilante and fascist-cop[6] has left him unable to clearly define himself in either category. "I never liked being called a hero. I just do what I think is right. Try to make a difference," he argues in this same issue. It is not the first time that he has pondered whether he is "doing more harm than good," but here the hero at the crossroads doesn't even have that choice. The inadequacies of the right-wing system have failed him, and his own leftist philosophy hasn't given the bowman adequate purchase on one side of the fence or the other. "I've crisscrossed the America of the 90s and found it wanting – badly," he declares in *Green Arrow* Vol. 2 #89 (Aug 1994). Not finding what he was looking for, he literally takes the choice of anarchy, or more accurately, Anarky: a *V for Vendetta* influenced figure fighting social ills in his own chaotic way.

Dooley's Anarky, originally created by Alan Grant and Norm Breyfogle as a Batman anti-villain in *Detective Comics*, comes closest to the Adams stories in his impassioned dissection of "America's gun epidemic -- or rather – addiction." Despite disagreeing with Anarky's decision to blow up the factory belonging to the "terrorists" who manufacture guns, Ollie decides to make his bow "mean something" by going against his own beliefs. "I may not agree with you," he muses, "But it's time to remember the right path... who knows what I'll find." So after a standing at the Crossroads of hero or vigilante, Green Arrow takes the 'third option' of rejecting the system entirely, embracing anarchy and blowing up the factory. It remains a divisive moment, especially given the perpetual gun debate that still rages in the United States. Yet for the unravelling of a hero, the penultimate chapter of 'Crossroads,' it's an example of the hero drawing a line, even if it doesn't make literal sense.

Where Angels Fear to Tread: A Hero Descending

If anything conclusively cut the last lingering bowstrings that tethered these heroes to the Silver Age, or at least the ideals of that era, then it was the deaths

---

[6] As suggested in Lampert, M. (12 Aug 2007). The Fate of an Archer! Retrieved 14 Aug 2015 from http://sequart.org/magazine/20018/the-fate-of-an-archer/ and discussed in detail throughout Chapter 7 of this book.

of Hal Jordan and Oliver Queen – especially given that the former met his untimely end by the latter's hand. The conclusion to 'Crossroads' was also a tie-in to DC's *Zero Hour* crossover event, wherein the assembled heroes of the DC Universe attempt to fight back the disintegration of time itself. Meanwhile, Hal Jordan, mad with grief over the destruction of Coast City, gains the enormous power of Parallax and tries to remake the Multiverse that existed prior to *Crisis on Infinite Earths*.[7] The tie-in issue, *Green Arrow* Vol. 2 #90 (Sept 1994) foreshadows the death of Oliver Queen. In Dooley's wordless issue, artist Eduarto Barreto divides each page into split narratives depicting alternative timelines. We witness Green Arrow chasing down a crook, although in one version he hesitates and is set on a path towards his own bloody demise. In retrospect, given that Oliver Queen's hitherto unknown son and successor would also witness his death just over a year later, the final scenes of Ollie standing over the corpse of his own doppelgänger is prophetic. It's also the conclusive mark of the second stage of this journey, as Ollie's descent into darkness turns into a freefall.

The mytheme of the hero's descent into the underworld is common across the mythology of many cultures, and while Ollie's fall from grace is not a literal descent into hell or another plane of existence[8], his journey across America takes him to some of the darker places of both the country and his own mind. A more apt model for this stage of Green Arrow's mythology is that of Aristotle's "tragic hero," a morally grounded figure who does not have any evil intent, but nevertheless commits great wrongs or injuries to those around him due to his human frailties, leading to their own misfortune and pervading sense that their destiny has brought them to that place.[9] Having killed a man to protect Dinah in *The Longbow Hunters*, and subsequently saddled himself with his former enemies out of a sense of obligation, Ollie's questionable allegiances and

---

[7] DC's ulterior motive for *Zero Hour: Crisis in Time*, both the event and the five-issue mini-series that held it together, was the publisher's attempt at reconciling the conflicting timelines that emerged after *Crisis on Infinite Earths*. Just as the latter unified the Multiverse into one Earth, *Zero Hour* was intended to fold the conflicting timelines into a single entity.

[8] This would have to wait until Kevin Smith's *Quiver* (2001 – 2002), during which Ollie fights actual demons, and be transported to Heaven to reunite with his reluctant soul. Smith's saga forms the basis of Chapter 9 of this book.

[9] Reeves, C. H.. (1952). The Aristotelian Concept of the Tragic Hero. *The American Journal of Philology*, *73*(2), 172–188.

romantic infidelities destroyed his relationship with Dinah and exiled him from his home. Now capable of killing, even if his original intent was to save Dinah, those same abilities have inevitably led him to a place where he must choose to sacrifice a friend because he's the only one that can do so. In a far too obvious metaphor for the mid-1990s reboots and renewals, legacy character Kyle Rayner / Green Lantern literally restrains the old guard of Hal Jordan, now driven mad as Parallax. After a long battle, Hal's power is drained, rendering him effectively impotent while he is held by his successor. At this opportune moment, Ollie's arrow penetrates the circle on his chest. Looking vaguely like a flipped version of the Mars symbol used to represent men, the whole sequence is a Freudian minefield.

Following the theme of ancient mythology, Oedipus was one of Sophocles' tragic heroes as well. In a reversal of sorts of that story, Oliver encounters his would-be successor in the wake of Hal's death when he returns to the ashram he visited at the end of the 'Hard Traveling Heroes' arc in order to cope with a previous accidental killing[10]. In *Green Arrow* Vol. 2 #0 (Oct 1994), Kelley Puckett begins his brief during a month of renumbered DC titles to tie-in with 'Zero Hour'. Ollie travels back to Seattle where he shaves off his beard and throws the remainder of his Green Arrow artifacts into the ocean. He finds Dinah's Sherwood Florist burnt out, and the physically and mentally broken Oliver Queen decides to return the ashes of his bow to Master Jansen at the Ashram Monastery. Here Puckett and artist Jim Aparo introduce the character of Connor Hawke, a young monk and Green Arrow fanboy that helps Oliver uncover the identity of the people out to kill him. Unbeknownst to Ollie, Connor is his biological son by former flame Sandra "Moonday" Hawke.[11] By allowing Connor to join his quest, Oliver inadvertently sets in motion the series of events that will lead to his own demise, and Connor becoming his successor to the mantle of Green Arrow. The Oedipal implications aside, it's a classic reimagining of the tragic hero trope as well. Puckett rounds out his short tenure on the book with the reintroduction of Eddie Fyers, Green Arrow's morally ambiguous ally, known for working on both sides of the law. He too has a part to play in this mythology.

---

[10] In the classic in *The Flash* Vol. 1 #217-219 (Sept 1972 – Jan 1973).
[11] Hinted at as early as *Green Arrow* Vol. 2 #91 (Nov 1994), and confirmed in *Green Arrow* Vol. 2 #96 (Apr 1995).

The final slide in the hero's descent came in the "Where Angels Fear to Tread" story arc,[12] as incoming writer Chuck Dixon borrowed a turn of phrase from Alexander Pope's *An Essay on Criticism* (1907). Dixon was already one of the most prolific comic book writers of the 1990s, having firmly established himself as a fan favourite writer at Marvel with *The Punisher Kingdom Gone* Graphic Novel, *The Punisher War Journal* monthly series and several other titles for the character. Catching the eye of editor and former Green Arrow scribe Dennis O'Neil, Dixon came to DC to not only run multiple Robin titles for several years, but he also became the key writer for Gotham City via seven years' worth of *Detective Comics* (1992 – 1999), a run on *Batgirl*, 70 issues of *Nightwing*, and co-creating and launching *Birds of Prey*, initially starring Barbara Gordon and Black Canary. In addition to creating the villainous Bane with Doug Moench and Graham Nolan, the character that would 'break the Batman' during the 'KnightFall' and 'KnightsEnd' arc, Dixon averaged seven titles a month at his peak. Known for his action writing, he later reflected that he was initially reluctant to begin writing for Green Arrow. "I took on this character with some trepidation," he reflected in the back-matter of *Green Arrow* Vol. 2 #137 (Oct 1998), his final regular issue of the series. "I mean, a guy with a bow and arrow in the 'shoot 'em up and leave 'em for dead' '90s?" Which might explain why it was only eight issues after the start of Dixon's regular run in *Green Arrow* Vol. 2 #93 (Jan 1995), the character of Oliver Queen was killed off.

Now established as a flawed and tragic hero, with all the pieces in place to seal his fate, Dixon at least offers Oliver Queen a chance at redemption via a heroic sacrifice. Oliver Queen divorced himself even further from the old guard by not wearing a costume at all, and under Dixon changed it completely to a more stylized red and brown spandex outfit with a hood. Unlike his previous costumes, born out of necessity on the island or adapted to the climate of Seattle, this was one based more in artist Jim Aparo's aesthetic leanings and the norms for costuming during the 1990s. In another telling signal, it was a matching costume to the one his son Connor was wearing, visually suggesting that the duo were now interchangeable. In his final months of publication, Oliver Queen argumentatively rejects his parentage of Connor on the flimsy

---

[12] *Green Arrow* Vol. 2 #96 through to *Green Arrow* Vol. 2 #100 (Sept 1995).

excuse of his deception,[13] and being the 1990s, eco-terrorists were the "villains" of the day, as Ollie finds himself on the wrong side of the moral high-ground when he joins Hyrax, the leader of the radical Eden Corp. Despite embracing anarchy even further, the tragic hero belatedly realizes that he has made an error of judgment, a classic motif of the archetype. Following a confrontation with Hyrax in *Green Arrow* Vol. 2 #100 (Sept 1995), who plans to destroy Metropolis with a weapon of mass destruction capable of levelling the city, Ollie finds himself strapped to the bomb as it heads towards the city. Appearing to him at this fateful moment is Superman, constructed here as a Christ-like figure, even sporting a messianic mullet hairstyle following his own resurrection. He offers Ollie a choice: losing his arm or dying with the plane. So it comes to pass in *Green Arrow* Vol. 2 #101 (Oct 1995), the perpetually stubborn Oliver Queen chooses a death that stays true to form with the character, electing to die in the explosion instead of losing the one thing that still gave his life purpose.[14]

The deaths of Hal and Ollie would remain in place for years, much longer than the traditional time-outs heroes such as Superman got for a publicity stunt, signalling the readiness of readers to embrace change, at least as long as there were elements of the familiar about them. The very fact that Green Arrow was almost immediately replaced gave readers nominal sense of continuity between eras, one aided by a budding partnership with Grell's character of Eddie Fyers, even if it was coupled with the shock of losing a character that was then 54 years old. Ollie's body, or lack thereof, isn't even cold when Black Canary endorses Connor as a successor in the same issue he dies in, by giving him the Howard Hill bow that Ollie once treasured as a totem. The mantle is now literally passed, with Dixon benefitting from the children's literature advice

---

[13] Much later, Brad Meltzer's "Archer's Quest" arc retcons this moment to establish that Ollie was aware of Connor since his birth, but abandoned him as an infant. The conclusion to that story was published in *Green Arrow* Vol. 3 #21 (Apr 2003).

[14] Almost a decade earlier, Frank Miller's seminal *Batman: The Dark Knight Returns* (1986) depicted an outlaw Oliver Queen operating as a counter-culture rebel against the oppression of an increasingly fascist government. The aged Ollie is a skilled archer, despite the loss of his left arm, something he blames Superman for. In Dixon's original script, Superman surgically removes Ollie's arm and flies him to safety, consciously recalling Miller's story. "That was what my editors wanted," he revealed in a personal interview, conducted 28 January 2016. See elsewhere in this book for full transcript.

The death of Oliver Queen in *Green Arrow* Vol. 2 #100. Art by Jim Aparo and Rodolfo Damaggio. © DC Comics.

to "kill the parents" and free up the next generation for their own adventures. It may not have been precisely based on the myth of the hero's descent into the underworld, but as the tragic hero met his ultimate end, his alter ego still achieved the corresponding immortality of the trope through the emergence of Connor Hawke as the new Green Arrow.

The Middle Path: A Hero Ascending

When looking at the earliest days of Green Arrow, we explored how Oliver Queen's alter ego was effectively a mix of several hero archetypes that already existed[15]. In Connor Hawke, Puckett's initial stories and the character that Dixon ran with for 47 issues already had the solid basis of a hero to emulate[16]. Indeed, despite being created by another writer, Dixon effectively developed Connor Hawke into a fully-fledged hero over the course of the next four years. So if Green Arrow was original built upon a pastiche and developed into his own identifiable character over the 40 years that followed, Connor Hawke shared at least some of those archetypes by virtue of being a variation on a theme. Like Green Lantern Kyle Rayner replacing Hal Jordan, himself an update of the Golden Age character Alan Scott, the Connor Hawke version of Green Arrow joined Barry Allen/Wally West (The Flash) and many more in a long line of legacy characters that carried on the 'family' name. The reasoning behind such a shift makes perfect sense, particularly in a decade when the two major publishers were trying to flip the panels to any angle that would make old ideas seem new again. A new character in an existing role gave the illusion of change towards a bold new direction, giving Connor the benefits of 50 years of continuity without their corresponding burdens.

Connor Hawke is deliberately set up as a reversal of Oliver Queen's infamous character traits. Connor's most prominent point of difference is his racial heritage, the son of half black and half Korean ex-hippie Sandra "Moonday" Hawke and the European ancestry of Oliver Queen[17]. Symbolically

---

[15] See chapter 1.

[16] Chuck Dixon's era follows Mike Grell and Judd Winick's respective runs as the lengthiest, lasting from *Green Arrow* Vol. 2 #93 (Jan 1995) to #137 (Oct 1998), and also incorporating *Green Arrow Annual* Vol. 2 #7 (1995) and *Green Arrow* Vol. 2 #1,000,000 (Nov 1998).

[17] Connor is sometimes incorrectly identified as the son of Japanese assassin Shado, conceived through the rape of Oliver Queen discussed in the previous chapter.

important for the more progressive DC Comics of the 1990s, Connor's appearance was often muddled by colorists and artists over the years, although these early appearances firmly establish his darker skin with his grandmother's Korean features, and the bright blonde hair of his father. As Green Lantern Kyle Rayner quips in Dixon's *Green Arrow* Vol. 2 #125 (Oct 1997), Connor is "kind of like one-stop multiculturalism." Yet having been in the monastery since he was 13 years old, Connor's worldview and experiences differ significantly from his father's as well, something Dixon provided an almost monthly reminder of throughout his run. Connor inherits Ollie's irresistible attractiveness to women, and barely an issue goes by without a waitress or deadly bombshell throwing herself at the affably clueless Connor. Sheltered in the ashram environment for five years, he is aware of his impact on women, but lacking his father's experience leaves him adorably unable to respond, even if the point is laboured as the years go by. His memory of his mother is one of absenteeism, which might also explain his difficult relationship with women, and while that is never specifically addressed, he later resolves this emotional crisis by discovering his mother was actually working to support him. In some ways, Connor Hawke is initially a 'Green Arrow' in name only, and despite his proficiency with a bow and kyudo archery, it is his martial arts and meditative qualities that define him in his early appearances. "Did I spend all those years in a monastery finding my spiritual center just so I could become a brawler," he ponders in *Green Arrow* Vol. 2 #106 (Mar 1996). Yet this is exactly what he does, keeping his arrows in their quiver more often than not, relying on the flying fists and feet of aikido and some Sankukai to take down opponents. Given the previous years had seen Oliver Queen resort to using deadly force, a Buddhist inspired approach of non-lethal combat and deep inner reflection was the polar opposite of the outward angst of the O'Neal/Adams legacy. As a vegetarian, Connor didn't even share his father's love of chili.

This is not to say that Dixon didn't recall those classic hits at multiple opportunities. The 1990s may have been all about shaking up the status quo for a new reader base, but even before the nostalgia of the early 2000s kicked in and marked the return of Oliver Queen, several arcs firmly reminded us of that

---

Despite several publishing mistakes that suggested otherwise, Shado and Oliver's child is canonically the much younger Robert, who shares a panel with Connor in Dixon's 2007 mini-series *Connor Hawke: Dragon's Blood*.

legacy. As early as *Green Arrow* Vol. 2 #104 (Jan 1996), a friendship is established between Connor Hawke and Kyle Rayner, the new Green Lantern. Recalling the firm bond between Hal Jordan and Oliver Queen, a fully-fledged 'Hard Traveling Heroes: The Next Generation' is launched with *Green Lantern* Vol. 3 #76 (July 1996), following the same numbering as the previous volume.[18] The roles of the heroes are reversed for the event, with Kyle initially taking on the role of the hot-headed liberal, while the sheltered Connor defers to the "proper" authorities. Indeed, it's Green Lantern who is showing the naïve Connor "how the world works" this time. Yet as Anderson (2013) points out, the heroes come off as initially less politically invested than their 1970s counterparts, indicative of the changing attitudes of college-age youth in the 1990s, but the existence of two mixed-heritage leads is itself a commentary on the progressive changes in the comic book industry.[19] It was a concept that evidently worked, so much so that it was repeated in "Hate Crimes," and later with the addition of The Flash in "Three of a Kind."[20] Often reminding us of the tradition that Green Lantern and Green Arrow share, with the spectre of their predecessors still looming large in their history, these fun crossovers also belied the difficulty DC had with completely breaking free of their Baby Boomer heritage.

With the spiritually-inspired Connor traveling across the globe having adventures with friend and mentor Eddie Fyers, was Dixon's era an update of Ollie's wanderings, with more than a dash of the 1970s television series *Kung Fu* thrown in for good measure? While there are some definite comparisons between the two that can be made, where Connor's journey under Dixon makes the most sense is as a version of the "monomyth" with an Eastern flair.

---

[18] The crossover event spanned *Green Lantern* Vol. 3 #76, *Green Arrow* Vol 2. #110 (both July 1996), *Green Lantern* Vol. 3 #77, and *Green Arrow* Vol 2. #111 (both Aug 1996). The Paul Pelletier cover of *Green Lantern* Vol. 3 #76 is a direct homage to Neal Adams' cover for *Green Lantern* Vol. 2 #76 (Apr 1970), just as Rodolfo Damaggio's cover art for *Green Arrow* Vol 2. #110 recalled Adams' *Green Lantern* Vol. 2 #87 (Dec 1971).

[19] Anderson, K. (2013). Green Lantern/Green Arrow. In R. Duncan & M. Smith (Eds.), *Icons of the American comic book from Captain America to Wonder Woman* (pp. 322-327). Santa Barbara: Greenwood.

[20] "Hate Crimes" takes place in *Green Arrow* Vol. 2 #125-126 and *Green Lantern* Vol. 3 #92 (Oct-Nov 1997), while "Three of a Kind" spans *Green Arrow* Vol. 2 #130-131, *The Flash* Vol. 2 #135, and *Green Lantern* Vol. 3 #96 (Mar-Apr 1998).

Broadly speaking, the monomyth is the idea that all heroic adventures are based on a common template, and was most famously espoused by scholar and mythologist Joseph Campbell. The cyclical nature of the journey is described by Campbell (1949) as follows: "A hero ventures forth from the world of common day into a region of supernatural wonder: fabulous forces are there encountered and a decisive victory is won: the hero comes back from this mysterious adventure with the power to bestow boons on his fellow man."[21] Campbell's 17 stages, mostly referred to as "The Hero's Journey," typically begins with the hero's call to adventure, the meeting of a mentor and crossing the threshold into a world they didn't previously know. Updated by Christopher Vogler for screenwriters in 2007, the end of the journey typically sees the hero returning to his or her ordinary world with something that improves it.[22] Vogler also spends time categorizing a series of character archetypes common to monomythic stories, not least of which are the mentor, the threshold guardian and the ally. While the monomyth, by its very definition, could be readily applied to just about any character arc, an exploration of Dixon's Connor Hawke stories reveal a strong adherence to these structures, giving the younger Green Arrow a distinctive journey from that of his father by the time it reaches its meditative conclusion.

Flung from one scenario to the next, the majority of these adventures may be considered Connor's ritualized 'trials,' but can just as easily be seen as his audition for the audience as well. The threshold the hero had to cross was one of accepting his own abilities and destiny, but in a very real sense he had to prove himself to a readership that had known a very different Green Arrow for over 50 years. Beginning with Connor's first solo arc in *Green Arrow* Vol. 2 #102 (Nov 1995), Connor leaves the isolated security of the Ashram Monastery thanks to a threat to its existence. Having lost its tax exempt status, the corporate Keever Enterprises wishes to tear down the site and build a Winky World theme entertainment park in its place. This is Connor's call to adventure, with Campbell's 'refusal of the call' evident in Connor's insecurities surrounding his ability to take up his father's mantle. "What am I *doing* here?" he muses in

---

[21] Campbell, J. (1949). *The Hero with a Thousand Faces*. Princeton: Princeton University Press.

[22] Vogler, C. (2007). *The Writer's Journey: Mythic Structure for Writers* (3rd ed.). Studio City, CA: Michael Wiese Productions.

the same issue. "I'm just pretending to be Green Arrow." After his initial adventures, he is more certain that this is his birthright: "That's what I want to do. What my father did. Look for wrongs and right them."[23] It isn't long, however, before Connor articulates this more clearly. In a crossover issue with Green Lantern, writer Ron Marz acknowledges the weight of Connor's role in the DC universe. "Being Oliver Queen's son was almost like... destiny. I don't think I consciously knew it... But it's as if I was training to take Ollie's place even before he died."[24] By the end of this arc, he has reconciled some of this legacy with his own nature, giving the self-reflective Connor the perspective he needs to embrace his hero's mantle. "My dad was a womanizer; the love 'em and leave 'em type," he muses in Green Arrow Vol. 2 #111 (Aug 1996). "I want to be the hero he was. Not the man he was." Connor articulates the type of hero he wants to be, realizing that some solutions only end in violence. However, he finds the middle path between "Eddie's way" of killing and non-violence, recognizing what it means to him to be a hero: "You can choose not to fight. But who's going to stand up for those who can't fight? That's the path I've chosen. That's the path my father chose. A path he followed until he died. Maybe that's where the path will lead me." This is the enlightenment that awaits Connor in his journey: the knowledge that he can be a son, a warrior, and remain true to his own code.

In the true tradition of the hero's journey, Connor was not alone on this path, with various allies, mentors, tricksters and even a princess helping to define his adventures. What is most interesting about the application of the hero's journey to Dixon's Green Arrow is the fluidity of character archetypes as the story progresses, with some characters not confined to playing singular roles. In the most direct and literal sense, Connor's "master archetype" is his ashram leader Master Jansen, an equally unworldly person who trained and guided Connor on his mission. Yet the ghost of Oliver Queen symbolically hangs over the hero, and what he represents leaves Connor at his own crossroads, especially given the conflicting mentor role that Eddie Fyers represents. As a confident and sworn protector, Eddie more likely represents the beleaguered

---

[23] Green Arrow Vol. 2 #108 (May 1996).
[24] In Green Lantern Vol. 3 (July 1996), the first issue of the 'Hard Traveling Heroes: The Next Generation' crossover, featuring legacy characters Green Lantern Kyle Rayner and Connor Hawke.

Connor Hawke, a new kind of archer, often operated without the aid of arrows. From *Green Arrow* Vol. 2 #132. Art by Doug Braithwaite and Robin Riggs. © DC Comics.

ally, a cynical older warrior type who at the very least respected Oliver Queen if he didn't agree with him all the time. In a flashback moment of *Green Arrow* Vol. 2 #107 (Apr 1996); Ollie describes Eddie as "a killer. He's what I was becoming before I went into the monastery." This is exactly the dichotomy that Grell set up during his tenure, staging Oliver's descent and ultimate death. Yet Connor is just as much a guiding light for Eddie, who slowly gives up his murderous habits as a result of his tenure with the young archer.

This leaves the role of mentor firmly in the hands of Oliver Queen himself. Eddie continues to guide and protect the fledgling hero, but meditations on his memories of his time with Ollie in the ashram gives Connor a new perspective. Using the *Kung Fu* comparison again, these vignettes are a version of Young Caine (played for television by David Carradine) interacting with his Master Po. In these sequences, Ollie is just as much a mentor figure as Obi-Wan Kenobi in the textbook hero's journey example of the *Star Wars* saga. Remembering the late archer's nuggets of wisdom ("Patience is at the heart of a hunter," advises a floating recollection of Ollie[25]) provides Connor with guidance at critical junctures, but so does his estranged grandfather and farmer Nathan Hawke, whose memories of the Korean War add additional comparative layers to Connor's warrior journey. Connor is never wanting for father figures and mentors, or the other archetypes for that matter. His stepfather Milo Armitage, an arms dealer who is abusive to Connor's mother, is a 'shapeshifter' type, constantly requiring a changing focus from the hero. For example, in *Green Arrow* Vol. 2 #124 (Sept 1997), Connor is conflicted by his mother's decision to support Armitage while he is on house arrest. Suspecting Armitage is still in the weapons trade, Connor is unable to tell his mother without proof. Despite finding evidence that his suspicions were true, Connor is forced to protect Armitage, who threatens to implicate Connor's mother in his wrongdoings.

The 'Lotus Seed' arc of Dixon's saga serves as a microcosm of this hero's journey. Beginning with *Green Arrow* Vol. 2 #112 (Sept 1996), Dixon infuses his hero's journey with Chinese folklore, playing out the monomyth in miniature across three issues. After encountering an assassinated man on the streets of San Francisco's Chinatown, Connor must take a key to the princess Lady Ren who is locked away in a hidden fortress (the Phantom City) in the Far East. To the surprise of Eddie Fyers, the Phantom City appears to be real, as does the

---

[25] Also in *Green Arrow* Vol. 2 #107 (Apr 1996).

Lady Ren. The supernatural surroundings play out a romantic love triangle, as the naïve hero Connor falls for the Lady Ren, who in turn believes him to be her reincarnated lover. Connor loses his virginity to Ren, crossing another personal threshold in the process, which angers the guardian protector Wei Fong. Wei is a threshold guardian, who pushes Connor to the limit by forcing him to give into his anger and nearly kill the guardian, an action that would have compromised the hero's moral code. Yet Connor has been deceived, for Lady Ren is also a classic shapeshifter archetype, playfully tempting him to embrace a less serious side, while literally transforming herself into a small animal to escape death. Having approached the Innermost Cave, and survived the Ordeal, it is time for Connor's reward. As he sleeps, a vision of Ren appears to him and informs Connor that the jade disc he carries is a calendar that shows him when he can return to the hidden city. For unbeknownst to Connor, it is implied that Ren will soon 'bear fruit' like the spring branches, suggesting that the fathering of illegitimate children runs in the Arrow family. Connor and Eddie begin their journey along the 'road back', but as followers of the classic monomyth will know, a final challenge awaits the hero archer.

In a much bigger sense, the Monkey Clan represents Connor's 'shadow' and the biggest ordeal he must face before crossing the return threshold. Only then can he achieve peace and enlightenment and some truth about Oliver Queen. In *Green Arrow* Vol. 2 #121 (June 1997), the disgraced Master Jansen reveals that the ashram has been taken over by the corporate Fritz Mueller, somewhat mirroring Ollie's own loss of his security blanket to big business. With the ashram now a celebrity spa resort in the Napa Valley, Connor challenges the resort's 'champion' to win back the ashram. The champion is Dixon's *Dectective Comics* creation, the mercenary assassin called the Silver Monkey, who brutally defeats Green Arrow. It marks a turning point for the character, who now has a barrier to 'the road back' to his ordinary world. Just as Kevin Eastman and Peter Laird's *Teenage Mutant Ninja Turtles* fled to the country after a stunning defeat, Connor returns to his grandfather Nathan's farm. Jansen identifies that "His honor is wounded. His belief in himself is low." In the following issue, the intrinsic heroic nature of Connor Hawke ensures that he will always protect the innocent, as he is thrown back into the fray, achieving a small victory and restoring his confidence. "Connor has achieved victory denied him at the Ashram," Jansen comments to Nathan. "I only hope that this restores the sunlight in his *heart*."[26] The notion is tested in *Green Arrow* Vol. 2 #127 (Dec 1997), when Connor's attempts at returning to a 'normal' life are blocked by the Silver Monkey, this time sent by Armitage. However, with the voices of Ollie and Jansen in his head encouraging him, he wins the battle. Amusingly trying to explain the incident to police, Jansen summarizes the entire saga: "It was about a young man trying to find his own way. A middle path between the teachings of his master and the influence of his father."

Dixon brings the saga to a close in an issue that is literally called 'Full Circle'. In the final ongoing issue prior to the temporary cancellation of the series, *Green Arrow* Vol. 2 #137 (Oct 1998), Connor seeks counsel with Superman, who not only tells Connor about Ollie's final moments but advises him that his home is "always worth fighting for." Having found his center, Connor elects to face Mueller's champion one last time, this time an old adversary named Suljuk[27]. Connor is victorious, and elects to stay in the ashram, and in the tradition of the monomyth he brings not one but two things with him to improve the ordinary world. The first is his own sense of balance, as both the character finally decides to put Oliver Queen to rest. "I've been carrying on in your name. Our name... But I'd like to think you wouldn't want me to *stay* in your shadow." Standing over his father's grave, he bids him farewell, although a flashback to six months earlier shows the green glow of Parallax over Ollie's grave, indicating that Oliver Queen will return. The other thing Connor brings back with him is Eddie, who makes the decision to give up his own wandering ways and remain with Connor in the ashram. Not only has the hero changed his own destiny, but that of his ally as well, perhaps starting Eddie on his own path to redemption for decades of killing. Their joint outside perspective brings balance to the 'ordinary world' of the ashram, now putting them in a better position to protect it from outside influences. Now at peace, the epilogue in *Green Arrow* Vol. 2 #1,000,000 (Nov 1998) has a present day Connor meditating in the ashram. He sees a future where a tribe of Green Arrows, descended from himself and Oliver Queen's other children, live in tranquillity until their life is threatened. The meditating Hawke comes to the realisation that completes his journey and hints at the next one: "Oliver Queen is alive."

---

[26] *Green Arrow* Vol. 2 #123 (Aug 1997)
[27] Last seen in *Green Arrow* Vol. 2 #107 (Apr 1996)

How useful is it to consider Connor's adventures as a representation of Campbell / Vogler's hero's journey? Dixon himself doesn't see the narrative as consciously adhering to the monomythic structure. "I hate all that Joseph Campbell crap. Whatever journey I sent Connor on was purely in pursuit of good stories."[28] After all, if the monomyth explains the fundamental commonalities between all heroic adventures, then surely it would follow that Connor Hawke's story would inevitably fall into its archetypes and stages anyway. Connor Hawke is unique in the history of Green Arrow precisely because he *can* be categorized in this way. Oliver Queen's publishing history spans decades and multiple writers, and was at least initially cobbled together on the back of heroes like Robin Hood, who had already experienced their hero's journey. There are certainly points in Ollie's history that fit the monomyth as well, not least of which are his hard traveling days with Hal Jordan, Grell's *The Longbow Hunters*, or the final descent as described earlier in this chapter. Yet under Dixon, we witness the complete journey of a novice to heroism, one in which the torch was conclusively passed from father to son and changed the shape of the Green Arrow myth for ever since.

Family Traditions: Fathers and Other Strangers

While Connor Hawke carved out his own legacy via a strong hero's journey under Dixon, when looking at Green Arrow's history in its totality, it is difficult to escape the view that this legacy era was merely a place-holder for the return of Oliver Queen. Connor's final meditations may have been to stop living under the shadow of his father, but the constant comparisons Connor made to his predecessor meant that the reader was invariably drawn towards doing the same. Indeed, the final moments of Connor's main run are spent over Ollie's grave, foreshadowing his return under Kevin Smith three years later. Yet taken on balance, the troubled era that followed Grell – and Dixon's epic tale of Connor Hawke – form a complete picture, one where the sins of the father don't simply define the actions of the son, but help him find a middle path between his two schools of teaching. The powers that be inevitably returned the cancelled series to publication in 2001 and restored a pre-Grell Oliver Queen persona in the role of Green Arrow. That series incorporated both Green Arrows, albeit awkwardly at times, to form something entirely new with a so-

---

[28] Chuck Dixon, personal interview, 28 Jan 2016. Full transcript in this book.

called 'Team Arrow' under a variety of writers, including Brad Meltzer's shock revelation that Ollie always knew about Connor from infancy, changing their dynamic significantly. Dixon himself returned to the character in the 2007 mini-series *Connor Hawke: Dragon's Blood*, expanding the relationship between Fyers, Connor and the assassin Shado. Nevertheless, this hero's descent and subsequent torch passing serves as a complete package, the story of the making of a hero that for once has a conclusive ending, at least for Connor Hawke. In the never-ending soap opera that makes up the mainstream comic canon, this saga itself might just be the elixir that is delivered to the (extra)ordinary world of Green Arrow.

Chuck Dixon Interview

Chuck Dixon has the distinction of being the writer who killed Oliver Queen. After coming to DC following a successful run on *Punisher War Journal* for Marvel, his workload increased exponentially, tackling an average of eight monthly titles during his most prolific period. Primarily working with the Batman universe, Dixon often brought his characters together, creating something of a Dixonverse of crossovers. For *Green Arrow*, he primarily dealt with the legacy character of Connor Hawke, the successor to Oliver Queen's mantle.

This interview was conducted via email on 28 January 2016, with several follow-up questions sent later for clarification.

RICHARD GRAY: At the time of writing Green Arrow, you were said to regularly have about seven titles coming out a month. How did you stay on top of that?

CHUCK DIXON: I was running on sheer enthusiasm as well as staying way ahead of schedule. And my wife handled everything grown-up so I could concentrate on the work. My kids wondered who that guy was who spent all day in that room full of comic books and toys.

RG: You were primarily known for your work on *The Punisher* at Marvel and the Batman universe at DC Comics in the early 1990s. Can you recall how you came to be involved with Green Arrow?

CD: I wrote a fill-in issue for the then current writer of *Green Arrow*. It was a rush job and the story turned out, admittedly, silly. I did it as a favor to the editor but promised that I'd never write another one. I didn't feel like I had an affinity for the character. Months later they asked me to take over the title. The addition of Connor Hawke made the series more interesting to me as writer. Here was a hook I could work with. I told them I'd write it for a year. I stayed for three.

RG: At the end of your *Green Arrow* run, you reflected that you were reluctant to tackle a "guy with a bow and arrow in the 'shoot 'em up and leave 'em for dead' '90s." Prior to coming to DC, or indeed taking on the title, did you have any other impression of Green Arrow as a character?

CD: He was a gimmick character to me for the most part. He was like Batman if Batman were all about the contents of his utility belt. Then Denny turned him into a bleeding heart which only made him less attractive to me. Grell turned him dark and I wasn't a big fan of that either. Are you sensing my reluctance yet? And I cast NO aspersions here. All the creators prior to me did great, heartfelt work. It just wasn't my kind of comics. The "bringing a bow and arrow to a gunfight" aspect was only part of the reluctance.

RG: Mike Grell had been writing the character for about seven years by the time you came aboard. 'Cross Roads' took a decidedly different spin to Grell. What were your intentions coming into the series?

CD: I meant to retain the cloak and dagger aspect that Grell laid down. That was all cool with me. I had no intention of veering away from Mike's stuff. He'd rebuilt the character in a new direction and that's what fans of the books expected. I wasn't about to rip his stuff apart and start over. All I really did was, over time, lighten the book up a little bit. My run isn't quite as grim as his was. But that fit because the bulk of my run was about Connor and the title took on a slightly different tone.

RG: You remained on the book from late 1994 until its temporary cancellation in 1998. Did you intend to stay on the book as long as you did?

CD: Nope. I only meant to write it for a year.

RG: Connor Hawke is credited as Kelley Puckett and Jim Aparo's creation, but your run made him his own character. Coming into the book, did you always know that you would be ultimately replacing Ollie with Connor?

CD: That was the plan. Though I didn't know what form that would take.

   And "my" Connor is Kelley's Connor. I did nothing to alter him one iota. He was fully formed when I took him over. Thanks, Kelley!

RG: The manner in which Ollie departed had some striking parallels with the hints we receive in Frank Miller's *The Dark Knight Returns* around how Oliver lost his arm. Were you consciously writing this possible alternative timeline?

CD: Originally, Ollie was to lose an arm in that issue. That was what my editors wanted. That's why I designed that convoluted trap with Ollie's arm stuck in that explosive device. In my original script, Superman cannot release Ollie from the trap and so surgically removes Ollie's arm with his heat vision then flies Ollie away (wrapped in his cape) at super speed, shielding Ollie with his own body from the effects of the explosion.

RG: One of the major threats to Ollie before his death is eco-terrorism and Hyrax. Green Arrow has always been political to some extent, or at least since O'Neil and Adams. Your own politics are on record, so what real-world events or trends informed your Green Arrow stories?

CD: I'd be lying if I said that some of what I wrote wasn't a reaction to Denny and Neil's run. I was working for Denny at the time, remember. He and I had some fun jabbing at each other. Those were simpler times when you could spar over politics then get back to work with no hard feelings.

I absolutely used eco-terrorism as a subject as a balance to the usual folderol about environmental issues. Al Gore was finding the environment as an issue at the time. But there were also outfits like Earth First committing tree-hugger jihad against oil and logging companies. The most fun I had was showing the city of Desolation years after Denny and Neil visited it. In my version, the citizens sued the big concerns that harmed them in the '70s and won huge settlements that turned this quiet little town into a community of flashy millionaires. To me, it was more a comment on how times had changed than anything else.

RG: Did you personally receive any reactions to killing off Ollie, from fans or other vested interests?

CD: Comics fans were so jaded about seeing their heroes kakked at that point that I heard very little about Ollie's "death."

RG: Connor's arc feels like a full circle, and in fact the last issue is called just that. It also strikes me that there's a classic hero's journey at play here, mixed with Eastern influences. Did you look to any classical models for Connor's journey from novice to hero?

CD: I hate all that Joseph Campbell crap. Whatever journey I sent Connor on was purely in pursuit of good stories.

RG: In fact, many of your stories – including Robin and the Batman universe – included specific references to martial arts styles and Eastern culture. Is this something that's fascinated you?

CD: Hong Kong action flicks were hot at the time and Batman and company are, essentially, empty hand fighters. It seemed like a natural extension of the characters. And I love those movies and that genre.

RG: In your "Year One" origin story for the *Green Arrow Annual* #7 (1995), you introduced the idea of Ollie (and subsequently Connor) having metahuman genes. What was the rationale behind this?

CD: That was an editorial mandate. I believe that this was an attempt to "amp up" Ollie and Connor so their place in the JLA (and the DCU in general) would be more likely. As the stories for the superheroes were becoming more and more outrageous, in terms of power and threat levels, two guys that shoot arrows were in danger of becoming irrelevant. In their opinion, not mine.

RG: When the main Green Arrow series ended in 1998, did you feel like you still had more to say? You certainly included Connor in several other titles you were writing.

CD: They wanted me to take on other work and something had to give. I knew that [they had] plans for Kevin to come on the book at some point so we decided on a cut-off point for me and I wrapped my stories up leaving a set-up for Ollie's resurrection.

I still used Connor in other titles. He'd become part of my regular cast and I liked the character a lot. I enjoyed the mini that Derec Donavan and I did a few years back.

RG: Kevin Smith was rapidly announced as the next writer on the book, but as we know that didn't happen for several years. Did you have plans for a story to bring Ollie back, or did you leave all the pieces there for your successor to take on?

CD: I was told generally how editorial wanted the return of Ollie to work and put everything in place for that.

RG: You got a chance to return to the character of Connor Hawke in 2007 with *Dragon's Blood*. Had your view of the character changed at all in the intervening decade?

CD: Not really. Except that he was now a true standalone character and I need to do a brand new story (mostly) free of his past continuity. The mini is meant to be read as a story complete unto itself. More a feature film or novel as opposed to a spin-off from the larger continuity.

RG: Following the end of *Green Arrow*, you kept things in the family so to speak by following Black Canary into the launch of the *Birds of Prey* ongoing. Canary is written as a spiritual successor to classic Ollie, in being passionate and idealistic. You described them collectively in 2000 as a "fertile clash of values."

CD: Everyone seemed to like them. I think it was the "buddy cop" mix of Babs and Canary. They really did, as Jordan Gorfinkel promised me, have a chemistry.

RG: You recrafted Green Arrow into something entirely new. Do these revisionist takes on established heroes hold a particular appeal for you?

CD: As long as they don't stray from the core of the character. As long as the character is instantly recognizable and relatable. I don't believe in breaking a franchise just for the sake of a story. Lucy van Pelt found in a shallow grave clutching a football would make for an interesting story, sure. But you've destroyed the property for the sake of a single storyline.

RG: You commented in your *Wall Street Journal* piece with Paul Rivoche that you felt your political views kept you from getting gigs at DC. Were there elements in these Green Arrow series you felt you couldn't discuss as a result of this?

CD: Everything was different then. I wasn't on the same planet as my editors politically but it didn't matter. It was only when a new crowd of editors came in that everything changed. The environment at the two majors goes beyond the political to cliquish. You not only have to have voted for who they voted for but you must like the music they like and wear the sneakers they prefer. I had an editor turn on me because I didn't like a movie he liked *as much* as he liked it.

RG: It's now almost two decades since your ongoing work with Green Arrow finished. Given the opportunity, are there any Ollie or Connor stories that you would want to tell?

CD: We'd need to discuss my page rate first.

Long Time, No See: Kevin Smith's Resurrected Saint and Brad Meltzer's Reformed Sinner

Death in comics is terminally impermanent. That's not to say that some deaths don't stick, but more often than not they are publicity stunts designed to sell more issues. While nobody could begrudge the big two publishers that prerogative, it does make readers question the meaning of those deaths in the canon. Is death inconsequential when the fictional world can be rewritten to bring anyone back? Peter David, best known for his 12-year run on Marvel's *The Incredible Hulk*, argues that this doesn't have to be the case if you can convince the audience of its gravitas[1]. At the very least, Oliver Queen's death was certainly more noticeable that other deaths, missing from the pages of DC Comics for over five years. So rather than simply ask what his death meant, which is largely covered in the previous chapter concerning the legacy of Connor Hawke, instead we should be asking what his *resurrection* represents. It fell to two writers from outside the comics industry – filmmaker Kevin Smith

---

[1] David, P. (2006). *Writing for Comics with Peter David* (p. 87). Cincinnati, Ohio: Impact Books.

and novelist Brad Meltzer – to begin the exploration of Ollie's new life. During this time, Green Arrow is cast as a returned saint, but just as importantly as a man who now had to live with the uncovered sins of his life.

The weight of Oliver Queen's death was accentuated by the absence of an ongoing Green Arrow series on the DC Comics roster. As early as February 1998, at least six months prior to the cancellation of Chuck Dixon's *Green Arrow* series, it was announced that Kevin Smith would be writing Green Arrow "sometime in the future."[2] As Dixon's *Green Arrow* was wrapping up its run, Smith's relaunched *Daredevil* for Marvel (with artists Joe Quesada and Jimmy Palmiotti) was already making positive waves. The 8-issue arc, 'Guardian Devil', remains one of the clearest examples of blind lawyer Matt Murdoch's constant struggle with his Catholic guilt, the kind of classic take Frank Miller, Ann Nocenti or Mark Waid's seminal runs played with. This spirituality and Catholicism didn't just make their way into *Dogma*, a film Smith was also wrapping up at this time, but his eventual Green Arrow run as well. *Green Arrow* editor Darren J. Vincenzo remarked in the back-matter for the Dixon's Green Arrow finale that the decision was made to relaunch the entire book for Smith's DC Comics debut. "He's already mapped out what he wants to do with his first story arc (which is, as I write this, planned to be a Prestige Format miniseries)... But, schedules being what they are, the relaunch cannot happen on the heels of this series."[3] The Prestige Format evaporated over the next few years, as seasons went by without any sign of the book. With Connor Hawke as the default archer, Green Arrow had returned to his days of existing in other people's books, prominently appearing in *Green Lantern* and Dixon's own *Robin* series. In a November 1999 online chat with fans to promote *Dogma*, a full year after the cancellation of *Green Arrow*, a fan asked whether we would see the book in 2000[4]. "I'm going to start writing *Green Arrow* very, very soon. I'm sure that DC will hold off on soliciting it until they have a good eight or nine issues in hand.

---

[2] The quote is attributed to comics news site Newsarama, who were predominantly known as a Usenet group at this time. It is (near) contemporaneously reported on http://manwithoutfear.com/daredevil-news-1998.shtml

[3] In the "Sherwood Forum" back-matter of *Green Arrow* Vol. 2 #137 (Oct 1998).

[4] "Kevin Smith on New Jersey, fatherhood and 'Dogma.'" (12 Nov 1999). Retrieved 17 Jan 2016 from http://edition.cnn.com/SHOWBIZ/Movies/9911/12/kevin.smith.chat/index.html?_s =PM:SHOWBIZ

Apparently, I have this reputation for lateness..." The reputation got some legitimacy, as the first issue would not arrive until February 2001, another year after this comment.

The delay only served to heighten the anticipation of the return, bringing Oliver Queen back at a time when DC was beginning to wind back the legacy characters of the 1990s and glorify the heroes of the Silver Age. Smith felt confident that he could make the book a success, telling Vincenzo that "if he was ever inclined to let me take a crack at it, I'd love to write 'Green Arrow', and that I felt I could put it in the top ten."[5] Smith's typical confidence wasn't unwarranted: once editor Bob Schreck took over the book and got the process moving, Smith's *Green Arrow* Vol. 3 #1 (Apr 2001) debuted in February 2001 at No. 6 overall on the Diamond Comic Distributors charts, along with being DC's No. 1 book, and remained in the Top 10 throughout his tenure[6]. To do so, Smith took an anachronistic approach to the Battling Bowman, recalling the often goofy hard traveling days of the Denis O'Neil/Neal Adams era, the sometimes overbearing Jiminy Cricket persona he provided the Justice League throughout the 1970s, and the urban hunter of serial killers of Mike Grell's 1980s. Smith's restored Green Arrow elevated Oliver Queen to a symbol of all that was once good about the comic book world, a legacy that Connor Hawke could never hope to compare with. Yet this only represents half of the story, for this beatified Oliver Queen was a metaphorical shell, and the reunion with his soul would also require him to answer for his past sins.

Quiver Full of Hollow: Kevin Smith and the Duality of Sainthood

Smith's first Green Arrow arc is called 'Quiver', and is primarily concerned with the rebirth of Oliver Queen. Building on the pieces that Dixon had left in his final issues, the 10-issue story opens in the expected Smith style, with his beloved Superman and Batman exchanging playful and taunting banner on a rooftop. Artists Phil Hester and Ande Parks immediately set about recreating some of Oliver Queen's key moments over the course of his then 60-year history, including Hal Jordan (now transitioning between Parallax and the godlike Spectre) seemingly bringing Ollie back from the dead at his memorial

[5] Giles, K. (1 May 2001). Kevin Smith Interview. Retrieved 17 Jan 2016, from http://comicbookresources.com/?page=article&id=128
[6] Miller, J. (18 Nov 2015). "Comic Book Sales Figures for February 2001." Retrieved 19 Jan 2016 from http://comichron.com/monthlycomicssales/2001/2001-02.html

site. Discovered in a dishevelled state in a Star City back alley by Stanley Dover, an elderly gentleman who appears to be running a charitable organization for the city, Ollie returns to the streets as Green Arrow. He is unaware that any time has passed, or indeed that he was dead to the world for years, apparently only possessing his memories up to the end of his *Hard Traveling Heroes* days. As the plot plays out, we discover that Ollie's body has been restored but not his soul, and it is revealed that Dover is a practitioner of black magic who seeks to use Ollie's "hollow" shell to transfer his own soul. This separation of soul and body becomes important to discussing Oliver Queen's resurrection, as it makes the returned archer something other than genuine, raising questions as to the moral responsibility (and corresponding culpability) he must now bear for a life he doesn't initially remember.

The Oliver Queen that Smith first reveals on the final page of the first issue of his arc is a husk of his former self in a literal and figurative way. His 'uniform' is a collection of rags resembling a costume, and his hair and beard have grown to unkempt lengths. In one of Hester and Parks' clever touches, he holds aloft a Clorox Bottle Arrow, later explained to be a crude recreation of his infamous Boxing Glove Arrow. Indeed, 'crude recreation' is the most apt term here, as it accurately describes the Ollie that Hal Jordan has resurrected. As we later learn, he is neither the pre-*Crisis* Green Arrow, nor a precise version of his Silver Age counterpart thanks to the absence of his soul. Physically restored to the body of his 'glory days', he comes across as a Mr. Rogers style saint on his first night out on the town. Rescuing the teenage prostitute Mia Dearden, destined to become the new Speedy in a later issue, he delivers a morally laden monologue to the runaway: "We all made mistakes, kiddo... You only get one childhood... Don't let a soul-sniper like this clown force you to grow up before you have to..."[7] The reference to a soul is somewhat prophetic given the events of the rest of the arc, but it is Mia who quickly identifies how removed the archer's words are from reality. "The way he *talks*," she muses to Stanley Dover in *Green Arrow* Vol. 3 #3 (June 2001), "It's like he's out of *another time*, or something." Which he is for all intents and purposes, although they more accurately conclude that he is in fact "kind of *stopped in time*." Confronted with an Aquaman who is willing to kill his nemesis, and a generation of heroes he doesn't recognize, the Oliver Queen that Hal Jordan restored is one not touched by the darkening of

---

[7] In *Green Arrow* Vol. 3 #2 (May 2001).

The final page of *Green Arrow* Vol. 3 #1. Art by Phil Hester and Ande Parks. © DC
Comics.

comics in the 1980s and 1990s. He is morally superior just by virtue of having skipped over the rough patches his comrades faced.

This "walking anachronism" is, of course, explained by the nature of his rebirth, but it also presents an interesting question about the weight of Ollie's guilt. Catholic guilt is something Smith is well familiar with, having publicly expressed some version of the latent pangs of the 'lapsed' believers throughout much of his professional career. Frank Miller had always made Catholic guilt a strand of Daredevil, most notably in the thematically similar *Daredevil: Born Again*, but Smith's *Daredevil: Guardian Devil* made it a central theme[8]. While it is not as overt in Green Arrow's 'Quiver' arc, the fantastical elements of literal angels and demons vying for Ollie's body are something the two works share. Yet this Ollie is able to absolve himself initially from any guilt, Catholic or otherwise, by virtue of the disconnection with his past. Meeting Dinah Lance/Black Canary for the first time since his revival, he has no memory of the infidelities or dubious choices he made prior to their painful separation. "If I hurt you in some way, I'm sorry," he explains in *Green Arrow* Vol. 3 #6 (Sept 2001). "But you can't hold me accountable for thing I don't *remember* doing." Dinah finds this all too convenient, but it's a valid point: Smith's Oliver Queen does not yet have to deal with the aftermath of his death, as he is born anew and as close to innocent as possible. By the end of the issue, Jason Blood turns into his alter ego, the demon Etrigan, in an attempt to kill the soulless Ollie, fearing his hollow form would be too great a temptation for the demons that might want it for themselves. "Take comfort in knowing you die a hero once again, sir," he calmly argues. "Your sacrifice here saves millions of lives." Yet for the same reasons that Ollie can absolve himself from his past sins, we must once again ask whether he is in a position to make this kind of decision. Can a soulless husk be any more responsible for the future fate of the world than for the actions he can no longer remember? When Ollie learns the truth about the duality of his current existence, he asks this very question. "Am I truly a person at this point?" he ponders in *Green Arrow* Vol. 3 #8 (Nov 2001). "Without a soul, what am I really?"

---

[8] Kelley, J. (10 Dec 2014). "Kevin Smith & Joe Quesada's *Daredevil*: The Comic that Saved Marvel." Retrieved 18 Jan 2016 from http://sequart.org/magazine/52690/kevin-smith-joe-quesada-daredevil/

Essential to Ollie's acceptance of his role as a tainted saviour is this notion of duality, a recurring human idea of the separation of a body from a soul that has gone to some 'other place', one that Thomas (2014) says is "perceived as a necessary condition of survival."[9] The idea that the soul has to pass some final hurdle to achieve immortality brings us back to that Catholic guilt, or any similar belief in an 'earned' afterlife, and in *Green Arrow* Vol. 3 #7 (Oct 2001) Smith makes this mythology a central part of his canon. Hal Jordan / Spectre has rescued Ollie at the last moment, just before the Demon had his way, and Green Arrow finally gets the explanation as to the duality of his present existence. Smith's version of Paradise has the souls of real-world celebrities like Abraham Lincoln or comedian Chris Farley, along with then-deceased Flash Barry Allen and ex-Robin Jason Todd. Most importantly, the hollow Ollie comes face-to-face with the older spirit version of himself, who explains that it was his own decision for Hal to recreate him with only the memories of the best years of his life. Which changes things significantly, as it was Ollie's *choice* to create a version of himself that was divorced from the responsibility of his past. "I was trying to spare you the grief of being me," Ollie's soul explains to his recreated self. "The night I took a life. I would never be the same after that. No matter how I'd search for peace."[10] Content to live off his 'reward' in Heaven, Ollie's spirit is reluctant to join his body at first. Yet Hal/Spectre sees what is patently obvious to any casual psychologist, pointedly telling Ollie "You're in a constant state of self-denial, seeing things only in black and white... skirting your responsibilities...that's classic Ollie."

Hal's redemption story mirrors Ollie's in Smith's 'Quiver'. While Jordan would not be fully restored for another few years, in Geoff Johns and Ethan Van Sciver's six-issue *Green Lantern: Rebirth* (Dec 2004 - May 2005), Ollie's resurrection was Hal's attempt at atoning for his past sins. Following his attempts to unmake the universe as Parallax during the *Zero Hour* event, one that was ultimately stopped by Ollie's arrow to his chest, Hal was now serving penance as the Spectre. Having saved the world by reigniting the sun, extinguished by the Sun-Eater during the 1996 *Final Night* crossover, Hal's

---

[9] Thomas, J. (2014). Death in Superhero Comics: How Not to End the Story. In O. Hakola & S. Kivistö (Eds.), *Death in literature* (pp. 269-286). Newcastle: Cambridge Scholars Publishing.
[10] *Green Arrow* Vol. 3 #8 (Nov 2001)

From *Green Arrow* Vol. 3 #2. Art by Phil Hester and Ande Parks. © DC Comics.

Spectre persona was a gilded cage just as much as Ollie's heavenly "reward." Rather than being the spirit of vengeance, Hal uses his powers for redemption, including the return of Ollie. However, Ollie's soul recognizes something in Hal that he can't quite see in himself yet. "You're a couple of screw-ups' last shot at righting some wrongs," spirit Ollie explains to his hollow in *Green Arrow* Vol. 3 #8 (Nov 2001), referring to the actions of himself and Hal. "You represented the best part of [Hal's] life. He wanted that back." So wrapped up in this apparently soulless husk of Oliver Queen is the vested interests of two redemption stories, neither of whom are willing to accept full responsibility for the weight of their actions.

The importance of choice has been a recurring motif throughout Ollie's career. We saw him struggle with it during Elliot S. Maggin's mayoral saga in the 1970s. During Grell's years, the choice to be a parent was taken away from him and Dinah as the result of trauma, and he responded by taking away her choice for vengeance. Similarly, the assassin Shado robbed Ollie of the choice to be a father by effectively raping him whilst he was unconscious. When his son Connor's life is in danger lest he return, the archer recognizes that he must take the responsibility he has been dodging and *chooses* to return to his heroic life. The decision he makes in *Green Arrow* Vol. 3 #10 (Jan 2002) is rife with meaning, especially if you take the totality of Ollie's life and death into the equation. When Oliver was killed[11], he was faced with a choice: lose his arm or die to save the people of Metropolis from an explosion. The closest thing to a god on Earth at that time, Superman, left the decision up to him, and the final chapter of 'Quiver' is partly a continuation of this idea of 'free will' that was so important to Smith's film *Dogma*. It's Ollie exercising 'free will' when he leaves the confines of heaven to return to Earth, sacrificing his prize of an eternal afterlife for a mortal existence. He does so because he believes it is the morally *right* thing to do. Or as the younger 'hollow' Oliver Queen more eloquently puts it: "Grow the hell up and take some responsibility here! You weren't here for him then, and you're not here for him now. Be a man, Ollie! For God's sake!" Parallels for long-time readers can be seen in Ollie's departure from the monastery back in *The Flash* Vol. 1 #219 (Jan 1973), and it's probably no coincidence that this is precisely the moment where 'hollow' Ollie's memories stop. Yet if further evidence was needed to suggest that this choice was about

---

[11] Back in *Green Arrow* Vol. 2 #101 (Oct 1995).

Oliver finally accepting some modicum of responsibility, then it's that he made the decision in order to protect his son, Connor Hawke, finally acknowledging the role of father and protector he had run from for most of his life. Indeed, "Father's Day" is the name of the issue, and the Smith's "Onomatopoeia" arc notwithstanding,[12] this acceptance sets up a number of the themes that Ollie has to deal with throughout Brad Meltzer's stories published later that year.

The Archer's Quest: Brad Meltzer and the Burden of Sin

"It all started with porn," writer Brad Meltzer quips in the afterword to the collected edition of *Green Arrow: The Archer's Quest*. Columbia Law School graduate Brad Meltzer was already a successful novelist when Green Arrow editor Bob Schrek approached him in January 2002, shortly before the end of Smith's run. Meltzer had been establishing his comic fandom for years. In his debut novel, *The Tenth Justice* (1997), character names Veidt, Kovacs and Dreiberg would be familiar to readers of Alan Moore's *Watchmen*. Sandman's Wesley Dodds and Michael Garrick (a nod to original Flash Jay Garrick) could be found in *The First Counsel* (2001). Meltzer had been reading Green Arrow comics since he was 12, and he shared a room with fellow comic book writer and future Green Arrow scribe Judd Winick during his college years. Indeed, the lead character in Meltzer's book *The Millionaires* (2002) is named Oliver. "Following Kevin Smith is like following a 500 pound gorilla," Meltzer commented before the release of *Green Arrow* Vol. 3 #16 (Oct 2002). "You're talking about someone who took a character who's been quite literally dead for years... and made him be the most popular title in the DC universe and arguably the comics universe..."[13] Nevertheless, Meltzer had his own clear vision of how he wanted Ollie's story to continue, with Oliver having to deal directly with the

---

[12] After finishing up his initially solicited 12-issue run, Smith felt as though he had one more story to tell. 'The Sound of Violence' is a 3-part arc running from *Green Arrow* Vol. 3 #13 (May 2002) to #15 (Sept 2002). Adding the first new member to his rogues gallery in years, Onomatopoeia is a serial killer targeting heroes without super-powers. He comes to Ollie's attention when he puts Connor in hospital with a bullet to the head. His signature motif is verbally imitating the sounds around him, such as the "BLAM!" of a gun. Smith would go on to reuse the villain in *Batman: Cacophony* (Nov 2008 - Jan 2009), pencilled by Walt Flanagan, as well as its sequel *Batman: The Widening Gyre* (Oct 2009 - July 2010).

[13] Blaschke, J. (21 Feb 2002). "Brad Meltzer: Revolution." SF Interview. Retrieved 19 Jan 2016 from http://revolutionsf.com/article.php?id=963

aftermath of his death for the first time. Taking inspiration from a conversation with a friend, Meltzer became fascinated with the idea of a "porn-buddy":

> When you die, your porn-buddy is the friend who goes to your house... and destroys all your porn so no one finds it. That is a beautiful idea... It's so ruthlessly brilliant. It works with any idea. And that's when it hit me. If anyone needs a "porn-buddy," it's someone with a secret identity.[14]

For if Smith's 'Quiver' was about a resurrected saint, making the choice to return to a life filled with regrets, then 'The Archer's Quest' is about the practicalities of living with past sins. What better way to delve into a discussion around the fringes of sin that to start with porn?

Smith's run marked a return to a classic version of Green Arrow for the publisher, a pattern that would follow for other books in the years to come. Following the events of "Quiver," in which the fraudulent Stanley Dover left his estate to Oliver Queen with the intent of taking over his identity, Ollie's fortune has effectively been restored and he has resumed his role as Star City protector Green Arrow. Smith had rebuilt the pieces of Green Arrow's shattered past, and now it fell to another writer to work out what to do next. "Smith has spent the last year and a half bringing Oliver Queen back from the dead," Meltzer told Newsarama in 2002. "Now I feel that it's the time to return him to his life."[15] Incorporating his "porn buddies" idea, Ollie and Clark Kent / Superman are visiting the site of Green Arrow's grave, and Clark shows him a series of photos of people who attended his funeral. One of these faces he doesn't recognize, and it turns out to be Thomas Blake, the Catman. In the course of the investigation, it is revealed that Ollie had made a deal with the villain known as The Shade prior to his death, and that if Oliver was ever to be killed, the Shade would personally take responsibility for tracking down all of Ollie's personal items so that they would not fall into the hands of enemies or be used against his loved ones. With a few items remaining for The Shade to track down, Ollie and his former sidekick Arsenal (a.k.a. Roy Harper / Speedy) commit to tracking down the final relics. Yet in the process of uncovering physical items from his past, the primary theme that Meltzer plays with is about a hero now having to deal with his past sins and mistakes in a direct way.

---

[14] Meltzer, B. (2003) A Word From Your Author. In B. Meltzer, P. Hester, & A. Parks (Authors), *Green Arrow: The Archer's Quest* (pp. 149-150). New York: DC Comics.
[15] Brady, M. (2002). "Q & A: Brad Answers All – Green Arrow." Retrieved 20 Jan 2016 from http://bradmeltzer.com/book/green-arrow/

Comics, and in particular DC Comics, have been cannibalizing their own past for decades in one way or another. Even at the birth of the Silver Age, it was revisionist takes on the Flash, Green Lantern, the Atom and Hawkman that defined the DC stable. Duncan and Smith (2009) argue that there has also been an "Era of Reiteration" since at least the 1980s, following the 50th-anniversary *Crisis on Infinite Earths*, a large number of 'Year One' projects and consciously nostalgic works like Kurt Busiek's *Marvels* (for Marvel) and Mark Waid's *Kingdom Come* – both gorgeously painted by Alex Ross – reached a "flashpoint for such nostalgia", motivated by a "desire to return to less complicated continuities."[16] By the early 2000s, it seemed that DC's primary *modus operandi* was about revisiting some of its past glories, with Sims (2010) identifying an industry "running on nostalgia rather than innovation, moving backwards instead of moving forwards."[17] Kevin Smith's "Quiver" was a prime example of those tides of change that introduced biracial legacy characters like Connor Hawke and Kyle Rayner being turned back, and by the end of the decade old guard characters Hal Jordan and Barry Allen had joined Oliver Queen back on the podium. Writer Greg Rucka (2003) reflects that Meltzer's arc does fall within this pattern, albeit as a deliberate attempt to evoke the O'Neil/Adams Hard Traveling Heroes journey. "It *is* sentimental. But it's a sentimentalism that is perfectly appropriate, never self-indulgent, never self-aware, and most-important, never self-loathing."[18]

That said, the six issues that make up "The Archer's Quest" are a sometimes leisurely journey through the past totems of Green Arrow's existence, and are often an excuse to pull out props from the history of the character and reunite the Golden Age team of Oliver Queen and Roy Harper. He collects the Diamond Tipped Arrow and membership plaque from his first *Justice League of America* story in 1961, and the Green Lantern and Flash costume rings his then-deceased friends Hal and Barry gave him. In *Green Arrow* Vol. 3 #18 (Dec 2002), he is literally hit with the derelict Arrowcar during a fight with the hulking Solomon

[16] Duncan, R., & Smith, M. J. (2009). *The Power of Comics: History, Form and Culture*. New York: Continuum.

[17] Sims, C. (6 May 2010). "The Racial Politics of Regressive Storytelling." Retrieved 21 Jan 2016 from http://comicsalliance.com/the-racial-politics-of-regressive-storytelling/

[18] Rucka, G (2003). Afterword. In B. Meltzer, P. Hester, & A. Parks (Authors), *Green Arrow: The Archer's Quest* (pp. 149-150). New York: DC Comics.

Grundy. Meltzer freely admits to this sentimental approach when asked. "Of course *Hard Traveling Heroes. Longbow Hunters...* everything with Dinah," he reflects. "But I also loved Ollie in the JLA... Those friendships were vital to me growing up."[19] The story makes perfect sense as a post-"Quiver" piece, with forensic psychiatrist (and comic book fan) Dr. Vasilis K. Pozios (2014) arguing that nostalgia is something people turn towards after a difficult transition.[20] The repeated issue opener of "I was dead. I came back to life" reminds us of the trauma, and Dinah observes in *Green Arrow* Vol. 3 #17 (Nov 2002) that "Oliver Queen is textbook duality... And the moment he starts making jokes... is the exact moment something's digging deeper underneath."

This returns us to the duality that we began exploring upon Ollie's resurrection under Smith. Green Arrow's dissimulation did not begin with the separation of his soul from his body, nor did it end with its restoration. The aforementioned Dinah could attest to that from her many years spent cohabiting with the man in Seattle. The extent of Ollie's deception becomes apparent in the final issue of Meltzer's arc, *Green Arrow* Vol. 3 #21 (Apr 2003) when it is revealed that the real reason Ollie collected his Justice League membership plaque was to retrieve a concealed photo of himself with Connor at birth. This establishes for the first time that Ollie knew about his son's existence but chose to abandon him. As a major retcon to the canon, it could be argued that Meltzer undercut some of the good will of the character and work of previous writers. Yet Meltzer's take is entirely consistent with Green Arrow's persona, with Ollie himself recognizing his own duality. "My best enemy has always been myself. Even when I take my mask off... I'm still wearing another." He doesn't even need to justify his own deception, the resurrected saint admitting his biggest sin to himself in purely pragmatic terms. "Why do people lie? Some do it to protect... Other do it to control... And a few of us... Just can't bring ourselves to tell the truth." Ollie's final choice in the arc is to maintain the secret, and once again avoid dealing with his past head-on, purely because things are going well with Connor in the present. The arc began with a secret unveiled, and it ends once again with the same. "You're a bastard, Ollie Queen,"

---

[19] Brad Meltzer, personal interview, 29 Feb 2016. Full transcript in this book.
[20] Rogers, V. (14 Nov 2014). The Psychology, Fan Science Behind Nostalgia-Fueled Convergence and Secret Wars. Retrieved 22 Jan 2016 from http://newsarama.com/22734-the-psychology-fan-science-behind-nostalgia-fueled-convergence-secret-wars.html

he muses to himself. "You knew. You always knew. And the worst part is... it's still your secret." So Green Arrow the sinner serves a penance of his own making, carrying the burden of truth to his second grave. It's a theme that Meltzer expanded upon in the controversial *Identity Crisis* mini-series, with Green Arrow carrying the moral weight of the secrets of a past generation, his human frailties once again making him the conscience of the group.[21]

Shades of Green

For most superheroes, the very act of putting on the mask creates a split personality and a twin set of faces they must present to the world. For Oliver Queen, where the running gag of his identity being somewhat less than 'secret' has been going since at least the 1970s, his deceptions have always been closer to home. So when DC Comics spent the better part of the new millennium resurrecting its dead saints, the problem became one of what to do with the legacy characters like Connor Hawke that had replaced the "outdated" models they were now bringing back. As comic book fans, but also writers from outside the world of superheroes, Smith and Meltzer understood this contradiction. Smith had his cake and ate it too with a Silver Age swashbuckler literally trying to reconcile with a soul that had been through the darkest times of the DC Universe, and finding that a complete person came burdened with his frailties as well as his strengths. Meltzer similarly embraced the human weaknesses of Oliver Queen via a nostalgic journey, radically changing his history and perhaps reader perceptions of Ollie's integrity, yet staying true to the character all the while. This is what makes Green Arrow a perpetually moving target, his ability to never remain one thing but contradictorily stay consistent while doing it.

---

[21] See chapter 3.

Phil Hester Interview

Phil Hester began working in comics during his studies at the University of Iowa, and has since been a writer and artist for virtually every major publisher. His tenure as the artist on *Green Arrow* with inker Ande Parks stretched from 2001 to 2005, where they worked with Kevin Smith, Brad Meltzer and Judd Winick on not only bringing Ollie back from the dead, but introducing iconic new characters such as Mia Dearden, along with villains Onomatopoeia, Constantine Drakon and Brick. More recently, he has applied his writing skills to the creator-owned *Mythic* and artistically on *The Thrilling Adventure Hour Presents*, both for Image Comics. Besides *Green Arrow*, he is perhaps best known for his art on *Swamp Thing* with writers Mark Millar and Grant Morrison, and co-creating the character of El Diablo, who appears in Warner's *Suicide Squad* film.

This interview was conducted on 26 February 2016 via phone.

RICHARD GRAY: In your introduction to *Sounds of Violence*, that was in 2003, you downplay your art style there in a modest manner. You talk about it being far removed from what you thought a Green Arrow book should be. What was it about Green Arrow that you thought was so far from what you've done before?

PHIL HESTER: Well, at least what I'd done for DC before was all Vertigo. I'd drawn *Swamp Thing* for a number of years, and I'd done short stories for Vertigo. Even my near-misses there were all for the Vertigo office. I almost drew *Doom Patrol*, and I drew *Black Orchid* for a little bit. I was sort of definitely in that 'not quite mainstream' camp at DC. And to me, as a fan, Green Arrow - at least the high points of Green Arrow's artistic legacy - were all sort of photorealism based. I'm 49, and most people my age when they think of Green Arrow think of Neal Adams, and if not Neal Adams, Mike Grell who is a shade of Neal Adams. Not to downplay Mike, I love Mike. He's in the Neal Adams camp. Even people younger than me, who came along with the Connor Hawke Green Arrow, were treated to Rodolpho DiMaggio, who also had a very - photorealist isn't the right word. I don't want to say accurate, he had really good drawing chops. My drawing is very cartoony, and very graphic and very flat, and almost abstract in some ways compared to those guys. So I never saw myself as a fit into that continuum. I guess that changed after I was there. [Laughs]

RG: Speaking of getting there, you mentioned your *Swamp Thing* run, and I understand that Kevin Smith is an admirer of that run.

PH: Yeah, that's why I wound up on the book I'm sure.

RG: Do you recall how that process came to be?

PH: Kevin originally wanted Joe Quesada to draw Green Arrow, coming off of their *Daredevil* run. Just around that time, Joe got this other job running

Marvel. [Laughs] Or at least running Marvel Knights I think. So I think Kevin just went down the list of comic book artists he knew or had worked with, and I had just done a one-shot with him at Oni called *Clerks: The Lost Scene*, which was about a scene they couldn't afford to shoot for *Clerks*. We just adapted it and made a one-shot out of it. I think I was also slated to do an adaptation of an unmade screenplay for *Mallrats 2*, and that didn't work out. So I think I existed in his memory somehow, also from that Swamp Thing run. I think he actually told me he'd bought a page from that run, somehow or other. I think he just moved down his list of guys he knew and liked working with, and I was after Joe, or Duncan Fegredo or somebody. In that orbit anyway. Bob Schreck, who was our editor at the time, had sort of been a champion of mine, trying to land me work when he was at both Dark Horse and DC. And DC, I don't think, was crazy about the idea of me drawing Green Arrow. But with both Schreck and Kevin behind me, they sort of acquiesced. I think my reputation up to then, like I said, was as a Vertigo guy, and I was definitely not in that Dan Jurgens mode that was the house style at the time.

RG: It's interesting, because the design that you land on for Green Arrow is a very classic look, but in the back-matter of the trade, the *Sounds of Violence* trade, there's a lot of different variations that you go through. Can you talk me through that process of how we get from those concepts to what we saw on the finished page?

PH: I'm going to pull the curtain back on the Wizard of Oz. That was manufactured after the fact for *Wizard Magazine*. They wanted me to do, before I started work on the book, DC wanted us to do a little press about it. And *Wizard* was like 'Can you show us all the designs you went through to create Green Arrow's look?' Green Arrow's look for me is basically the Neal Adams look, just a little more - at least stylistically - streamlined. So they're like 'Well just make something up.' [Laughs] So I created a lot of different versions of what it could be, and I don't know if I did it specifically for *Wizard*, but we wound up doing some finished pieces that wound up in *Wizard* based on those. There was also probably the fact that I had a lot of downtime between when I knew I got the book, and when we actually got scripts to work on. So it's entirely possible I just was just noodling around with costume ideas before, without any request from DC that I do so. There might have just been some idle sketches, but there was never any real consideration given to changing his costume. It was always going to be the Robin Hood outfit.

RG: That's fantastic. It's a classic look, but that is something I have learned this day.

PH: And it's not the last time. Around that time, I did a couple of issues of *Ultimate Marvel Team-Up* with [Brian Michael] Bendis. And we had the Hulk in it, or Ultimate Hulk. I guess that was the first time anyone saw Ultimate Hulk, and Bendis was like 'Just do what you consider the ultimate version of the Hulk.' And I'm like, well: that's the Hulk! The guy with purple pants and green skin. So we did the story, and *Wizard* was like 'Hey, can we get some behind the scenes sketches of any alternate versions you did of the Hulk?' I didn't really, I just drew the Hulk the way the Hulk looks. For *Wizard's* sake, I did a couple of alternate takes, and now I'm sure it exists in whatever comic book trivia show lore that I did a couple of different versions of Ultimate Hulk before we landed on the one in the book, but it's actually the other way around.

RG: I'm never going to trust behind the scenes pages again.

PH: Sure. You can't trust *Wizard*, you can't trust any of that. [Laughs] You have to do all your own scholarship from now on.

RG: Well, this may be a redundant question given what you've just said, but I did notice in some of those sketches, you did have notes around "definitely not a compound" bow. Did you do any research into archery and archery equipment?

PH: Yeah, quite a bit. I think it was a point of Kevin's that we wanted to say that Ollie had the best upper body strength of a normal human in the DCU. So the idea that idea that he would use a compound bow is kind of silly. He could just use a traditional pull bow, and get the kind of pull weight that a normal person would need a compound bow to generate. Also, compound bows are so terrible to draw. It's like drawing a bicycle in every panel, it's terrible. So yeah, I did a lot of research. Also, being from the Midwest, I don't think any kid gets out of high school without a couple of months of archery from physical education. So I've shot plenty of bows and arrows, but yeah. I did load up on a bunch of books and magazines to not look totally ridiculous when it came time to draw the act of nocking and shooting the arrows.

RG: Apart from Ollie, of course, you got to create a number of new characters for the series. Mia is one of those characters you got to introduce. When you first came on board, did you go in with a sense, in designing her, that she would ultimately be the new Speedy?

PH: Yes. That was in Kevin's mind, and what we thought would happen. But at the time Kevin was really into confounding fan theories. So if people guessed a twist or turn in the book, he'd go the other way. When Mia showed up, everybody immediately started at cons and letters saying 'Oh, she's going to be Speedy.' Kevin really backed off that, and didn't do that in his run. We didn't do that until Judd's run actually. So he always intended for her to be Speedy, but when people jumped his guess, he decided forestall that for a little while, I guess, just to mess with people. [Laughs] Or just to confound expectations a little bit. So yeah, we thought that she was going to be Speedy, but it took us a couple of years to get there.

RG: So when you do eventually design the costume for Speedy, under Judd, were there certain points Judd wanted in that costume design, or were you given free rein?

PH: I was given free rein. I did quite a few versions before we landed on the one that DC accepted. I have to tell you a funny story about that. I think the year that we designed that, and the year that she came out, I only got to draw that costume in a couple of panels, because that was my last issue of Green Arrow. But still, I felt like that was what I'm leaving with, I designed this one last major character and I can go out the door. Then at the San Diego Con that year, I got to the airport and I got in a cab and I pulled up to the front. This was back when it was still crazy busy, but you could actually pull a cab up to the front of the convention center. I got out, and the very first human being that I saw when I stepped out of the cab, was a young woman cosplaying as Speedy, as that new version of Speedy. But I didn't say anything to her, because there's no way to say that without sounding like a total creep. [Laughs] 'Oh, you know I designed that outfit?' There's no cool way to say that. So I just kind of chalk that up to cosmic karma or whatever.

Yeah, we did quite a few versions. You know there's a dream sequence earlier, when she's dressed up as Speedy there? I liked that one, and I submitted that again, but DC definitely wanted a new take. We wound up with that sort of cape and cowl version, the cape and hood version I should say.

RG: On a similar topic, with Onomatopoeia, who was one of the characters you introduced in Kevin's last run on the book, he has a very simple, but enigmatic look. Did Kevin Smith come in with definite ideas about what he wanted out of that character?

PH: I would say Kevin designed that character. I mean, he never put a pencil to paper, but the way he described it was so exacting that we pretty much gave him back what he asked for. One design of that was the design we went with.

Kevin had very definite ideas about the way that character looked, and I complied with that.

RG: Jumping off from that, were there certain points where you found yourself influencing the direction of the series based on designs, or different ways you wanted the art to go?

PH: Oh, yeah. I mean, Kevin was very considerate in that regard. Right off the bat, he said 'Who do want to be in the book? What kind of guest stars do you want to draw?' Immediately I said Batman and the Demon, because everybody loves Batman, and I think my art style lends itself to drawing the Demon. So I wanted to draw the Demon, and Kevin's like 'Yeah, sure that will work.' I said I like the Spectre and Deadman too, and he said 'Yeah, we'll get all that in there.' And Kevin is a little bit younger than me, but we're in that same age group where those Alan Moore issues of *Swamp Thing*, where Swamp Thing goes to hell and tours the afterlife in his astral body, were huge, huge influencers on us. So Ollie going to heaven and meeting himself, and taking that tour of those dark corner DCU characters definitely sprang from that Alan Moore run of *Swamp Thing*. I was like, 'I want to draw all those characters please,' and we got to do that.

RG: Just because we sort of touched on it briefly there, the idea of Kevin Smith's script versus a Judd Winick script or a Brad Meltzer script. What does a Kevin Smith script look like as opposed to say somebody else you've worked with?

PH: Kevin's scripts are huge, because he sort of writes like he talks. If you've heard his podcasts, or any of his speaking engagements, he's very cogent - and when I said good, I don't mean that in any negative sense - he speaks very eloquently. But he talks a lot. [Laughs] So his scripts are very like that. He was new to writing comics, and oftentimes he would have just massive word balloons in panels. If you go back and look at the book, I think a lot of people would be shocked by how talky the book is. So yeah, we sort of had to budget for balloons. It was good for me as a storyteller, it made me more disciplined about the way I blocked shots to allow for balloons to be read in the proper order. It taught me a lot of ways to communicate clearly when I know there's going to be a lot of exposition in the dialogue, you know, what I can include or leave out for an effective panel. So it was a challenge I learned a lot from. But I don't think it impacted the book in a negative way. I think that's what people bought their tickets for. That's Kevin's strength, is his dialogue. People picked up *Green Arrow* for that snappy repartee, and it was my job to facilitate it or get out of the way when it was time for the dialogue to shine.

In Brad's case, Brad came from the world of novels. What he would write looked a lot more like letters to me. They were sort of long missives to me about the mood of the setting, and what he was trying to convey emotionally with each scene, and the dialogue that would follow. Then Judd, Judd's scripts were the easiest because Judd is also an artist. So Judd understands how much heavy-lifting I can do with the artwork. So his scripts were, I would not call them minimal, but they were more conventional in that there were stage directions and dialogue, and him trusting me to do more than Kevin or Brad. Maybe trust is the wrong word, because both guys were sort of new to comics, so I don't think it was a matter of them trusting me or not. I think it was a matter of them not being 100% sure how much they had to carry, and how much they could expect an artist to carry.

RG: Under Judd, one of the characters you got to introduce was Brick, and he's now one of a number of your characters that have made their way to the screen in *Arrow*. How do you feel about the depictions, if you're watching the shows, of some of those characters so far?

PH: It's tough to - you can't get attached to those characters, because they're going to go through so many changes on their way to the screen that they're sort of not yours by the time that they're there. In a way, it's like, I can't remember who described it. Maybe it was Steve Rude. I think it was Steve Rude when he was talking about a run of Nexus where they had a lot of fill-in artists. Like fantastic fill-in artists, like Mike Mignola, Paul Smith. I think later he admitted to not having read those issues, because it was like seeing somebody else going out with your girlfriend. [Laughs] And in a way, once I was done with *Green Arrow* for a long time, even though I'm a fan of Tom Fowler and Tom's my friend, but I didn't read it right away when Tom was drawing the book. It's kind of a little bit painful, and I'm not going to do that. That's sort of the way I feel about the TV show too. I think the TV show is really well made. I'm not a regular watcher, but I think it's really cool. It's a little bleaker and more hard-edge than I think Green Arrow probably should be. I think *The Flash* show has a closer tone to what I think the Green Arrow show should probably be, but what do I know? They're both big ratings hits.

Yeah, the way they're depicted. I don't worry about the way they're depicted once they're out of my hands. I'm going through that again with *Suicide Squad* having a version of El Diablo I co-created in it. It doesn't look at all like him, but it's definitely based on the Chato Santana version. I just have to go with the flow [Laughs]. There's no use fighting it.

RG: Is *13 Steps* still happening?

PH: Well, it was optioned and then a teleplay was written by Javier Grillo-Marxuach, who worked on *Lost* and works on *The 100*. He's a super talented writer, and he really got the characters and everything. The teleplay is really cool, but it did not get picked up by Sony who optioned it in the first place. But it's been optioned again, but we'll see if something happens with that. I don't count on any of that stuff until the check actually clears the bank, then it's for real.

RG: I should say that when I've been talking about your designs, and your artwork, I'm of course talking - particularly in the case of Green Arrow - of a longtime collaboration with Ande Parks. How did that come about?

PH: Ande and I have known each other since probably right after college. The Midwest, well you know from living in Australia, that people from Europe don't understand how big our countries are. How far away everything is. [Laughs] To be local is like a three-hour drive, that's local - and three hours in Europe can take you across ten countries. So the quote-unquote "comics scene" in the Midwest goes from Minneapolis to Chicago to Kansas City to Omaha, you know, to St. Louis. It's huge. So even though I'm from Iowa and Ande's from Kansas, we're sort of part of the same comics scene. I met him at a Kansas City convention, and we're both about the same age, and we both had the same appreciation for - this is about the time of the Image Revolution - and both Ande and I had an appreciation for older, more classic cartoonists. We're both fans of Wally Wood, and Jack Kirby and Will Eisner and Mike Ploog. You know, throwback guys. It wasn't even a reaction to what was hot at the time, it was just what we appreciated. So we seemed to share similar aesthetics, so we started doing fanzine work together at the time. We did a couple of series here and there for some indie publishers. Then Ande got work at DC before me, inking Catwoman over Jim Balent, which was not like an aesthetic fit for him. At that same time, I started doing Swamp Thing. Kim DeMulder was inking me, and that wasn't necessarily an aesthetic fit for me. So we were sort of like these star-crossed lovers that were separated by fate. It took *Green Arrow* for us to be united on a big showcase book, and I'm glad that happened because our partnership has been pretty constant since we were in our early 20s, it's just that nobody knew about it until we hooked up on Green Arrow.

RG: Are those kind of collaborations important in comics, and is it a different thing when you're working with a rotating roster, for example?

PH: I think it's important. Like I said, we share similar aesthetics so we had the same goal in mind when we set out to do a page together. Again, I'm in love with the romance - [Laughs] however limited it may be - I'm in love with the romance of the cartoonists life. Part of that was growing up with [Joe] Sinnot and Kirby, [Neal] Adams and [Tom] Palmer, you know [Joe] Simon and Kirby. You know, those duos meant a lot to me. To be a part of a duo like that was like carrying on that legacy, and I still feel that way and I'm glad we did it. Of course, since then, lately, Ande's become a very prolific writer and semi-retired from inking. I've done more writing lately than drawing, but I'd always welcome the chance to work with him again.

RG: Just as a sidebar on that topic, do you have a preference at this stage in your career for writing over pencilling?

PH: Not to be snarky, but writing is a lot easier. [Laughs] I don't mean in terms of it being less creative, or less intellectually demanding, but it's less physically demanding. You know, I'm not up at three in the morning bent over a drawing table writing scripts. You can type a car chase in five minutes, and a car chase takes five days to draw. So there's definitely a difference in the amount of labor required. Ideally, I'd like to find a project where I'm suited to do both at the same time on the same book, but it just hasn't worked out that way too often, except a few indie projects. I think most editors and publishers see me as one or the other, but that's okay as long as they see me as one *of* the other, you know? [Laughs] One of the two is fine, as long as I can become gainfully employed I'm ok. They both have different challenges and rewards and I enjoy both, but one's a little less taxing. Especially, I'm a family man, so the time you spend with your family as an artist is limited because you have to be holed up in your studio more. So to let go of that a little bit to write was very helpful to me.

RG: Just bouncing off something you've said there, talking about the difficulties between the two styles there, do you recall throughout that lengthy run you did, was there a particularly challenging piece of art that really pushed you throughout that *Green Arrow* run?

PH: To me the only really big challenge, at least during Kevin's run, the biggest challenge was, again, dealing with how much dialogue there was on each page and how much ground we were trying to cover story-wise. It's kind of a compressed story, actually. During Brad's run, the challenge for me was - I think what's most engaging about Brad's run - is that he really contrasts the mundane aspects of Ollie sort of trying to hold his normal family together, and contrasting that with the bizarre superhero adventures he'd get on. So, in one scene you're drawing him in a fist-fight with Solomon Grundy, and then in the next you're showing him looking for puppies at the pound with his son. So, that was the challenge of Brad's run. I think the challenge of Judd's run was that the cast expanded a lot during Judd's run, and there were a lot more people to draw. Making them distinct is difficult for me, because my work is stylized. Again, I don't draw photo realistically so trying to find different looks for every character that walked in through the book was a challenge for me.

RG: We're talking here about three different writers you worked with over that run. Judd was, of course, on it for a very long time. I believe you were on there for about 40 issues. Was the intention going in ever to stay that long?

PH: Oh, yeah. Ande and I were both of the same mind when we left. It was our choice. I think when we started, DC wasn't ecstatic about the fact we were on the book. Then by the time we left, they were sort of shocked that we would want to leave. It didn't have anything to do with the work we were doing with Judd, which was satisfying, it's just that we were sick of drawing the same character for four years and we were ready to draw something else. We were a little bit restless, because at one point during Kevin's run there was talk of - and boy, I wish this would have happened because I'd have a swimming pool right now - there was talk of us leaving *Green Arrow* as a team, and moving on to a Batman book. Like a lot of things with Kevin, he gets out over his skis a little bit, because he gets really enthusiastic about something, and something else draws him away. During the peak of our *Green Arrow* run, we thought we were going to leave 'Sound of Violence' and go do a *Brave and the Bold* revival. It was going to be Batman teaming up with whoever Kevin wanted to write, and we wanted to draw. It would have been awesome, it didn't work out that way. So by the time of our fourth year on *Green Arrow* rolled around we were kind of like 'we want to see what else we can do' at DC or Marvel, but probably at DC. We wound up moving over to *Nightwing* from *Green Arrow*. Which I guess was sort of a Bat-book [Laughs], close to a Bat-book. So we were okay with it.

RG: There were so many cameos from Batman in Kevin's run, it was practically a Bat-book for a while.

PH: It was! You know, it was for a while, and that's what made us so charged up about going and doing a Bat-book afterwards. Also, we thought that's going to be a license to print money. If Kevin could make *Green Arrow* DC's Number One book, what's he going to do for Batman?

RG: Just on that, coming in [Kevin] was very confident about making that a top ten book, and it very much hadn't been prior to that. What were your impressions of Green Arrow coming into the book?

PH: I was always a fan, but I have always been a fan of underdog characters. My favourite superhero is Ragman. I love Swamp Thing. I love Stalker. I love the things that are never long for this world. Seriously, the only really popular characters that I like are Spider-Man and Batman. Otherwise, I like the weirdos. So I think at the time, Doug Mahnke was drawing Justice League – and Doug's from the Midwest like I am – and we were at a convention once. Doug has that more European look to his work, a little more Moebius or Enki Bilali than a normal superhero artist. We were at some banquet or something, and we were looking at each other like "Can you believe we're drawing DC's one and two books? Us?" It's weird. It was sort of the dawn of the writer age, also. That's when writers really started moving the needle more than artists, around 2000. Also, it was kind of a nadir for sales. We were DC's number one book and we were probably selling about 120,000. Even today, a Star Wars book will sell a quarter of a million copies. Matt Wagner teased us once, we were at his house, and I said, "Man, this is a nice house." He was like, "*Batman/Grendel!*" He was like, "Yeah, royalties from *Batman/Grendel* paid for this." At the time, we got a royalty cheque for *Green Arrow* #1 that was like five grand. We thought that was great, because we didn't know any better. He slapped us on the back and he was like, "You guys picked the wrong time to have DC's number one book." Thanks, buddy. I have to say, DC's royalty system is so fantastic. I make money from *Green Arrow* every year. Not a lot, but you know, a nice little Christmas bonus every year from *Green Arrow*.

RG: It probably helps that they keep republishing it. There was that beautiful Absolute Edition that came out late last year.

PH: I was happy to see that. Also, there are a couple of goofs in the original run, even in the collections of the original run, that we finally got a chance to correct with this Absolute Edition. Maybe I'm the only person who knows about the goofs, and I'm the only person who knows about the corrections, but it eases my mind that they're actually in there now.

RG: Would you like to unburden and share about them?

PH: Well, there's a sequence in 'Sound of Violence' that has previously been printed out of order. There's a two-page scene where Ollie is in the operating room watching Connor being operated on, and he's in the observation theatre, and there were two pages printed out of order. Nobody caught it, and it kept getting reprinted that way and finally it got fixed. Also, there were some coloring errors in the way the Demon was depicted throughout the run that we finally got to fix. So yeah, those were kind of little nagging things that got stuck with me.

RG: I'm going to be scrambling to go back and check that now.

PH: Well, in the earlier editions, Guy Major colored the Demon as if he were shirtless. So his chest was always yellow, but he still had the red cuffs. I kept going 'Man, he's got a shirt on in all of these.' Oh yeah, we'll get to that. We were in such a rush on that book because Kevin, of course, is notorious now for being late with scripts. I don't think its necessarily about he's late or lazy or anything like that, I think it's that he's got so much stuff going on. He was making film... so we'd get scripts when we got them. So the idea of going back and making sure the Demon was colored properly was pretty low on the priority list.

RG: You got a chance to return to kind of a version of Green Arrow in the *Arrow* and *Flash* tie-in comics. How different was the approach to the character then?

PH: I just treated it like it was a completely different character, because physically he's different and the continuity's so different. I treated it like it wasn't my Oliver Queen. It's easy to do on that Flash and Green Arrow book. The Flash book itself is a different continuity, it's the TV continuity. It was an easier separation to make, but it was fun to draw him again, although a different version. And I'd done a cover for that book also, the *Arrow* book, in the past. It's a cool costume. It's actually, I think, a more - I don't want to run anybody down - but I think that TV costume is actually a more iconic costume than the New 52 costume.

RG: It definitely has a lot more DNA with say, Grell's run than it does with the New 52.

PH: It's simpler. The New 52 one is a nightmare to draw.

RG: Have you had a crack at that one at all, the New 52 version?

PH: Just for fans. Just for commissions at shows and stuff. I'm like, 'Boy oh boy, can I just draw the Robin Hood one, or at least the *Longbow Hunters* one? Help me out here.'

RG: When you're illustrating from a source, like those TV shows, do you feel obligated to be faithful to the look of the human cast? Or is it more interpretive than that?

PH: We were told we didn't have to be, as long as it was in the spirit of the cast. You know. Nobody had likeness approval, which is a bugaboo for a lot of artists, certain actors have likeness approval. They can make you redraw something a hundred times, but they didn't have any of those agreements in place, at least on *The Flash* book that I worked on. So nothing I drew had to look exactly like the actors, but it had to be in the ballpark.

RG: Speaking of designs, Green Arrow has had some significant redesigns as we've spoken about - the New 52 costume you've just mentioned. Do you ever look at those costumes and start tinkering in your own mind what you would do differently?

PH: Oh, yeah because I'm a nerd, so I'm still doing the same thing I did when I was 13 and drawing my version of Iron Man in my algebra notebook. I still do that in the back in my mind. I think you'll find every artist has quote-unquote "their take" on every character. I definitely have a dream take on Green Arrow or Superman or Spider-Man or any of these iconic characters. I sort of have an idea in the back of my head of how I'd handle them differently.

RG: Do we have to wait for the equivalent of a *Wizard* article to look at your alternate concept sketches?

PH: Yeah. [Laughs] I'll have to make up more back-matter. I'll have to invent more back-matter.

RG: I asked you a little while ago about what your view of Green Arrow was going into the book. Now that you've had an extended stay on the character, and had some time away from it, how did your view of the character change in that period?

PH: It's tough to say, because I think the writers I worked with shared my view of him. That he was sort of this irascible but loveable rogue, but a guy who would always do the right thing. He was sort of the Han Solo of the DC Universe, but also at the same time a very conscientious person. Even in Frank Miller's *Dark Knight Returns*, he's that person. He's that grumpy conscience of the DCU. I think that stayed intact throughout all the runs I worked on, that character. There was also this idea that he was sort of like the John Wayne of liberalism. [Laughs] You know? He was still a Pinko, but the kind that would eat meat, wear leather jackets and sleep around a lot. He was kind of a John F. Kennedy Democrat. Yeah, I think everybody I worked with on the book shared those kind of feelings about Oliver Queen. Of course, you know with the television show and the further iterations of the character, some of that stuff comes and goes. But I think with at least people my age, that's almost set in stone.

An alternate approach to Green Arrow for the cover of TV tie-in *Arrow* #3. Art by Phil Hester and Eric Gapstur. © DC Comics.

RG: I guess to pull this all together, is there a moment throughout those 40 issues that you're most proud having produced and given to the world?

PH: Yeah. Ok, this is so inside baseball. The day I decided to be a comic book artist for real, came when I was probably 12 years old, or 13. The Frank Miller *Daredevil* issue where Daredevil fought the Hulk. I don't know if you know the issue I'm talking about, it's called 'Blind Alley.' I actually own a page from it. I saved up, as soon as I got into comics, I saved up my money and bought an original page from that, because that issue meant a lot to me. Brad knew that, and he's like, "You know what, I'm going to give you an issue like that." That was the issue of Green Arrow where he fought Solomon Grundy for basically an issue. He let me choreograph a lot of that, and to me it had the spirit of that "Blind Alley" issue of *Daredevil*. So it was a way of me connecting with my [Laughs] origins as a comic book artist. When I read that issue of *Daredevil*, I thought this is what I really, really want to do, and I'm going to try to do this. 20 years later, I got to actually pay homage to that.

Brad Meltzer Interview

Columbia Law School graduate Brad Meltzer was already a successful novelist when he succeeded Kevin Smith as the writer on *Green Arrow*. With his political thrillers *The Tenth Justice* and *The First Counsel*, he showed a lifelong comic book fandom, naming his characters after characters from *Watchmen* and the original Justice Society of America. Following his Green Arrow run, Meltzer delivered one of the most powerful post-9/11 musings in comic with *Identity Crisis*, an often controversial murder mystery in which Oliver Queen was one of the chief protagonists, and the conscience of the Justice League. Since then, Meltzer has worked on *Justice League of America* (for which he won an Eisner Award) and *Buffy the Vampire Slayer* in comics, launched a series of children's books, a TV series called *Decoded* and continued to release more bestselling novels.

The following interview was conducted via email on 19 February 2016.

RICHARD GRAY: You have always been very open about your lifelong comic fandom. Indeed, your novels namecheck characters from *Watchmen*, Sandman and in *The Millionaires*, Ollie himself. As a fan and reader, what was your impression of Green Arrow as you were growing up?

BM: Activist. Hothead. Unafraid. Stubborn. That was all I needed. I never saw anything like him. He was a fully formed conscience.

RG: In 2002, you were known primarily as a novelist. How did you first come to be involved with the Green Arrow series?

BM: Bob Schreck. For years, I'd been hiding comic book references in all my novels. The character in *The Millionaires* was even named Ollie. Then DC editor Bob Schreck noticed. At the time Kevin Smith was leaving *Green Arrow*, and it was the number-one-selling superhero book for DC. So Bob came to me and said, "If we bring in another comic writer, everyone's going to go, 'Where's Kevin Smith?' But if we bring *you* in, you may sell some novels, but nobody knows you in comics." I know it sounds crazy now, but back then, no one was coming from different mediums and going into comic books except for Kevin, God bless him. And Bob said, "Would you be interested in coming in? You'll either fail on a big stage or you'll succeed on a big stage." And I said, "I'll take that shot."

RG: You once described the success of Smith's run as "like following a 500 pound gorilla." Did you feel any sense of pressure at the time? Did you ever get the opportunity to confer with Smith about the baton pass?

BM: Kevin was pure class. I hadn't even met him yet – he hadn't read a thing I'd done – but he went out and told everyone: "I can't wait to read Meltzer's run, and you should read it too." That's the definition of class. But did I feel pressure? It was their #1 book and I'd never written a comic. I was never more terrified, never more excited.

RG: For your arc, you returned Green Arrow to life, but did so with his warts and all. It strikes me that few other DC characters could get away with being this consistently flawed. How do you feel Green Arrow compares with other characters in this regard?

BM: That's the best part of Ollie. Bruce, Clark and Diana can be on their pedestals. But Ollie is always flawed, always half-wrong, always half-right, and always half-cocked -- and therefore always like us. Today, we're seeing a few more characters like him. I still maintain they've veered Tony Stark into Ollie's well worn territory. But Ollie was the first.

RG: The original rough pitch of 'The Archer's Quest' was a four issue series. When did the decision get made to extend it, and what changed? For example, I see that Ollie's "big secret" about Connor is dropped in the penultimate issue instead.

BM: When I started, I just said "Four issues." I had no idea how pacing worked in a comic. And then when I started, I fell in love a bit more each day. Bob was kind enough to put up with me as it unfolded. I always knew the ending. I just didn't realize how much more character work I wanted to do along the way.

RG: The road-trip motif reads as a tip of the feathered cap to *Hard Traveling Heroes*, and you cover a lot of nostalgic ground in 'The Archer's Quest.' Were there any particular past arcs or stories that were narrative touchstones for you?

BM: Of course *Hard Traveling Heroes*. *Longbow Hunters*. And c'mon... everything with Dinah. Even old Wolfman/Perez Titans stories for some great Roy cameos. All the obvious haunts. I always loved the Roy dynamic. But I also loved Ollie in JLA, when his best fights and moments were with his fellow Leaguers. If Barry and Hal were best pals... and Ollie and Hal were best pals, well... that dynamic meant Ollie and Barry have a shared friendship (and competitive side) too. Those friendships were vital for me growing up.

RG: The big revelation of Ollie's true relationship with Connor changes the way we look at Chuck Dixon's run, and perhaps the ones before it, yet it still feels completely in line with the flawed Ollie. Were there any alternative editorial directions that came up in preliminary discussions?

BM: Not about Connor. DC was completely supportive on that. They knew Ollie was capable of it – and it fit with his M.O.: making a grand decision that blows up in his face.

RG: By the end of "Archer's Quest," Ollie is left with a secret, but also with a family. It feels like a mixed emotional ending. Where did you feel the next chapter in Ollie's life/career would progress?

BM: I knew Judd was coming, so I wasn't worried. If Kevin was bringing Ollie back from the dead, my only goal was to bring him back to his life. He had to find family again. To me, when Ollie forgets that, that's when he gets lost.

RG: Speaking of burdens, having read through 75 years' worth of Green Arrow, there was a point where Ollie becomes the conscience of the Justice League. Was that one of the driving factors of *Identity Crisis*?

BM: He's *always* the conscience of the Justice League. Show me anyone who fought, argued, kicked and screamed more at his fellow members. Indeed, one of the things I really wanted to focus on in *Identity Crisis* was his long animosity with Hawkman. In the 70s, I believed them hating each other just for politics. But as I got older, their disagreement couldn't just be about Democrat/Republican. Their venom and animosity needed to come from something far deeper.

RG: Although published a few years later, is it fair to say that *Identity Crisis* is a response to post-9/11 world?

BM: That was the goal. Dan DiDio said to me: "After 9/11, remember how we felt about all first responders? We were worried that every time a police officer or firefighter put on their uniform, they might die." Dan asked if I could bring that feeling back to the DC Universe: that when our heroes put on their costumes, we'd be worried they weren't coming back.

RG: *Identity Crisis* had its own set of revelations and shocks. One major site claimed that "every hero comes out of *Identity Crisis* looking like a jerk, a victim or a pariah." As a fan of comics yourself, how do you feel about the book being held up by some critics as one of the examples of the darkening of comic books?

BM: It's consistently been on the worst comics ever list, best comics ever list, and top selling comics ever list. But the best and most consistent thing I hear is simply this: *Identity Crisis* is the book that brought me into comics. There's no better compliment than that.

RG: You continued your association with Team Arrow by including Black Canary and the renamed RoyHarper/Red Arrow on your *Justice League of America* run. What qualities did they bring to your version of the League?

BM: I wanted that Green Arrow/Green Lantern/Canary dynamic back. But I didn't want to simply pull out the past and keep it stagnant. I could've written

Roy, Hal and Dinah for 10 more years on that book. And Hawkgirl mixed in there too.

RG: Having now contributed several major Green Arrow works to the canon, has your view of the character changed from your earlier recollections?

BM: Ollie is one of the few character that, like Batman, the deeper you dig, the more you find. And not just about Ollie. About yourself.

RG: If you returned to comics, do you think you have any more stories to contribute to the modern version of the Emerald Archer?

BM: For. Sure.

Not Dying, Living: Judd Winick and the Return of Relevant Comics

There was nothing inherently political or rebellious about Green Arrow when he was created. "Oliver Queen was born with a silver spoon in his mouth," reads Judd Winick's character description in *Green Arrow* Vol. 3 #47 (Apr 2005). "He was the very definition of a millionaire playboy." The product of elitism, the millionaire (and later billionaire) playboy was personal friends with the police commissioner and other captains of industry alike throughout the Golden Age. Although initially a far cry from the Robin Hood outlaw archetype that he was partly based on, it was this same myth that Denis O'Neil and Neal Adams drew upon when reworking Ollie Queen as the loudmouthed conscience of the Justice League. It was such a good fit that the scourge of 'fat cat' businessmen everywhere became defined by this trait over the years, argumentative on every point and principled to a deadly fault. Yet while the character maintained a conscious politicization during the subsequent decades, and his life under Elliot S. Maggin and Mike Grell in particular intersected with the hot button issues of the day, few had channeled their own world views so directly into Green Arrow as O'Neil's journalistic approach. At least, that is, until Judd Winick took over the helm in 2003 and focused Ollie's outrage into personal and universal relevance. "Judd is Oliver Queen," artist Phil Hester told

Italy's *Amazing Comics*. "I tease him that if John Wayne were a liberal he would be Judd."[1]

Writer and cartoonist Judd Winick first came to the attention of the wider public after appearing on the early reality show, *The Real World: San Francisco* in 1994. As one of the housemates, it was there that he met Pedro Zamora, an AIDS positive educator and activist. Their friendship and Zamora's death later formed the basis of the beautiful and heartbreaking graphic novel, *Pedro and Me*, released in 2000 and winning Winick his first GLAAD award, an Eisner nomination and several other notable awards.[2] Influenced from an early stage in his career by Kyle Baker's *Why I Hate Saturn* and the Berke Breathed *Bloom County* works, Winick shifted his focus away from superheroes for a short time. His meta-series *The Adventures of Barry Ween, Boy Genius* (Oni Press, 1999 – 2002) garnered Winick a dedicated fan base, before moving into more mainstream fare with DC's Green Lantern. Yet in the 36 issues he wrote between 2000 and 2003, Winick never stopped making socially relevant comics. In *Green Lantern* Vol. 3 #137 (June 2001), a character reveals he is gay to Lantern Kyle Rayner, speaking about the rift it had created with his parents. Later, Winick tackles homophobia more directly in 'Hate Crime' in *Green Lantern* Vol. 3 #154 (Nov 2002), when Kyle Rayner's gay friend is brutally attacked and left for dead.

Taken as a whole, Winick's Green Arrow stories are a rollercoaster of an action yarn that rarely give the heroes a break, but they are rarely apolitical. Following a short crossover run with *Green Lantern*, with Ben Raab swapping over temporarily on the writing duties for *Green Arrow*, Winick became the regular writer for the archer with *Green Arrow* Vol. 3 #26 (July 2003) through to the renamed *Green Arrow and Black Canary* Vol. 1 #14 (Jan 2009). In Winick's debut issue, Ollie and Jefferson Pierce (a.k.a. Black Lightning) joke about being on different sides of politics, while Ollie sympathizes with saboteurs who are trying to stick it to the "corporate sacks of pus" who use immigrant labor for their urban redevelopment plans. Winick's second arc, 'City Walls,' returns to a

---

[1] Guarino, D. (15 Oct 2003). *Amazing Comics* - Phil Hester interview - English Edition. Retrieved 26 Jan 2016 from http://amazingcomics.it/interview_phil_hester.htm

[2] GLAAD is short for the Gay and Lesbian Alliance Against Defamation. Other awards for *Pedro & Me* included several American Library Association (ALA) citations and the 2000 *Publisher's Weekly* prize for Best Book to name a few.

theme of the 'evil that men do' as a mystical barrier goes up around the Star City limits and summons demons whenever a crime is committed. In the face of an uncaring automated response to crime and punishment, Ollie must partner with mobsters and crooked cops alike to take down the threat, and it is Winick's first indication that his Ollie may be willing to get his hands dirty to justify his means to an end. It's a recurring theme throughout Winick's run, especially as he leads into Ollie's mayoral tenure, when Green Arrow experiences yet another reinvention to reflect the realities of the world around him. It's also an acknowledgment on the part of Winick that while his politics mirror the experiment in 'relevant' comics of the 1970s, it's a far more complex landscape that the character now inhabits. "A few *fascist* politicians or a freakshow *dictator* are looking *pretty* good to me right now," Ollie muses in *Green Arrow* Vol. 3 #37 (June 2004). "*Those* cast I can handle."

As the successor to Kevin Smith's resurrected saint and Brad Meltzer's flawed sinner, Winick is one of the most prolific and sustained writers of Green Arrow stories outside of Grell's epic arc in the 1980s and 1990s, and while his work is invariably action-packed, it is never anything less than infused with socially relevant undercurrents. Even when facing down giant troll-like monsters, Winick was commenting on corporate responsibility and undocumented workers. As Black Canary and Green Arrow started down the long road to the altar, Ollie would have to break the cycles of distrust he had built around himself for decades. Before Mia Dearden would become Speedy, she would face being a teenager with HIV. In this chapter, three threads from Winick's run are examined to tease out Ollie's role as an educator, as a political actor as he once again throws his hat into the mayoral race, and as the partner in crime of Black Canary.

Wanting to Fight: The Education of Green Arrow

Some of the most important developments in the Winick era concerned the character of Mia Dearden, who was destined to be the new Speedy since Kevin Smith first introduced her. Just as Green Arrow had taken on the role of teacher to Green Lantern in the 1970s, and Roy Harper / Speedy had in turn schooled Ollie about the realities of drug users, Mia became a mouthpiece for educating readers and Green Arrow alike about HIV and the AIDS virus. Following the conclusion of 'City Walls,' in which Mia's first outing in the field results in her having to choose to kill a man to save the city, Ollie can't help but see parallels with his own choices. "This young woman who I drew close to me... *solely* to give her a new life... only to *protect* her. And I made her a *murderer*."[3] In the 'New Blood' story arc that follows, the former teenage prostitute and drug user tests positive for HIV. At first she tries to shrug it off, but over the course of many issues, we get to witness her personal growth and that of her adopted family. The comic book issues ring true, echoing some of the biography that Winick had illustrated for his friend Pedro Zamora.

Mia Dearden continues the educational work of Zamora, with Winick now having the advantage of a broader comic book audience to speak with. The subject of HIV education had been close to Winick's heart since his earliest work, and the *Green Arrow* Vol. 3 #44 (Jan 2005) issue and storyline gained international attention and mainstream news coverage. The cover is a melancholy portrait of Mia, surrounded by a dominant white background. Beneath her profile shot are the lowercase words "h.i.v. positive" highlighted in red, with the creator names beneath it in black. The simplicity of the cover belies the weight of the issues-based narrative, one that covers a lot of ground in a short period of time. During an interview with CNN, Winick noted that his Green Arrow story was still a human tale at its core. "We're telling a story about a horrible situation and someone rising above it."[4] Like Zamora, Mia is tested positive at the age of 17, and makes the decision to deliver a speech to her fellow students at a school assembly. It mirrors a scene that Winick selected for inclusion in 2000's *Pedro and Me*. In the latter, Zamora is quoted as saying "I am here to tell you that you should be *very* frightened of AIDS, not people living with AIDS... I am not dying. I am *living* with AIDS. *Living*." Mia repeats these words almost verbatim in *Green Arrow* Vol. 3 #45 (Feb 2005). "I'm not someone you should be scared of," she tells the assembly. "You should be *very* frightened of AIDS, not *people* with AIDS. I'm still me. *HIV* has changed many things in my life, but it *hasn't* changed who and what I am. *I'm still me*." Here we see Mia quite literally taking on the role of Zamora, educating both the reader and Ollie at the same time. Throughout the arc, the dialogue covers T-cell counts, the differences between HIV and AIDS, viral loads, combination drug therapy and the cost of insurance in America. As Polite Dissent (2004) suggests in their

---

[3] *Green Arrow* Vol. 3 #40 (Sept 2004). It is the first issue of the 'New Blood' story arc that runs until *Green Arrow* Vol. 3 #45 (Feb 2005).
[4] Marquez, M. (Presenter) & Winick, J. (Guest). (23 Oct 2004). *CNN Live Saturday* [TV episode]. Atlanta, Georgia: CNN.

From *Green Arrow* Vol. 3 #45. Art by Phil Hester and Ande Parks. © DC Comics.

medical-based analysis of the issue, the details are right, even if Winick leans towards being overly didactic in a handful of moments.[5]

The parallel role that Mia adopts by the end of the issue is in formally becoming Green Arrow's sidekick and the new Speedy. Artists Phil Hester and Ande Parks, on their last issue since becoming the regular artists under Kevin Smith, update the red costume with a yellow cape and cowl, firmly bringing the Green Arrow / Speedy partnership into the new Millennium. Ollie, counter to his liberal leanings, has a tough time dealing with Mia's diagnosis, undoubtedly mirroring his poor reaction to his former ward Roy Harper being "a junkie." No longer content with sitting idly by on the sidelines, Mia argues that "Whatever time I have... however long that may be... I want to do the thing that is the *most* important to me." In a beautiful moment of transmogrification, the superhero metaphorically steps off the page to become real, as a fictional character becomes the representative not just for the AIDS cause in the DC Universe, but as an avatar for Pedro Zamora. Winick simply stated in the aforementioned CNN interview, "I figured one hero story should follow another." Continuing to play out this story, while the action oriented saga of the super-powered mob overlord Brick remained the overarching narrative, Winick puts the story first by ultimately making Speedy's seroconversion another aspect of her character. Speaking with Conan (2004) for World AIDS Day, Winick discussed the parallels between superheroes and advocacy:

> We write it with the 14-year-old and the 45-year-old in mind. We write it so that a younger reader will understand it, and take it in, but also write above them... Truly what are superhero stories about? They are about fighting evil, they're about beating the bad guys and they're about our heroes overcoming obstacles, and what could be a greater obstacle than a young woman who's facing a life threatening illness, and to turn around and want to do good? To want to fight, and want to try and help the world.[6]

Yet neither Winick nor Mia wishes to simply use her medical condition as a defining trait. In *Green Arrow* Vol. 3 #46 (Mar 2005), Ollie gets Mia to join the Teen Titans, a junior Justice League with a long history of sidekick membership.

---

[5] Polite Dissent. (19 Dec 2004). Retrieved 1 Feb 2016 from http://politedissent.com/archives/460

[6] Conan, N. (Presenter) & Winick, J (Guest). (1 Dec 2004). Reflections of AIDS in Pop Culture. [Radio broadcast]. In L. Bishop (Producer), *Talk of the Nation*. Washington, D.C.: NPR.

She chooses not to share that she is HIV positive with the group, arguing that she wants to be known as "a fighter. As a teammate. As a person. Otherwise, I'm just going to be the kid on the team with AIDS."

While Winick might take the story-first approach and narrowly avoid writing a *purely* didactic tale, he still acknowledges the role of educator that comics, and the subsequent media attention, plays. "Comics have a long history of telling lessons," he is quoted as saying in *The Washington Post*. "They tell stories through metaphor, but sometimes I feel we don't need the metaphor. Why should it be that Mia contracts some alien virus?"[7] The mixture of characters and reactions, including the uncertainty that Ollie feels about this new knowledge, recognizes that the reader community will have a similarly mixed take on the issues. Yet being dissatisfied with the modern conversation around HIV and AIDS, Winick's stated aim was simply to put the discussion back on the agenda. "If in a small way we elevate a discussion on the subject, a discourse, it is worth it… It took a superhero for us to talk about it… I think we should be discussing this more and more."[8] To further draw parallels to the *Green Lantern/Green Arrow* morality tales discussed earlier in this book, Moore (2003) identifies that classic series as exposing social ills along with the "inadequate response of those who were encountering them for the first time."[9] This is arguably Winick's intent here as well, bringing a subject back to the agenda for a generation that didn't go through the AIDS crisis of the 1980s and 1990s, and for whom sex education comes from a variety of conflicting sources. Green Arrow represents the reader the same way Green Lantern did, providing the emotive response to Mia's educational monologues.

Family Relations: Oliver Queen as a Father

For the first time decades, Winick's Oliver Queen is (for the most part) a contented family man. It was a role he craved throughout Mike Grell's *The Longbow Hunters*, a role that Dinah Lance/Black Canary didn't want to share with him given their chosen professions. The choice was taken away from them in violent circumstances, and after also being raped by the assassin Shado, the

---

[7] Breznican, A. (14 Oct 2004). "'Green Arrow' Comic Book Targets HIV." *The Washington Post*. Retrieved 2 Feb 2016 from http:// washingtonpost.com/
[8] Ferber, L. (Dec 2004). Positively Heroic. *HIV Plus*, 7(8), 26-27.
[9] Moore, J. T. (2003). The Education of Green Lantern: Culture and Ideology. *The Journal of American Culture* (26), 263–278.

child of that union was kept far away from him. On the flip-side of the coin, Ollie spent years running from the son he did know about, denying that Connor Hawke was his own and angrily leaving him again prior to Ollie's dramatic death[10]. However, bridges have been mended in Winick's era and past indiscretions are forgiven, with the extended Team Arrow now consisting of Ollie's son Connor, Mia (Speedy), his long-term love, Dinah and his adopted ward Roy Harper (Arsenal / Red Arrow). His past darkness and need to isolate himself from the rest of his contemporaries is replaced with a strong sense of family. "I have lived many places and have spent a good chunk of my life bunking in high-tech flophouses," Ollie expresses in *Green Arrow* Vol. 3 #50 (July 2005). "I like having a home." Yet as soon as has he expressed that, the narrative gods promptly blow up that domicile. Winick's central theme in the subsequent 'Heading Into the Light' arc is that of villains targeting him where he hurts the most, with Ollie and his family in the crosshairs of Dr. Light and Merlyn the assassin archer.

Central to Green Arrow's change of path in the next act of Winick's saga is the manner of Ollie's defeat at the hands of the villains. Referencing Brad Meltzer's *Identity Crisis* (and in fact calling the issue "Identity Crisis... Again"), Green Arrow comes to the realization that someone knows who is under his mask in *Green Arrow* Vol. 3 #52 (Sept 2005). In confronting Ollie much later, the revealed rogue Dr. Light identifies why Green Arrow's weakness is his family. "Men and women like you don't fear death. You fear weakness... vulnerability. You fear pain. More inside than out."[11] Dr. Light was already made more sinister than his ridiculous Silver Age counterpart by Meltzer, and Winick turned Merlyn - who really had been something of a one-note villain – even more deadly than he'd ever been before. Working in concert with Dr. Light's machinations, the story culminates in *Green Arrow* Vol. 3 #59 (Apr 2006), with the targeted Team Arrow in tatters. Being forced to make a choice between saving his family and his city, Ollie watches helplessly from a rooftop as Merlyn pushes the button that triggers explosions across the city. "In a moment, Oliver Queen lost everything", Winick writes in a caption, before Merlyn impales the hero on two of Ollie's own arrows. It is a powerful scene so instantly classic that it was

---

[10] In Chuck Dixon's "Where Angels Fear to Tread" and Brad Melzter's "The Archer's Quest," discussed in chapters 8 and 9, respectively.
[11] *Green Arrow* Vol. 3 #57 (Feb 2006).

mirrored as the season finale to the first year of the *Arrow* TV series[12]. The moment is significant, and devastatingly emotional, because Ollie is defeated not just because he was outmaneuvered by his foes, but because he was so dedicated to family.

While not a political statement per se, it was a bold move on Winick's part to make the biggest decision of the arc one about choosing between the fate of his family and his city. The Kobayashi Maru[13] moment meant that the positive direction Ollie had been following since his resurrection had perhaps been fated to end in disaster. The Catholic guilt of Kevin Smith might suggest that his past sins were coming back to haunt him, and the burden of knowledge and secrets involving Dr. Light literally brings him to his knees. More importantly, Winick's arc suggests that those who stand up and try 'Heading Into the Light' (as the stories are named) are the most radical figures of them all. It was not Green Arrow's skill as an archer that fired Merlyn's blood, but instead what his history and identity represented. "When I first heard your entire story I thought I'd never stop throwing up," Merlyn spits at Ollie in *Green Arrow* Vol. 3 #57 (Aug 2005), referring to his early ordeal on the island, and subsequent choice to become a hero. "It makes you dangerous. A symbol that any man can fight the fight if he manages to find the will to do so."

In attacking Ollie's family and light-bearing structures, Merlyn is toppling what Green Arrow symbolically represents. Repeatedly in Green Arrow's history, the notion of "what one man can do" has been the thematic glue that held together the character's major turning points. Winick knowingly plays on the notion in this arc, framing it within the Internet savvy 21st century where global protest movements stand up against the faceless multinational corporations of the world. Indeed, Winick had played with grassroots movements in the 'City Walls' arc, as Green Arrow led a small army of cops and crooks against the forces of evil. No stranger to dying, Ollie's symbolic 'death' here is crushing those ideals. Does that mean that resistance against the machine is futile? Absolutely not, and instead Winick asks Oliver Queen to

---

[12] "Sacrifice." *Arrow*, season 1. Aired 15 May 2003.

[13] The Kobayashi Maru was the no-win scenario presented to Captain Kirk when he was in the Starfleet Academy in the *Star Trek* TV and film series. Kirk, of course, cheated and won the scenario, and didn't have to face the consequences until years later.

reinvent himself for this new world, something he has been adept at throughout his entire career.

"Vote 1" For Oliver Queen... Again: Ollie for Mayor Redux

Back in Kevin Dooley's 'Crossroads' event, discussed in detail in Chapter 8, Ollie encountered a *V for Vendetta* inspired anti-villain known as Anarky. It exposed Green Arrow to a choice that required him to reject the system entirely and embrace the anarchist principles of chaos. Yet when they meet again in James Peaty's fill-in issue of *Green Arrow* Vol. 3 #52 (Aug 2005), Anarky reminds Ollie of Mark Twain's old adage that "the radical of one century is the *conservative* of the next." With his focus on family and the building of a home in Star City being a major focus of Winick's arc, it's difficult to argue with Anarky's assessment of Ollie. He's no longer the windmill-tilting destroyer of sacred cows that he was in the 1970s, or the angry isolationist of the 1980s and 1990s. Nevertheless, Winick's next move made Ollie firmly a part of the establishment that he'd so often railed against, and returned to a storyline that Elliot S. Maggin had initiated all the way back in 1971. Following the destruction of a third of his hometown, and DC Comics' *Infinite Crisis* event, the publisher took the opportunity to jump all of its books for a *One Year Later* gimmick. Much had changed for Oliver Queen, not least of which was that he was now the elected mayor of a fractured Star City.[14]

Winick uses this storyline once again as a filter to explore 'relevant' style comics, albeit flipping the script by recasting the outraged Ollie as a *part* of the system. In *Green Arrow* Vol. 3 #61 (June 2006), Winick poses a question that defines the remainder of the volume. "In general, the *Man* is the establishment. What becomes of the rabble rouser, the trouble maker, the rebel -- when he *becomes the Man*?" As both mayor of the troubled Star City, literally divided by a wall that keeps the destroyed sections in ghetto conditions, Ollie must balance out his two lives as the protector of the city in his new hooded costume and as the official face of the institution, one that is answerable to committees, the media, the electorate and political in-fighting. Amidst demands that he tear down the wall and balance the city's budgets, Winick depicts a left-wing politician also facing the reality of balancing free-market ideals with the social welfare of a city. This arc is the logical progression of Denny O'Neil and Neal

---

[14] From *Green Arrow* Vol. 3 #60 (May 2006).

Adams' classic works. Ollie's public face readily admits to the media that they probably see him as "some whacked-out *commie* bucking corporate America at the cost of the city's people." Yet by the same token, his costumed life sees him siding with citizens who want to blow up the divisive wall. True to form, the media turns on Green Arrow for his nocturnal activities while attacking Oliver Queen for his decisions to perform mass same-sex marriages, rather than focusing on his economic recovery policies. Ollie plays the media game by insisting that the marriages will benefit the Star City economy, but Winick recognizes the typical knee-jerk reactions of the conservative media. Indeed, the warring pundits on television are reminiscent of Frank Miller's motif in *Batman: The Dark Knight Returns*, once again suggesting that this darker world requires a different kind of hero to protect it.

The two roles Ollie plays are the same sides of the duality that he has always warred with, but the darkness he has been brushing up against rears its head in this arc as well. Ollie justifies his flamboyant public displays as mayor as a means of keeping attention on the plight of his beloved city. "If that means I marry a few gay people, break a few state tax codes, and piss off the *talking heads*, well, *that* is what it costs to come to this *circus*."[15] However, this kind of justification extends to his costumed life as well, with Ollie retraining himself and reinventing what Green Arrow means. Starting with *Green Arrow* Vol. 3 #66 (Nov 2006), and continuing through to *Green Arrow* Vol. 3 #68 (Nov 2006), Winick fills in the gaps and shows us how Ollie, Connor, and Mia spent time recuperating after their devastating loss. Ollie hires assassin Natas to train him in the ways of willfully killing, something he had consciously purged from his system in the past. He learns swordplay and how to think like a tactician rather than a fighter, skills he employs to capture longtime foe and assassin Deathstroke. It's a step that Connor describes as "about one foot over the line," as Ollie also learns to properly adopt the Robin Hood mantle by robbing from the rich to fund his heroic deeds. Winick adds the aptly named confidants Frederick Tuckman and John Smalls in the Friar Tuck and Little John roles to add to Ollie's band of merry men. Even so, Natas warns Ollie that he will ultimately have to make a choice. "Taking down companies and *profiting* from their demise... but you *still* try to make it an act of *goodness*. You still think of yourself as a *hero*." To punctuate the point, the artistic team of Scott McDaniel,

---

[15] *Green Arrow* Vol. 3 #65 (Oct 2006).

Andy Owens, Guy Major – a great collection of stylistic successors to Phil Hester and Ande Parks – recraft Green Arrow's costume as a blend of Neal Adams' classic design and the hooded look of Mike Grell's urban hunter. For this is what Winick's Green Arrow *has* to become to survive in this harsher and more complex political landscape, a combination of the best and darkest aspects of his character. Ollie puts it best as he describes himself in *Green Arrow* Vol. 3 #71 (Apr 2007) as "Vigilante. Mayor. Playboy. *Hypocrite*. And the guy with *swords* to your *throat*."

It might seem that Winick's run is a somewhat cynical view of the path of the hero in a complex world, but despite brushing against the demons of his nature, Winick created a Green Arrow that never stopped heading towards the light. What brings down Oliver Queen's mayoral tenure in the end has nothing to do with his track record or the good/bad he has done for the city in either of his guises. He is revealed to be secretly funding the rogue vigilante team known as the Outsiders[16], and the ensuing media circus forces him to resign his position as mayor. He willfully takes a dive in the polls against a corrupt opponent to ensure the protection of his social welfare programs along with Mia's past and secrets, sacrificing himself politically to stay true to his ideals and his devotion for family. Yet Winick, and by extension Ollie, has one final trick up his sleeves. "I've had to do a *great* many things to save this city," he argues in *Green Arrow* Vol. 3 #73 (June 2007). "*Some* things were at best 'questionable.' Others... I *won't* lie to you I'm *ashamed*. But I *want* to set as much *right* as I can. As *mayor*... and as *the man with this bow*." Ultimately, his qualified victory is a compromise between ideals: he resigns as mayor rather than being elected out, but uses the establishment's legal frameworks to ensure that his 'Friar Tuck' compatriot Frederick Tuckman slides into his vacant position. Ollie's mayorship is a parallel for the democratic leaders, such as US President Bill Clinton, who are perhaps remembered more for misleading the public on their indiscretions than for their many contributions to world politics. Winick is assuredly aware of this as he has Ollie apologize to the Star City public

---

[16] The Outsiders have seen many line-ups, and are essentially a team that doesn't fit into the mainstream pockets of the DC Universe. The iteration that was contemporary with this run of Green Arrow was also written by Winick, who recast them as a covert bounty hunter team that included former sidekick Roy Harper (Arsenal) on the roster. Ollie's revelation of funding them left him in an awkward position with the voting public.

for lying to them. Yet for all of the corruption and politicking on display, Winick optimistically avoids the fate that Maggin gave Ollie's mayoral campaign, allowing him to have some modicum of victory as he literally brings down a wall, and proposes marriage to the long-term love of his life.

Green Arrow and Black Canary: For Better and For Worse

After being in a relationship that spanned decades of publishing changes, Oliver Queen finally popped the question to Dinah Laurel Lance in *Green Arrow* Vol. 3 #75 (Aug 2007). Winick had planned to leave the book after that issue, with Ollie no longer mayor and set-up as a clean slate for subsequent writers, but he remained on for a wedding special and to launch the next volume of the Green Arrow and Black Canary saga in the process.[17] Yet several key questions remain when contemplating this run, one that was a major event for DC Comics and involved large chunks of the DC roster of characters at various points[18]. What was it that had changed in the character of Green Arrow to warrant this new commitment, and was this really a good idea?

To answer the first part, Ollie's proposal certainly marked a major change in his character, one that Winick strips down to its bones before building him back up again. Green Arrow is not *just* a new kind of fighter and tactician, but Dinah notices his emotional changes as well, after discovering he has been celibate for a year. "I was waiting for you," Ollie explains in *Green Arrow* Vol. 3 #74 (July 2007). "I wasn't going to *pursue* you anymore... I wanted to be a *better* man... for *you*. I *wanted* you to come *back* to me." As for whether it is a good idea, Wonder Woman wonders aloud in the *Green Arrow and Black Canary Wedding Special* whether any of the heroes should be married to each other. "We should

---

[17] Schedeen, J. (28 Sept 2007). "Green Arrow/Black Canary Interview." Retrieved 3 Feb 2016 from http://ign.com/articles/2007/09/28/green-arrowblack-canary-interview

[18] Following *Green Arrow* Vol. 3 #75, the wedding saga continues with *Birds of Prey* Vol. 1 #109 (Oct 2007), *Black Canary* Vol. 3 #1-4 (Sept-Oct 2007), the *Black Canary Wedding Planner* Vol. 1 #1, and the *Green Arrow and Black Canary Wedding Special* Vol. 1 #1 (both Nov 2007). The scarcely related *Justice League of America Wedding Special* Vol. 2 #1 (Nov 2007) is mostly a "bachelor party," but it is still a step up from the *Black Canary Wedding Planner*'s flimsy excuses to have Wonder Woman, Vixen and Black Canary modeling lingerie for each other. This is not a high point in the history of Black Canary or Green Arrow. They are collectively republished as *Green Arrow / Black Canary: Road to the Altar* and the *Green Arrow / Black Canary: The Wedding Album* trade collections.

be with people who are an oasis," she says referring to Clark Kent and Lois Lane, "who live outside this life." It is difficult to not recall the so-called '*Moonlighting* curse,' in which the lead couple finally consummated their sexual tension, starting the path to the decline of the series' ratings and its eventual cancellation. Former *Green Arrow* writer and artist Mike Grell, who first showed Ollie and Dinah together in a realistic relationship, feels that these couplings are always fraught.

> The problem with relationships in comics is that a lot of the writers don't seem to understand how to do a story where people are functioning as a couple without marrying them off. They feel compelled to marry them off. That's the death-knell. One of two things happens: either the wife immediately gets pregnant, or is killed off, or something happens.[19]

Grell is at least partly right about this inevitability, something Winick addresses by the end of the *Green Arrow and Black Canary Wedding Special.* The wedding itself is somewhat problematic, albeit all in good fun. There's passionate fighting and equally passionate making up from the titular leads that we've come to expect, an all-out brawl when villains attack and despite some gorgeous art from Amanda Conner, there's also a delightfully terrible wedding dress that is a white variant on Black Canary's fishnets and corset look. The issue ends with Ollie attacking Dinah on their wedding night, forcing her to 'kill' him with an arrow through the neck. Of course, it turns out to be just a doppelgänger in the form of the shape-shifting Everyman, and a manhunt begins for the kidnapped archer in the new volume *Green Arrow and Black Canary.*[20]

Initially pairing Connor Hawke and Black Canary, the publication title of *Green Arrow and Black Canary* is significant because it does not imply that Canary is a sidekick or a super-wife, but rather implies partners and equals, the way *Green Lantern/Green Arrow* did in the 1970s. The title font is even styled to

---

[19] Mike Grell, personal interview, 29 Mar 2015. See full transcript in this book.
[20] Collectors should note that the numbering gets a little confusing around here. This series begins with the *Green Arrow / Black Canary Wedding Special*, continues in *Green Arrow and Black Canary* Vol. #1 (Dec 2007) and carries this title until issue #29 (Apr 2010), before reverting to the plain and simple *Green Arrow* for issues #30 through 32. However, despite the name change, this is not considered to be 'Volume 4.' This would start with writer J.T. Krul in *Green Arrow* Vol. 4 #1 (Aug 2010). That latter series lasted 15 issues, until DC Comics rebooted their entire line in 2011 under the 'New 52' banner.

look like that classic run. Initially under Winick, and with gorgeous art and covers by Cliff Chiang, their relationship is tested in the same way that Grell pushed it, grappling with the notion of their marriage, adding in the kidnapping and brainwashing of Connor Hawke and fully integrating the notion of "family" into Team Arrow. Connor even briefly exhibits metahuman healing powers, losing his archery skills, but retaining his martial arts abilities. So on some levels Grell was absolutely right in thinking that the marriage would not last, for it ultimately collapses under the weight of Green Arrow's cold-blooded murder of the villain Prometheus in James Robinson's *Justice League: Cry for Justice* #7 (Apr 2010)[21]. Yet before the darkness once again consumed Oliver Queen, and this version of the character received his final push towards the light, Winick gave him a brief moment of happiness. In the wake of some of the most horrible events to ever befall a single hero, Ollie chose to better himself and seek out the better angels of his nature. This final step may not be as didactic or overtly politically as some of Winick's previous arcs, but instead of taking the easy path of crushing Ollie under yet another mountain of dirt, he chose to take time out and take stock of the positive elements in his life. What is more radical than that?

Brighter Days: From Relevancy to Humanism

Judd Winick's arc remains both one of the most sustained and engaging runs, bringing back old villains and introducing new ones that will stand the test of time, but it is also a thoughtful collection of practical musings on issues that concerned the writer deeply. "I'm known as a guy getting up on the soap box ... but that's okay," he later reflected. "I'll take the rap for that because I really do think that, one, it was always to serve and tell the stories the best we could... that was the No. 1 goal, and, two, if we could actually get a message out there and get a discussion out there."[22] For our perpetual moving target Green Arrow,

---

[21] Green Arrow had killed before, and spent time repenting in an ashram, but this is the first time he had done so willfully. Yet in a bold move, DC Comics and writer J.T. Krul held him accountable for his crimes. In an ambitious crossover that collectively known as *Justice League: Rise and Fall*, Ollie is ultimately confronted by the League, has his engagement ring returned to him by Dinah, and turns himself in for his crimes. Parts of this saga are also discussed in Chapter 3.

[22] Patankar, A. (2013, Oct 23). "Q&A: Judd Winick Shares 'Storyboards' Behind *Pedro and Me.*" *University Wire.* Retrieved from http://search.proquest.com/docview/1443992627?accountid=12763

another reinvention took place, evolving a little bit further out of nostalgia of the Kevin Smith and Brad Meltzer eras, and pushing the boundaries of Ollie's moral code. Ollie was not depicted as one side of the coin or the other, but rather a complex hero who had to tread either side of the moral line, and those areas in between, in both of his identities. Winick returned O'Neil and Adams' conscious relevancy to the Green Arrow stories, nudging this concept into more complex territory. The political hot potatoes of HIV, anti-economic liberalization groups, media pundits and pressure groups, and even marriage equality were prominent, but the core messages of family, the ability to change one's fate and not being burdened by the past were broader brush strokes. As such, Winick's politics moved out of mere relevancy and into a kind of universality, one where the politics may have been ostensibly left in keeping with Ollie's historical persona, but coupled with a maturity that moved the character more into a humanist stance, one where the notions of right and wrong are based on the common good, and more importantly, living in the here and now and making the world a better place.

Someone Else, Something Else: Green Arrow on Screen and the Visual Language of *Arrow*

If Green Arrow has been a perpetually moving target in the pages of comic books, then his television counterparts never stood still. This volume has mostly concentrated on the printed adventures of the Emerald Archer, and for a very good reason. As difficult as it may be to believe, the first 63 years of Green Arrow's existence saw only *one* appearance on screen. Perhaps it's because his identity shifted so radically throughout his career, and unlike the top tier characters Superman and Batman, Ollie Queen's adventures hadn't been exploited on radio and television in the 1950s. In this chapter, some of those screen appearances will be examined, with particular attention paid to the visual language of the TV series *Arrow*, one that uses the language of comics to shift time and create a parallel set of stories. Even more importantly, this piece ponders whether or not this format shifting works, and whether those ties to the comic book origins are more of a hindrance than a helper.

Since 2004, Green Arrow has appeared in multiple animated and live action adventures over the course of his long career, but how accurate are these appearances to their comic book counterparts - and does it even really matter?

Throughout Green Arrow's history, he has shown an incredible versatility in changing and adapting to the needs of the writers, some of whom completely rewrote his origin to either build upon existing continuity or retcon it to suit a wider story. Where comics are often slavish to continuity, even in the face of contradictory storylines, television and other media has the advantage of picking and choosing what elements it adapts. Some of these elements are lifted from the adventures of other characters, while are others aren't found in the source material at all. So is Arrow merely a greatest hits package put to screen, or a keystone in the vast landscape of parallel worlds that DC Comics has created?

"Great Flaming Arrows!" Will the Real Green Arrow Please Stand Up?

Super Friends was an animated adaptation of stories from the DC Comics canon that ran from 1973 to 1986 in various guises, featuring the core Justice League members of Aquaman, Batman and Robin, Superman and Wonder Woman. It also featured regular appearances from other DC heroes, along with characters specially created for the screen, such as the ethnically diverse Apache Chief, Black Vulcan, El Dorado, Samurai and the alien shapeshifters known as the Wonder Twins, complete with their own canine sidekick, Wonder Dog.[1] Green Arrow's singular appearance in the series came in the fourteenth episode of the first season, an oddity titled 'Gulliver's Gigantic Goof.' With all of the Super Friends shrunk by the misguided environmentalist Dr. Gulliver, who aims to shrink the world's population to save resources, "the world's greatest archer" and "staunch member of the Justice League of America" is called away from his mission "at game headquarters in Bornego." Despite also shrinking, he manages to fight off ants with a pencil, build a makeshift bow out of a paperclip, a needle and a car antenna, and hilariously rides his own Hover Arrow (and later Wonder Dog!) to become instrumental in saving the League.

---

[1] While running for most of this time period, the show's 109 episodes appeared under several guises: *Super Friends* (1973-74), *The All-New Super Friends Hour* (1977-78), *Challenge of the Super Friends* (1978-79), *The World's Greatest Super Friends* (1979-1980), back to *Super Friends* (1980-83), *Super Friends: The Legendary Super Powers Show* (1984-85), and then changing name completely for *The Super Powers Team: Galactic Guardians* (1985-86). Green Arrow appeared in the first season of this run.

Voiced by Norman Alden[2] and spouting catchphrases like "Great flaming arrows!" and "By Robin Hood's bow!", it's an odd version of the character that has no direct comparison in the comic books. With the exception of the odd random issue, most notably in Mike Grell's run much later, Green Arrow spent little time outside of the major urban environments of the United States. Nevertheless, the character is unmistakably the Emerald Archer, even if no direct reference is made to alter-ego Oliver Queen. His costume is based on the Neal Adams redesign, which was then only a few years old. His quiver was full of trick arrows, including a Grapple Arrow, a Fireworks Arrow and a variation on his Bolo Arrow. Indeed, the whole scenario was vaguely reminiscent of the 'Doom of the Star Diamond' story from Green Arrow's first Justice League adventure in *Justice League of America* Vol. 1 #4 (May 1961). Even so, it started a tradition of Green Arrow appearances that were analogous to a comic book counterpart, even if they weren't strictly based on one particular version.

Many of Green Arrow's appearances in other media were mostly one-shots, forced to pick a version of the character that was easily explainable to audiences in a handful of scenes. The *Justice League Unlimited* (2004-2006) animated series immediately positioned the character as the Denny O'Neil / Neal Adams version, reluctant to join due to his "leftist" politics, but firmly established by the end of the run as a necessary component in the League's conscience.[3] In *The Batman* episode "Vertigo," where the character is voiced by *The Nerdist*'s Chris Hardwick, writer Stan Berkowitz recreates Ollie's origin story to make the villain Count Vertigo instrumental to his backstory, as a scientist who worked for Ollie, before using his powers to push the hero overboard from his ship and towards the fateful island. This version, also based on the Adams look and carrying a variety of trick arrows, is uncharacteristically motivated by revenge towards Vertigo.[4] In *Batman: The Brave and the Bold* (2008-2011), Ollie's appearance shifts to the beardless Golden/Silver Age version of the archer. Voiced by James Arnold Taylor, he shares a friendly rivalry with Batman, acknowledging their similarities during the earlier years of both characters in print. There's even an episode set in the future that references a version of Ollie

---

[2] Alden also voiced Aquaman for the series, and is perhaps best noted amongst genre fans as the voice of Sir Kay in Disney's *The Sword in the Stone* (1963) and as the coffee shop owner Lou Caruthers in *Back to the Future* (1985).
[3] Explored in more detail throughout chapter 3.
[4] "Vertigo." *The Batman*, season 5. Aired 6 Oct 2007.

in *Kingdom Come*. In *Young Justice* (2010-2013), the irregular Green Arrow appearances (voiced by Alan Tudyk) replace the archer with surrogates, including Roy Harper (variously as Speedy, Red Arrow and later Arsenal) and primarily the 15-year-old female archer, Artemis. Introduced as Green Arrow's "niece," she is in fact the daughter of villains Sportsmaster and the Huntress, and conflicted about her place in the world. In the live-action TV series *Smallville*, Green Arrow (Justin Hartley) was introduced in the show's sixth season in 2006 as an expert 'thief' and an anti-hero, but later becoming a trusted ally of Clark Kent on his path to becoming Superman. *Smallville* created something new out of existing pieces so that an audience had something as universal as Robin Hood to latch onto as a touchstone.

The recurring problem of maintaining a singular identity for Green Arrow on screen is exacerbated by the nature of these appearances, and with the exception of *Smallville*, Green Arrow was given few opportunities to experience the same sustained character building that a serial comic book affords. It results in a brand identity that is difficult enough when the character is a Batman or a Superman, but problematic when the character has never really had a public limelight. This was what made the long-gestated film proposal *Green Arrow: Escape from Super Max*, developed by writers Justin Marks and David S. Goyer, a baffling prospect. While it never got beyond the script stage, it proposed a Green Arrow movie that would introduce the character *in medias res*, before sending him to the titular super max prison alongside some of the DC Universe's biggest villains. It became what Goyer described as "the most elaborate heist we've ever seen, involving superpowers. Because the prison itself kind of has superpowers!"[5] In other words, it was planned as a Green Arrow movie that was mostly about the character out of costume. Even with the *Arrow* TV series on screens regularly from 2013, a series of animated shorts, aired as part of Cartoon Network's DC Nation block, cast a younger Green Arrow (voiced by Will Friedle) with a talking electronic bow (Kevin Michael Richardson) fighting Onomatopoeia's hitherto unseen Onomatopoeiabots, a version of Judd Winick's monolithic Brick, and the obsessive Cupid alongside a radically different version of Black Canary (voiced by Kari Wahlgren). It is difficult to know what DC

---

[5] Adler, S. (13 Aug 2008). "Green Arrow Plans Jail Break with Help from Joker, Lex Luthor in Upcoming Film." Retrieved 7 Feb 2016 from http://mtv.com/movies/news/articles/1592718/story.jhtml

Entertainment were thinking by having three completely different versions of the character across the comic book, these shorts and the *Arrow* series.

About the most accurate any short got was the *DC Showcase: Green Arrow* animated short film released in 2010, with a character design based on the then-current combination of Adams' costume and the addition of Mike Grell's hood. Voiced by Neal McDonough, it featured the archer having to protect a Vlatavan royal as she is attacked by Merlyn (Malcolm McDowell) and Count Vertigo (Steven Blum). It plays like a microcosm of Green Arrow history, ticking off the major rogues as Ollie ultimately teams up with Black Canary (Grey DeLisle) to defeat them, before successfully proposing marriage to his long-time love[6]. Yet as faithful as this short was, at 11 minutes it only just scraped the surface of what the character was about, meaning that the news of an ongoing live-action series was something long-term fans could get excited about.

Saving This City: The Arrowverse and the Multiverse

At the time of publication, the television series *Arrow* is entering its fifth season, and has spawned spin-offs in *The Flash* and *Legends of Tomorrow*, along with paving the way for numerous other DC inspired television series such as *Supergirl*, *Gotham*, *Constantine*, and *Lucifer* on other networks. With the end of the long-running *Smallville* in 2011, after a decade on the air of The WB (and later CW), the network decided it was time that the archer had his own series. On 12 January 2012, it was revealed that executive TV producers/writers Greg Berlanti and Marc Guggenheim, who had also both worked on Warner's *Green Lantern* (2011) film, would be working on a new Green Arrow series with Andrew Kreisberg, a former writer for the comic series. A week later, the show was officially dubbed *Arrow* when it received a pilot order at the CW. For the first time since that character's inception in 1941, Green Arrow would be

---

[6] Originally released a bonus feature on the *Superman/Batman: Apocalypse* DVD/Blu-ray, the short is directed by Joaquim Dos Santos and written by Greg Weisman. The latter partly based the story on an unpublished Black Canary mini-series he had first pitched to DC Comics back in 1984. Delays on the art, by Mike Sekowsky, and eventually Mike Grell's *Green Arrow: The Longbow Hunters*, kept it from ever seeing the light of day. However, Wiseman incorporated the idea of Ollie proposing to Dinah in this animated short, finally completing something he'd set out to do 26 years earlier. A terrific examination of this unseen mini-series can be found in Wells, J. (2011). "Failure to Launch: The Black Canary Mini-Series That Never Took Flight." *Back Issue!* (46), 45-52.

headlining his own TV series. In February 2012, Canadian born Stephen Amell was cast as Oliver Queen and his vigilante alter ego. Amell had only been in a handful of films in both Canada and the US, but already had a Gemini Award under his belt for his role in Canadian sci-fi series *ReGenesis*. He had also grabbed some attention in major recurring roles in HBO's *Hung* and ABC's *Private Practice* throughout 2011.

The CW's *Arrow* is a loose but spiritually faithful adaptation of DC's Green Arrow. Oliver Queen (Stephen Amell) returns to his native Starling City after spending five years on a "hellish island," or so we're led to believe, after which he becomes the hooded vigilante known variously as the Hood/Vigilante/The Arrow/Green Arrow as the show progresses. The show initially sets up the titular character as an anti-hero, primarily concerned with hunting down a list of people his father had given him who had "failed" the city. He slowly lets people into the fold, including his 'driver' John Diggle (David Ramsey), his tech guru Felicity Smoak (Emily Bett Rickards) and eventually a supporting crew known as Team Arrow, fighting crime as the city's hero. Yet for the first season at least, the show plays to the conventions of a CW soap drama just as much as it does an action series, with Oliver clashing with his mother Moira (Susanna Thompson) and new stepfather, his bratty teen sister Thea (Willa Holland) rebelling against whatever is put in front of her, and his best friend Tommy Merlyn (Colin Donnell) secretly involved with his ex-girlfriend Laurel Lance (Katie Cassidy), whose sister Sara was killed during the shipwreck because she was engaged in an affair with Ollie. Their father is Detective Quentin Lance (Paul Blackthorne), who not only blames Ollie for Sara's death, but is actively trying to bring down "The Vigilante."

When compared with the core Green Arrow comics of the 70 years that preceded the show, there is a lot that might be considered to be 'missing' or altered from the text. In an attempt to ground the show in a semblance of reality, Star City is bafflingly renamed Starling City. Oliver Queen begins the show as a joyless killer, closer in tone to Marvel's Punisher, and over the next few years his arc aims to make him more into the hero that comic book fans will know. Yet smaller changes are also puzzling: Laurel Lance shares a similar name to the comic book Black Canary, but in a second season twist it is revealed that Sara Lance (Caity Lotz) survived the shipwreck and trained with the League of Assassins, briefly becoming Arrow's partner. Sara's third season death effectively allows for Laurel to become the Black Canary, even as fandom dictated that the on-screen couple of Ollie and Felicity (known online as

'Olicity') dominated as the the preeminent love story for the series. It was only in 2017, during the show's fifth season, that the character of Dinah Drake was introduced as the new Black Canary, complete with a metahuman sonic scream. Troubled street rat Roy Harper (Colton Haynes) suits up as Arrow's sidekick, but when that actor was contracted out of the series, the red-hooded role went to Ollie's sister Thea, teased with the nickname 'Speedy' from the beginning. Yet even though these elements are familiar, it is difficult to point to a single Green Arrow run that it has lifted its story elements from, with smatterings of Mike Grell, Judd Winick and even Golden and Silver Age characters making their way into the series. It demonstrates the versatility of television in being able to cherry-pick the best bits of the source material, but also the irreverence of Hollywood in not being tied to comic book canon.

Nevertheless, *Arrow* remains faithful to the spirit of its comic book origins, even if it's not always Green Arrow comics that inspire the television stories. What it does pull from the comics are characters from almost eight decades of history, from modern creations like China White to 21st century spins on Silver Age caricatures such as William "The Clock King" Tockman. They are not simply the formulaic cartoon characters that they were in the 1940s and 1950s comics at the start of Ollie's comic book origins, and instead they initially come with some personal connection to the core group of characters. Sara and Laurel Lance as the respective Black Canaries each dated Ollie in their past. Palmer (played by former Superman Brandon Routh), is introduced in *Arrow*'s third season. He eventually becomes the Atom, and co-lead in the spin-off *Legends of Tomorrow*, albeit one who shares some DNA with Marvel's Iron Man. Assassin Deadshot is believed to have been responsible for the death of Diggle's brother. Merlyn, the most nefarious of all of Green Arrow's villains, is also one of the Queen family's friends and later revealed to be the real father of Ollie's sister Thea. Slade Wilson (Manu Bennett), better known to comic book fans as Deathstroke the Terminator, actually spent time on the island with Ollie in flashback, an uneasy ally and one of the people who trained him in martial arts and archery. Joining them are Mike Grell's creations of Shado (Celina Jade) and Eddie Fyers (Sebastian Dunn), the former still a skilled archer who is kidnapped by the latter. Neither follow their heritage from Grell's *The Longbow Hunters*, as they both meet their deaths on the island. Even with these multitude of changes, *Arrow* is systematically ticking off boxes from comic book lore to create something that *feels* authentic. This isn't always totally "Green Arrow" canon, incorporating villains Firefly, Deathstroke, Deadshot, Huntress and even

Poster for the second season of television's *Arrow*.

a less-hulkish Solomon Grundy. The villains span the entire DC Universe, introducing Brother Blood, the Bronze Tiger and the ambiguous motivations of Amanda Waller, A.R.G.U.S., and her Suicide Squad.

So why do this kind of obvious appropriation? It's not as though Arrow doesn't have a rogues gallery of his own from his 75 years in the vigilante business, albeit a less defined one that Batman's. Through the show's seasons to date, they have brought in Merlyn, Count Vertigo, China White, Cupid, Brick, and Dodger. The cynical response is that *Arrow* has become a backdoor Batman TV series, while Warner keeps the Dark Knight rights tied up for the big screen. Even the *Gotham* television show only deals with a pre-cowl Bruce Wayne. When asked, artist Neal Adams recognizes the influence of his Batman work. He cites the third-season fight between Ra's Al-Ghul, but doesn't see it as an issue.

> We call it the Neal Adams show. I don't know how we can call it anything else. The Neal Adams and Denny O'Neil show. But they've got a lot of Deadman in there, and I did an awful lot of Deadman... But they're clearly getting in Batman, with Ra's Al-Ghul and the League of Assassins and all that, and the whole nine yards. And they know it, and they talk about it... You can't fault them for that. A lot of people are clandestine, they steal my stuff all the time but kind of hide it. These guys are just out there... "You got anything else? We'll take it. We're just having a good time." And they are – they are having the damnedest time.[7]

On a far more practical level, these Batman villains provide a universal lubricant by which new viewers can ease into often complex comic book concepts. After all, Ra's Al-Ghul had been introduced to mainstream audiences only a few years earlier via actor Liam Neeson's portrayal in Christopher Nolan's *Batman Begins* (2005) film and its sequels. Like those films, *Arrow* aimed for the 'realistic' and 'gritty' facade of the Nolan films, working on the assumption that audiences would accept the fantastic notion of superheroes if there were no superpowers and the lights remained off. So it's a very particular brand of Batman being borrowed initially, the crypto-fascist Frank Miller moodiness that has been used to smother the hope of the *Man of Steel* (2013) and *Batman v Superman: Dawn of Justice* (2016), and later adopted by 20th Century Fox to kill the potential sense of wonder in *Fantastic Four* (2015). In an infinite Multiverse, a comic book concept that allows for multiple versions of reality to be simultaneously true, it's entirely possible that this Oliver Queen took the life

---

[7] N. Adams (personal interview, 8 Feb 2016). Full interview can be found in this book. The episode he refers to is "The Climb," *Arrow*, Season 3 (aired 10 Dec 2014).

that was intended for Bruce Wayne. It is even more likely that *Arrow* uses Batman's mythology as shorthand for casual audiences.

Being 'grounded' was, as the term implies, merely a foundation. The tactic ultimately paid off, with *Arrow*'s fourth season allowing itself to go deep into comic book territory. Euphemisms were finally dispensed with, as 'the Arrow' announced himself to the city as 'Green Arrow'. Some of the cheeky humor of the comics began to slip in, and as Thea slipped on the red hood, Green Arrow officially had a sidekick named Speedy. Even the location fell in line and became known as Star City. Partially influenced by sister show *The Flash*, also produced by Greg Berlanti and his colleagues, *Arrow* was allowed to drift away from the grounded grittiness and introduce metahumans and broader comic book concepts. In the fourth season, the primary antagonist is Damien Darkh (Neal McDonough), the magically enhanced semi-immortal ex member of the League of Assassins. *Arrow* doubled-down on its magical leanings, introducing iconic DC character John Constantine in the fourth season's 'Haunted', with actor Matt Ryan reprising his role as the character from the recently cancelled NBC series *Constantine*. His role wasn't merely an Easter Egg either, arriving to reunite the briefly deceased Sara Lance's resurrected body with her soul. Later in the season, the crew chooses to go up against Darkh in the episode 'Taken' with the help of Vixen (Megalyn Echikunwoke), a fellow hero magically enhanced with the abilities of any animal thanks to her Tantu Totem heirloom[8]. So it seems that *Arrow* decided that audiences would accept the outlandish plots of comics, as long as they were accompanied by familiar villains and a decent dose of romantic subplots.

When the characters of *Arrow* come closest to their comic book counterparts in the comic books, at least in the episodes of the show to date, it is primarily through the use of alternative realities and speculative timelines. The *Legends of Tomorrow* spin-off episode 'Star City 2046' takes the crew of

---

[8] In August 2015, the producers of *Arrow* expanded the universe created in *Arrow* and *The Flash* by adding a short animated series called *Vixen* to the online streaming service CW Seed. Set in the same universe as the two original shows, and by extension the 2016 spin-off *Legends of Tomorrow*, the show featured the voices of Megalyn Echikunwoke as the title character, and Stephen Amell, Grant Gustin (*The Flash*) and various other actors in cameos. Echikunwoke reprised her role in live action for *Arrow*'s fourth season, specifically 'Taken', *Arrow*: Season 4 (Aired 23 Feb 2016).

time traveler Rip Hunter's vessel to the ravaged future of Oliver Queen's home[9]. There they encounter a post-war world that has fallen to the forces of darkness, with only a familiar looking archer that calls himself Connor Hawke (played by Joseph David-Jones) trying to keep the peace. Oliver Queen, who is initially said to have been missing for years, is a fractured shell of his former self when eventually discovered in the ruins of his 2016 headquarters. Finally sporting his trademark beard, albeit by way of some questionable makeup and prosthetic applications, he is missing an arm and no longer the city's primary protector. This is an Oliver Queen that is carrying the burden of having failed his city 30 years prior. It's a logical progression from the darkness that *Arrow* presents on a weekly basis, with the corresponding *Arrow* episodes of the weeks surrounding the *Legends* episode concentrating on the complex web of lies that Ollie must constantly weave to keep his family safe. In a handful of scenes, the *Legends of Tomorrow* episode reminds viewers that the Green Arrow depicted in *Arrow* is a "version" or a "reflection" of the one readers know. Ollie 2046 (a.k.a. "Old Man Ollie") is not precisely the version seen in Frank Miller's *Batman: The Dark Knight Returns*, and Connor Hawke is in fact John Diggle's son, and not Ollie's as he is on paper. This Ollie is physically transformed to resemble the version "fans" might want to see, although it does so within the confines of its own universe. For example, it's indicated that it was Deathstroke's son that took Ollie's arm, and not an unseen incident with Superman, a character who wasn't allowed on the CW network until spin-off *Supergirl* shifted there for its second season in late 2016. Nevertheless, there is a direct line from *Arrow* to what this possible future, indirectly hinting that infinite versions of Green Arrow and Ollie – including everything from Neal Adams to Kevin Smith – potentially lay waiting in between.

Rather than looking at *Arrow* as something lesser because it is a potpourri of influences, it should instead be seen as another of the infinite worlds that occupy the DC Universe. *Arrow* is simply another aspect of the vast Multiversal architecture introduced by Julius Schwartz in the Silver Age of comic books. Mark Waid and Grant Morrison played with the idea of Hypertime, described as a repudiation of the typical approach to continuity in which the only valid version is the current continuity. In 1998, Waid published *The Kingdom*, a kind of sequel and prequel to his own alternative reality mini-series, *Kingdom Come*.

---

[9] "Star City 2046," *Legends of Tomorrow*, season 1 (aired 25 Feb 2016).

There he introduced this notion of Hypertime. "Hypertime is our name for the vast collective of parallel universes out there, in which you can somewhere find every DC story ever published," he explained to *Comic Book Resources*. "Instead of continuing the sisyphian task of building a continuity on shifting sand (to mix a metaphor), why not instead invent a mechanism through which inevitable continuity fluxes can be explained?"[10] To put it in far simpler terms, and to repeat a much used catchphrase, "It's all real." DC may have abandoned elements of this Hypertime concept in print, Morrison's 2015 *The Multiversity* and the line-wide Convergence event of the same year notwithstanding, but it has never been more apt than it is with the growing television universes. *Arrow* executive producer Andrew Kreisberg confirmed in late 2015 that they were building what they called the "Arrowverse," incorporating *The Flash* and time-travelling spin-off show *Legends of Tomorrow*.[11] The Arrowverse is simply another aspect of Hypertime, and this version of Green Arrow has appropriated elements from counterparts and comrades in various realities. Either that or these are just particularly excellent examples of superhero comics that the producers wanted to see on screen by any means necessary.

Legends of Yesterday: *Arrow* and the Flashback Paradox

Comic books and live action film and television are not the same thing. This seemingly common sense statement is not always common practice, as countless Hollywood movies and TV shows struggle with the middle ground between the two visual languages. Wolk (2007) has stated that comics are neither visual prose nor static movies, and they are a "medium with its own devices... traps and liberties."[12] Ludwig (2015) builds on this in relation to translating comics to film, drawing a distinction between more faithful adaptations, which are the same stories told in two different mediums, and "fidelity" or creating "equivalent, rather than identical, effects across the

---

[10] Yarbrough, B. (31 Dec 1998). "Waid on the Keys to 'Kingdom', Defining Hypertime and Overturning 'Crisis.'" Retrieved 10 Feb 2016 from http://comicbookresources.com/?page=article&id=1515
[11] Bucksbaum, S. (3 Dec 2015). "'Supergirl,' 'The Flash' EP Shoots Down Crossover Rumors." Retrieved 10 Feb 2016 from http://www.hollywoodreporter.com/live-feed/supergirl-flash-ep-shoots-down-845560
[12] Wolk, D. (2007). *Reading Comics: How Graphic Novels Work and What They Mean* (p. 14). Cambridge, MA: Da Capo Press.

different media."[13] Most films tend to fall into loose adaptations of existing storylines, such as *The Amazing Spider-Man 2* (2014) and the infamous "Death of Gwen Stacy" arc. *V for Vendetta* (2006) makes a decent stab at Alan Moore and David Lloyd's original works, even if they are removed from the immediacy of their inception inside of Margaret Thatcher's Britain. *Iron Man 3* (2013) takes large chunks of Warren Ellis' 'Extremis' story, and remixes in new versions of the villainous Mandarin. Then there's slavish adaptations such as Frank Miller's *Sin City* (2005), *300* (2006), and *Watchmen* (2009), where respective directors Robert Rodriguez and Zack Snyder spent as much time adapting the look of the panels as they did in converting its dialogue to screen. *Arrow* sits somewhere in the middle of these two types of translations, adapting elements of Green Arrow and other DC stories while creating something "equivalent, rather than identical" to the Green Arrow of the comic book medium. It has done this through the appropriation of content from the source material, as discussed, but it also does it through the use of comic book language such as narration and time-shifting.

The cast of *Arrow, The Flash,* and *Legends of Tomorrow.* © The CW.

---

[13] Ludwig, L. (2015). *Moving Panels: Translating Comics to Film* (p. 2). Edwardsville, IL: Sequart Organization.

Television undoubtedly plays with a different set of rules to the comic book sources,[14] but it also does have the temporal limitations of cinema either. Like comics, television plays out in a serial format with cliffhangers and the never-ending soap opera of constant drama that has sustained superhero comics since the 1930s. A brand new television show doesn't come burdened with decades of history, but in some cases it has to at least acknowledge that it exists. By way of comparison, *Marvel's Agents of S.H.I.E.L.D.* television series exists within the broader Marvel Cinematic Universe, and it can't go into some corners of comic book history for fear of contradicting upcoming big screen ventures. By the same token, it does have the luxury of dozens of episodes a year to tell character-based stories, and frequently does. *Arrow* began as an exemplar of this kind of storytelling, for better or for worse, in its first season. From the pilot episode, *Arrow* employs a flashback motif to explore the five years prior to Ollie's current adventures. Each season contained weekly scenes that switched back to five years prior, with the idea initially being that by the end of each season, audiences would also be caught up with the hero's "missing years". Those flashbacks were used to unfurl a mystery, at least at first, with the majority of episodes peeling back a piece of time spent on the island. It initially made sense for the show, as it managed to deal with the journey of Ollie from pampered rich kid to a deadly tattooed man with a bow without overburdening the audience with all of the exposition at once in the pilot. The Green Arrow comics, on the other hand, had typically partitioned off this story into standalone tales and mini-series.[15]

Flashbacks are neither unique to comics or television, but it is a language comic books are adept at. In a single panel, readers can be transitioned from the present day Sydney, Australia to Ancient Egypt with only a narrative bubble,

---

[14] This section expands upon the ideas first presented in an article the author wrote for the Sequart online magazine. It can be found at: Gray, R. (17 Nov 2015). "The Flashback Paradox: How Comic Book Television Deals with Remembrance of Things Past." Retrieved 6 Feb 2016 from http://sequart.org/magazine/61270/the-flashback-paradox-how-comic-book-television-deals-with-remembrance-of-things-past/

[15] Andy Diggle and Jock's *Green Arrow: Year One* and Mike Grell's *Green Arrow: The Wonder Year* to name a few, although the island story has been reimagined a number of times since Jack Kirby and Ed Herron's 'The Green Arrow's First Case' in *Adventure Comics* Vol. 1 #256 (Jan 1959). In the next chapter, Jeff Lemire introduces a new element that suggests Ollie was predestined to arrive on the fated island.

a tonal shift or an artist's pencil needed to create the shift. Flashbacks are typically used to take the reader or viewer back to a point in the narrative's past in order to add crucial information that is now pertinent to the main story. In the case of *Arrow*, it may have been to demonstrate where Ollie first learned a particular skill, received a scar or first met a character that had reemerged in his current life. Comic books do it all the time because it is easy to travel back and forth in time in sequential art. This approach falters when *Arrow* feels obligated to keep using those flashbacks, and the adherence to the comic book structure hampers forward momentum. By the third season, the strain on the flashback motif was even beginning to cramp believability. Throughout that season, many of the flashbacks concentrated on Hong Kong initially, as Ollie is forced to work for the shadowy semi-government A.R.G.U.S. organization on a series of seedy and violent errands. They are mostly an excuse to bring back characters killed off in the first two seasons, but while it is one thing to acknowledge that Ollie left the island during the five years away, missions to Hong Kong certainly pushed credibility to the point of breaking. The real offender was 'The Return', which tweely flipped the script by having the present day storyline play out on the island, while the flashback was a return to Starling City five years earlier. Instead of reading as a poignant moment in Ollie's development, he was the superhero equivalent of the ghost of Christmas past, trapped in a narrative bubble and shrouded in foreshadowing.

By the same token, the existence of this technique within the show's infrastructure allowed the aforementioned cameo of John Constantine in both Ollie's past and present. While viewers of the cancelled *Constantine* would have already been familiar with the character, *Arrow* could not assume that their distinct demographic was familiar with the occult detective. The flashbacks meant the show could introduce Constantine not only to new audiences, but to a younger Oliver Queen. In the present day scenario, it was then simply a matter of Ollie asking for Constantine's help in restoring Sara's soul. Brian Ford Sullivan and Oscar Balderrama's script uses the well-trodden comic book convention of the crossover, one that had also been a tradition of *Arrow* and *The Flash* since their respective third and first seasons. (These too use the literal language of comic books, with episode titles like 'The Brave and the Bold' and 'Flash vs. Arrow'). Yet the episode is also an example of what happens when the conventions of those two worlds collide. The compressed nature of comic book storytelling can convey complex concepts in a short period of time, or alternatively would play it out over several issues. This entire saga plays out on screen in under 45 minutes, resulting in a narrative that feels rushed to an artificial conclusion. Grateful fans would have been no doubt happy to see Matt Ryan back on screen, having only been given 13-episodes of *Constantine* by the television gods, but the net result was something that wasn't entirely faithful to either show, nor to either medium.

These examples merely confirm that Green Arrow works differently in the very distinct mediums of comic books and television. They don't speak to the nuance or *Arrow*'s own rhythms that has developed over the last few seasons. It has its own heightened dramatic language, its own complex plots and narratives, its own set of characters, and crucially its own successes that ensure the Venn diagrams of their respective audiences only overlap in part. Yet this did not stop DC Entertainment from trying to retranslate that language back into a comic book format. On 14 September 2012, DC Entertainment announced that there would be a new digital first series based on *Arrow*. It featured stories from the show's executive team of Marc Guggenheim and Andrew Kreisberg, and was billed as "a weekly comic which ties directly into a TV series with stories that fill in important gaps in the television narrative and written by the show's writing staff."[16] It launched via DC's digital app on the TV show's premiere date of 10 October 2012, a day that DC Entertainment declared "Arrow Day" across North American comic book stores, and a print copy of the first issue featured a cover by none other than Mike Grell. Monthly print editions followed from November 2012, and for the first time in Green Arrow's seven decade history, there were two monthly Green Arrow titles on the shelves. After all, the Batman family could have a dozen monthly titles, surely the Emerald Archer deserved a second one?

For a media tie-in comic, the kind that are notoriously associated with unknown artists and are typically targeted at non-comics readers, there was a surprisingly large number of Green Arrow veterans involved. Most importantly, Mike Grell not only provided the cover art for the first two issues, but interior pencils on several of the subsequent releases. This marked the first time he had officially worked on the character since the 1990s. With TV series writers Guggenheim, Kreisberg, and Ben Sokolowski, also attached to the book, it kept

---

[16] Phillips, B. (14 Sept 2012). "New Digital Comic Based on CW's *Arrow* to Launch on Oct. 10." Retrieved 11 Feb 2016 from http://dccomics.com/blog/2012/09/14/new-digital-comic-based-on-cws-arrow-to-launch-on-oct-10

a consistent tone with the television series and provided potential new comics readers with something familiar from the on-screen version. In 2014, the tie-in comic took a different tact, renaming itself *Arrow: Season 2.5* and acting as a bridge between the show's second and third seasons. So now the language has shifted into something else, a dialogue between television and comics that tells one seamless narrative, one where the complete telling requires the unique visual languages of each of the mediums.

My Name is Oliver Queen: Owning the Green Arrow Mantle

In the space of a few short seasons, *Arrow* has transformed itself from something that *television* audiences might have *expected*, to a form more in line with what *comic book* readers are accustomed to. The CW network that it screens on in the United States had become known for its demographic strengths among females 18-34 thanks to successes with *Gossip Girl*, *90210*, *Supernatural* and *The Vampire Diaries*, leading some to dub the melodramatic family squabbling and frequently shirtless men of the first season of *Arrow* as "9021-Arrow." Yet as the direction of the show, and indeed the network with the additions of *The Flash, Legends of Tomorrow* and DC's Vertigo inspired *iZombie* debuting, we witness a show that is confident in embracing its inner geek. Indeed, the show is no longer afraid to refer to its own character as Green Arrow. What *Arrow* has actually achieved is remarkable, not simply interpreting a version of the Green Arrow comics for the screen, but in creating a whole new universe via its spin-offs *The Flash* and *Legends of Tomorrow*. *Arrow* is not merely an adaptation as a result of this, but the lynchpin for an entirely new universe within DC's vast Multiversal infrastructure.

Arrow is another phase in the saga of the moving target that is Green Arrow. While it is difficult to point to any one version of Green Arrow that the show has lifted its interpretation from, it's undeniably got the vibe of an Emerald Archer comic from the last 30 years. For a generation, *this* may be the defining version. In fact, the show has become so influential that it has fed back into the mainstream comics as well. In Jeff Lemire and Andrea Sorrentino's tenure on *Green Arrow* Vol. 5,[17] new layers were added to the island story, and the character of John Diggle – purely a television creation, albeit named after comic writer/editor Andy Diggle – was introduced into the comic book canon.

---

[17] *Green Arrow* Vol. 5 #17 (Apr 2013) to *Green Arrow* Vol. 5 #34 (Oct 2014).

Arrow showrunner Kreisberg went deeper down the rabbit hole when he and Sokolowski briefly took over writing duties on the DC Comics version of the character, introducing a version of TV love interest and tech guru Felicity Smoak. The character is an interesting mix of cross-appropriation from Firestorm and Batman comics to begin with,[18] and her introduction into the mainstream comic book universe as a version of her TV persona is indicative that Green Arrow's television counterpart is as much a part of the spectrum of influences as any other version is now. While the comic book goes through its own radical changes under a completely rebooted DC Universe, as explored in the next chapter, *Arrow* has become the defining Green Arrow for an era as much as any comic book version. Or to put it another way: it's all real.

---

[18] The character of Felicity Smoak first appeared in *Firestorm* Vol. 2 #23 (May 1984), created by Gerry Conway and Rafael Kayanan. Originally the manager of a computer software firm and stepmother to one half of the Firestorm character, the version reintroduced to *Green Arrow* Vol. 5 #35 (Nov 2014) is based firmly on the television version of the character as portrayed by Emily Bett Rickards. In the fourth season of Arrow, Smoak is paralysed by an assassin's bullet, and becomes Overwatch, a character analogous to Barbara Gordon's Oracle, another loaner from the Batman mythology. Smoak is almost a microcosm of the whole incestuous mythology exchange that has populated *Arrow* from its first episode.

I Was a Green-Age Werewolf! Year One and the Origin That Never Ended!

This book began with the premise that Green Arrow is a moving target, a character born of a pastiche origin that is continually being updated to reflect his place within the current continuity of the DC Comics canon. More than that, thanks to the multitude of influences that creators Wort Weisinger and George Papp - along with all of the other Golden and Silver Age creators pulled on – Green Arrow was intrinsically in search of an identity. It's a pattern he has pursued for most of his career, although it is arguable that it was never truer than in the current era of comic books. The 21st century has seen the comic book industry in a perpetual state of reinvention, scrambling to meet the competing demands audiences being pulled in competing directions by a mix of medias. The century to date has been something of a strange dichotomy for the character, on one hand consolidating all the best bits he had to offer in the previous century, while spending the better part of recent memory abandoning those concepts for something new and undefined.

The post-2000 period of comic books has always been tricky to define, and for the purposes of this chapter at least, needs to be considered with a new moniker. The Modern Age of Comic Books can be traced to the changes that came out of *Crisis on Infinite Earths* (1986). Voger (2006) has extensively defined the "conscience-deprived heroes... typified by implausible, steroid-inspired physiques" since the late 1980s as the Dark Age of comics[1]. Morrison points to the 'Renaissance' of the new millennium, a mixture of comics that recall and glorify the past (*Kingdom Come, Marvels*), take all eras of comics together (his own *All-Star Superman*) or remix them entirely to create something new (Mark Millar's *The Ultimates*).[2] Yet surely that renaissance finally came to an end at DC Comics with the New 52. In May 2011, following the reality-altering crossover event called *Flashpoint*, DC Comics made the announcement that they would "launch a historic renumbering of the entire DC Universe line of comic books with 52 first issues," starting all of their books again with new creative teams and ideas from issue one[3]. It was a bold move, one aimed at gaining new readers who didn't want to be saddled with the decades of history of a character before dipping their toes into the universe. After all, DC Comics did feature some of the longest continually running comic books in the history of the medium, with *Action Comics* and *Detective Comics* up to issues #904 and #881 respectively by the end of their first volume runs. So what do we call this brave new world that actively pushes aside the Modern Age of Comics and sets its own continuity?

The contention here is that in the place of the nebulous Modern Age, a period that has now spanned over 30 years of comic book history, we should start rightly referring to the Contemporary Age of Comic Books. This certainly follows the naming conventions of the broader art movement, and the terminology accepted by art historians. By definition, this contemporary work is continually in a state of flux, and as much of a moving target as Green Arrow himself. Using the loosest of possible definitions, the wider "contemporary art movement" can broadly be defined as a rejection of the ethos of the modern art that preceded it, and is made by artists living today. Extending this to the

---

[1] Voger, M. (2006). The Dark Age: Grim, Great & Gimmicky Post-Modern Comics (p.6). Raleigh, NC: TwoMorrows.

[2] Morrison, G. (2012). Supergods: What Masked Vigilantes, Miraculous Mutants, and a Sun God from Smallville Can Teach Us About Being Human (p. 423). New York: Spiegel & Grau.

[3] Hyde, D. (2011, May 31). "DC Comics Announces Historic Renumbering of All Superhero Titles and Landmark Day-and-Date Digital Distribution." Retrieved 14 Feb 2016 from http://dccomics.com/blog/2011/05/31/dc-comics-announces-historic-renumbering-of-all-superhero-titles-and-landmark-day-and-date-digital-distribution

comic book medium, or more precisely narrowing its definition to sequential art, comics produced at DC Comics following *Flashpoint* have consciously rejected the work of the Modern Age regardless of their standing.

Outside the comics world entirely, the Occupy Wall Street movement also began in September 2011 in the United States. Rapidly spreading across the world, the various protests had different agendas, but were all unified by a common belief that the global financial system undermined the rights of minorities and poorer socio-economic brackets. This is by no means suggesting that the decisions of DC Comics brains trust were influenced by pro-democracy protest movements, but the crackle of energy in the air at the time was paralleled in the radical overthrow of the old guard and replacing them with new and unfamiliar versions of iconic totems. Of course, in this instance it was the corporations doing the overthrowing, and the comic-book reading masses willingly handing over cash. The strategy worked, with 17 "New 52" titles from DC Comics in the Top 20 books of the September 2011 sales charts.[4] A sense of empowering democratization did come with the launch of DC Entertainment's digital platform, liberating consumers from entering dusty old comic book stores and buying their comics directly from the publisher in hi-res digital formats that took advantage of new tablets and touchscreens. Yet by 2015, DC's *Convergence* event wrapped up the New 52 branding with an event that briefly restored the old guard by battling characters from various continuities against each other. Simultaneously, Marvel's *Secret Wars* event saw Jonathan Hickman, Esad Ribić and Ive Svorcina literally deconstruct the entire Marvel multiverse, and put it back together with the bits and pieces that they chose to keep from various universes. The mad scramble to stuff the genie back inside the bottle was fruitless, and in a world where the public were devouring specific film and television versions of beloved characters to the tunes of billions of dollars, all the retcons in the world couldn't alter the simple reality that comic books could never go back "home".

The Contemporary Age, as we will now call it, has arrived. It even comes complete with its own origin story. With the prevalence of strong creator-owned voices at publishers like Image Comics and Dark Horse Comics, it's an age in which artistic and creator driven work continues to reinterpret and

---

[4] Miller, J. (Oct 2011). Comic Book Sales Figures for Feb 2001. Retrieved 19 Sept 2016 from http://comichron.com/monthlycomicssales/2011/2011-09.html

reimagine what has come before, as well as projecting ahead to the future. For DC Comics, it has been about finding a balance between the continuing soap opera of superhero stories and finding something accessible to new readers. For the villain of the Contemporary Age is the diminishing audience for the source material, and not a month seems to go by without one member of the comics or mainstream press prematurely penning the obituary for comic books. In this final chapter, Green Arrow's never-ending origin story is explored, taking four case studies over a ten-year period of the industry tearing down icons and rebuilding them: the pre-New 52 *Green Arrow: Year One*; Judd Winick's first official origin story of rebooted New 52 universe; Jeff Lemire's revisionist take on that, and finally Benjamin Percy's unlikely foray into the horror genre that ironically led to a restoration of some of the most endearing qualities of the character.

From Peter Pan to Robin Hood: Expanding Jack Kirby with *Year One*

When the Golden Age version of Green Arrow was created in 1941, he did not receive an origin right away. When he did, in the pages of *More Fun Comics* Vol. 1 #89 (March 1943), it was not the more recognizable island story that has been reused and remixed since the late 1950s, but rather a less familiar tale of an archeologist in search of Native American artefacts in the Lost Mesa. Kirby's origin story from *Adventure Comics* Vol. 1 #256 (Jan 1959), in which Ollie Queen must learn to survive on a deserted island, has more or less remained the template since. In the intervening years, the story had been retold multiple times, each of them adding new information to Ollie's island odyssey to help us better understand the man behind the mask/hood, or in the case of writer Chuck Dixon and artist Rick Burchett's *Green Arrow Annual* Vol. 2 #7 (1995), the editorially driven implication that Ollie's marksmanship was actually the result of metahuman abilities.[5] That retcon not only changes the very crux of the 'what can one man do?' theme that has always underpinned Green Arrow, but was also rapidly forgotten by DC in the following years. The origin has been told at least three times by Mike Grell: briefly in *The Longbow Hunters*, again in *Secret Origins* Vol. 2 #38 (March 1989), and more extensively in *Green Arrow:*

---

[5] Chuck Dixon's 1995 story is called 'Year One', and it is not to be confused with the Andy Diggle and Jock story discussed for the majority of this section.

The Wonder Year.[6] In the wake of the renewed popularity of the character off the back of Kevin Smith, Brad Meltzer and Judd Winick's runs, DC decided that a definitive and updated origin story was needed. This became the six-issue mini-series *Green Arrow Year: One* from writer Andy Diggle and artist Jock.

As with each of the origin stories that had been told over the decades, *Green Arrow: Year One* is primarily aimed at updating the origin to a modern setting. The established team of Diggle and Jock (*The Losers*) brought the Emerald Archer screaming into the 21st century in 2007, drawing on the same gritty realism of Diggle and Jock's other works. Speaking with Re/Action in 2011, Diggle explained his motivations behind updating the character:

> I took this inherently hokey character, which I always thought was really cheesy and laughable and just crap, and thought, well, okay, how would I turn that into an Andy Diggle comic? [W]ith *Green Arrow Year One*, I realised that a) no one had told that origins story for about thirty, forty years, whatever it was, and b) it's a hunted man thriller, rather than a superhero story. There's no spandex, there's no superpowers, there's none of that. It could happen in the real world.[7]

While Diggle may not have been aware of *The Wonder Year*, it *had* been several decades since the origin was updated. The structure of the story remains essentially the same, with Oliver Queen a boorish trust-fund baby ("Oliver Queen, the champagne anarchist") who is more of a thrill-seeker than an actual adventurer, a Peter Pan type who delays growing up by filling his life with extreme pursuits. After being betrayed and washed up on an abandoned Starfish Island after a drunken night, he must learn to survive on an island. The smugglers of the original tale have been updated to enslaved native island dwellers, forced to manufacture heroin under the thumb of 'China White'.

Necessarily recalling Frank Miller and David Mazzucchelli's *Batman: Year One* (1987) with its title, Diggle's *Green Arrow: Year One* doesn't attempt to contradict anything that came before and instead aims merely to expand on the mythos and update it for millennial audiences. Even so, artist Jock also follows Mazzucchelli's deep shadows and a recognition that the minimalism of pen and ink are where heroes are most real. Like Kirby's Green Arrow, Ollie's first tools and costumes are built out of a sense of necessity and ingenuity. A leaf-spring suspension blade, broken bottles and rusty nails form his first bow, while a

---

[6] All covered in detail in chapter 7.
[7] Re/Action (5 Mar 2011). Interview: Andy Diggle. Retrieved 14 Feb 2016 from http://reactionblog.livejournal.com/3594.html

"mold-encrusted hunk of sail canvas" forms his first green hood ("just to keep the sun off, you understand.")[8] This is a far more practical alternative to the leaf suit that Kirby illustrated in 1959, but nevertheless serves the same practical function that it did almost 50 years prior to that. Like earlier versions, trick arrows are invented on the fly, with a Knock-Out Arrow and a Flare Arrow combining materials already at hand. After an injury, Ollie is nursed back to health by pregnant islander Tatiana, during which time he briefly becomes addicted to opium, adding layers of additional meaning in retrospect to his outrage over Speedy's heroin addiction during the 'Hard Traveling Heroes' arc. Jock's psychedelic art here recalls Neal Adams' full page drug freak outs, although Jock leans more towards the mindfreak than the 1960s counterculture poster that Adams looked to. Yet Diggle and Jock's work departs from Kirby in one key aspect: the naming of the hero. While the previous and subsequent stories had attributed the name 'Green Arrow' to either crooks or the press, Diggle's script gives the name some additional meaning. Inspired by his heroic deeds, Tatiana tells him the villagers have nicknamed Ollie "Auu Lanu Lau'ava," which literally translates to Green Arrow. This simple twist is designed to give a name, originally the result of appropriation and simple marketing[9], some relevance in the over-explanatory modern era.

Destiny is an element that is introduced into this version of the origin, one that will be picked up by Jeff Lemire several years later in the New 52. It is perhaps unsurprising when taking a six-and-a-half page story, and retelling it in the decompressed format of modern comics, that new elements should arise. As mentioned, Dixon tried his hand at it with the metahuman motif back in 1995. In *Green Arrow: Year One* #4 (Oct 2007), Ollie returns to a salvaged Pacific Queen ship to find the Howard Hill longbow he dropped on deck. Ollie muses "It's been waiting for me. It's *always* been waiting," implying some kind of force of nature that was always destined to bring Oliver Queen and the bow together. It's at odds with the practicalities of the first bow and outfit, although unlike Lemire's later reworking, it doesn't contradict anything we already know. The Howard Hill bow is something Grell established Ollie had a personal connection with in *The Longbow Hunters*. The larger narrative of China White's drug empire is consciously rejected by Ollie as an attempt to protect the villager's way of

---

[8] *Green Arrow: Year One* Vol. 1 #2 (Sept 2007).
[9] See chapter 1.

From *Green Arrow: Year One* #2. Art by Jock. © DC Comics.

life. "Downplay the whole thing," he tells them in *Green Arrow: Year One* Vol. 1 #6 (Dec 2007). "You know, tell 'em it was just rowdy mutineers, or a couple of stoner hippies growing weed or something." Which is exactly what Grell had done in his versions, explaining that his legend overtook the reality. Instead, we have Oliver Queen finally electing to control his own destiny, defying the "dumb luck" that washed him aboard the island and choosing to forego recognition in lieu of working towards a 'better deal for the little guy' as Green Arrow. Indeed, it fully embraces the Robin Hood elements of the Green Arrow myth, neatly summarizing the parallels between the two: "Rich dude. Gave it all up to fight the power, help the poor. Free the oppressed. Like that." Even more than that, *Green Arrow: Year One* is a complete story without having to rely on prior knowledge, but is still vastly enhanced by it.

The All-New Battling Bowman: The New 52 and the Contemporary Age of Comic Books

When the DC Universe rebooted with the New 52, the theory was that anything was fair game. Some titles remained fairly static in the continuity, principally the established Batman and Green Lantern universes. For other characters like Green Arrow, it was a bit like being back in DC's Golden Age of comics, except the heroes were definitely not being seen for the first time by a hungry war-torn audience. Given how formulaic and scattershot some of the early Weisinger/Papp stories are, the comparison is an unfortunate one, except now a commitment to a silly idea or villain took several issues, rather than six to eight pages, to pay off. In the opening arc 'The Midas Touch', Queen is ostensibly running Q-Core out of Seattle, or not running it properly to the chagrin of the head of the board of directors Emerson, an old friend of his father. Ollie's band of merry men and women now included the Oracle-like hacker Naomi and an engineer named Jax, who aid his extra-curricular activities from afar[10]. For new readers, Ollie was another jet-setting billionaire with a tech support crew. For old readers, there was very little trace of the Green Arrow they knew beyond the obvious moniker. A rapid succession of writers followed initial scribe J.T. Krul, with Keith Giffen and Dan Jurgen co-scripting until a third writer came on board with *Green Arrow* Vol. 5 #7 (May 2012). By this stage, writer Ann Nocenti took Ollie far away from the Seattle he was

---

[10] From *Green Arrow* Vol. 5 #1 (Nov 2011).

already neglecting, and if he isn't attempting a *ménage à quatre* with triplet assassins, he's running from genetically modified wolves in the Yukon. The rapid misadventures mirror the Golden Age version of Green Arrow in their attempt to find him an identity, but also in the folly of incongruous villains and a lack of cohesive identity.

It fell to long-time Green Arrow writer Judd Winick to put the first stamp on the Battling Bowman's renewed origin. Told as part of the New 52's "Zero Issues" anniversary event, *Green Arrow* Vol. 5 #0 (Sept 2012) is a one-shot re-envisaging of the events leading up to Ollie being stranded on the island. The pre-island storyline conclusively cans the events of *Green Arrow: Year One*, with wild-child Ollie having turned his clerical position on his father's oil rig into a party hub. In the midst of a fight with his long-term girlfriend Leena, a group of terrorists attack. Led by the disposable new villain Iron Eagle, Ollie tries to fend them off with rudimentary archery skills. Unfortunately, his plan fails and he inadvertently causes the destruction of the oil rig, along with killing Leena and badly burning his friend Tommy Merlyn in the process. Ollie, of course, lands on the island and is forced to survive, while a badly burned Tommy wakes up and is set on the path to becoming Green Arrow's adversary and fellow archer, Merlyn.[11]

This addition follows the trends of superhero cinema, combining the origins of the hero and villain for the sake of compression. In *Spider-Man* (2002), Norman Osborn is simultaneously transformed in an experiment just as Peter Parker is undergoing his metamorphosis. In both of Fox's *Fantastic Four* (2005 and 2015) origin films, the birth of Victor Von Doom as a villain is linked with the origins of the heroic team. In comics, many of the main rogues came along in quick succession in the years that followed their initial origins. Batman's Joker came along a year after his first tale in 1939, and Penguin and Two-Face in the two years subsequent to that. Ra's al Ghul didn't come along until 1971, the same year Merlyn was introduced in print with the other League of Assassins members. Yet the films *Batman* (1989) and *Batman Begins* (2005) had the Joker

---

[11] Originally introduced as Arthur King in *Justice League of America* Vol. 1 #94 (Nov 1971), the archer was retroactively one of Ollie's inspirations to take up archery as "Merlyn the Magician." His later involvement with the League of Assassins made him one of Green Arrow deadliest recurring enemies. Tommy Merlyn, on the other hand, has a personal vendetta against Queen, with King a separate character in this continuity.

and Ra's Al-Ghul not only active as the hero began his journey, but instrumental to his origin story as well. In Dixon's aforementioned story, he tied Ollie's origin to that of villain Nicholas Kotero, a character Dixon was introducing to Connor Hawke's life in the main comic concurrently. Tying the hero's origin to that of the villain makes them inexplicably tethered, an important if sometimes frustrating shorthand narrative technique used when rebirthing a character for new audiences.

Taken by itself, the New 52 origin story turns one of the cleanest character arcs in comics history, and the journey of what one man can do, into nothing more than a footnote. During Jeff Lemire's tenure on the book, discussed in the next section of this chapter, the writer took the opportunity to expand on Winick's origin story. In a short and compressed piece for *Secret Origins* Vol. 3 #4 (Sept 2014), mirroring the kinds seen in the Golden Age, Lemire and legendary artists Denys Cowan, Bill Sienkiewicz and Marcelo Maiolo portray the island as Ollie's "crucible." More significantly, Lemire follows Diggle in suggesting that there was an element of destiny to Ollie's time on the island, as the archer discovered "who he was *predestined* to be, loomed over him like some monolith he feared he'd never scale." However, this was not the full extent of Lemire's notion of destiny, taking it one step further with his ongoing run and changing the nature of Ollie's origin conclusively for the Contemporary Age.

The Prodigal Origin: Jeff Lemire and Predestination

In his debut issue of *Green Arrow* Vol. 5 #17 (Apr 2013), Lemire's first order of business is to strip the New 52's Oliver Queen back to his essential elements. Much like his loss of fortune in the 1960s, Ollie returns from his jet-setting to find Emerson has sold Queen Industries to Stellmoor International. At the same time, Ollie is framed for Emerson's subsequent murder; his Q-Core base is detonated with his support crew seemingly killed in the blast, and he is suddenly on the run without money or resources. "He had everything he could ever want handed to him, yet he could never really live up to this legacy his father had," Lemire explains. "So in my story, basically we just tear everything down and he loses everything right away and he has to rebuild himself."[12] Emerson evokes Green Arrow's origin before his death, remarking that "aside

---

[12] Jeff Lemire, personal interview, 6 Feb 2013. Full transcript in this book.

from your ordeal on the island, you've never had to truly fight for anything in your life." Yet the most intriguing aspect of the first issue relates to the nature of his time on the island, with the enigmatic new character of Magus dropping the truth bomb that Ollie "was never supposed to leave the *island*." It is the second seed of a wider arc involving the predestined nature of Ollie's time on the island, and the start of one of the richest and most complex origin tales in the history of the character.

Lemire evokes Mike Grell in his back-to-basics approach, not only eschewing the trick arrows but introducing Grell's character of Shado into the New 52, the first writer to do so in a significant way since Chuck Dixon's *Connor Hawke: Dragon's Blood* in 2007. Even this is subverted by Lemire, with the New 52 version not enamored with the much younger Ollie. Instead, it was Ollie's father Robert that caught the assassin's passions, resulting in their daughter Emiko, a skilled young archer and Ollie's half-sister. The greater revelation is that Ollie's island ordeal was not one of mere coincidence. "You didn't really think you washed up there with *only a bow* by mere happenstance, did you?" asks his de facto spiritual guide Magus[13]. Returning Ollie to the island that was once his temporary home, Lemire introduces the notion of the Outsiders – seven ancient houses formed around totem weapons such as the arrow, the spear, the fist, the shield, the sword, the axe and so on – and an ancient "Green Arrow" relic that was the obsession of the power-seeking Robert Queen. Oliver discovers that not only is his father Robert still alive, and sporting the classic Green Arrow beard in a wonderful visual reference from artist Andrea Sorrentino, but was one of his masked tormentors on the island[14]. As such, Oliver's father had a direct hand in his transformation from spoiled playboy to costumed vigilante, an ill-fated and sinister attempt to force a son into the legacy of his father.

So the destiny elements enter into the origin by way of the arrow totem that is said to grant the bearer ultimate power and control of the Arrow Clan, yet the actual predestination comes by way of human intervention. At the very least, Ollie was robbed of the choice of how his life would proceed, even if he was "wasting it" from the perspective of friends and family. It's a choice that he manages to regain somewhat, when he defies his 'family heritage' by snapping

---

[13] *Green Arrow* Vol. 5 #21 (Aug 2013).
[14] *Green Arrow* Vol. 5 #28 (Apr 2014).

the Totem Arrow and passing on a new legacy to his sister. "Just because he raised you as a monster," he tells her in *Green Arrow* Vol. 5 #31 (July 2014), referring to Komodo, her villainous adopted father, "it doesn't mean you have to become one." Ollie could just as well be talking about himself, as he at last embraces his role as the protector of Seattle, solidifying Lemire's run as one extended origin story and leaving Oliver Queen "finally able to become the hero I've always wanted to be."

Lemire's additions to earlier island sagas demonstrate how changing details in a character's origin can alter his entire perception for audiences. Lemire's Oliver Queen is no longer just a man forced to survive on the land and choosing to be a hero, but rather a passive pawn of ancient machinations that he later chose not to embrace. Ollie being on the island deliberately, and indeed tortured by his father, darkens this version of the character by necessity. Of course, Lemire's changes to prior DC canon extend to new versions of Richard Dragon, Red Dart, and the addition of John Diggle from television's *Arrow*. Lemire manages to have his cake and eat it too, projecting events forward five years in the *Green Arrow: Futures End* Vol. 1 #1 (Nov 2014) tie-in issue, that also happens to be the concluding chapter of his run. Count Vertigo has evolved into a cult of copycats, and Emiko is operating as the new Green Arrow following Oliver Queen outing himself as the vigilante. Ollie's public face has "franchised non-profit social aid" and he continues the fight in his own way from shadows, officially passing the mantle to Emiko for good. It's a reminder that Green Arrow doesn't have to be one thing, or even one person as Connor Hawke previously demonstrated.

Primal Instincts: An Origin Story for Ollie's Beard

Modern writers are faced with the problem of what new direction to take Green Arrow in after 75 years' worth of stories, and numerous origin tales in between. After all, this is a character who was stranded on a island, known for carrying a Boxing Glove Arrow, has ridden on the back of a giant doppelgänger in a parallel dimension, has fought a little girl who looked like Richard Nixon, and had even come back from the dead. So in 2015, writer Benjamin Percy did the one thing nobody had thought of before.

He started to turn Green Arrow into a werewolf.

More specifically, in *Green Arrow Annual* Vol. 5 #1 (Dec 2015), Percy and artist Szymon Kudranski had Oliver Queen contract the Lukos virus that slowly turned him into a vicious wolfy monster. What follows is the most convoluted way of creating a New 52 origin story for Green Arrow's beard, a convenient by-product of Ollie's battle with his most primal instincts. The irony was that it was done following some serious social commentary that was perfectly in keeping with Green Arrow's history. Despite the stated horror elements that the author introduced, Percy still hit on some of the fundamentals of the character. 'The Night Birds' arc, specifically *Green Arrow* Vol. 5 #42 (Sept 2015), involves a red-eyed albino leading an army of robotic cephalopods called the Panopticons, but it is still essentially a story about social justice. There are issues of race explored, not to mention a protest movement in the very city that hosted the well-publicized "Battle of Seattle" WTO protests in 1999. The Panopticon robots themselves are not just a clever-clever reference to 18th century philosopher Jeremy Bentham, who is in fact named-checked in the book by Emiko, but are also a piece of commentary on the use of drones on domestic soil and the excessive militarization and use of police force as seen in Ferguson and Baltimore in 2015. Yet Percy's focus in the series, illustrated with deliberately inky darkness by series artist Patrick Zircher, is one based in horror. Here Green Arrow is literally transformed, a classic form of body horror where the hero inside is at war with his external visage. There's never been a more apt way of describing the Contemporary Age's Green Arrow.

Yet all of this was merely Percy's prelude to the main event, with the writer making good on the promise of a Green Arrow that paid tribute to the legacy of the character. As DC approached the fifth anniversary of the New 52 and their 'Rebirth' event in 2016, the stories typified the search for direction since the inception of this version of the character in 2011. Five years after the commencement of the New 52, DC announced that June 2016 would be the start of their 'Rebirth' event. While the continuity of the New 52 would still stand, it provided an opportunity for DC to bring back some of the characters and stories that got thrown out with the bathwater post-*Flashpoint*. On a larger scale, people not seen for five years, including Wally West, Aqualad, and Ryan Choi (The Atom), to name a few, returned to continuity. The much missed Ted Kord and Ray Palmer, who had enjoyed appearances in the television universes in this time, had their pre-Flashpoint personas restored to life. Monumentally, it canonized the interference of Doctor Manhattan from Alan Moore and Dave Gibbons' *Watchmen* as the catalyst for the initial changes, forcing readers to change their perceptions of the last five years of DC Comics, and hopefully restore some good will in the process.

On a much smaller scale, although equally enormous for fans of Green Arrow, was the reunion of DC's former sweethearts, left separated just prior to the *Flashpoint* saga, and the ultimate restoration of another furry friend. "Readers are aching for the reunion of Green Arrow and Black Canary, and we're finally going to give it to them." said writer Benjamin Percy in the solicitations. "Also returning? Green Arrow's goatee."[15] Black Canary had enjoyed her own adventures in this period, radically being made over as Dinah Drake, who after a fallout with Barbara Gordon/Batgirl, takes on the role of lead singer of a band called Ashes on Sunday. Escaping her vigilante past, Dinah goes by the name D.D. and leads the band until all of their lives are threatened, due to her mute guitarist Ditto (actually an alien Sound Wave given human form) and the powers Dinah derives from their association. When Percy took over the 'Rebirth' version of Green Arrow, he took this version of Black Canary and explored how that classic relationship would work not only in the context of a new century, but in their vastly different personality traits. This was a Green Arrow and Black Canary meeting for the very first time, but simultaneously couched within the nostalgia of a decades-long love story.

From the second page of the rebooted *Green Arrow* Vol. 6 #1 (Aug 2016), aptly named "The Death and Life of Oliver Queen, Chapter One," we witness a bearded Green Arrow fighting side-by-side with Black Canary in her classic fishnets and leather jacket. Emiko, a major concession to the New 52 and speaking for the reader, perhaps sums it up best: "Excuse me while I enjoy this fangirl moment." Recalling the Elliot S. Maggin, Gerry Conway and Joey Cavalieri era of the 1970s and 1980s, a period that consciously rebuilt Green Arrow as a working class hero, Ollie and Dinah are a clash of cultures. Ollie attempts to reconcile his riches with his attempts to do legitimately wide-changing social work with the corporate way that Queen Industries is being run in his name. As we saw in the early days of the book, there's a dichotomy between Queen as a billionaire and Green Arrow as a Robin Hood for the 21st century. Percy poses the same question Judd Winick did a few years before, pondering how Queen can fight "the man" when he has come to represent (at least to the Seattle public) everything that "the man" stands for. Dinah, meanwhile, is continuing to

---

[15] From "DC Comics' Rebirth Arrives in June 2016 Solicitations" (28 Mar 2016). Retrieved 30 Mar 2016 from http://comicbookresources.com/article/dc-comics-rebirth-arrives-in-june-2016-solicitations-2016

search for her independence, and what it means to be Black Canary outside the context of a band or a team. She rebels against Queen's place in the cultural hierarchy, but is attracted to him because of the man behind the beard. It's a perfect mirror to those earlier "Bronze Age" issues, and just as crucially provides a parallel source of passionate antagonism that won't make this coupling a smooth one. Once again, they come to the page as equals, warriors on separate but similar paths, intersecting, fighting and making love in equal measures.

Visually, Otto Schmidt's art in the initial issues of this series recalls a much later version of that couple. There are moments in the debut issue where the couple share a post-coital embrace in bed, Schmidt's lithe and brightly colored figures nakedly sharing each other's company and conversation. The intimacy of the scene necessarily recalls a similar scene in Mike Grell's *The Longbow Hunters*. In the follow-up issue, Schmidt knowingly references Grell and Ed Hannigan's art from the first volume of Green Arrow, reintroducing Shado and nodding to the "Here There Be Dragons" arc of almost 30 years prior. The vision of Ollie tumbling through a fever dream of angels and dragons summons the stories of the past, and recontextualizes them for modern readers. It's a visual quotation of the past that both rewards the faithful and intrigues the initiate. You could be familiar with every story mentioned in this increasingly lengthy book, or picking up the adventures of Dinah and Ollie for the very first time, but the weight and importance of their association is conveyed in just a handful of panels.

Percy and Schmidt's approach is akin to the one taken with television's *Arrow*. As explored in the previous chapter, it is difficult to point to just one version of Green Arrow that his live action counterpart draws inspiration from. This 'Rebirth' is not a return or sequel to any particular Green Arrow story, but rather an amalgam of all the elements that made him an enduring character in the first place. It's no wonder that the writer commented in a 2016 interview that "We're channeling the zeitgeist."[16] Where his pre-*Rebirth* stories were mired in a tension between horror fiction and a clear love of the character, consciously keeping Oliver Queen out of his costume and concentrating on

---

[16] Rogers, V. (2016, May 5). "Ollie is a 'Social Justice Warrior' in Rebirth Green Arrow." Retrieved 18 Sept 2016 from http://newsarama.com/29144-rebirth-green-arrow-writer-ollie-is-a-social-justice-warrior.html

various dilemmas of a personal and lupine nature, Percy allows himself to strip away all the editorial baggage that came with the publisher's then-current edict and restore The Green Arrow. The definite article, you might say. In the aforementioned interview, he expands on this by talking about the character's predilection towards issues-based causes. "Green Arrow is a social justice warrior. Green Arrow has his finger on the pulse of the moment," he clearly states in the same interview. The choice of language is an interesting one, given that by 2016 the term "Social Justice Warrior" (or commonly "SJW") had become a pejorative term for anybody promoting socially progressive views on civil rights, feminism, identity politics or political correctness. In the wake of several high-profile cyber-mob harassment cases of women within the gaming industry, commonly dubbed "Gamergate," Heron, Belford and Goker identify how the use of "social justice warrior" is used to "to imply that the target of the term is a wishy-washy left-wing liberal who seeks to engage in the discussion for personal validation rather than out of any deep-seated conviction. [The term attempts] to neutralize opposition through inferred degradation of the motivations."[17] As derogatory as its intention might be, it's hard to imagine a more perfect descriptor for the Oliver Queen we have seen evolve as a mouthpiece for the liberal left since the late 1960s. Percy embraces the term by taking it back, using it as a positive badge for Ollie, and puts it in the hands of a literal superhero. If 1970s Oliver Queen could speak directly to the audience, he'd probably tip his dusty cap to Percy for crafting a put-down as classy as this.

In the context of these *Rebirth* stories, the modern version of the character becomes less of a tension between old and new than it does about establishing continuity between those earliest tales from the 1940s and the one represented in Percy's work. This is not to say that there is a continuous canonical narrative that links those stories together, as the various reboots, continuity fixes and alternate timelines have ensured no such thing really exists for this character by 2016. However, there is a thematic continuation between the pre-*Flashpoint* and post-*Rebirth* iterations of Green Arrow. Think of it this way: if the pre-*Flashpoint* Ollie was plucked out of time (as he was in the 2016 *Convergence* event, a forerunner to *Rebirth*), he would see a lot of

[17] Heron, M. J., Belford, P., & Goker, A. (Nov 2014). Sexism in the circuitry: Female participation in male-dominated popular computer culture. ACM SIGCAS Computers and Society, 44(5), 18-29.

commonalities with his post-*Rebirth* counterpart. The latter would be physically younger and arguably less experienced with a bow, but he is instilled with all the spiritual characteristics that make the "classic" Ollie. In time, the actual finer details of their divergent histories will drop away, or at least become unimportant, and the contemporary Green Arrow will become indistinguishable from any other elements of his history anyway. After all, if the reader is presented with a character that has the same skill set, the same core values, and is developing the same relationships, can it not be said that this is the same Green Arrow, give or take a few continuity tweaks?

The Origin That Never Ended: Green Arrow as a Moving Target

Origin stories are important when discussing a character, and they are often the hook that allows us to recognize the human side of the fantastic. Superhero films so frequently begin with them so that unfamiliar audiences have something to latch onto. Hatfield, Heer, and Worcester (2013) elevate this notion by saying that origin stories tap into the "tension between psychological rigidity and a flexible and fluid sense of human nature."[18] Romagnoli and Pagnucci (2013) go so far as to add that origin stories represent a Fixed Compositional Point for heroes, as "no matter the reinterpretation, reimagining, reboot, retcon, re-whatever, a superhero's origin remains fixed."[19] With Green Arrow, this is only half-true, and the *tabula rasa* that Denny O'Neil found when first tackling the Emerald Archer in the late 1960s still had the underlying island story at its core. Yet even that origin story isn't fixed, with writers half a century later finding new ways to scour the island, turn over rocks and uncover some new piece of archeology that points to something we never knew about Green Arrow before. Whether it is metahuman powers, predestined arrow totems or being best friends with one's enemies before they turn bad, each layer potentially changes all that we thought we knew about a timeless character. Is it just that those origins are now too simplistic for modern palettes, or that they were so solid to begin with they lend themselves to

---

[18] Hatfield, C., Heer, J Considerations.' In C. Hatfield, J. Heer, & K. Worcester (Eds.), *The Superhero Reader* (p. 3). Jacks., & Worcester, K. (Eds.). (2013). 'Historical on: University Press of Mississippi.

[19] Romagnoli, A. S., & Pagnucci, G. S. (2013). *Enter the Superheroes: American Values, Culture, and the Canon of Superhero Literature* (p.111). Lanham, MD: Scarecrow Books.

reinterpretation with each new generation? In the case of Green Arrow, it's a little from each column, as the character has rarely stopped evolving and having new origin stories over the course of 75 years.

When we think about different types of targets, we recognize that they come in various shapes and sizes. They can be made of paper, steel, rubber or have an electronic scoring system attached. Targets can be round, shaped like humans or other objects, or even made into a virtual form via video games. They have advanced with the technology of the world at large, and of the weapons that fire at them. Yet despite their shifting form, their function has remained resolutely the same. Scoring targets, which we most frequently recall when we reflect on the form, contain different values but almost all of them have a dead center, or a 'bullseye' that is fixed and absolute. Green Arrow, the world's greatest archer in the DC Comics Universe, is filled with nuance and layers as well, but as this book has demonstrated, he has always been a core part of that universe and its pantheon of heroes. The Green Arrow that was born in 1941 may have been a little bit of a Batman clone – along with being equal parts Robin Hood and the 'Indian' to the Vigilante's cowboy – but he has evolved into so much more since then. Never standing still, few characters have changed with the times so much as Green Arrow yet remained essentially the same character at his heart. He's been a rich playboy, shot into space, travelled the hard roads of America with his super best friend, and been a journalist, a mayor, a killer, a monk, a lover, a cheater, a husband, a father, and a son. Green Arrow has been broken, killed and reborn, reinvented and reinterpreted by dozens of writers. He has used his role to educate and provoke, carried the weight of the Justice League's conscience, risen through their ranks and fallen just as hard.

Yet after 75 years, he is still one of the comic book industry's longest-running survivors. As he enters the home stretch towards a century of fighting the good fight, there is little doubt that he will continue to grow and change, whether it is through the passing trends of an editorial mandate, or because he has naturally progressed that way. More than anything, Green Arrow is a hero. He is also nothing but a man. He is a moving target.

Jeff Lemire Interview

Jeff Lemire, along with artists Andrea Sorrentino and Marcelo Maiolo, took over the creative duties on the main Green Arrow title in early 2013 until late 2014. Lemire is known as a writer and artist on acclaimed works such as the *Essex County Trilogy*, DC Vertigo's *Sweet Tooth*, *The Underwater Welder* and *Descender*. For DC Comics he has also been the writer behind *Animal Man* and *Justice League Dark*, and at the time of the second interview, he was the ongoing writer for Marvel's *Hawkeye*.

The first part of this interview was conducted in February 2013, just prior to the release of *Green Arrow* Vol. 5 #17 (Apr 2013), the first issue of Lemire's run. Recorded originally for the Behind The Panels podcast, interviewers are Richard Gray and David McVay.

RICHARD GRAY: Green Arrow is out in stores this week. I understand you've been living with that character for the better part of the last year. Was Green Arrow really on your radar before that?

JEFF LEMIRE: No, not at all. I mean, I grew up reading DC stuff. I was always a DC Comics fan over Marvel stuff as a kid for whatever reason. I grew up in the mid-80s, so you were either into the X-Men or the Teen Titans. For whatever reason, I went for the Teen Titans, so I was always a DC guy. Green Arrow was never really a character, other than seeing him in Justice League, he was never really someone that I cared for as a kid or whatever. I think that maybe that was just because back then, he didn't really have his own monthly book or anything. I guess long story short, he never really was on my radar.

When I got the book, I was looking for another DC project. Something that was a little bit closer to the center of the DC universe than *Animal Man or Swamp Thing*, and *Justice League Dark* and all the stuff I'd been doing which I love, and still love doing, they're all really horror books. They're kind of off in their own little corner. I thought it would be fun to do something a little more close to the center of the DC universe but still something that I could have my own take on it, and bring my own voice to it. When Dan DiDio suggested Green Arrow to me, it just seemed like the potential was there to do a really cool *noir* crime, kind of superhero epic. When I thought about it that way, I got really interested in the character.

And I also really like the character of Oliver Queen now, just in terms of the redemption story of this guy who was born into privilege. He had everything he could ever want handed to him, yet he could never really live up to this legacy his father had. So in my story, basically we just tear everything down and he loses everything right away and he has to rebuild himself. So I kind of like redemption stories. There was definitely a lot there for me to play with.

RG: You kind of touched on there that Green Arrow is now at the center of the DC universe in a lot of ways, and of course, there's a TV series that's a big flagship for CW as well. Has there been any pressure on you to conform Arrow to a certain mould?

JL: No, not at all. It was weird. I got the gig in July of last year [2012], and the show was in production but I certainly hadn't seen it yet. So I really had to develop my own take and story well before, months before the series premiered. So they really developed separately, and even now there's no pressure for me to try and make the character more like the TV show version or make the storylines sort of in line with what they're doing. They really are separate things. Which is good, I'm glad I have that freedom. But at the same time, it's really nice that there's so much more awareness around the character at the moment, and the TV show's doing so well in the [United] States. It's just more people potentially that could tune into the comic, and that's a good thing for me.

DM: With that in mind, what are your impressions of the TV series? Are you a fan?

JL: Yeah, you know, it's pretty good. It's TV, so there are limitations and they have to sort of follow a certain format every week, and stuff like that with network television. I think considering that they've done a pretty good job of creating a really grounded take on a vigilante superhero. I think that people who are enjoying the TV show but maybe haven't read the comic, or don't read comics in general, will find the transition to our comic somewhat easy. Just in terms of – I approached it in a really grounded way as well, you know, it's a superhero comic but he's not fighting really outlandish supervillains every week and doing lots of crazy stuff. It really is a street-level crime-noir story, and much more grounded in reality. I think aesthetically there's a crossover there that I hope will help people bridge that gap.

RG: Well, just on the topic of that grounding of the character, I know you've mentioned Mike Grell and [Brian Michael] Bendis and [Frank] Miller's respective takes on Daredevil [in past interviews]. Does this mean your take will see a return to the 'urban hunter' Ollie?

JL: Oh yeah, that's the only version I had any interest in doing. That was sort of right away what I pitched, definitely a return to the Mike Grell era. This hero of the gutters, this hero of the street, really urban hunter basically kind of character. That's really what I was after. You know, the Mike Grell stuff holds up quite well actually, when you read the whole run that he did. Some really amazing character work in there. That's really what inspired me, was that and also Denny O'Neill's *Question* comics from the 80s, I really love those. More recently, stuff like Bendis' run on Daredevil. Some of the more recent Batman stuff. These really, kind of, street-level superhero stories that were successful. It's the kind of thing I'm trying to tap into without ripping those guys off.

RG: It's music to my ears, because Grell's run is really one of my favorites.

JL: It's amazing.

RG: On that note, are you planning on being in for the long haul for this title?

JL: I sure hope so, you know. You never know what's going to happen. It's not always in my control. As long as the book's successful, and they let me keep going, I really want to try and do a sustained run on this book.

RG: And coming to this book as both a writer and an artist, coming to someone else's creation in a lot of ways, is it easy to start working with a different artist, in this case Andrea Sorrentino, not knowing up front if they're going to get your vision of the character?

JL: When I do stuff that I draw myself, especially stuff that's creator owned, I get to control every aspect of the storytelling, and that's really rewarding obviously. The fun side of working for DC, aside from working with these characters that I love, is the collaborative aspect. So I know that when I start Green Arrow, it's not my Green Arrow, it's *our* Green Arrow. It's the by-product of both of our visions coming together. The same thing when I did *Animal Man* with Travel Foreman, and now Steve Pugh. For me, it's really easy when I do DC stuff to let go of the visual side of it and completely leave that up to the artist. I worry about plot, and character, and dialogue and things like that, and I let them inform all the visual stuff. Having said that, I did have a pretty specific vision for the kind of book I wanted Green Arrow to be. We chose an artist specifically that we thought would be in line with that, and Andrea – if you've seen his work on *American Vampire* – he does very stark, black and white, kind of noir-ish work to begin with. So I thought he would be a really cool look for a superhero comic, you know the intention of having a superhero drawn in that style I thought would be really interesting and fit that vision. So it's kind of a mix of both things: of letting him bring his voice to it, and trying to choose the right artist that fits your vision of the books.

RG: It would almost be a shame to see it in color, having had a look at some of the sketches.

JL: Oh yeah, it's really weird. The good thing is that he colored the first issue himself, so it really is his vision. I had this idea where certain panels, key moments in action in the layouts, would actually stay in black and white with just green as a spot colour. We did that throughout the first arc, and it really worked well. It's a mix of colour and black and white, and really strange visual techniques he tried himself. It's pretty cool. It's actually pretty experimental for a monthly superhero comic.

From *Green Arrow* Vol. 5 #22. Art by Andrea Sorrentino. © DC Comics.

RG: That's very cool, and I look forward to seeing it later this week. With the rest of DC's New 52, you're obviously still busy with Animal Man and Justice League Dark, did that contribute at all to the end of *Sweet Tooth*?

JL: Oh no, not at all. That was a book, when I developed the idea, that story wise it was just a natural conclusion. I was doing three monthlies while I was working on *Sweet Tooth* and it wasn't a problem. Now I'm actually working on a new book for Vertigo called *Trillium* which we'll launch later this year. One book that I'm writing or drawing, and two or three monthlies. So no, it certainly didn't have any effect on ending *Sweet Tooth* the way it did. That was always on my own terms.

DM: I guess we'd have to ask the same question we'd ask of Brian Michael Bendis – have they cloned you? How do you fit this much in?

JL: I don't know. I guess I just have a really good work ethic and I'm very disciplined. But when you love what you do, and your job is your passion, it's really easy to want to do it all the time. So for me I'm always wanting to work. It's not hard for me to balance a lot of projects and get really excited by them.

RG: Well, in addition to those monthly titles, you've also managed to *release The Underwater Welder* in the last six months as well, a standalone comic, a creator-owned comic. What determines the format that you ultimately present it in? In this case, it was a graphic novel as opposed to say an ongoing series like *Sweet Tooth*.

JL: Generally the stuff I do on my own is graphic novel format, and *Sweet Tooth* was kind of an anomaly in that. I never imagined that I would do a monthly comic. It just didn't seem like something that was possible. I always just did graphic novels, but when the opportunity to pitch for a monthly book came up, I pitched *Sweet Tooth*. So that was almost a special circumstance. While I do prefer the more standalone, close-ended stories – where I can tell a beginning, a middle, and an end – in one big chunk, rather than the ongoing thing where you're uncertain where it will end, and how it will end. I don't think I'll do another ongoing monthly for a while. Even *Trillium*, my next Vertigo monthly, will be a limited thing. A 10-issue thing.

RG: And what do you read in terms of your influences, comics or otherwise?

JL: Comics right now, the stuff that I'm into, I follow writers. I'm really into Jason Aaron's stuff, I'm liking – I loved *Scalped*, obviously, which ended, but I'm really enjoying his Thor and his X-Men. I'm following [Jonathan] Hickman as well. I find myself reading a lot more prose lately, just because I spend so much time thinking about comics all day, I almost need a break at night, and I need to read something else. So I've been reading a lot more prose, which is good because it's kind of been informing my work in a different way.

RG: On the topic of graphic novels, you've sort of mentioned that you couldn't have really told *Underwater Welder* in any other format. Some of your previous novels have received some pretty major acclaim around the world, in particular *Essex County* which I believe was shortlisted as one of the Essential Canadian Novels of the decade. Which to me demonstrates a changing attitude towards graphic novels in a way.

JL: Yeah, definitely.

RG: Do you feel there's a different attitude between say, Canada and the US about that?

JL: I just think Canada's a bigger country, but obviously a smaller population. So whenever any author or filmmaker that is successful, gets a bit more attention within the country just because there's so few of us. My books, which were firmly rooted in Canada – the narrative was set in Canada, and it's about a small Canadian town – yet they were still successful in the US, it got a lot of attention in Canada. In general I think, obviously, the attitude and attention towards the medium is changing all the time. Even five years ago, I don't think you would have seen a book like *Essex County* shortlisted for an award like that. So it's great, and I think there's just so much good stuff being put out, that's the thing. 25, 30 years ago, when *Maus*, and *Watchmen* and *The Dark Knight*, kind of reached that public awareness, and introduced the public to the idea of the graphic novel. I think the reason it didn't catch on as much back then was that after people read those two or three major works, there wasn't as much stuff for them to find. Whereas now, if you read *Essex County* you can go to the bookstore and find dozens of amazing graphic novels. There's such a broad range of stuff, so many different genres, there's something for everybody really. It's just going to get better and better.

RG: On that topic, what advice would you give to people trying to break into that industry these days?

JL: I can only talk about what I did. For me, I just knew that, ironically my drawing style and what I wanted to write about really didn't fit with DC or Marvel. So I didn't try to get into DC or Marvel. I didn't try to write superhero comics or anything. I just did my own thing, and self-published at first, and told the stories I wanted to tell. I didn't really worry about what was popular or what publishers might be interested in. As the result of that I wound up working for DC, because I guess I had my own voice and developed my own style, and inevitably they would look for people like that who would bring new energy for these characters that have been around for 50 or 60 years. I guess, just follow your own voice and not worry about what you think editors are looking for, or what's popular at the moment. If the story you really want to tell doesn't seem really commercial, it shouldn't influence you. You just have to do what you're passionate about. If you're digging what you're doing, chances are someone else will too.

DM: Interestingly, in your introduction to *Underwater Welder*, Damon Lindeloff talks about the fact that it's the greatest *Twilight Zone* never produced. It made me wonder whether you've ever thought about moving your material to an animated form?

JL: Honestly, I love comics so much, and I don't feel like I have an interest in working in other mediums. Comics can do so much more than film or television can do. For me, creatively, it's so much more direct. I can sit down, and whatever I put on paper is what people see, whereas if you're working in film you have to filter your ideas through so many different people, and it's so expensive. It's really hard to maintain a vision like that. For me, film and TV aren't nearly as rewarding as creating comics. I have no interest in pursuing it personally, but having said that, if someone else were interested in adapting my stuff, that's totally a different situation. As long as I wasn't involved, it's always interesting to see someone else interpret your ideas.

Part 2

The second part of the interview is more reflective, picking up the conversation on 27 February 2016 via email. By this stage, Jeff Lemire had left the DC Comics fold to concentrate on his creator-owned comic *Descender* for Image, set to be adapted into a film by Sony, along with his two headlining titles for Marvel, *Extraordinary X-Men* and *Hawkeye*.

RG: When we first spoke, the first issue of your Green Arrow run was just about to hit shelves. Now that it's been well over a year since your last issue, how has your view of Oliver Queen as a character changed throughout the process?

JL: Well, it's hard for me to answer that, because to be totally honest with you, once I leave a project, I don't really think about it again. So I can't say Ollie has really been on my mind since I left the Green Arrow book. But I will say that he is probably only one of two characters I ever wrote on a work for hire basis that I feel like I could return to one day. I still feel there could be a lot of potential to continue with Ollie and The Green Arrow mythos.

RG: It's no secret that Green Arrow struggled to find direction as a character at the inception of the New 52. 'The Kill Machine' arc begins dramatically: he's broke, attacked, seemingly loses his friends and his building explodes. Was this your way of stripping Ollie back to basics to give yourself a blank slate?

JL: Absolutely. I hated the New 52 Green Arrow. To be blunt, it was terrible. They had taken away everything that was unique and interesting about the character. His social consciousness, his age and his life experiences. Him being a man of the people. That was all gone as they attempted to make him a young, hip Tony Stark clone. And it didn't work at all.

But it did give me a great opportunity. I decided I could take this unlikable Oliver Queen and we could actually see his transformation into the more mature, socially conscious, street-level. Green Arrow and Ollie Queen. So I started by burning down his house and laying a new foundation.

RG: Your Green Arrow stories are the first to truly subvert the "island" story that been around since the 1950s. Did you always intend to give the New 52 its origin story coming aboard?

JL: No, that developed quickly though. As I dug and got into things I realized what an absolute goldmine that Island was. It was so full of mystery and potential. I credit the *Arrow* TV show for showing me that. They really mined the secrets of the island in the first season. I had no intention of copying what they did, but I could do my own version of that in the comic.

RG: The notion of the totemic Outsiders is an intriguing one, and very different to what has come before in the origin mythos. Where did it come from?

JL: That was actually all Anne Nocenti. She was doing *Green Arrow* right before me and then moved over on to write the Katana series. So she has started to develop this idea of The Outsiders and the various Weapon clans. When I came on *Green Arrow* we talked a lot and we saw potential in expanding her idea and having it eventually culminate in a crossover of sorts between GA and Katana. Unfortunately her Katana series got cancelled before we got to it, so I took the lead and worked it all into a more Green Arrow-centric mythology.

Aside from transforming Ollie into the Green Arrow I knew and loved, my other main objective was doing some major world building and expansion of his mythology. The weapon clans and Outsiders offered a great gateway to that.

RG: You said to me a few years ago that Mike Grell's urban hunter is the "only version I had any interest in doing." So I find it interesting that you flip the script on a number of his key characters. Shado has always been comparable to Elektra to me, so here you reinvent her as well. With Emiko are you picking up on Grell's loose end of Shado's child?

JL: Yes, for me I don't ever want to just do nostalgia. It's not that interesting to me. I love the Grell stuff but that doesn't mean I want to just recreate it. I want to capture the essence of that stuff but I want to make it my own as well. And some of the reinvention was necessary due to changes in the New 52 world as well.

RG: Richard Dragon is another character you get to put a spin on, following in the footsteps of other Green Arrow writers Denny O'Neil and Chuck Dixon. In the past though, he's always been a hero. Why the dramatic change?

JL: It's hard for me to remember exactly where all the changes on Dragon stemmed from. Some of this stuff was done on the fly, as the monthly deadlines can get a bit aggressive as you get into a run, so sometimes you just make decisions and go with your gut. I do seem to remember Wil Moss, my editor, suggesting some of these changes to Dragon.

Including a version of Dragon seemed like a natural fit with the tone of what we were doing. All those late 80's DC characters like Question, Grell's Green Arrow, Butcher. That was the well of inspiration I was pulling from. Again, I wanted to recreate the "feeling" that those books gave me when I read them, but not just rip them off or copy them. I wanted to put my own spin on them.

And of course I say "I", but I really mean "we" because Andrea Sorrentino was my partner in all of this. He was as responsible for the tone and feel as I am.

RG: Speaking of classic villains, your take on Count Vertigo draws on so much pathos. Is it important that we feel something for the villain?

JL: If we can't feel for them, or relate to them, then they're not really very good villains. They just become two-dimensional cardboard cutouts. So, yes, I wanted to make Vertigo into a really tragic and tortured guy. Someone who you may not be able to agree with, but you can at least feel for him.

RG: Andrea Sorrentino's art is magnificent in this series. How much of that idea of the mixture of color and black and white and using different techniques as the series progressed?

JL: I feel like Andrea and colorist Marcelo Maiolo really evolved as a team over the course of the series. You can see them getting more experimental and making bolder choices as the series progressed. And their evolution perfectly mirrored Ollie's growth as a character. It all worked perfectly.

RG: Those flashback sequences use different techniques as well, with an Eastern influenced parchment paper. Were these specific things you indicated in the script, or things that Sorrentino came to you with?

JL: That was all Andrea's idea. Not in the script at all. He just went for it and it worked great. That's why we shared storytelling credit. It really was one of those rare, perfect collaborations.

RG: You also got to work with Deny Cowan and Bill Sienkiewicz. Were these artists that you sought out for those backups?

JL: Yes! I requested them. Like I said, *The Question* was a huge influence, so I really fought to get those guys on board and Wil Moss totally got it and made it happen. That is one of the thrills of my career working with those two. I have one of the original art pages from our stories and it hangs proudly on my studio wall.

From *Green Arrow* Vol. 5 #23. Art by Andrea Sorrentino. © DC Comics.

RG: At the start of your run, we spoke about the *Arrow* TV show and the comic being two separate things. Yet you also introduce the character of Diggle, a direct lift from the series: was this a case of you finding yourself influenced by some of the show?

JL: Yes. I avoided the show for my first couple of arcs, really wanting to do my own thing. Then when I felt like we'd found our footing, I checked out the show, looking for any inspiration it could provide. And the two things I pulled from it were, the idea to explore the mystery of the island, and also the Diggle character, who was great and I felt, a great compliment to Ollie.

RG: Events and tie-ins were regular throughout your run - *Villains Month, Zero Year, Futures End* - but you tended to use them as flashbacks. As a writer, do you find these narrative breaks a hindrance or a help?

JL: They are usually a pain in the ass, but for whatever reason, with *Green Arrow* they just felt like opportunities. Maybe it was because we were in a groove and feeling confident in what we were doing so we could take these things as they came and treat them as fun challenges. But for whatever reason, they really worked for us, they offered us new ways to expand and explore the mythology and history we were building. Again, for me *Green Arrow* was all about building. You don't often get the chance to do as much as we did to develop a character and their world.

RG: In your final regular issue, Ollie says "I'm finally free... able to become the hero I've always wanted to be." Was this a matter of wiping the slate as clean as you'd left if, with a new status quo?

JL: Yeah, to me this was the end of "phase one". We wiped away all the shit that DC had stuck the character with when they did the New 52, had built a new origin, mythology for Ollie and set him on the right track to being that more socially conscious, street-level hero I always liked.

Unfortunately, for various reasons, this was also the end of our run so I never got to explore what I saw as "phase 2"

RG: Your last issue on Green Arrow was the Futures End tie-in, five years in the future with Emiko taking up the mantle. Was this a blueprint for where you felt the series should go?

JL: That was it. The next arc would have been "The New Green Arrow." It would have had Emiko becoming Green Arrow and Ollie hanging up the costume and focusing on figuring out who the hell Oliver Queen was. He would have opened a homeless shelter and drug rehabilitation center in Seattle, named after his

Mother, and this would be his focus, while also training and supervising Emiko and Naomi, who would be the new Red Dart.

I pitched the idea, but various things conspired to prevent us from continuing.

RG: Do you think it's *time* for a female Green Arrow in DC's near future?

JL: I haven't given it much thought. I liked the Emiko character and felt it was a good story to tell. I don't think of these things as "female character" or "male character". It's just about whatever story I'm excited to tell.

RG: By way of comparison, you're now writing *Hawkeye* for Marvel, where there has been a female counterpart to the titular character. What similarities do you seen between DC and Marvel's leading archers?

JL: They are *very* different, which is the only reason I took the *Hawkeye* gig. Aside from the fact they are all archers, there is really no similarities between the characters or the tone of the books. Archery is a much bigger factor in Green Arrow's mythology and his character. It is central to who is, where as with Hawkeye it's almost arbitrary. The archery is just a means to an end. Bows and arrows are what they use to be heroes, but it could easily be anything else and wouldn't change them as characters, I don't think.

And on a personal level Hawkeye is almost the exact opposite of Ollie. Clint Barton was an orphan raised in poverty and the circus. Ollie inherited the legacy and wealth of his family. Very different origins and life experiences.

RG: Do you feel you said everything you had to say about Green Arrow, and if not, where would you potentially see him going?

JL: As I outlined, I had an idea for the next phase of my run, but it was not to be. But I don't really feel dissatisfied or like I didn't complete something. I think our run holds together really well, and along with *Animal Man* is the thing I'm most proud of from my time at DC. No regrets.

Acknowledgements

Moving Target is dedicated to my late grandparents, Barbara and Ossie Gray. I get the feeling they'd dig what I've put together here.

This book wouldn't be possible without the kindness, support, and tolerance of so many people, and thanking them all would necessitate a second volume. First and foremost, thanks must go out to Mike Phillips and Julian Darius at Sequart, who took a chance on this antipodean author and supported a passion project. These guys get their books and films out on a magical mixture of blood, sweat, and pure affection for the medium, and I only wish that their enthusiasm and patience could be bottled. Of course, that connection wouldn't have been possible at all without writer extraordinaire and friend Ryan K. Lindsay (*The Devil is in the Details*), a man who is not only generous with his contacts list, but a veritable font of advice for anybody who is serious about this business of writing. Fellow Australian Louie Joyce, a regular collaborator with Ryan, is responsible for the phenomenal cover art of *Moving Target*. A terrific artist who makes me hopeful people will judge this book by its cover.

Everybody who has tolerated my Green Arrow obsession over the years gets a hearty salute, chief among which are Nima Afshar and Jaime Lawrence, both of whom suggested this book should happen just to keep me quiet. The Behind The Panels boys, David McVay and Dave Longo, spent literally hundreds of hours hearing me bang on about Green Arrow, talking me off ledges, and giving me the space to explore this project behind a microphone. As my buddy Alex Doenau once put it, "You were a kid with a dream who grew into a man with a beard who's going to talk to a man about a man with a beard. It warms my heart." Our daily chats keep me sane and grounded. My editor at Newsarama, the Dashing David Pepose, tolerated some malleable deadlines on reviews as a result of me being knee-deep in fictional archery. John Dee is the only Green Arrow who has ever asked me to have breakfast with a man in green pleather at 6am, and his sage advice has helped keep me on the straight and narrow. My oldest friend, filmmaker Ivan Kovac, led the way by living the dream and reminding me of what I could do if I put my mind to it. You inspire me, old friend. Closer to home, mere thanks would be inadequate for Amy Allenspach, a partner in crime in all things, and someone who has absorbed *so much* more about Green Arrow in a year through osmosis and impromptu live readings than most comics readers do in decades. Of course, I need to thank my mother, Stephanie Gray: it goes without saying I wouldn't be here without you.

I was also lucky enough to engage with some of the creators who worked on the Green Arrow comics across the years, not least of which are Neal Adams, Mike Grell, Chuck Dixon, Phil Hester, Brad Meltzer and Jeff Lemire. These wonderful people were not only generous with their time, but gracious enough to allow us to use their interview material for publication in this book. Phil also generously wrote the foreword to this tome, and I am both humbled an excited by its inclusion.

Last, but in no way least, if it isn't obvious enough, this book was born out of a love for an archer that is perhaps the most human of all DC's heroes. The book began its life back in 2013 as a series of articles for Behind The Panels, and expanded rapidly to this tome you are now holding, but the love of Green Arrow has been decades in the making. So here's to Mort, George, Jack, Denny, Neal, Elliot, Joey, Mike, Chuck, Kevin, Brad, Judd, Jeff, Benjamin, Stephen, and just about anybody else who has been instrumental in bringing life (or new life) to the Battling Bowman. This book is a massive "thank you" to all of you.

Richard Gray
Somewhere in Oliver Queen's Trophy Cabinet
June 2017

About the Author

Richard Gray is a writer, critic and probable dilettante. Since 2013, he has been a regular columnist at Newsarama.com's Best Shots. Richard is the editor of TheReelBits.com, where he also writes about film and television, and regularly appears on Australia's ABC Radio and various podcasts.

His writing has appeared in diverse places as diverse as Sequart.org, Filmink, METRO Magazine, and dozens of online sources. He is a member of the Online Film Critics Society.

Moving Target: The History and Evolution of Green Arrow is Richard's first book. You can find his unfiltered train of thought on Twitter @DVDBits, where he will give you his opinion whether you want it or not.

Richard lives in Australia and is in your future.

ALSO FROM **SEQUART**

THE BRITISH INVASION: ALAN MOORE, NEIL GAIMAN, GRANT MORRISON, AND THE
    INVENTION OF THE MODERN COMIC BOOK WRITER

CLASSICS ON INFINITE EARTHS: THE JUSTICE LEAGUE AND DC CROSSOVER CANON

AND THE UNIVERSE SO BIG: UNDERSTANDING *BATMAN: THE KILLING JOKE*

IMPROVING THE FOUNDATIONS: *BATMAN BEGINS* FROM COMICS TO SCREEN

GOTHAM CITY 14 MILES: 14 ESSAYS ON WHY THE 1960S BATMAN TV SERIES MATTERS

BOOKS ON GRANT MORRISON:

GRANT MORRISON: THE EARLY YEARS

OUR SENTENCE IS UP: SEEING GRANT MORRISON'S THE INVISIBLES

CURING THE POSTMODERN BLUES: READING GRANT MORRISON AND CHRIS WESTON'S THE FILTH IN THE 21ST CENTURY

THE ANATOMY OF ZUR-EN-ARRH: UNDERSTANDING GRANT MORRISON'S BATMAN

BOOKS ON WARREN ELLIS:

SHOT IN THE FACE: A SAVAGE JOURNEY TO THE HEART OF TRANSMETROPOLITAN

KEEPING THE WORLD STRANGE: A PLANETARY GUIDE

VOYAGE IN NOISE: WARREN ELLIS AND THE DEMISE OF WESTERN CIVILIZATION

WARREN ELLIS: THE CAPTURED GHOSTS INTERVIEWS

BOOKS ON SCI-FI FRANCHISES:

A GALAXY FAR, FAR AWAY: EXPLORING STAR WARS COMICS

A LONG TIME AGO: EXPLORING THE STAR WARS CINEMATIC UNIVERSE

NEW LIFE AND NEW CIVILIZATIONS: EXPLORING STAR TREK COMICS

THE SACRED SCROLLS: COMICS ON THE PLANET OF THE APES

BRIGHT LIGHTS, APE CITY: EXAMINING THE PLANET OF THE APES MYTHOS

OTHER BOOKS:

HUMANS AND PARAGONS: ESSAYS ON SUPER-HERO JUSTICE

MOVING PANELS: TRANSLATING COMICS TO FILM

THE WEIRDEST SCI-FI COMIC EVER MADE: UNDERSTANDING JACK KIRBY'S 2001: A SPACE ODYSSEY

THE DEVIL IS IN THE DETAILS: EXAMINING MATT MURDOCK AND DAREDEVIL

TEENAGERS FROM THE FUTURE: ESSAYS ON THE LEGION OF SUPER-HEROES

MINUTES TO MIDNIGHT: TWELVE ESSAYS ON WATCHMEN

WHEN MANGA CAME TO AMERICA: SUPER-HERO REVISIONISM IN MAI, THE PSYCHIC GIRL

THE FUTURE OF COMICS, THE FUTURE OF MEN: MATT FRACTION'S CASANOVA

THE BEST THERE IS AT WHAT HE DOES: EXAMINING CHRIS CLAREMONT'S X-MEN

MUTANT CINEMA: THE X-MEN TRILOGY FROM COMICS TO SCREEN

DOCUMENTARY FILMS:

DIAGRAM FOR DELINQUENTS

SHE MAKES COMICS

THE IMAGE REVOLUTION

NEIL GAIMAN: DREAM DANGEROUSLY

GRANT MORRISON: TALKING WITH GODS

WARREN ELLIS: CAPTURED GHOSTS

COMICS IN FOCUS: CHRIS CLAREMONT'S X-MEN

For more information and for exclusive content, visit Sequart.org.